DESIGN RESEARCH ON LEARNING AND THINKING IN EDUCATIONAL SETTINGS

The key question this book addresses is how to identify and create optimal conditions for the kind of learning and development that is especially important for effectively functioning in the 21st century. Taking a new approach to this long-debated issue, it looks at how a design research-based science of learning (with its practical models and related design research) can provide insights and integrated models of how human beings actually function and grow in the social dynamics of educational settings, with all their affordances and constraints. More specifically:

- How can specific domains or subject matters be taught for broad intellectual development?
- How can technology be integrated in enhancing human functioning?
- How can the social organization of classroom learning be optimized to create social norms for promoting deep intellectual engagement and personal growth?

Part I is concerned with broad conceptual and technical issues regarding cultivating intellectual potential, with a focus on how design research might fill in an important niche in addressing these issues. Part II presents specific design work in terms of design principles, models, and prototypes.

Design Research on Learning and Thinking in Educational Settings is intended for all educational researchers, instructional psychologists, learning science researchers, and students who have an interest in educational innovations in teaching and learning particularly aimed at intellectual gains.

David Yun Dai is Associate Professor of Educational Psychology and Methodology, Department of Educational and Counseling Psychology, University at Albany, State University of New York.

THE EDUCATIONAL PSYCHOLOGY SERIES

Robert J. Sternberg and Wendy M. Williams, Series Editors

For additional information on titles in the Educational Psychology Series series visit www.routledge.com/education

DESIGN RESEARCH ON LEARNING AND THINKING IN EDUCATIONAL SETTINGS

Enhancing Intellectual Growth and Functioning

Edited by
David Yun Dai

Routledge
Taylor & Francis Group

NEW YORK AND LONDON

First published 2012
by Routledge
711 Third Avenue, New York, NY 10017

Simultaneously published in the UK
by Routledge
2 Park Square, Milton Park, Abingdon, Oxon OX14 4RN

Routledge is an imprint of the Taylor & Francis Group, an informa business

Library of Congress Cataloging in Publication Data
Design research on learning and thinking in educational settings: enhancing
  intellectual growth and functioning/[edited by] David Yun Dai.
    p. cm.—(Educational psychology series)
  Includes bibliographical references and index.
  1. Cognitive learning. 2. Learning, Psychology of. 3. Critical
  thinking—Study and teaching. I. Dai, David Yun.
  LB1062.D485 2011
  370.15′2--dc23   2011012781

ISBN: 978–0–415–88050–3 (hbk)
ISBN: 978–0–415–88051–0 (pbk)
ISBN: 978–0–203–84957–6 (ebk)

Typeset in Bembo
by Florence Production, Stoodleigh, Devon
Printed and bound in the United States of America on acid-free paper
by IBT Global

For David N. Perkins

CONTENTS

PREFACE

This book addresses a long-debated issue with a new approach. The key question is how to identify and create optimal conditions for the kind of learning and development especially important for effectively functioning in the 21st century, such as deep understandings of core concepts, theories, and principles essential for knowing the world around us, making causal reasoning and solving complex problems that have direct consequences on the well-being of the society, and exercising creative and critical thinking that transforms information into personal knowledge that is truly generative and productive. Not everyone agrees that these lofty goals are achievable through carefully arranged learning environments. For some critics, only some highly intelligent people can attain deep knowledge and higher-order thinking. Contributors in this volume share a more optimistic outlook, viewing learning outcomes as shaped by the way learning is organized or "designed" in a fundamental way.

It is usually easier to demonstrate learning gains if particular content knowledge (say, what are the structural regularities of a triangle) is targeted, than if learning is about, say, gaining a mathematical disposition or way of thinking regarding trigonometry. The characteristic solution to this problem is that only learning outcomes that are easy to measure get attention and pushed to the forefront. Design researchers take a different tack. Instead of asking whether we have the right input and measurable output, they turn research attention to "design" issues: how we can create the optimal learning conditions for particular learners with particular content, and how these conditions leverage personal and environmental resources and address critical constraints in developing higher-order thinking and achieving high-end learning. We argue that design research provides a new way or epistemology of approaching the topic, with respect to how we investigate instructional treatment and learning conditions, how we define and assess constructs of learning gains, and how we make evidence-based claims.

The book is structured in two parts. Part I, "Issues, Theories, and Methods," (Chapters 1–5) is concerned with broad conceptual and technical issues regarding cultivating intellectual potential, with a focus on how design research might fill in an important niche in addressing these issues. Chapter 1 delineates an overarching framework for the volume. It provides a historical perspective on learning and intelligence, and argues that the two are intertwined. It also provides an architecture of design research that helps identify different issues at different phases of design research. Then, Chapter 2 presents an argument, based on "relational ontology," that environments can be optimally structured to develop dispositions to act and think more intelligently. Chapter 3 further provides a pedagogical model for promoting creative and critical thinking across school subjects. Chapter 4 raises the issue of assessing learning gains and higher-order thinking in dynamic learning situations with reliability and validity in design research, and proposes new ways of conceptualizing the matter. Chapter 5 delineates the process of conducting design research on the topic of designing technology-supported interventions for children with twice exceptionalities. Together, the five chapters lay out a foundation for design work aimed at high-end learning and design-enhanced intellectual functioning.

Part II, "Models, Tools, and Pragmatics," (Chapters 6–10) presents specific design work in terms of design principles, models, and prototypes. Chapter 6 reports a pedagogical innovation in using measures and motions as a metaphoric basis for developing mathematical understanding of rational numbers for elementary school students. Chapter 7 discusses a model that builds on Ann Brown's work on fostering community of learners, featuring distinct norms shaping the participatory structure of learning. Chapter 8 extends Scardamalia and Bereiter's work on knowledge building, and presents a principle-based model of adaptive collaboration supported by technology and aimed at self-sustained inquiry and deep understandings. Then, Chapter 9 reports an after-school program designed to develop identity as well as competencies in history, science, and technology. And Chapter 10 focuses on assessment of causal reasoning and problem solving online, while learners are learning to play a computer game that involves application of principles of physics. Finally, the Epilogue synthesizes the chapters in terms of advances and challenges of identifying and creating optimal conditions for learning and cultivating intellectual potential through design research, conceptually and methodologically.

A common thread connecting this body of research is its emphasis on reciprocal interaction of practice, theory, and research: theoretical conjectures guide practice. Enacted practice informs research, research enriches or modifies initial theoretical conjectures, and theory in turn further improves practice. These processes operate in an iterative and cyclic manner to achieve an ever-refined theoretical understanding of particular learning conditions, as well as its pedagogical means and ends (e.g., a design prototype). The validity and viability of the resultant theoretical and practical models no longer follow the principle of falsification, as in natural science, but are judged based on their optimality relative to achieving particular goals, given the resources, constraints, and values, as is the case in engineering or design sciences. Given the social-contextual and developing nature of conceptual understanding and high-order thinking, learning outcomes are understood not as isolated individual phenomena but as growth trajectories in the dynamic context of person–task transactions and social interactions. Moreover, the timescale of participation and action also becomes significant if one is to observe meaningful transitions in feeling, thinking, and action. These changes in the scope of research design present a double-edged sword. They undermine the conventional definition of what constitutes "effectiveness" and "validity," yet at the same time pose new challenges as to how to make evidence-based claims about optimal conditions for specific learning gains in the midst of environmental noises and complications and many uncertainties. Several common themes emerge from the research reported in this volume: (a) how learning and thinking about important matters can be scaffolded and otherwise pedagogically supported; (b) how distinct norms can be created and maintained to engage and enhance learning and thinking; (c) how assessment can be designed diagnostically to trace and monitor the progress; and (d) how technological tools can be developed to assist all the above functions. The extent to which design research can successfully address these questions will ultimately determine whether it is a viable research methodology for bringing significant changes to educational practice.

The book is intended for all educational researchers, instructional psychologists, learning science researchers, and graduate students who have an interest in educational innovations (including technological ones) in teaching and learning, particularly aimed at intellectual gains, such as conceptual development, critical thinking, problem solving, and creativity. Because it adopts a new research methodology in investigating learning and thinking in educational settings, the book also has a distinct methodological orientation that may be interesting to research methodologists: for example, how we redefine the issues of reliability, validity, and generalizability in instructional psychology and learning as a design or normative science.

ACKNOWLEDGMENTS

Thanks are due to State University of New York at Albany for a sabbatical, and to the US State Department for a Fulbright scholarship, granted to me during 2008–2009, as this book project was launched and taking shape during that period. I would also like to thank Naomi Silverman for encouraging me to pursue this project, and anonymous reviewers for their helpful feedback on the book proposal. My writings for this volume benefited from many discussions I had with the graduate class of Advanced Educational Psychology I taught in the fall of 2010. I appreciate and value the emergent professionalism and self-sustained development of scholarship the students demonstrated in many Blackboard discussion sessions. I would also like to thank Robert Sternberg for his helpful advice in the early conceptualization of this volume, and Yehan Zhou and Stella Li, my research assistants, for providing much needed editorial assistance. And finally, this book is dedicated to David Perkins, a mentor and friend, for the ideas I drew from several conversations with him, in Chicago, Montreal, and through emails, and from his many writings, which benefited this project, directly and indirectly.

David Yun Dai

PART I

Issues, Theories, and Methods

1

FROM SMART PERSON TO SMART DESIGN

Cultivating Intellectual Potential and Promoting Intellectual Growth through Design Research

David Yun Dai

Education seeks to develop the power and sensibility of the mind. On the one hand, the educational process transmits to the individual some part of the accumulation of knowledge, style, and values that constitutes the culture of a people. In doing so, it shapes the impulses, the consciousness, and the way of life of the individual. But education must also seek to develop the processes of intelligence so that the individual is capable of going beyond the cultural ways of his [her] social world, able to innovate in however modest a way so that he [she] can create an interior culture of his [her] own. (Jerome Bruner, 1966, "After John Dewey, What?")

From Smart Person to Smart Design

What makes people intelligent? This question is often interpreted to mean what makes some people smarter than others? The entire history of research on intelligence uses what I call the smart person paradigm; that is, intelligence is a property of the individual mind. We can trace the logic through the use of language: if a person acts *intelligently*, then he or she is *intelligent*, and we might further infer that he or she possesses high *intelligence* (see Lohman, 2001). The reification, of course, requires evidential support. Research efforts have abounded in the past century to pin down exactly what makes one more intelligent than others. What I briefly mention in the following section are but a few distinct examples.

The year was 1978. In an effort to understand how intelligence works, Campione and Brown (1978) drew insights from the performance of children with mental retardation. What they found lacking in these children in a "transfer of training" task was "executive control" (including metacognition), which is responsible for generalizing and deploying routines and strategies in new situations. "As retarded children do not spontaneously fill in gaps in training, their performance gives clues to the kinds of 'gap-filling' which is automatic, or relatively so, for the more intelligent problem-solver" (pp. 287–288). A similar conclusion was drawn from Borkowski and Peck (1986), based on research comparing gifted and regular children on a metamemory task requiring filling in the gaps left by instruction. They found that gifted children did better with fewer trials in the "gap-filling" task and were able to make a far transfer. Similar work based on the then dominant information processing theory led Resnick and Glaser (1976) to propose a definition of intelligence as the ability to learn in the absence of direct or complete instruction. Indeed, the gap-filling capacity was one of the design principles underlying the Aptitude-Treatment Interaction approach (ATI; Cronbach & Snow, 1977; Snow, 1994). This is but only one version of smart person accounts (see, for example, Carroll, 1993; Cattell, 1971; Jensen, 2001).

Now, fast forward to 2005. In an online chess tournament organized by Placechess.com, two amateur chess players as a team became the final winner, defeating some grand masters on their way to the tournament championship. Secret? They "trained" and used three computers to conduct highly skillful analyses, whereas the grand masters were only equipped with mediocre computer programs. Many lessons can be drawn from this event. The most distinct are technological support (computers doing some highly complex calculations and analyses), collaboration (putting heads together, mutual stimulation and evaluation), executive control (deliberation on multiple sources of information and decision-making), and online and offline learning (reflecting on situations and problem solving). To be sure, the role of intelligence in the two amateur players cannot be discounted, which in a way resembles the executive, metacognitive control in the gap-filling research paradigm. However, there is no doubt that the high-level intellectual performance they demonstrated is not possessed by them individually, surely not a property of their minds, but distributed between the two individuals, between the individuals and their environment (conditions and constraints related to chess games) and tools (computer programs) they used. Indeed, there is even an implicit "design" in the distribution of intelligence: taking advantage of what human beings are good at, and what computer programs are good at (see Kasparov, 2007). This and many other social circumstances led Barab and Plucker (2002) to question: what makes an act intelligent; smart person or smart context?

Comparing the intellectual preoccupations in the 1970s and 1990s or 2000s, one cannot help but notice the changes in zeitgeist. Those leading scholars who used to espouse the smart person paradigm back in the 1970s and 1980s have shifted their focus to context (e.g., Brown, 1997; Glaser, 2000; Resnick, 2010; Snow, 1992). Without denigrating the smart person paradigm, it is indeed high time that we consider the problem of "smart design": how intelligent acts can be enhanced by deliberate arrangements of person–task transactions and environmental support.

Learning and Intelligence: How the Twin Got Separated and Came Back Together

In Alfred Binet's original conception as well as its more contemporary rendition (e.g., Carroll, 1997), learning is about making adaptive changes through experience, and intelligence is about the ability to make adaptive changes, and the growing potential to become increasingly more intelligent through learning. It follows that intellectual development and learning should be closely related: intellectual functioning enables effective learning, and learning should facilitate further intellectual growth. A child who has a habit of trying to figure out things will be smarter over time than a child who is used to getting ideas from others. However, while individual differences in cognitive abilities have always been treated as an important determinant of learning (e.g., Ackerman, 1988; Carroll, 1997; Haier, 2001), the history of research on learning seems to have little to do with enhanced intelligence until recently (Ceci & Williams, 1997; Kyllonen, Roberts, & Stankov, 2008; Perkins, 1995). Why is this? One reason is that for a long time intelligence has been considered genetically determined and biologically constitutional; one can gain knowledge through learning, but one's level of intelligence remains virtually unchanged (see Jensen, 2001). Methodologically, it has to do with the divide between what Cronbach (1957) called two disciplines of psychology. While applied research focuses on psychometric testing and adopts an individual differences approach to the study of intelligence, from Spearman (1904) to more recent efforts (see Carroll, 1993; Deary, 2002), basic research on learning takes a situational approach, aimed at understanding the basic underlying processes and mechanisms, how new responses get strengthened, and gradually become habitual, or how information gets encoded and how it is retrieved for use. Concerns over how active learning enhances an intellectual grasp of matters and achieves its adaptive value in a particular functional context became secondary.

Although Estes (1986) pointed out the role of learning and knowledge in enhanced intellectual functioning, it is not until more recently that intelligence has been conceptualized as contextually bound and developing in nature (Ceci, 1996; Lohman, 1993; Sternberg, 1998). One prominent psychometric theory of intelligence (Cattell, 1971) makes a distinction between crystallized intelligence and fluid intelligence, with the former influenced by learning experiences and supported by knowledge (Hunt, 2008), and the latter more biologically determined and difficult to change. However, recent studies (Jaeggi, Buschkuehl, Jonides, & Perrig, 2008) show that even fluid intelligence can be improved through working memory training. A view of intelligence as distributed between the person, the environment, and tools and resources around, rather than a property of the mind (Pea, 1993; see Gresalfi, Barab, & Sommerfeld, this volume) further opens the door for more contextual, dynamic, and incremental accounts of how intelligence (i.e., the human mind) functions and develops through learning experiences.

In addition to the parting of the "two disciplines of psychology" (Cronbach, 1957), child development research has also witnessed a long separation of learning and intellectual development. While learning is considered an intake of specific content information, which is processed and stored in long-term memory to be retrieved later, intellectual development is considered as having its own preordained structural properties and development, devoid of any content and context dependency; progression in cognitive functions will occur sooner or later, regardless of what kind and duration of learning experiences or input one might have (e.g., Piaget, 2001). This more or less Cartesian view of development of mental functions as separate from embodied experiences has been challenged in recent years (see Fischer & Bidell, 2006; see also Siegler, 2000, for a discussion of learning redux in developmental research). From a micro-developmental point of view, Kuhn (2002) argued that learning so much resembles development in its complexity, organization, multifacetedness, and dynamic quality, that "we now recognize learning to be more like development" (p. 111).

Taken together, a broader conception of learning, thinking, and intellectual development seems in order, which would fully incorporate the normative notion of learning aimed at optimal intellectual development.

Learning as an Intellectual Act, and Learning Outcomes as Intellectual Growth

Psychology has come a long way in realizing that learning and thinking are fundamentally intertwined, and that, to a large extent, learning is about learning to feel, think, and act in a more sophisticated, intelligent way. As Resnick (1987) pointed out, the seemingly simple task of learning to read involves development of higher-order cognitive functions, such as nuanced understandings of the syntactic and topical nature of a text, and the active process of filling in gaps (e.g., making inferences, building coherence), and detecting discrepancies in making meaning out of a text. Likewise, learning of basic mathematics should be treated as an interpretative (i.e., intellectual) enterprise, so that "mathematics is seen as expressions of fundamental regularities and relationships among quantities and physical entities" (Resnick, 1987, p. 12; see also Resnick, 1988), rather than merely a set of computation routines, created by geniuses and meant to be committed to one's memory. It is time, indeed, to advocate a thinking curriculum (Resnick, 2010) that goes beyond the transmission metaphor of learning and the warehouse model of knowledge (Schank & Cleary, 1995), and integrates what we know about the interplay of knowledge and intelligence to elucidate how knowledge can be built to facilitate good thinking and intellectual growth. A broadened view of learning also includes participation in various domains of social practice, to experience the world in new ways, to form new affiliations with various groups of people who are doing meaningful work, and to gain resources to prepare for future learning (Gee, 2007).

Although theoretical expositions of learning in the emergent learning science are abundant, with many new proposals and renditions (see Sawyer, 2006), the following three principles are particularly in line with a focus on learning as an intellectual act.

(a) Learning is Perspectival

To learn at the intellectual level is to gain new perspectives or broaden one's intellectual horizon, to feel, think, and talk about a particular topic or act upon a particular class of situations in a more intelligent way (Gee, 2003; Gresalfi et al., this volume). Lampert (1990) distinguished this type of knowledge as knowledge-about, that is, the knowledge of the functionality of a particular method or way of knowing in the larger context of social practice (see also Gee, 2003), which is different from knowledge-of, the knowledge of a particular procedure or concept itself. The perspectival principle also implies that, for a given topic or issue, there likely exist multiple perspectives, each having its own assumptions, logic, and values (Bruner, 1996). The perspectival view of learning highlights the educational value of directing attention and developing sensitivities to various ways of meaning making for adaptive and productive purposes. Affectively, it takes the sequential processes of recognizing, appreciating, and valuing to gain particular perspectives. A child who starts to appreciate a particular way of looking at the world (e.g., through Picasso, Hawkin, or Mother Teresa) is changing his or her mental compass in a fundamental way.

(b) Learning is Instrumental

This principle suggests that learning and doing cannot be separated (Schank & Cleary, 1995); the pursuit of learning always serves some intellectual, practical, and social purposes, be it scientific discovery, engineering a product, or environmental protection. Dewey (1997) put it this way:

> Intellectual organization originates and for a time grows as an accompaniment of the organization of acts required to realize an end, not as the result of a direct appeal to thinking power. The need of thinking to accomplish something beyond thinking is more potent than thinking for its own sake. (p. 41)

Therefore, human motivations are always deeply involved in any socially organized, goal–directed learning activities; it is important, therefore, that students feel "a need to know" (Wise & O'Neill, 2009, p. 90). Learning is optimal when the purposes, structure, and tools of a relevant domain of knowledge are made clear to learners, so that they know why to engage in an activity and how to find and use available tools and resources to achieve their goals. The instrumental principle also implies that contents of knowledge need to be connected so that the learner can see how the parts are linked to the whole in a domain in serving larger functional purposes. The metaphor of "learning your way around" (Greeno, 1991; Perkins, 1995) is powerful in explaining how learning as an intellectual act is to build conceptual understandings of the deep structure or "design grammars" (Gee, 2007, p. 28) that serve to organize seemingly discrete factual and procedural information and turn it into "usable knowledge" (Bransford, Brown, and Cocking, 2000, p. 16). While the history of learning theories was replete with atomists who portrayed learning as a linear accumulation of bits and pieces of knowledge in building a whole (see Hilgard, 1948), the navigation metaphor of learning suggests that learning is an act of navigating complex conceptual spaces and understanding how a particular component is connected with other components in the workings of a machinery, a group of people, an ecosystem, so on and so forth, so as to inform our action in a related practical setting. To be sure, honing skills and consolidating procedural and conceptual instruments take much instruction, training, and deliberate practice over time (recall the 10-year rule in the development of expertise; see Ericsson, 2006). It is important, however, to distinguish between technical proficiency and conceptual understanding in skill development. Technical proficiency reflects the kind of procedural competence that works in a fixed way, thus reproductive in nature. Only conceptual understanding can make one's thinking truly productive in that it enables one to adaptively solve problems for which no ready solution is available (Hatano, 1988). The instrumental view of learning is an antidote to the type of learning that produces inert knowledge, which is a major problem in modern education (Whitehead, 1929). It is the use of knowledge in problem solving that propels extended learning and knowledge building.

(c) *Learning is Reflective*

Dewey (1933) takes reflective learning as the central task of education: "The real problem of intellectual education is the transformation of more or less casual curiosity and sporadic suggestions into alert, cautious, and thorough inquiry" (p. 181). Learning is reflective to the extent that the learner reflects on the nature of social practice they participate in, and of instruments and tools they are using or mastering, and of thinking processes and strategies that they are deploying. Reflection, then, means more than metacognition. Rogers (2002) summarized Dewey's delineation of reflective thinking as based on four criteria: (a) meaning-making, (b) a rigorous way of thinking, (c) community of reflective practice, and (d) a set of attitudes conducive to reflection. Reflective learning naturally leads to what Gee (2003) called critical learning: "the learner must be able consciously to attend to, reflect on, critique, and manipulate those design grammars [the organizational rules of a knowledge domain or social practice] at a metalevel" (pp. 31–32). What one gains through such reflective thinking is metaknowledge (e.g., knowledge about the nature and process of knowing, thinking, and doing in a domain of social practice) and strategic understandings of when and how knowledge can be used to achieve one's goals. It is worth noting that a reflective stance, like experiencing new perspectives, has both cognitive and affective entailments; as Dewey argued, "there is no integration of character and mind unless there is fusion of the intellectual and the emotional, of meaning and value" (quoted in Rogers, 2002, p. 858; see also Dai & Sternberg, 2004).

To illustrate how these principles are reflected in classroom teaching, I paraphrase an account of a science class quoted by Herman and Gomez (2009, pp. 72–73), with my comments inserted in the brackets:

> In a 9th grade environmental science class, students began by discussing a car on a hot day and the difference between the outside and inside temperature of a car. Then students conducted a lab with 2-liter soda bottles, measuring the temperature differences inside the covered versus uncovered bottles. [*Comments*: A question about an everyday phenomenon drove the discussion and experimentation; students experienced a scientific mode (i.e., a new perspective) of understanding something occurring frequently in everyday life.]
>
> During the post-lab discussion, the teacher probed students on why the temperature increased, and uncovered a misconception that light and heat energy are the same thing, and that they both can pass through a barrier like glass (in the case of the car), or plastic wrap (in the lab). The students were perplexed when their observation of what happened to the covered bottles was at odds with their assumption. [*Comments*: misconceptions and perplexity instigate a need to know, which prompts instrumental learning; students became more reflective on their own beliefs.]
>
> To resolve the puzzle, students read the text about the greenhouse effect and annotated with partners to help dissect the reading. Students discussed what they had found and tried to explain the lab results. Connections were drawn between the covered bottles and the greenhouse effect, tying together the opening example of the car, the experiment, the greenhouse effect, and global warming. [*Comments*: texts were used as a resource for resolving a lingering question; students learned to coordinate evidence and theory in formulating reasoned arguments; they experienced collaboration as a mode of shared inquiry; they made connections between what they did in school and a major challenge in the 21st century, which should lead to significant perspectival, instrumental, and reflective gains.]

Finally, the students returned to their lab group to answer questions that synthesized all of this information and ultimately how the greenhouse effect is the mechanism for global warming. [*Comments*: time for synthesizing, organizing, and reflection.]

In short, these students, through carefully structured activities, were gaining a new way of looking at what occurs around them every day and developing an appreciation of how to think, talk, and act like scientists (perspectival learning), on top of acquiring substantive knowledge. The students' desire for knowledge was driven by making an inquiry that was socially important and personally meaningful; they were building, through the inquiry process, new technical and conceptual instruments for observing, reasoning, and problem solving (instrumental learning). Through discussion, sharing, and reflection on the inquiry process and outcomes, the students were also gaining insights about themselves as learners, about the nature of scientific inquiry, sources and evidence of veridical knowledge; they were also likely to value science when they saw how it improves human conditions and contributes to the welfare of the larger society (reflective learning). This type of learning, which engages thinking and reflection, is in stark contrast to learning as regurgitation and passive absorption of prescribed knowledge, as was apparently the case in the teacher's earlier rendition of the same unit of curriculum (see Herman & Gomez, 2009, pp. 72–73). Consequently, intellectual growth can be defined as follows:

- *Perspectival gains*: Do students gain new perspectives because of the learning experience? Is there evidence of newly acquired or enhanced sensitivities to important matters in the world? Do students come to appreciate and value certain ways of looking at and thinking about the world that they were not aware of before?
- *Instrumental gains*: Do students acquire the kind of foundational knowledge and skills to organize the knowledge in a way that allows them to effectively navigate the problem spaces, including those ill-structured ones? Do they demonstrate the ability to use knowledge and external resources and tools adaptively and productively? Do they show increased motivation to further pursue knowledge in the service of understanding and problem solving that has real life significance?
- *Reflective gains*: Do students show metacognitive gains regarding how and how well they tackle the challenge at hand? Do they show epistemological gains in terms of deep insights into the nature and structure of a domain of knowledge and social practice? Is there evidence of a more critical stance toward information and knowledge claims with respect to its validity and use? Do students show attitudinal changes regarding the value of the knowledge pursuit they have been engaged in?

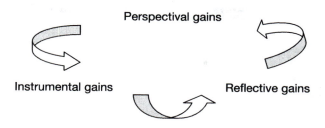

Perspectival gains

Instrumental gains

Reflective gains

FIGURE 1.1 Reciprocal interaction of perspective, instrumental, and reflective learning.

The three aspects of learning tend to reciprocate and work in a cyclic fashion to form new organization of intellectual functioning. Perspective gains, owing to their framing effect, facilitate instrumental learning. Instrumental gains, by getting deep into the structure and workings of a domain, facilitate reflective learning. And reflective gains further enhance perspectival learning. Viewed this way, learning outcomes should be treated, not in a piecemeal and static fashion, in terms of what one is able to recall or do given a short period of instruction, as the traditional learning and transfer research paradigm implicitly prescribed, but as a dynamic change in the scope, organization, and use of knowledge, and the way the mind is truly empowered to act upon the world (Kuhn, 2002; Schank & Cleary, 1995). In essence, perspectival, instrumental, and reflective learning is by nature generative, adaptive, and productive (Bruner, 1960, 1979). In the same vein, research on transfer should take a more dynamic, developmental view, as evolving representations of contexts and situations in which utilities of certain knowledge are salient (Bereiter, 2002; Royer, Mestre, & Dufresne, 2005).

From this point of view, instruction should be redefined, not as dispensing particular pieces of subject knowledge onto the heads of students, but as supporting and guiding such an intellectual act of making meaning out of presented information and situations and promoting intellectual growth. Optimal teaching, then, involves "smart design," in the sense that (a) learning environments are orchestrated in such a way that the learner's cognitive, affective, and motivational resources are leveraged to optimize intellectual acts and growth; (b) supporting tools and resources are made available to provide affordances and address emergent learning-related constraints and needs; and (c) timely guidance and instruction are provided to enhance meaning making and knowledge building. A smart design, then, is not only producing smart learning in terms of making people smarter in feeling, thinking, and action; it itself is a smart system in its adaptivity to new possibilities and constraints.

Why Design Research? A Need for a New Epistemology of Research on Teaching and Learning

There are profound consequences of such a new conception of learning as involving significant amounts of gaining new perspectives about the world, building instruments and tools for understanding and practical problem solving, and reflecting on knowing and knowledge relative to intricacies and complexities of the part of the world being acted upon.

Learning theory and instructional theory are no longer separate, the former descriptive, and the latter prescriptive (Bruner, 1966; Glaser, 1976; Shuell, 1993). Rather, how instruction mediates learning and thinking at a particular point in development for optimal intellectual growth is a main concern. In other words, instructional design is a normative enterprise constrained by evidence-based principles and reasoning.

Given the nature of design science versus analytic science (Collins, 1992), and the ambition and scope of the "smart design," the traditional research apparatus simply cannot handle the complexity and interactivity of multiple components, and the extended timescale of evolving behaviors of such a system. Taking things apart to see how each component works within a short time frame can be effective up to a point; but, ultimately, putting it all together to see how the system functions as a whole over time entails a new approach. In sum, we need a new methodology that is apt to handle the complexities and responsive to emergent possibilities and constraints involved in designing such a learning environment. Dede (2004) asked: "If design-based research is the answer, what is the question?" (p. 105). It seems that design research is well poised to address the central question of interest here.

While sharing certain common interests and concerns with the traditional research on instructional design and learning–teaching interactions, design research, alternatively called design experiment, design studies, design-based research, espouses a different epistemology. Design research, as Brown (1992) initially envisioned, is "an attempt to engineer innovative educational environments and simultaneously conduct experimental studies of those innovations. This involves orchestrating all aspects of a period of daily life in classrooms" (p. 141). More recently, Collins, Joseph, and Bielaczyc (2004) defined design research as having a design focus and involving assessment of critical design elements, while closely examining "how a design plays out in practice, and how social and contextual variables interact with cognitive variables" (p. 21). It is important to note that switching from the comfortable lab to the messy classroom as a venue for research is not merely intended to carry out theoretical applications in practical settings; it is a strategic move to embrace complexity and find new inspiration from the real-life interactive systems (Brown, 1994; Greeno & the Middle School Mathematics Project Group, 1998). Whereas the traditional instructional design research is concerned with engineering a sequence of activities in light of how expertise is developed (e.g., Glaser, 1976) or, in the program evaluation sense, how well a particular instructional program achieves its goals (Isaac & Michael, 1995), design research is concerned not only with building practical models, but also with building theories in situ (Barab & Squire, 2004), or what diSessa and Cobb (2004) called "ontological innovation." What distinguishes design research from the traditional research on instructional designs is the reciprocal interaction of theory, practice, and research in situ, and its iterative, formative, and progressive nature.

Although drawing inspiration from "design" disciplines and professions such as architecture, engineering, and industrial design (Simon, 1981), design work in teaching and learning has both similarities and differences compared with physical design work. Like all design sciences (Simon, 1981), design research in education is concerned with building, testing, modifying, and disseminating new practices and artifacts for particular educational purposes; it has to simultaneously address multiple constraints in achieving its goals; it involves a process of negotiation and bootstrapping, resulting in many cycles of research and development in situ; it uses technical rationality, via building formal models and replicable procedures, as well as reflective rationality, via reflection-in-practice and reflection-on-practice (Schön, 1983). Research evidence to support a particular claim is based not on the rule of falsification, as in natural science, but on optimality of a design relative to achieving its goals, given resources, constraints, and values involved in the design work (cf. Glaser, 1976; Simon, 1981).

However, there are unique properties of design research on teaching and learning. First, design work in education deals invariably with open systems rather than closed systems; the parameters of an open system can never be fully pre-specified, and the end state is not fully determined. In other words, design work in education is by nature an ill-structured domain (Spiro, Feltovich, Jackson, & Coulson, 1991). In contrast, there is complete information for building a house or airplane, both in terms of its structure and the environment in which it will function. Second, design work on teaching and learning involves designing actions and processes for human beings who have their own dispositions to act in certain ways; this constraint is not present for object-based or most agent-based (e.g., designing a robot) design work. Third, as a consequence, any instructional design so developed is a soft design, a design with certain degrees of freedom, as it involves enactment through human actions and interactions. In contrast, a "hard" design would specify every computational detail, leaving little room for variation (other than allowing sometimes for random selection of pre-programmed routines). Taken together, design research in teaching and learning deliberately situates itself at a level of complexity commensurate with that of real-life teaching and learning conditions (Greeno & Middle School Math Project Group, 1998).

Four essential epistemic features can be identified of design research on teaching and learning in general, and designing teaching and learning with the aim of cultivating intellectual potential and promoting intellectual growth in particular.

Authenticity

Authenticity does not only mean that contexts, problems, conditions, and resources set up for learning maintain high degrees of resemblance to those in the real world; the perspectival, instrumental, and reflective learning itself is *authentic* in the sense it carries real meaning and significance to the participants. In other words, there is real human agency in action (perceiving, acting, feeling, and thinking), with real consequences (ends, solutions, and products). The environmental science class discussed earlier illustrates what an authentic learning activity looks like.

Complexity

The teaching–learning system is by nature complex in that there are many interactive elements, social and technical, interpersonal and intrapersonal, that have non-trivial consequences in terms of what actually transpires. Sometimes the complexity can be decomposed to simpler problems or components; for example, constraints specific to individual functioning can be identified and addressed (see Bannan, this volume). But many times, multiple components are responsible for a particular emergent pattern of teaching–learning interaction, which cannot be reduced to any single element acting alone, as interaction can produce emergent properties at the system level.

Emergence

Design work enacted in situ is always "work in progress." Design research on teaching and learning has the dual role of building a theory-driven practical model while simultaneously modifying and refining its conceptualization. Emergence in the design space means that there are emergent properties (new affordances and constraints) during enactment that can only manifest themselves in dynamic situations, and thus need to be captured during the enactment. From an epistemological perspective, emergence as a principle dictates that design research is very much a process of conceptual development and change, from initial conjectures to full-fledged theoretical models. The metaphor of Neurath's boat that Carey (1999, p. 316) used to characterize conceptual changes fits the dynamic, paradoxical nature of design work in situ: building a boat while in the middle of the ocean—water conditions and the functionality of the boat, available materials and tools all dynamically constrain how the boat is built.

Formalism

Design research is supposed to produce a design of some sort. By formalism, I mean both an overt, distinct structure of a practical model, and covert underlying theoretical underpinnings; they both indicate what Gee (2007) called *design grammars*, or what I would prefer to call "design logic." Practically, an instructional model achieves formalism when affordances and constraints of a given learning condition are specified, and the processes by which affordances are realized and constraints satisfied are also explicated to permit the deployment of a set of definable tools and executable procedures in implementing the model (i.e., prototype) in new situations. The design logic here mirrors the process of formalization: an ever-refined understanding of affordances and constraints in such a detailed fashion that a theory can be developed to elucidate underlying components, relationships, and processes within the boundary of a certain teaching–learning situation.

In sum, a smart design aimed at engaging intellectual acts and facilitating intellectual growth in educational settings is situated in authentic contexts, with authentic tasks and purposes. It has a level of dynamic complexity that can only be understood at multiple levels of interactions. Thus design work needs to be tuned into emergent properties and refine its conceptualization iteratively. As a result, practical models can be "formalized" with distinct theoretical underpinnings.

In essence, what I advocate here is a theory of education-based, design-enhanced intelligence and intellectual development. As a matter of fact, much of what diSessa and Cobb (2004) called "ontological innovation" is in line with the notion of design-enhanced intellectual functioning and growth. Such a theory of intelligence would serve the dual goal of making educational innovations that solve recurrent and urgent problems, and building theories that address questions of how intelligence works and why it works at various levels of analysis. Indeed, such an education-based theory of intelligence could easily incorporate those developed in the last century (Campione & Brown, 1978; Resnick & Glaser, 1976), but put them at a proper level of analysis, while pointing out that new educational technology can assist students in performing cognitive (or meta-cognitive) functions traditionally considered difficult for some individuals (e.g., White & Fredericksen, 2005). In short, *design research is poised to address the complex issue of cultivating intellectual potential in its emphasis on agency, structure, and resources, and its focus on how they work together to produce trajectories of intellectual growth.* It can potentially resolve a deep conundrum of the separation of person accounts and situation accounts in psycho-educational research (Cronbach, 1957, 1975), and the separation of descriptive and normative accounts of development in developmental research (White & Frederiksen, 1998). As a result, such an evidence-based theory would gain more explanatory power than descriptive theories of learning, intelligence, or development.

Challenges to the "Smart Design": A Wicked Problem?

While promoting high-end learning and intellectual growth is a lofty goal, can design research measure up to the task? There are at least three distinct challenges. The first challenge comes from those social pessimists who believe that, when it comes to intelligence, there is not much that educators can do (see Dweck, 1999, for the discussion of an entity view of intelligence). For many of them, transfer, a major concern over whether education can help students extrapolate, generalize, and use what they learn, is epiphenomenal to individual differences in intelligence (Detterman, 1993). This view is in line with early theories of intelligence (e.g., Campione & Brown, 1978; Resnick & Glaser, 1976). More recent theorists also argue that the biologically secondary nature of most human knowledge dictates a more modest view of the active learning and transfer (Geary, 1995), or that the lack of knowledge and expertise fundamentally constrains students' ability to benefit from a constructivist pedagogy aimed at engaging high-level intellectual acts such as problem solving and critical thinking (Kirschner, Sweller, & Clark, 2006). Although there is convincing evidence for the effectiveness of some instructional methods, such as mastery learning, in which highly targeted facts, procedures, and ideas are concerned (e.g., see Bloom, 1984 for learning gains by two standard deviations), solid evidence for learning gains in terms of enhanced adaptivity, deep conceptual knowledge, and critical thinking is still lacking, making some educators and researchers skeptical of such a thing as a "thinking curriculum" advocated by education leaders (e.g., Resnick, 2010). Although obscured in the horizon of many design researchers whose theoretical lens is more social-cultural, the question of ATI (Cronbach & Snow, 1977) and differential treatment effects for individuals still lingers (see Ceci & Papierno, 2005).

The second challenge is epistemological, regarding the efficacy of design research in resolving the issue of enhancing intelligence. The problem of enhancing intelligence through education is an "open problem." Compared with closed problems, for open problems, initial state(s) and goal state(s) cannot be easily defined, and operators to move initial states to goal states are unclear (Kelly, 2009). In other words, the problem may be fundamentally an ill-defined one. It may even represent "a wicked problem" (Kelly, 2009, p. 75), a kind of problem that involves elements or constraints that make its solution potentially unattainable. There are also concerns over methodological rigor, such as lack of control (hence, questionable internal validity) and subjectivity in observing, assessing, and interpreting classroom events, situations, and outcomes, as design researchers are hardly bystanders, neutral to what they are observing. The messiness of classroom teaching and learning itself is a daunting challenge. Should the three-strikes (falsification) rule apply if we have a hard time obtaining solid, convincing evidence in the midst of various "noises" surrounding the classroom (Mayer, 2004)? Are we opening a Pandora's Box methodologically by venturing into the classroom as a main venue for research? Is the enterprise we are pursuing tractable?

If it is not tractable, then such a research program will not be sustainable (Lakatos, 1978).

The third challenge has to do with the purposes of design research: is it mainly practical, fashioning innovations that can directly benefit learning and help solve pressing problems, or theoretical, aiming at fundamental understanding? Barab and Squire (2004) and diSassa and Cobb (2004) stressed theory building as a hallmark of design research, while others argue that design research striving for improved practice is by nature eclectic (Kelly, 2009). Of course, we can conceptualize design research as fitting into the Pasteur's quadrant (use-inspired research) in Stokes's (1997) framework, seeking fundamental understanding of effects of some artifacts and practices in a functional context. However, a theoretical orientation would naturally seek explanations that have generalizability as well as coherence, while omitting unnecessary local details and practical constraints, and a practical orientation would be attuned to local conditions and make pragmatic decisions based on available tools and resources. Their priorities can be quite different. Dede (2004) called for a distinction between design and "conditions for success" for a particular design. Thus, a design can be intact itself, even though its practicality may be an issue to be reckoned with in implementation. For example, a design may entail high-level pedagogical content knowledge on the part of the teacher (Shulman, 1987), but that not all teachers are well equipped in this regard does not make a related pedagogical argument less compelling (see also Collins et al. (2004), for the distinction between a design and its implementation). However, if the impetus of design research is to effect changes in the real world (Barab & Squire, 2004), then a design needs to address practical, social, and technical constraints in a direct manner. A "hothouse" design involving intensive resources and support systems may turn out fragile in real classrooms, where resources and infrastructure are not even close to what the designers expect.

Embracing and Untangling Complexity: A Multiple-Level, Multi-Phase Analysis of Design Work

Although dealing with the complexities of classroom life is a daunting task, there are strategies and analytic tools with which to impose order. Greeno and the Middle School Math Project Group (1998) discussed two strategies currently used in research. One strategy is to conduct task analysis of subsystems and components at the individual level, such as cognitive analysis of individual behavior; a problem with this strategy is that there may be emergence of new properties, operators, and outcomes in the higher-order interactive systems that cannot be predicted by the behavior of lower-level components. The other strategy is to study the higher-level interactive systems directly. A drawback is that such analysis might overlook details of individual-level functioning. The two strategies might complement each other. However, an approach that can integrate these two levels of analysis is to propose a multi-level analytic framework that can avoid reductionistic temptations to make individual participants look like isolated islands, while at the same time giving sufficient attention to individual-level constraints on realizing higher-level interaction (Sawyer, 2002).

Levels of Analysis

Any complex system can be seen as a multi-level system (Newell, 1990; Simon, 1981). For the sake of analyzing classroom teaching and learning, I suggest a three-level analytic system, the activity, intentional, and computational levels, with each level having its own properties, constraints, and principles. The first is *activity (interactivity) level*, which is mainly concerned with context, agency, purpose, and structure, and resources revolving around a learning activity. At this level, design analysis is strategic: decisions have to be made on (a) what are desired goal states; (b) what kind of tools and resources are needed to achieve the goal states; and (c) how should learning be organized and structured to achieve the goal states?

As the design work gets to psychosocial processes, the intentional-level analysis will be introduced; that is, how affordances of a learning activity are perceived and acted upon by the learners individually or interactively in a group setting, and what kind of intentional-level action and interaction needs to be activated. Note that the three aspects of learning, perspectival, instrumental, and reflective, all involve intentionality or directed consciousness in the form of affects, desires, and thoughts (Searle, 2004). Active learning and meaning making are interpretative acts, and thus the design analysis needs to preserve its unique subjective properties, such as intention, positional identity, and intersubjectivity. For example, Brown and Campione's (1994) postulation of shared inquiry (e.g., seeding and migration of an idea) is meaningful only under the assumption of a common intellectual space traversed by many, and the commitment to norms of practice shared by a group of participants (see also Bereiter & Scardemalia, 1993; Zhang, this volume). Learning as critical interpretation (Lehrer & Pfaff, this volume), as active investigation and the development of dispositions to think and act (Gresalfi, Barab, and Sommerfeld, this volume), as participation and identity development (Polman, this volume), all operate at the intentional level.

As design analysis gets further down to algorithmic or computational level, then the issue of how intentional-level actions are realized (or fail to be realized) at the individual level can be further elucidated. In other words, how instructional mediation plays out at the psychological level, and how individual-level enabling and constraining factors interact with instruction and social interaction can be identified. Indeed, we can discuss constraints imposed by cognitive architecture (Kirschner et al., 2006) and its functional properties (e.g., comparing architectural ideas by Barsalou, 2003; Glenberg, 1997; Sun, 2007; Sweller, Kirschner, & Clark, 2007).

The utility and importance of discerning levels of analysis in design work becomes clear when we realize how we can be caught up by the failure to pay due respect for unique properties and principles at each level of analysis. In a recent debate on pedagogy or instructional approaches (Tobias & Duffy, 2009), "constructivists" and "instructionists" talked past each other (Duffy, 2009; Wise & O'Neill, 2009) precisely because they discuss issues at the different levels of analysis. While constructivists espouse more ambitious goals of promoting active learning and critical thinking and developing the person, instructionists are more worried about the lower-level constraints, such as lack of knowledge and cognitive overload. Each level of analysis has its own properties and principles that need to be heeded; however, to argue that lower-level constraints can be a basis for prescribing higher-level learning goals amounts to arguing that physicists know better than civil engineers about how to build a bridge.

Multi-Phase Design Architecture

In addition to levels of analysis, complexities of design work can be managed by segmenting different components and phases of design work, each tackling a particular aspect and phase of learning activity. For instance, Calfee and Berliner (1996) used *someone (teacher) teaching something (content) to someone (learner) else in some setting (context)* as a basic script of the dynamic teaching–learning system. The "How People Learn" framework focuses on four main components as central issues of designing learning environments: community, learner, knowledge, and assessment (Bransford et al., 2000). There seem to be two critical issues all design work has to deal with. The first is how instruction can be responsive and adaptive to behavioral, cognitive, and motivational characteristics demonstrated by a learner or a group of learners (Snow & Swanson, 1992); the second is how to balance and integrate content representations and thinking processes in teaching (Baxter & Glaser, 1997) and assessment (Anderson & Krathwohl, 2001). Figure 1.2 presents an architecture of design research on teaching and learning that honors the conventional wisdom and practice in educational psychology, while emphasizing the dynamic emergence of theories and models of teaching–learning grounded in practice, research, and reflection in situ. As Glaser (1976) envisioned in probably the earliest exposition of design research in instructional psychology:

> The design process essentially involves the generation of alternatives and the testing of these alternatives against practical requirements, constraints, and values. This is not done in a single generation-and-test cycle, but through an iterative series involving the generation of alternatives, testing them (through actual small-scale studies or through simulation), describing revised alternatives, testing them, and so on. (pp. 7–8)

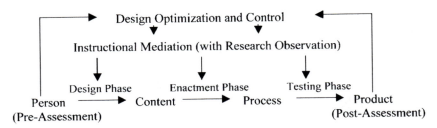

FIGURE 1.2 An architecture for design research on teaching and learning.

In this flowchart (Figure 1.2), Instructional Context serves as an overarching guide for design work on goals, specific components, structure, interactions, and resources. The arrows indicate the direction of information flow in design work. The information flow starts with Person (the learner), individually or as a group, which directly informs instructional mediation of the person–content interface. This is the "design phase," typically occurring offline (i.e., before enactment): how to represent subject matters and structure the learner–content interaction in a way conducive to the desired learning outcomes.

As the information flows from Person and Content to Process, design research enters the "enactment phase": designed learner–content interaction occurs, and related instructional mediation is carried out "online" (in real-time teaching) by teachers or teachers/researchers. Simultaneously, design researchers document what thought processes are engaged through what kind of instructional mediation, and how content is represented and processed.

When Process leads to Product, the design work enters the "testing phase": how well the designed interactions work, as manifested by learners' overt behavior and performance. This information would flow back to Design Optimization and Control to create feedback and feedforward loops, and another cycle of design work starts for optimization and improvement of a design and a modified and refined underlying theory. In the following section, I will discuss each component in the context of enhancing intellectual functioning and promoting intellectual growth, or, more specifically, how perspectival, instrumental, and reflective learning can be engendered through teaching–learning interactions and realized at the individual level.

Instructional Context

Instructional contexts are mainly concerned with goals, structure, and resources for designing a learning environment and sequence of learning activities (an activity-level analysis). Thus, any design has a normative side (what kind of knowing and knowledge is desired and valued in the learning enterprise), a pedagogical side (how learning should be structured and mediated to achieve the set goals), and a pragmatic side (what resources are available for that purpose).

The following questions are central when we try to integrate learning with concerns over intellectual gains: What is the nature of the subject matter we are teaching vis-à-vis the current level of the child's knowledge and thinking, how it is connected to the larger social world in which children live, and how it might broaden the intellectual horizon of the child in question. A recurrent debate in this regard has been between those who insist in teaching basic knowledge and skills and those who advocate teaching for deep understanding and higher-order thinking. Siegler (2001), for example, questioned whether it is realistic to teach grade school children for deep disciplinary understanding of math and science (see also Kirschner et al., 2006).

There are three root metaphors of the structure of learning, transmission (or acquisition), construction, and participation (cf. Greeno, Collins, & Resnick, 1996), which help organize learning in pedagogically different ways. For those who promote "higher literacy" and believe that students need to know that "mathematics, biology, history, physics, and other subjects of the school curriculum are distinctive ways of thinking and talking" (Wineburg & Grossman, 2001; see also Gee, 2003), the notions of learning as participation and (knowledge) construction are central, though social transmission of knowledge is also meaningful in the form of cognitive apprenticeship. How we can teach the mind to respond to new situations more adaptively and critically is at the heart of cultivating intellectual potential and promoting intellectual growth. For this purpose, learning of disciplinary content in proper contexts of use is instrumental for supporting such intellectual growth.

Person as an Enabling as Well as Constraining Factor

The person (the learner) is both an agentic presence and constraining factor for design work. Under the cognitive framework or acquisition metaphor, the person is often conceptualized as providing an initial state, and instruction is designed to bring the person from an initial state to a goal state, however defined (Glaser, 1976). Researchers using the participation metaphor of learning conceptualize the learner in terms of what kind of entry (timing, medium, and support) is appropriate for ushering the person into the realm of a particular social practice, be it mathematics or literature.

Many putative learning-related constraints have been proposed, most of which have to do with abilities and prior knowledge (Snow & Swanson, 1992). A recurrent theme summarized by Newell (1990) is the preparation–deliberation trade-off: the more offline preparation (e.g., more prior knowledge), the less the demand on online deliberation. Cognitive load theory (CLT) deals with this trade-off in a more elaborate way (see Plass, Moreno, & Brunken, 2010). Arguments against inquiry-based or more constructivist-oriented teaching are often based on the assumption that students don't have the necessary knowledge preparation to engage in high-level thinking and problem solving (Kirschner et al., 2006; see Tobias & Duffy, 2009). With respect to levels of analysis, the arguments typically conceptualize constraints as located at lower-level mechanisms and operations, such as working memory capacity limits and lack of cognitive schemas to reduce the cognitive workload. Regarding this objection to higher-level meaning making in learning, the question is how much does a person have to know about a domain before he/she can develop deep insights into the "modus operandi" of a domain as a form of social practice? Here, the distinction between perspectival and instrumental learning becomes useful. It seems that gaining a new perspective through experiencing things differently or in more specialized and principled way (knowledge-about; see Lampert, 1990) may not be as demanding in terms of prior knowledge as building and practicing "instruments" for problem solving (knowledge-how). A key pedagogical strategy is to start informally and experientially (e.g., developing an intuitive basis for deep understanding, using metaphors and other means; see Lehrer & Pfaff, this volume) and move gradually toward formalization (Bruner, 1979; see also Bransford et al., 2000).

Individual differences in cognitive and affective functions are often used as a basis for differentiated treatment. Indeed, the ATI research is built on this premise (Cronbach, 2002; Cronbach & Snow, 1977; Snow & Lohman, 1984). Glaser (2000) suggested that we move away from the abstract notion of "aptitude" and take a more diagnostic approach regarding what one can or cannot do. To combat a static, unqualified notion of "aptitude," Snow (1992) proposed aptitude– situation as a union; that is, aptitude is always relative to situations. This more proximal, situational construal of aptitude makes it possible to encourage and foster active and critical learning and intellectual development regardless of their "entry" level, while addressing whatever constraints and impediments might be present vis-à-vis the learning task at hand (see Bannan, this volume, for a detailed account of designed interventions with twice exceptional children).

There is an increasing realization that children should be considered not merely as a constraining factor, but as an enabling one, a resource to draw on. The fact that the human brain is predisposed to predict patterns, even when an array of stimuli is random (Gazzaniga, 2000), and that children as young as five or six years old are routinely and spontaneously engaged in conscious meaning making of their experiences of the world (e.g., making "representational redescription"; Karmiloff-Smith, 1992), makes it clear that learners should be an active part of design work, rather than sitting at the receiving end, "acquiring" the knowledge and skills prescribed by others. The two examples used by diSessa and Cobb (2004) to demonstrate "ontological innovation" in design research, metarepresentational competence and sociomathematical norms are cases in point. The former refers to a body of knowledge students bring to bear upon the learning materials in a way potentially leading to critical and creative interpretations and representations, and the latter refers to norms of mathematical discourse that encourage intellectual autonomy in taking part in mathematical practice. Both are instances of agency emergent from classroom discourses that the design researchers leveraged for more advanced academic and intellectual development. That learners can effect a more productive learning environment by acting on the subject matter intelligently, critically, and creatively should be a major consideration in design. It brings opportunities as well as uncertainties to design work (see Engle, this volume; Gresalfi et al., this volume; Langer, this volume; Zhang, this volume).

Content Representation: Designing the Person–Content Interface

Design work in this phase is basically designing the person–content interface. It involves analysis of affordances and constraints: what a situation enables and affords the learners to do and accomplish, and what constraints need to be addressed in order to materialize these affordances. The key issue to be addressed is representation, because how students interact with an instructional situation is mediated by perceptions and interpretations of that situation. This is a distinct intentional-level analysis. By content representation, I mean not only representation of the subject matter, but also that of a learning situation (e.g., in what context and how a topic is introduced, and a problem is presented, and what is the purpose of introducing the topic or problem), as the latter can influence students' perceptions and representational strategies regarding the former.

The normative question of treating learning as an intellectual act is how an instructional situation and its informational content can be designed to induce perceptions and interpretations conducive to perspectival, instrumental, and reflective learning.

For this purpose, both the medium and substance of representation are important. Medium concerns *how* information is presented and represented, and substance concerns *what* is presented and represented. For illustration purposes, we can roughly classify media as text-based, discourse-based, and action-based, and substance as content knowledge (facts, concepts, and theories, etc.), reasoning schemas and strategies (proportional vs. causal reasoning, use of metaphors and analogy, inferring design grammars, etc.), and complex problem solving (cases, critical instances, projects, etc.). Putting them in a larger instructional context, a curricular/instructional activity has three levels of representation: (a) representation of subject matter as part of the curriculum content in its purposes, structure, and functionality; (b) representation of the informational content as part of a larger body of domain knowledge and its epistemic value and practical utilities (i.e., Popper's World 3; see Popper, 1972); and (c) representation of content being learned as a cultural way of knowing and part of social practice that produced this body of knowledge (i.e., recognizing it as a particular kind of socially sanctioned meaning making or problem solving. "Knowing about a social practice always involves *recognizing* various distinctive ways of acting, interacting, valuing, feeling, knowing, and using various objects and technologies, that constitute the social practice" (Gee, 2003, p. 29; italics original).

Medium and Message

Text-based representations include a variety of verbally mediated forms of communication aimed at disseminating information and knowledge or presenting a particular argument. A text can contain propositions, facts, claims, narratives, or expositions, from which meanings (structures, functions, relationships) can be drawn and made about the world (states of affairs, human conditions, etc.). However, text-based representations are for most part mediated by language and, to a lesser degree, pictures. Text comprehension (e.g., critical reading) is an act of reasoning and meaning making par excellence, involving critically interpreting and understanding the underlying logic of a text vis-à-vis a particular topic. Texts are most frequently used for representation of a culturally created body of knowledge, World 3 in a Popperian sense (Popper, 1972). One example is concept-oriented reading instruction (Guthrie, Wigfield, & Perencevich, 2004). However, texts can also be built to represent the cultural practice that produces knowledge. Palincsa and Magnusson (2001), for instance, reported their research on second-hand investigation by deliberately building a text in the form of a scientist's notebook, mixing genres of narrative, exposition, description, and argumentation, to represent scientists' doing, feeling, and thinking in a scientific domain. Learners, while reading the notebook, would mentally simulate the thought processes (i.e., emulating, vicariously, a modus operandi) scientists go through, and gain insights into the nature and processes of scientific inquiry. The context for the use of texts becomes a critical consideration in such instructional contexts, as is also the case in the teaching of the greenhouse effect discussed earlier, where text material is used as a tool with which to understand real-world problems students encountered. In other words, a text, and the just-in-time knowledge it presents, is used instrumentally to understand and solve a problem.

Discourse-based representations refer to representations engendered during or after significant amounts of teacher–student, student–student communication and interaction. Discourse-based representations are important because most of academic learning involves interpretation or sense making, namely delving into the various realms of meanings (Gee, 2003; Phenix, 1964). Resnick's (1987) teaching of mathematics as an ill-structured discipline and Lampert's (1990) pedagogy of engaging fifth graders in mathematical guesses were early examples of building deep understanding of a topic through discourse-based representations. In fact, they afford metarepresentation of underlying logic and "rules" for generating and justifying knowledge claims (Kuhn, 2002). Lehrer and Pfaff's (this volume) use of measurement as a basic metaphor for understanding rational numbers is also a discourse-based tool, frequently used to engage students in

"epistemic conversation." Langer's (this volume) envisionment-building in literature and social studies, and Zhang's (this volume) creative knowledge practice
also rely heavily on discourse-based representations.

Action-based representations are based on situated inquiry and problem-
solving activities. Guided discovery, problem-based and project-based learning,
skill-based simulations and games, all have a distinct action component in the
sense of having a problem to solve and a task to accomplish. An action may involve
texts and discourses but has added value in its affordances for real-time, in situ
actions and representations (and metarepresentation) of a particular way of
knowing and thinking as a professional practice (Gee, 2003; Shaffer, 2004). Action-
based representations are embodied because such representations are ingrained in
actions, motivations, perceptions, affects, attitudes, and values, rather than taking
the abstract, symbolic form. Although the efficacy of action-based instructional
activities for students who have limited knowledge and skills to work with is
questioned (Kirschner, 2009), it can be argued that they provide an experiential
basis for grounding the otherwise decontextualized abstract concepts and theories.
As Barsalou (2003) suggested, an action-based dynamic conceptual representation
can be tailored or fine-tuned to "the constraints of situated action" (p. 553), thus
more easily activated to support future action. The learning conditions created
in the environmental science class discussed earlier afford such an action-based
dynamic conceptual representation of "greenhouse effect" that enables the
students to act upon the knowledge (i.e., transfer) more readily and effectively.

A design may mix two or more forms of medium, as is usually the case with
most designs. A critical question for perspectival, instrumental, and reflective
learning is *how to put a particular content in a larger context so that representations become
potent for connections to its perspectival reference and instrumental value.* An age–old issue
in learning theory is the part–whole problem. Hilgard (1948) delineated the history
of learning theories as divided between those who view learning more
atomistically, as installing building blocks one by one to build an ever more
complex repertoire of knowledge and skills, and those who view learning as a
process of mapping out the structural whole in which various pieces of knowledge
will find their respective place (see also Perkins, 2010). Without taking a too
polemic view on the debate, it can be argued that situated actions coupled with
guided inquiry may engender representations that are intellectual in nature; that
is, they afford metarepresentation of knowledge as the result of human endeavor
to understand and change the world.

Process and Instructional Mediation: Engineering a Sequence of Learning Activities

This is an enactment phase of design work. The key question is how to engineer
a sequence of learning activities that maximally utilize personal, technological,
and social resources to achieve perspectival, instrumental, and reflective gains,

while at the same time addressing possible developmental, social, and individual difference constraints regarding cognitive readiness, affective valence, and motivational inclinations. This is where the person, content, and context issues need to be integrated and addressed simultaneously: (a) How to leverage students' knowledge, abilities, and motivations while addressing potential constraints at the individual and interactive levels (Person); (b) How to direct attention and thinking to engender proper content representations in the service of overall learning goals (Content); (c) How to orchestrate important design elements of classroom teaching (pedagogical tools, technological support, social organization of learning) to enable optimal learning conditions for intellectual growth (Context). In short, while early phases of design work may take things apart to see how they work separately, in the enactment phase one has to put everything together to see how it works as a whole. Most important social-contextual, interactive factors (activity level) and psychosocial variables (intentional level) in a given learning situation are now clearly defined, substantiated, and operational at this stage of design work, and enactment will ultimately get the computational level in terms of execution and detailed implementation. They set the stage for the work of instructional mediation.

Instructional Mediation: Engage, Guide, and Organize

Instructional mediation is the real-time mediation of the person–content–context interaction. Instructional mediation of learning as an intellectual act can be seen as a pedagogy of enhanced thinking: *how to engage, guide, and organize learning and thinking in the direction of gaining new perspectives, mastering new instruments, and fostering new reflective insights*. The mediation process can be explicit (e.g., taking the form of direct teaching or guidance), or seamless (e.g., embedded in problem-solving activities); it can be a built-in feature of an instructional medium (e.g., how a text or game is structured to engage, guide, or organize active and reflective learning), or through a human agent (e.g., the teacher) (Dai & Wind, in press; Palincsa & Magnusson, 2001). Instructional mediation inevitably utilizes three resources: pedagogical tools, technological support, and social organization in addressing learner-related, content-related, and context-related constraints. In the following, I briefly discuss how gaining perspectives, mastering instruments, and fostering reflective insights have their own distinct entailments, and how each can be engaged, guided, and organized, with a caveat that they work in a reciprocal, cyclic fashion.

Instructional Mediation of Perspectival Learning

In line with ecological psychology, the essence of perspectival learning is the education of attention and perception (Gibson, 1977). Although working memory capacity and cognitive load are distinct, relevant issues for learning new materials

(Plass et al., 2010), Saariluoma (1992) found from his research on chess that a more critical element in performance errors is perceptual (apperceptions) in nature, rather than memory capacity. In other words, learning involves a reorientation of attention and restructuring of perception, or reorganization of one's interpretative apparatus (Piaget, 2001; Sinatra & Pintrich, 2003). Because of the perceptual nature of perspectival learning, affect or feeling becomes a crucial factor. The moment one says "it makes sense" or "how come this happened?" indicates a state of feeling and consciousness that is anything but emotionally neutral. Two constraints follow: people only try to actively interpret a situation when there is perceived novelty or perplexity (Hatano, 1988); and perspectival gains would not occur unless a learner is open to changing beliefs and values (following the recognize–appreciate–valuing sequence).

Instructional Mediation of Instrumental Learning

Learning is instrumental in that learning helps one achieve intellectual, social, and practical goals of solving problems relevant and meaningful to the learner. In the greenhouse lesson cited earlier, the teacher engaged students in figuring out the temperature changes inside a car or soda bottles, thus creating "a need to know" (Wise & O'Neill, 2009). A major pedagogical strategy for cognitive and affective engagement is to position learners to acquire content knowledge that has a direct bearing on important, real-life circumstances (Barab, Gresalfi, & Ingram-Goble, 2010). Besides engagement, guiding attention, reasoning, and organizing problem solving through modeling, scaffolding, and granting authority, and collaboration is what most inquiry-based learning models highlight (see Hmelo-Silver, Duncan, & Chinn, 2007; Schmidt, Loyens, van Gog, Paas, 2007; White & Fredericksen, 1998; 2005; see also Engle, this volume; Zhang, this volume). Consider the "gap-filling" notion of intelligence discussed in the beginning of this chapter: children who are spontaneously engaged in coherence-building, or bridging-the-gap self-explanations, are seen as more intelligent than those who are not. If so, instructional mediation for those less prone to fill in the gaps can take the form of encouraging inference-making and self-explanations, which enable the learners to develop a disposition to seek explanation and consequently a schema for reasoning about a given class of phenomena or events (Siegler, 2002). Even constraints that sit deeply in the learner's cognitive infrastructure (e.g., attention deficit) can be remedied to some extent by external, technology-supported systems (see Bannan, this volume), analogous to prosthetic devices for the physically handicapped. To be sure, instrumental learning means mastery of conceptual and technological instruments and tools that take many years of deliberate practice to build and solidify (Ericsson, 2006), and the nature of instrumental learning as progressive deepening (de Groot, 1978; Newell, 1990) may put further constraints on how fast one can achieve technical proficiency and expertise in a domain. Yet, the instructor should never lose sight of their real-life utilities or instrumental value as supporting problem solving (Shulman & Quinlan, 1996).

Instructional Mediation of Reflective Learning

To use Schön's (1983) framework, both reflection-in-practice and reflection-on-practice can be instructionally mediated through engagement and guidance. For example, in epistemic games that mimic professional practices (Shaffer, 2004), Shaffer and his colleagues deliberately built a reflection cycle into the gameplay, so that the epistemological grounding of such professional practice can be reflected upon. White and Fredericksen (2005), in their work on inquiry-based learning in science, developed a technology-based support system designed to enhance metacognition. In his mathematical teaching, Lehrer (Lehrer & Pfaff, this volume) engaged students in an epistemic conversation, meant to be reflective on the fundamentals of mathematical thinking. Viewed in a broader context of learning, reflective learning is a natural consequence of instrumental learning (see Figure 1.1). People engage in reflection, not because of its intrinsic interest, but because of the consequentiality of learning (Barab et al., 2010; see also Derry & Lesgold, 1996, for reflective learning in training settings).

Product: Assessing Learning, Developing a Prototype, and Building a Grounded Theory

If the enactment is a process of orchestrating and engineering, the transition from a focus on process to a focus on product indicates a testing phase for design work. Here, the term "testing" has three dimensions: (a) whether the process produces a desired state or trajectory individually or collectively (the effectiveness criterion); (b) whether the process produces a design prototype that has well-defined components and procedures that make it scalable and applicable to a range of instructional situations (the practicality criterion); and (c) whether the process produces a grounded theory that has all constructs and interrelations well defined and assessed and has a level of generality that enables it to explain how learning can be optimized to support thinking and development (the validity criterion).

Does the Process Produce a Desired State or Trajectory (the Effectiveness Criterion)?

Current assessment practices for effectiveness of a program are still in the transition from a traditional approach that assesses discrete pieces of knowledge to a more formative, diagnostic approach that aims to enhance learning (Shepard, 2000). For assessment of intellectual growth, what one learned serves the purpose of thinking more intelligently about a topic. At least the following taxonomy of intellectual gains can be discerned: (a) foundational knowledge (facts, procedures, and concepts, and goals of a discipline or domain of social practice); (b) conceptual understandings (reasoning schemas at a more complex level) regarding a subject or domain; (c) meta-awareness of the epistemological grounds of the knowing process and knowledge claims; (d) the transformation and productive use of knowledge for intellectual or practical purposes (i.e., problem solving); (e) refined habits of mind, such as a critical stance, a disposition to reason, seek explanations and make educated guesses, to extrapolate, to suggest viable alternatives, and probe for further understanding, to engage in counterfactual thinking (suspense of disbelief), or, simply put, to think more intelligently (Gresalfi et al., this volume; Halpern, 2008; Perkins & Ritchhart, 2004). The traditional psychometric approach is inadequate in dealing with the challenge (see Moss, Pullin, Gee, & Haertel, 2005, for a sociocultural argument against psychometric perspective on testing); yet, without some metrics of performance and behavior, making claims about positive changes becomes difficult (see Kelly, this volume). At any rate, the assessment of learning gains of interest would have to take innovative approaches, capturing these qualities dynamically in situ, rather than in a paper-and-pencil task (see Gresalfi et al., this volume; Shute & Kim this volume; and Zhang, this volume; see also Gee & Shaffer, 2010). Assessment in design research is by nature formative, not only in the sense of improving design, but also assisting in further defining the parameters of a problem that a design attempts to address.

Does the Process Produce a Design Prototype that has Well Defined Components and Procedures that Make it Scalable and Applicable to a Range of Instructional Situations (the Practicality Criterion)?

The second criterion determines whether a design is practically viable and implementable. It is still open to debate as to the degree in which a design needs to be "proceduralized" so that instructors can implement it with high fidelity, or should be principle based and remain flexible for adaptation to local situations (see Dede, 2004; Engle, this volume; Zhang, this volume). The issue concerns the extent to which a design can realize full technical rationality or formalism in terms of specifying all details of implementation from the social–interactive level all the way down to the psychological level. Given that we still don't know much about how to engineer psychological processes in an algorithmic fashion, a design may have to stay at a level that is not fully specified through technical rationality. Therefore, a fair amount of reflective rationality is still needed on the part of implementers to materialize a design that, in many respects, remains principle based and demands critical (and sometimes creative) interpretations in implementation. Another issue is the extent to which a design can maintain its quality and integrity while remaining realistic for implementation, for example, not taking inordinate amounts of resources and expertise. Dede (2004) alerted design researchers to a distinction between a design and its conditions for success. There seems to be a trade-off between idealism and realism.

Does the Process Produce a Grounded Theory that Has All Constructs and their Interrelations Well Defined and Assessed and Has a Level of Generality that Enables it to Explain How Learning Can Be Optimized to Support Thinking and Development (the Validity Criterion)?

Design research ultimately aims at producing evidence-based claims that potentially change the existent educational practices (Barab & Squire, 2004). Moreover, it generates theoretical ideas that illuminate important parts of education and instructional practice and thus deserve the label "ontological innovations" (diSessa & Cobb, 2004). Design research aimed at high-level intellectual functioning and growth should do no less. At a minimum, it needs to specify person-based, content-based, and context-based affordances for, and constraints on, learning as an intellectual act in a way that informs instructional mediation, leading to social and psychological processes that materialize affordances in terms of enabling perspectival, instrumental, and reflective gains. To the extent it illuminates how feeling, thinking, or acting is (or can be) engaged, guided, and organized in authentic learning and performance situations, it becomes an education-based, fully integrated theory of learning, intelligence, and intellectual development.

Process Optimization and Control: Design–Test–Modification Iteration and Theory Building

This is the metalevel, executive function of design work. Part of the executive function is control: how to manage the temporal, socially and psychologically dynamic activity of learning that involves interactivity of multiple agents and resources within a certain temporal and social boundary. Historically, researchers preferred to use simple units of analysis that contain minimal elements for enhancing internal validity (i.e., doing controlled experiments; Campbell & Stanley, 1966). Design research deliberately uses a unit of analysis that encompasses a broad range of social and psychological parameters and has a high level of complexity. A strategic issue design researchers have to wrestle with is how to define and manage the boundary of a design, open and responsive to important clues and new leads, while not overstretching to the point of unmanageable complexity. For example, should a design involve institutional support, such as teacher training and capacity building? Earlier, I elaborated on instructional mediation. But what about teacher learning and growing with students? Such a component may require cultural and institutional changes of a school and complicate implementation. However, without such a component, a design may be fragile and unsustainable in real classroom settings.

Beyond control and management issues, the main purpose of the executive function of design work is optimization, a prominent feature of design work (Glaser, 1976): how a system can be attuned adaptively to emergent constraints, properties, and new affordances, while maintaining an initial principled stance. The optimization mainly relies on two mechanisms: feedback and feedforward. Feedback mechanisms rely on information that flows from person, content, process, and product to inform effectiveness of learning vis-à-vis set goals and objectives, including identifying emergent person-related, content-related, and process-related constraints (see Polman, this volume). Feedforward mechanisms rely on information from the person, content, process, and product to envision emergent affordances and new possibilities (e.g., students' newly found or acquired skills create new learning opportunities). It should be noted that both feedback and feedforward mechanisms are not merely to improve practice; it is a process of theory building as well. In fact, the "ontological innovations" diSessa and Cobb (2004) elaborated on are all based on feedforward mechanisms, inventing new theoretical constructs that become a leverage point for enhancing intellectual functioning (see also Zhang, this volume).

Significance of This Line of Work

In this introduction chapter, I attempt to delineate a history of how we have come to a point where it is viable to think about learning, teaching, and thinking as intertwined rather than separate issues, and how design research may help build an agenda to promote intellectual growth and formulate an education-based theory of intelligence and intellectual development along the way. A perusal of the literature on design research will reveal that most prominent concerns of design research have been on students' deep conceptual knowledge and higher-order thinking; yet the design research community remains silent regarding the challenges from the psychometric research that shows distinct individual differences in intellectual functioning and development, or from those skeptics who argue that the constructivist movement aimed at promoting higher-order thinking in education has yet to produce creditable supporting evidence beyond the rhetoric (e.g., Kirschner et al., 2006; Mayer, 2004; 2009). There are three imperatives that make this line of work important: theoretical, empirical, and practical.

The Theoretical Imperative

Intelligence has for a long time been seen as a property of the mind, a trait possessed by the person. Perkins (1995) concluded that all extant intelligence theories fall into three classes: the first kind, neural intelligence, emphasizes the role of biological underpinnings for high-level functioning; the second kind, experiential intelligence, emphasizes domain experience as a basis for high performance; and the third kind, reflective intelligence, stresses the role of the reflective guidance in enhanced intellectual functioning. While neural intelligence is presumably less malleable, experiential and reflective intelligence can be enhanced by social interventions. Also, in the spirit of distributed intelligence (Gresalfi et al., this volume), design research has the potential to contribute to "smart design," even a new kind of theory of intelligence, fully situated in education settings, use-inspired, grounded in empirical evidence of realized intellectual potential and growth, reflecting optimal design as much as power of mind. In other words, can we go beyond the Flynn Effect (Neisser, 1998) to reach a new level of sophistication in intelligent designs and designed intelligence? To social optimists as well as pessimists, this is a test of nature and nurture in a fundamental way. Design efforts to cultivate intellectual potential and promote growth will ultimately demonstrate how nurture (with all its pedagogy, technology, and resources) can stretch the limits of human potential, and how nurture may be constrained by nature (Dai, 2010).

The Empirical Imperative

Whether design research is a viable method for generating theoretical as well as practical models of enhanced intellectual functioning and growth depends on whether "smart learning" indeed results from the design work. This is particularly true in the larger policy and funding context (Kelly, this volume). Finding proper ways of assessing the progressions in learning and thinking continues to be a main challenge. In that regard, technological breakthroughs in assessment of intellectual functioning in situ and growth over time in design research are critical in producing credible evidence, which can convince stakeholders of education and skeptics that a more ambitious education agenda aimed at high-end learning and higher-order thinking is indeed viable. In addition, design research aimed at promoting deep understanding and higher-order thinking has yet to confront evidence of individual differences in learning and thinking (Ceci & Papierno, 2005) head-on, rather than treating this body of literature as irrelevant. How individual participants differentially benefit from a particular design, and how a design is adaptive to individual difference constraints are also legitimate questions (Snow, 1992). Design research has to show that, while the more able may indeed gain more with education interventions (Ceci & Papierno, 2005), almost all students can gain intellectual grounds when instructional designs engage their agency and address their needs or particular constraints. Design research will also need to fashion a new language of interpreting data and making evidence-based claims, switching from simple, linear cause–effect mapping to more complex, multi-level affordances–constraints, means–ends analysis. Validity needs to be redefined from the new epistemic stance in terms of whether insights gained from the research help bring about meaningful, positive changes (Barab et al., 2010). As a new methodology, design research is well poised to achieve both relevance and rigor; however, it is still in its early stage of development, and there are more questions than answers regarding its nature and efficacy. For example, just as a design study can be underconceptualized and overproceduralized, as Dede (2004) pointed out, it can also err on the opposite, overconceptualizing and under-proceduralizing, falling short of operationalization and substantiation, with a design remaining "theoretical."

The Practical Imperative

Design research is normative, concerned with what "ought to be" (Simon, 1981). There is an inherent aspect of educational innovation in it. The past century has witnessed a sea change in social and economic development, facilitated by dazzling scientific and technological advances, yet the structure of schooling, as well as how curriculum is structured and delivered for the same period, remains virtually unchanged (Collins & Halverson, 2009). In the spirit of designing for a better future, design researchers should take on the challenge of designing learning environments for optimal development of the young generations. New conceptions of learning and instructional psychology that integrate learning, thinking, and development are just one way to meet the challenge of the new world, a global knowledge economy, which demands a workforce capable of making adaptive changes and productively using knowledge in problem solving and decision making, of capturing new opportunities and dealing with uncertainties in an ever-changing work environment and job market. The design research community ought to contribute its scholarship to the public discourse on competencies and skills needed for the new century (e.g., Partnership for 21st Century Skills, 2008). The topics of building deep conceptual knowledge, enhancing complex problem solving, critical thinking and creativity, of promoting self-direction and collaborative skills along with academic ones ought to be part of the research agenda for design researchers. When everything is said and done, it is the consequential validity that ultimately determines the viability and promise of design research.

Acknowledgments

I would like to thank Sasha Barab, David Perkins, Keith Sawyer, and Jianwei Zhang for their thoughtful comments on an earlier version of this chapter. I also appreciate the helpful feedback provided by Jeannette Ellis, Robyn Long, and Yue Ma.

References

Ackerman, P. L. (1988). Determinants of individual differences during skill acquisition: Cognitive abilities and information processing. *Journal of Experimental Psychology: General, 117*, 288–318.

Anderson, L. W., & Krathwohl, D. R. (Eds.) (2001). *A taxonomy for learning, teaching, and assessment*. New York, NY: Longman.

Barab, S. A., & Plucker, J. A. (2002). Smart people or smart context? Cognition, ability, and talent development in an age of situated approaches to knowing and learning. *Educational Psychologist, 37*, 165–182.

Barab, S., & Squire, K. (2004). Design-based research: Putting a stake in the ground. *The Journal of the Learning Sciences, 13*, 1–14.

Barab, S. A., Gresalfi, M., & Ingram-Goble, A. (2010). Transformational play: Using games to position person, content, and context. *Educational Researcher, 39*, 525–536.

Barsalou, L. W. (2003). Situated simulation in the human conceptual system. *Language and Cognitive Processes, 18*, 513–562.

Baxter, G. P., & Glaser, R. (1997). *A cognitive framework for performance assessment: CSE technical report*. Los Angeles: National Center for Research on Evaluation Standards, and Student Testing, Graduate School of Education, University of California, Los Angeles.

Bereiter, C. (2002). *Education and mind in the knowledge age*. Mahwah, NJ: Lawrence Erlbaum Associates.

Bereiter, C., & Scardamalia, M. (1993). *Surpassing ourselves: An inquiry into the nature and implications of expertise*. La Salle, IL: Open Court.

Bloom, B. S. (1984). The 2 sigma problem: The search for methods of group instruction as effective as one-to-one tutoring. *Educational Researcher, 13*(6), 4–16.

Borkowski, J. G., & Peck, V. A. (1986). Causes and consequences of metamemory in gifted children. In R. J. Sternberg & J. E. Davidson (Eds.), *Conceptions of giftedness* (pp. 182–200). Cambridge, UK: Cambridge University Press.

Bransford, J. D., Brown, A. L., & Cocking, R. R. (2000). *How people learn: Brain, mind, experience, and school*. Washington, DC: National Academy Press.

Brown, A. L. (1992). Design experiments: Theoretical and methodological challenges in creating complex interventions in classroom settings. *Journal of the Learning Sciences, 2*, 141–178.

Brown, A. L. (1994). The advance of learning. *Educational Researcher, 23*, 4–12.

Brown, A. L. (1997). Transforming schools into communities of thinking and learning about serious matters. *American Psychologist, 52*, 399–413.

Brown, A. L., & Campione, J. (1994). Guided discovery in a community of learners. In K. McGilly (Ed.), *Classroom lessons: Integrating cognitive theory and classroom practice* (pp. 229–270). Cambridge, MA: The MIT Press.

Bruner, J. S. (1960). *The process of education*. Cambridge, MA: Harvard University Press.

Bruner, J. S. (1966). *Toward a theory of instruction*. Cambridge, MA: The Belknap Press of Harvard University Press.

Bruner, J. (1979). *On knowing: Essays for the left hand*. Cambridge, MA: Belknap Press of Harvard University Press.

Bruner, J. (1996). *The culture of education*. Cambridge, MA: Harvard University Press.

Calfee, R. C., & Berliner, D. C. (1996). Introduction to a dynamic and relevant educational psychology. In D. C. Berliner & R. C. Calfee (Eds.), *Handbook of educational psychology* (pp. 1–11). New York: Simon & Schuster Macmillan.

Campbell, D. T., & Stanley, J. C. (1966). *Experimental and quasi-experimental designs for research*. Chicago: Rand McNally.

Campione, J. C., & Brown, A. L. (1978). Toward a theory of intelligence: Contributions from research with retarded children. *Intelligence, 2,* 279–304.

Carey, S. (1999). Sources of conceptual change. In E. K. Scholnick, K. Nelson, S. Gelman, A., & P. H. Miller (Eds.), *Conceptual development: Piaget's legacy* (pp. 293–326). Mahwah, NJ: Lawrence Erlbaum.

Carroll, J. B. (1993). *Human cognitive abilities: A survey of factor-analytic studies*. Cambridge: Cambridge University Press.

Carroll, J. B. (1997). Psychometrics, intelligence, and public perception. *Intelligence, 24,* 25–52.

Cattell, R. B. (1971). *Abilities: Their structure, growth, and action*. Boston: Houghton Mifflin.

Ceci, S. J. (1996). *On intelligence: A bio-ecological treatise on intellectual development* (2nd ed.). Cambridge, MA: Harvard University Press.

Ceci, S. J., & Papierno, P. B. (2005). The rhetoric and reality of gap closing: When the "have-nots" gain but the "haves" gain even more. *American Psychologist, 60,* 149–160.

Ceci, S. J., & Williams, W. M. (1997). Schooling, intelligence, and income. *American Psychologist, 52,* 1051–1058.

Collins, A. (1992). Toward a design science of education. In E. Scanlon & T. O'Shea (Eds.), *New directions in educational technology* (pp. 15–22). New York: Springer-Verlag.

Collins, A., Joseph, D., & Bielaczyc, K. (2004). Design research: Theoretical and methodological issues. *The Journal of the Learning Sciences, 13,* 15–42.

Collins, A. M., & Halverson, R. (2009). *Rethinking education in the age of technology*. New York: Teachers College Press.

Cronbach, L. J. (1957). The two discipline of scientific psychology. *American Psychologist, 12,* 671–684.

Cronbach, L. J. (1975). Beyond the two disciplines of scientific psychology. *American Psychologist, 30,* 116–127.

Cronbach, L. J., & Snow, R. E. (1977). *Aptitudes and instructional methods: A handbook for research on interactions*. New York: Irvington.

Cronbach, L. J. E. (Ed.) (2002). *Remaking the concept of aptitude: Extending the legacy of Richard E. Snow*. Mahwah, NJ: Lawrence Erlbaum.

Dai, D. Y. (2010). *The nature and nurture of giftedness: A new framework for understanding gifted education*. New York: Teachers College Press.

Dai, D. Y., & Sternberg, R. J. (2004). Beyond cognitivism: Toward an integrated understanding of intellectual functioning and development. In D. Y. Dai & R. J. Sternberg (Eds.), *Motivation, emotion, and cognition: Integrative perspectives on intellectual functioning and development* (pp. 3–38). Mahwah, NJ: Lawrence Erlbaum.

Dai, D. Y., & Wind, A. P. (in press). Computer games and opportunity to learn: Implications for teaching students from low socioeconomic backgrounds. In S. Tobias & J. D. Fletcher (Eds.), *Computer games and instruction*. Greenwich, CT: Information Age Publishing.

Deary, I. J. (2002). G and cognitive elements of information processing: An agnostic view. In R. J. Sternberg & E. L. Grigorenko (Eds.), *The general factor of intelligence* (pp. 151–182). Mahwah, NJ: Erlbaum.

Dede, C. (2004). If design-based research is the answer, what is the question? A commentary on Collins, Joseph, and Bielaczyc; diSassa and Cobb; and Fishman, Marx, Blumenthal,

Krajcik, and Soloway in the JLS special issue on design-based research. *The Journal of the Learning Sciences, 13,* 105–114.

de Groot, A. D. (1978). *Thought and choice in chess* (2nd ed.). The Hague: Mouton.

Derry, S., & Lesgold, A. (1996). Toward a situated social practice model for instructional design. In D. C. Berliner & R. C. Calfee (Eds.), *Handbook of educational psychology* (pp. 787–806). New York: Simon & Schuster Macmillan.

Detterman, D. K. (1993). The case for the prosecution: Transfer as an epiphenomenon. In D. K. Detterman & R. J. Sternberg (Eds.), *Transfer on trial: Intelligence, cognition, and instruction* (pp. 1–24). Norwood, NJ: Ablex Publishing Corporation.

Dewey, J. (1933). The process and product of reflective activity: Psychological process and logical forms. In J. Boydston (Ed.), *The later works of John Dewey* (Vol. 8, pp. 171–186). Carbondale, IL: Southern Illinois University Press.

Dewey, J. (1997). *How we think.* Mineola, NY: Dover Publications. (Originally published in 1910.)

diSessa, A. A., & Cobb, P. (2004). Ontological innovation and the role of theory in design experiments. *The Journal of the Learning Sciences, 13,* 77–103.

Duffy, T. M. (2009). Building lines of communication and a research agenda. In S. Tobias & T. M. Duffy (Eds.), *Constructivist instruction: Success or failure?* (pp. 351–367). New York: Routledge.

Dweck, C. S. (1999). *Self theories: Their role in motivation, personality, and development.* Philadelphia, PA: Psychology Press.

Ericsson, K. A. (2006). The influence of experience and deliberate practice on the development of superior expert performance. In K. A. Ericsson, N. Charness, P. J. Feltovich & R. R. Hoffman (Eds.), *The Cambridge handbook of expertise and expert performance* (pp. 683–703). New York: Cambridge University Press.

Estes, W. K. (1986). Where is intelligence? In R. J. Sternberg & D. K. Detterman (Eds.), *What is intelligence? Contemporary viewpoints on its nature and definition* (pp. 63–67). Norwood, NJ: Ablex Publishing Corporation.

Fischer, K. W., & Bidell, T. R. (2006). Dynamic development of action and thought. In W. Damon & R. M. Lerner (Eds.), *Handbook of child psychology* (6th ed., Vol. 1, Theoretical model of human development, pp. 313–399). Hoboken, NJ: John Wiley & Sons Inc.

Gazzaniga, M. S. (2000). Cerebral specialization and interhemispheric communication: Does the corpus callosum enable the human condition? *Brain, 123,* 1293–1326.

Geary, D. (1995). Reflections of evolution and culture in children's cognition. *American Psychologist, 50,* 24–37.

Gee, J. P. (2003). Opportunity to learn: A language-based perspective on assessment. *Assessment in Education, 10,* 27–46.

Gee, J. P. (2007). *What video games have to teach us about learning and literacy.* New York: Palgrave/Mamillan.

Gee, J. P., & Shaffer, D. W. (2010). Looking where the light is bad: Video games and the future of assessment. *Edge, 6,* 3–19.

Gibson, J. J. (1977). The theory of affordances. In R. Shaw & J. Bransford (Eds.), *Perceiving, acting, and knowing* (pp. 67–82). New York, NY: Wiley.

Glaser, R. (1976). Components of a psychology of instruction: Toward a science of design. *Review of Educational Research, 46,* 1–24.

Glaser, R. (2000). Cognition and instruction: Mind, development, and community. *Journal of Applied Developmental Psychology, 21,* 123–127.

Glenberg, A. (1997). What memory is for. *Behavioral and Brain Sciences, 20,* 1–55.

Greeno, J., & the Middle School Mathematics Through Applications Project Group (1998). The situativity of knowing, learning, and research. *American Psychologist, 53,* 5–26.

Greeno, J. G. (1991). Number sense as situated knowing in a conceptual domain. *Journal for Research in Mathematics Education, 22,* 170–218.

Greeno, J. G., Collins, A. M., & Resnick, L. B. (1996). Cognition and learning. In D. C. Berliner & R. C. Calfee (Eds.), *Handbook of educational psychology* (pp. 15–46). New York: Simon & Schuster Macmillan.

Guthrie, J. T., Wigfield, A., & Perencevich, K. (Eds.) (2004). *Motivating reading comprehension: Concept oriented reading instruction.* Mahwah, NJ: Laurence Erlbaum Associates.

Haier, R. J. (2001). PET studies of learning and individual differences. In J. L. McClelland & R. S. Siegler (Eds.), *Mechanisms of cognitive development: Behavioral and neural perspectives* (pp. 123–145). Mahwah, NY: Lawrence Erlbaum Associates.

Halpern, D. F. (2008). Is intelligence critical thinking? Why we need a new definition of intelligence. In P. C. Kyllonen, R. D. Roberts & L. Stankov (Eds.), *Extending intelligence: Enhancement and new constructs* (pp. 293–310). New York: Routledge.

Hatano, G. (1988). Social and motivational bases for mathematic understanding. In G. B. Saxe & M. G. Gearhart (Eds.), *Children's mathematics* (pp. 55–70). San Francisco: Jossey-Bass.

Herman, P., & Gomez, L. M. (2009). Taking guided learning theory to school: Reconciling the cognitive, motivational, and social contexts of instruction. In S. Tobias & T. M. Duffy (Eds.), *Constructivist instruction: Success or failure?* (pp. 62–81). New York: Routledge.

Hilgard, E. R. (1948). *Theories of learning.* New York: Appleton-Century-Crofts.

Hmelo-Silver, C., Duncan, R. G., & Chinn, C. A. (2007). Scaffolding and achievement in problem-based and inquiry learning: A response to Kirschner, Sweller, and Clark (2006). *Educational Psychologist, 42,* 99–107.

Hunt, E. (2008). Improving intelligence: What's the difference from education? In P. C. Kyllonen, R. D. Roberts & L. Stankov (Eds.), *Extending intelligence: Enhancement and new constructs* (pp. 13–30). New York: Routledge.

Isaac, S., & Michael, W. B. (1995). *Handbook in research and evaluation* (3 ed.). San Diego, CA: EdITS.

Jaeggi, S. M., Buschkuehl, M., Jonides, J., & Perrig, W. J. (2008). Improving fluid intelligence with training on working memory. *PNAS, 105,* 68290–66833.

Jensen, A. R. (2001). Spearman's hypothesis. In J. M. Collis & S. Messick (Eds.), *Intelligence and personality: Bridging the gap between theory and measurement* (pp. 3–24). Mahwah, NJ: Lawrence Erlbaum.

Karmiloff-Smith, A. (1992). *Beyond modularity: A developmental perspective on cognitive science.* Cambridge, MA: MIT Press.

Kasparov, G. (2007). *How life imitates chess.* New York: Bloomsbury USA.

Kelly, A. E. (2009). When is design research appropriate? In T. Plomp & N. Nieveen (Eds.), *An introduction to educational design research* (pp. 73–87). Enschede, Netherlands: SLO-Netherlands Institute for Curriculum Development.

Kirschner, P. A. (2009). Epistemology or pedagogy, that is the question. In S. Tobias & T. M. Duffy (Eds.), *Constructivist instruction: Success or failure?* (pp. 144–157). New York: Routledge.

Kirschner, P. A., Sweller, J., & Clark, R. E. (2006). Why minimal guidance during instruction does not work: An analysis of the failure of constructivist, discovery, problem-based, experiential, and inquiry-based teaching. *Educational Psychologist, 41,* 75–86.

Kuhn, D. (2002). A multi-component system that constructs knowledge: Insights from microgenetic study. In N. Granott & J. Parziale (Eds.), *Microdevelopment: Transition processes in development and learning* (pp. 109–130). Cambridge, UK: Cambridge University Press.

Kyllonen, P. C., Roberts, R. D., & Stankov, L. (Eds.) (2008). *Extending intelligence: Enhancement and new constructs.* New York: Routledge.

Lakatos, I. (1978). *The methodology of scientific research programs.* Cambridge, UK: Cambridge University Press.

Lampert, M. (1990). When the problem is not the question and the solution is not the answer: Mathematical knowing and teaching. *American Educational Research Journal, 27,* 29–63.

Lohman, D. F. (1993). Teaching and testing to develop fluid abilities. *Educational Researcher, 22*(7), 12–23.

Lohman, D. F. (2001). Issues in the definition and measurement of abilities. In J. M. Collis & S. Messick (Eds.), *Intelligence and personality: Bridging the gap between theory and measurement* (pp. 79–98). Mahwah, NJ: Lawrence Erlbaum.

Mayer, R. E. (2004). Should there be a three-strikes rule against pure discovery learning? The case for guided methods of instruction. *American Psychologist, 59,* 14–19.

Mayer, R. E. (2009). Constructivism as a theory of learning versus constructivism as a prescription for instruction. In S. Tobias & T. M. Duffy (Eds.), *Constructivist instruction: Success or failure?* (pp. 184–200). New York: Routledge.

Moss, P. A., Pullin, D., Gee, J. P., & Haertel, E. H. (2005). The idea of testing: Psychometric and sociocultural perspectives. *Measurement, 3,* 63–83.

Neisser, U. (Ed.) (1998). *The rising curve: Long-term gains in IQ and related measures.* Washington, DC: American Psychological Association.

Newell, A. (1990). *Unified theories of cognition.* Cambridge, MA: Harvard University Press.

Palincsar, A. S., & Magnusson, S. J. (2001). The interplay of first-hand and second-hand investigation to model and support the development of scientific knowledge and reasoning. In S. M. Carver & D. Klahr (Eds.), *Cognition and instruction: Twenty-five years of progress* (pp. 151–193). Mahwah, NJ: Lawrence Erlbaum.

Partnership for 21st Century Skills (2008). 21st Century Skills Education and Competitiveness Guide. Retrieved from www.p21.org/documents/21st_century_skills_education_and_competitiveness_guide.pdf (accessed July 22, 2011).

Pea, R. D. (1993). Practices of distributed intelligence and designs for education. In G. Salomon (Ed.), *Distributed cognitions: Psychological and educational considerations* (pp. 47–87). Cambridge, UK: Cambridge University Press.

Perkins, D. N. (1995). *Outsmarting IQ: The emerging science of learnable intelligence.* New York: Free Press.

Perkins, D. N. (2010). *Making learning whole: How seven principles of teaching can transform education.* San Francisco: Jossey-Bass.

Perkins, D., & Ritchhart, R. (2004). When is good thinking. In D. Y. Dai & R. J. Sternberg (Eds.), *Motivation, emotion, and cognition: Integrative perspectives on intellectual functioning and development* (pp. 351–384). Mahwah, NJ: Lawrence Erlbaum.

Phenix, P. H. (1964). *Realms of meaning.* New York: McGraw-Hill Book Company.

Piaget, J. (2001). *The psychology of intelligence.* London: Routledge. (Originally published in 1950.)

Plass, J. L., Moreno, R., & Brunken, R. (2010). *Cognitive load theory.* New York: Cambridge University Press.

Popper, K. P. (1972). *Objective knowledge: An evolutionary approach.* Oxford, UK: Clarendon Press.

Resnick, L. B. (1987). *Education and learning to think.* Washington, DC: National Academy Press.

Resnick, L. B. (1988). Treating mathematics as an ill-structured discipline. In R. Charles & E. Silver (Eds.), *The teaching and assessment of mathematical problem solving* (pp. 32–60). Reston, VA: National Council of Teachers of Mathematics.

Resnick, L. B. (2010). Nested learning systems for the thinking curriculum. *Educational Researcher, 39,* 183–197.

Resnick, L. B., & Glaser, R. (1976). Problem solving and intelligence. In L. B. Resnick (Ed.), *The nature of intelligence* (pp. 205–230). Hillsdale, NJ: Lawrence Erlbaum.

Rogers, C. (2002). Defining reflection: another look at John Dewey and reflective thinking. *Teacher College Record, 104,* 842–866.

Royer, J. M., Mestre, J. P., & Dufresne, R. J. (2005). Introduction: Framing the transfer problem. In J. P. Mestre (Ed.), *Transfer of meaning: From a modern multidisciplinary perspective* (pp. vii–xxvi). Greenwich, CT: Information Age Publishing.

Saariluoma, P. (1992). Error in chess: The apperception–restructuring view. *Psychological Research, 54,* 17–26.

Sawyer, R. K. (2002). Emergence in psychology: Lessons from the history of non-reductionist science. *Human Development, 45,* 2–28.

Sawyer, R. K. (Ed.) (2006). *The Cambridge handbook of the learning sciences.* Cambridge, UK: Cambridge University Press.

Schank, R. C., & Cleary, C. (1995). *Engines for education.* Hillsdale, NJ: Lawrence Erlbaum.

Schmidt, H. G., Loyens, S. M. M., van Gog, T., & Paas, F. (2007). Problem-based learning is compatible with human cognitive architecture: Commentary on Kirschner, Sweller, and Clark (2006). *Educational Psychologist, 42,* 91–97.

Schön, D. A. (1983). *Reflective practitioner.* New York: Basic Books.

Searle, J., R. (2004). *Mind: A brief introduction.* New York: Oxford University Press.

Shaffer, D. W. (2004). Pedagogical praxis: The professions as models for postindustrial education. *Teachers College Record, 106,* 1401–1421.

Shepard, L. A. (2000). The role of assessment in a learning culture. *Educational Researcher, 29*(7), 4–14.

Shuell, T. J. (1993). Toward an integrated theory of teaching and learning. *Educational Psychologist, 28,* 291–311.

Shulman, L. S. (1987). Knowledge and teaching: Foundations of the new reform. *Harvard Educational Review, 57*(1), 1–22.

Shulman, L. S., & Quinlan, K. M. (1996). The comparative psychology of school subjects. In D. C. Berliner & R. C. Calfee (Eds.), *Handbook of educational psychology* (pp. 399–422). New York: Simon & Schuster Macmillan.

Siegler, R. S. (2000). The rebirth of children's learning. *Child Development, 71,* 26–35.

Siegler, R. (2001). Discussion of Part I and II. In S. M. Carver & D. Klahr (Eds.), *Cognition and instruction: Twenty-five years of progress* (pp. 195–203). Mahwah, NJ: Lawrence Erlbaum.

Siegler, R. S. (2002). Microgenetic studies of self-explanation. In N. Granott & J. Parziale (Eds.), *Microdevelopment: Transition processes in development and learning* (pp. 31–58). Cambridge, UK: Cambridge University Press.

Simon, H. A. (1981). *The sciences of the artificial.* Cambridge, MA: The MIT Press. (Originally published in 1969.)

Sinatra, G. M., & Pintrich, P. R. E. (2003). *Intentional conceptual change*. Mahwah, NJ: Lawrence Erlbaum.

Snow, R. E. (1992). Aptitude theory: Yesterday, today, and tomorrow. *Educational Psychologist, 27*, 5–32.

Snow, R. E. (1994). Aptitude development and talent achievement. In N. Colangelo, S. C. Assouline & D. L. Ambroson (Eds.), *Talent development* (Vol. 2, pp. 101–120). Dayton, OH: Ohio Psychology Press.

Snow, R. E., & Lohman, D. F. (1984). Toward a theory of cognitive aptitude for learning from instruction. *Journal of Educational Psychology, 76*, 347–376.

Snow, R. E., & Swanson, J. (1992). Instructional psychology: Aptitude, adaptation, and assessment. *Annual Review of Psychology, 43*, 583–626.

Spearman, C. (1904). "General intelligence" objectively determined and measured. *American Journal of Psychology, 15*, 201–293.

Spiro, R. J., Feltovich, P. L., Jackson, M. J., & Coulson, R. L. (1991). Cognitive flexibility, constructivism, and hypertext: Random access instruction for advanced knowledge acquisition in ill-structured domains. *Educational Technology, 31*(5), 24–33.

Sternberg, R. J. (1998). Abilities are forms of developing expertise. *Educational Researcher, 27*(3), 11–20.

Stokes, D. E. (1997). *Pasteur's quadrant: Basic science and technological innovation*. Washington, DC: Brookings Institute Press.

Sun, R. (2007). The importance of cognitive architectures: An analysis based on CLARION. *Journal of Experimental and Theoretical Artificial Intelligence, 19*, 159–193.

Sweller, J., Kirschner, P. A., & Clark, R. E. (2007). Why minimally guided teaching techniques do not work: A reply to commentaries. *Educational Psychologist, 42*, 115–121.

Tobias, S., & Duffy, T. M. (Eds.) (2009). *Constructivist instruction: Success or failure?* New York: Routledge.

White, B. Y., & Fredericksen, J. R. (1998). Inquiry, modeling, and metacognition: Making science accessible to all students. *Cognition and Instruction, 16*, 3–117.

White, B. Y., & Fredericksen, J. R. (2005). A theoretical framework and approach for fostering metacognitive development. *Educational Psychologist, 40*, 211–223.

Whitehead, A. N. (1929). *The aims of education*. New York: The Free Press.

Wineburg, S., & Grossman, P. (2001). Affect and effect in cognitive approaches to instruction. In S. M. Carver & D. Klahr (Eds.), *Cognition and instruction: Twenty-five years of progress* (pp. 479–492). Mahwah, NJ: Lawrence Erlbaum.

Wise, A. F., & O'Neill, K. (2009). Beyond more versus less: A reframing of the debate on instructional guidance. In S. Tobias & T. M. Duffy (Eds.), *Constructivist instruction: Success or failure?* (pp. 82–105). New York: Routledge.

2

INTELLIGENT ACTION AS A SHARED ACCOMPLISHMENT

Melissa Gresalfi, Sasha Barab, and Amanda Sommerfeld

Traditionally, intelligence has been thought of as an individual attribute that people carry across contexts. Both our measurements of intelligence (they take place outside of any familiar context of learning, using protocols that make assumptions about the separation of content and context) and the ways we talk about intelligence (someone *is* "smart" or "gifted," rather than someone might *act* smart) indicate our overwhelming belief that intelligence is ultimately a property of an individual. In this chapter, we propose a different vision of intelligence, one that focuses on how we learn to act in ways that are recognized as more or less intelligent, and the role of the environment in making an individual appear intelligent or not. Specifically, we propose a way of thinking about intelligence that highlights the kinds of *disposition* we develop to act in particular ways, and consider how those dispositions develop in relation to learning opportunities with which learners are presented over time.

We come at this issue from a relational ontology that makes particular assumptions about the location of knowledge and intelligence as a shared or distributed accomplishment rather than an individual one. In other words, we purport that what it means to act intelligently is spread across individuals (both the person acting intelligently and those others in the immediate context), and is inseparable from available tools (such as computers or dictionaries), norms and expectations (whether risk taking is supported or punished), opportunities for action (for example, procedural versus more conceptual expectations for action), and personal history (such as knowing how to understand a particular interface or participate in a particular context) to environmental particulars of the immediate situation. In this way, a relational ontology focuses attention on the individual-in-context, and how people use the world around them to scaffold their meaningful participation. It is according to this perspective, for example, that

Vygotsky (1978) discussed zones of proximal development in learning, as opposed to someone's internal abilities. A relational ontology moves away from individual–environment and mind–body dualisms, and instead focuses on how the two interact, resulting in what we believe to be a better model for thinking about intelligence (Barab, Cherkes-Julkowski, Swenson, Garrett, Shaw & Young, 1999).

Importantly, when defining intelligence as relational, we are not simply talking about intelligent *functioning*, such as how a computer allows the statistician to more effectively calculate the effects of interacting variables. We are also referring to the *disposition* to calculate statistics for making sense of the world: what one is able to do is inextricably bound with the opportunities one has had to practice what is required in a particular context, and whether one has the motivation to exploit these opportunities. In other words, we argue that acting intelligently in the real world is about more than how much you know, but also involves the ways one engages with a situation in a particular manner (Gresalfi, 2009; Perkins & Ritchhart, 2004; Perkins, Tishman, Ritchhart, Donis, & Andrade, 2000), highlighting the situated nature of intelligence. Additionally, it also focuses on the timescale of intelligence—that acting intelligently is a function of histories of experience that enable one to recognize situational requirements and thereby to act on the world in legitimized ways. This chapter is, therefore, both about defining intelligence as a relational activity and about advancing an ontological characterization of the necessary elements for supporting and ultimately understanding performances of intelligent accomplishment. Through this framework, it then becomes possible to consider who is recognized as capable and likely to perform intelligently in particular contexts.

Building on this relational ontology and what we define as the necessary ontological elements of acting intelligently, we then describe two significant implications of this perspective. The first is that the recognition of someone as intelligent is an intensely political act that is shaped by local norms and values and that has significant consequences for the individual. In this way, the act of intelligence recognition can have significant implications for the kinds of identity that individuals develop. The second implication is that intelligence is distributed over space and time, and cannot be perceived as a momentary activity, as implied by our methods of intelligence testing. This latter implication is significant both in terms of how one learns to participate in ways that are recognized as intelligent, and in terms of the assessments we use to recognize someone as intelligent. Thus, as a whole, considering intelligence from a relational ontology assumes that both enduring experiences, and the sociopolitical context in which these experiences are situated, constitute the nature of intelligence as it is ultimately recognized.

We begin the chapter with a brief overview of our assumptions about the location of intelligence, which we refer to here as "knowing." We trace the argument about the nature of knowing between two conceptualizations: one that focuses on what individuals know and are able to do, and a second that broadens the conceptualization of knowing to consider the inseparability between what people do and the resources that are available to them. We then consider how intelligence develops through participation with a set of practices that come to be recognized and reified in particular ways. Finally, drawing on data from our own curricular designs, we share examples of how opportunities to learn can be designed such that they are likely to evoke a more robust accomplishment that leverages multiple environmental elements, including more productive dispositions. We close with a discussion of transfer, reflecting on what a more sequestered learning environment affords, as opposed to the trajectories we have been designing to intentionally evoke the enlistment of multiple environmental elements and to evoke legitimate situational motivation.

On Intelligence and Knowing

There is a long history of treating knowing and learning as properties of an individual that can be assessed separately from the contexts in which he or she learns. In addition to the significant quantity of research that has been conducted based on this assumption, most theories of intelligence, though divergent in their definitions, follow this line of reasoning. While some theorists have promoted the existence of innate intellectual abilities that determine an individual's underlying cognitive capacity across tasks (e.g., Spearman's g), other theorists have instead hypothesized that intelligence can best be considered as having both fluid and materialized (i.e., crystallized) characteristics that are differentially affected by education and life experience (c.f., Horn & Cattell, 1967). Despite their differences, across these theories is the shared assumption that intelligence resides within individuals, regardless of the situational requirements. Even Gardner's theory of multiple intelligences (1983), which seeks to expand conceptualizations of intelligence from solely cognitive competencies to include relational, artistic, and kinesthetic abilities, upholds intelligence as residing within individuals. Based on this perspective, research and assessments follow suit, with standardized intelligence tests being conducted by unknown evaluators, outside of the contexts in which people learn, and intelligence quotients being derived through comparison of individual scores to age- or grade-based norms.

These histories demonstrate the popular acceptance of the idea that intelligence lies within people. However, debates within the intelligence research community challenge the universality of such perspectives, with some researchers such as Snow (1992) arguing for a pluralistic conceptualization of intelligence that recognizes the role of context in shaping what we are able to do and how our actions are recognized as meaningful in any given moment of time. For example, Sternberg (2007), among others, has pointed out that intelligence is recognized quite differently among different cultures, and that the results of intelligence tests likely are most revealing of the congruence between an individual and the norms and values of the dominant culture. Indeed, Sternberg notes that:

> the identification of a general factor of human intelligence may tell us more about how abilities interact with cultural patterns of schooling and society, especially Western patterns of schooling and society, than it does about the structure of human abilities. (2007, p. 150)

In the sociological literature, Pierre Bourdieu (1984) attends to the intersection between individuals and their surroundings by considering the ways in which individual attributes are differentially legitimized based on the values of the context. He notes that, because contexts demand particular attitudes and skills for success, what could be considered valuable behaviors or abilities in one setting could be meaningless, or even detrimental, in another. Consistent with such thinking, in discussing the limitations of traditional theories of aptitude, Snow (1992) stated that the "conceptual limitation derives from our tendency to think of persons and situations as independent variables, rather than [to see] persons-in-situations as integrated systems" (p. 19). Advocating a similar perspective, Barab and Plucker (2002) discuss intelligence as couplings distributed across individuals and their environments in the service of particular goals: "we characterize ability or talent as a set of functional relations distributed across person and context and through which the person–in–situation appears knowledgeably skillful" (p. 174). In this way, they treat intelligence, not as a causal entity bound up in the individual, but as an epiphenomenon arising out of the dynamic transaction between the individual, the physical environment, and the sociocultural context.

Likewise, McDermott (1993) paints a compelling picture of the ways in which intelligence, or, in his work, perceived lack of intelligence, is actually a process of recognition and participation that is only partly based on what the individual in question is actually doing. In his essay entitled "The Acquisition of a Child by a Learning Disability," McDermott describes the ways that particular contexts made a student's performance as a learning–disabled child relevant, while other contexts did not evoke such a characterization. In discussing how these different moments of recognition came to occur, he states that:

> On any occasion of his looking inattentive, for example, it took Adam to look away at just the right time, but it took many others to construct the right time for Adam to look away; it took others to look away from his looking away, and still more to discover his looking away, to make something of it, to diagnose it, to document it, and to remediate it. (p. 273)

Through this analysis, McDermott makes it clear that earning the label "intelligent" is an accomplishment, not merely of an individual, but of the individual within a context that holds particular expectations, values, and norms.

Taken as a whole, theorists conceptualize intelligence as a form of participation that is fundamentally connected with, and constitutive of, the contextual particulars through which it occurs. These discussions about the nature of intelligence intersect with a notion of learning that considers the extent to which individuals and contexts are interconnected. Many theorists have shared numerous examples that help to clarify the extent to which learning and knowing must be understood in light of the affordances of the contexts in which people are participating. This work, often referred to as theories of *situative cognition* or *sociocultural theory*, claims that *what* someone comes to know cannot be separated from the situation in which one has come to learn it. As an example, a student can be presented with opportunities to learn mathematics by watching a teacher carefully work through examples and then practicing those examples. Alternatively, a student can be presented with opportunities to learn mathematics by being given a complex problem without a set solution path, which he has to work out in collaboration with peers and consultation from the teacher. These two dramatically different kinds of opportunity to learn impact the nature of the content that one is likely to engage and ultimately understand (Boaler, 2000; Boaler & Greeno, 2000; Gresalfi, 2009; Gresalfi, Martin, Hand, & Greeno, 2009; Schoenfeld, 1988).

These learning opportunities also determine what would be viewed as intelligent engagement with the material, or, more generally, what we take as intelligent action. Whereas intelligent behavior in the first example may primarily involve listening, intelligent behavior in the second example would primarily involve communicating mathematical ideas. This work therefore calls into question the extent to which it makes sense to consider intelligence as a stable internal trait that can be considered separately from the contexts in which one is acting. In this chapter, we consider how "intelligence" (or behavior that is recognized as intelligent) might develop by discussing two paired ideas: how opportunities to learn shape the forms of engagement that are offered to people at given moments in time, and how that engagement is recognized as indicative of intelligence.

How Contexts Co-determine Intelligence

In this chapter, we argue that what an individual can do in any moment in time is tied to what they have opportunities to do and what is valued in the context as worthwhile to do. Indeed, although even a chained prisoner can exercise agency (by deciding to thrash and yell versus stand quietly), the forms of agency that we can exercise at any given time are largely shaped by the particular situation in which we are acting. Although this may seem an obvious point, it is one that is often overlooked when it comes to considering what someone has learned or is able to do. For example, standardized tests are notoriously interpreted as reflections of individual competence and predictors of future performance. By being identified as "standardized," these tests supposedly evaluate abilities regardless of contexts, thus serving as a way to compare students from different backgrounds and predict future academic outcomes. However, what are not considered in these standardized scores are the kinds of learning opportunity with which the students have been presented. As a result, although the tests purport to differentiate students in terms of ability, what they instead provide are indications of the extent to which the test is aligned with students' ways of knowing (Boaler, 2000; Gresalfi, Martin et al., 2009).

For us, considering the kinds of opportunity to learn that are presented to a student is inseparable from our analysis of what students are ultimately able to do. Our understanding of learning draws heavily on ecological psychology, which builds on Gibson's (1979) theory of perceptual affordances, and claims that what happens in any particular moment is based on a co-constructed set of possible actions defined by the affordances of the environment for a particular action, the intention of the agent to take up those affordances, and the effectivities of the agent to actually realize those affordances. Affordances refer to the set of actions that are offered by a particular object (for example, a chair affords sitting, but a door does not). Effectivities refer to an individual's ability to realize those affordances (a chair affords sitting for a human, but not, typically, for an alligator). And finally, the extent to which an affordance is realized depends on the dynamic intention that emerges (just because one could sit on a chair doesn't mean that one does so, depending on the situation) (Barab et al., 1999; Gibson, 1979; Greeno, 1994; Gresalfi, 2009; Shaw, Effken, Fajen, Garrett, & Morris, 1997; Shaw, Kadar, Sim, & Repperger, 1992). Thus, understanding what happens at a particular moment requires unpacking what was possible (what was afforded), and whether and how those affordances were recognized and realized.

This focus on interaction acknowledges that, although a particular opportunity to learn might be *possible*, it is not *obligatory*, for the extent to which an affordance is realized depends in large part on the goals and intentions, along with the abilities, of the agent (Greeno & Gresalfi, 2008). There are many aspects of a situation that might be included in the elements of a relational ontology that define if an individual–environment system has acted intelligently. For example, having a computer might allow an individual to be judged a good writer, whereas without the computer he might appear to be a poor writer. Likewise, a student writing a fictional story might appear to be a less effective writer than if she was writing to convince a congressman of why a particular law that has personal significance is problematic.

In both cases, determining whether a person is "intelligent" has to be combined with a consideration of the resources, motivations, and histories that are supporting that person to act in more or less intelligent ways (along with, of course, the standards of the setting that shape what will be recognized as intelligent behavior). Here, we focus on three aspects of educational situations that we believe co-constitute intelligent action:

- the nature of the task and how it frames activity, and the tools and resources that are available to support activity;

- the norms and rules that shape how particular activities are recognized and valued; and
- the personal histories and dispositions of the learner.

Each one of these is briefly expanded below and then contrasted in terms of two different learning situations.

The Role of Tasks in Shaping Intelligent Action

When considering an educational activity, one of the first salient elements is what the students are working on. The task that has been set for students plays a significant role in the nature of the activity that unfolds. Clearly, some tasks are more interesting than others, and tasks—of course—target different conceptual ideas. Perhaps most importantly, tasks frame both the purpose and the nature of one's activity and, in so doing, have the potential to position students differently relative to the activity. As an example, and foreshadowing the analysis that will follow, students can engage in dramatically different tasks relative to learning about coordinate plotting. The task could be to practice coordinate plotting by locating a series of ordered pairs on a coordinate graph. This task frames students' participation in terms of *procedural engagement*—students practice the method for coordinate plotting and ensure that they can plot any ordered pair, regardless of their value.

Alternatively, the task could involve asking students to find a lost professor in a 3D virtual world by navigating around an island to find particular points on a map. This task frames students' participation in terms of procedural and *consequential* engagement (considering the implications of the steps that one has carried out), as students can directly see the outcome of their choices based on what happens to them in the 3D space (Gresalfi, Barab, Siyahhan, & Christensen, 2009). The nature of the task is also impacted by the tools and resources available for its completion; other students, tools such as calculators or a textbook, and even the feedback from the 3D space are all resources that support (or thwart) students' engagement with the tasks. Thus, what students are able to do as they engage in a task is framed by the structure, constraints, and affordances of that task, as well as the resources and tools available to complete the task. As a consequence, the extent to which they act intelligently in relation to that activity is a joint accomplishment between what the task affords, how particular resources support students to perceive and act on the task, and, ultimately, which affordances of the task students realize.

The Role of Norms in Shaping Intelligent Action

Of course, the extent to which a task affords intelligent activity depends in large part on the way the activity is framed, both in the immediate local context and in the context of students' experience more broadly. Classroom environments, institutional expectations, teachers' goals, and broader cultural values play a significant role in the way the task and students' engagement with the task ultimately plays out (Cochran-Smith & Lytle, 1999; Henningsen & Stein, 1997; Squire, McKinster, Barnett, Leuhmann, & Barab, 2001; Stein, Smith, Henningsen, & Silver, 2000). As a consequence, the very same task could be set in two different classrooms with ultimately very different consequences in terms of the ways that task is introduced, positioned, and ultimately taken up by the participants. To be clear, norms and values frame participation both at a micro level, as they contribute to the expectations of how work proceeds locally, and at a macro level, as larger cultural values shape the extent to which the task or activity is deemed meaningful or worthwhile. As an example of the former, some classrooms have developed norms for discussion that involve students making conjectures, challenging each other, and justifying their ideas. Other classrooms have developed norms for discussion that involve offering answers only, and relying on the teacher to correct an inaccurate response if one is given. These different norms would dramatically shape the kinds of conversation that unfold in the classrooms and how those modes of interaction are reinforced, in part because of the differential valuing of forms of engagement.

At a more macro level, the extent to which the activity is valued also plays a role in individuals' engagement with it—if the task is deemed valuable and personally meaningful, students are more likely to expend effort in attempting to resolve it. In contrast, if the task is not valuable, it is more likely to be ignored or engaged superficially. To be clear, this is not an issue of some students being more motivated than others, but, rather, a consideration of how the task or activity fits into the larger sociopolitical context that shapes the meaning and value of the activity (Eccles et al., 1983; Gutiérrez, 2004; Hand, 2010).

In her book *Unequal Childhoods*, Lareau (2003) provides several examples of such contextually legitimized behaviors, including children's ability to debate. She observes that verbal reasoning in an argument is highly valued in some families, while in others it is discouraged. As a result, she notes that these home contexts prepare students differently to interact with adults, and reports divergent patterns of interaction between students and teachers based upon the interactional norms of their families. In those families where being able to justify ideas with verbal support is valued, students learn how to interact in this manner and are, therefore, able to apply this skill to the classroom setting, where it is also highly valued. For those children for whom such a behavior is not valued in their home setting, application of such an interactional style in the classroom setting is more difficult. In this example, it is not the children's ability, per se, that determines their behavior, but rather how that behavior is valued (and therefore practiced) in different contexts.

The Role of Dispositions in Shaping Intelligent Action

A final element of intelligent action involves, of course, the behavior of the individual in a particular context. Although, as previously stated, contexts afford particular opportunities for action, they do not *determine* individual behavior, and thus there is an interplay between the kinds of opportunity to act that are possible, and what individual students actually do. This intersection can be considered at micro levels of interaction, but can also be considered over a longer time span, as individual actions accrue into *emergent continuities* over time (Gresalfi, 2009). In this case, we are referring to the kinds of disposition that students have towards engaging information—that is, the predictabilities in whether, when, and how students take up particular opportunities to learn. Dispositions concern what individuals do given what they have opportunities to do, and therefore involve both elements of the system in which an individual is participating as well as individual proclivities for acting on particular opportunities. Just as we cannot understand intelligent action without considering the context, we cannot understand intelligent action without understanding why individuals act in the way they do. In this work, we understand individuals' proclivities as being made up of an interaction between intentions and effectivities in relation to available affordances. As an example, in any classroom, a teacher may offer an explanation of a new procedure or rule. This explanation is an affordance for understanding that new rule. The extent to which a student is able to act on that explanation, that is, to use it in order to solve a new problem, is dependent on both his effectivity for doing so and his intention to use that explanation—that is, his understanding of the explanation and his recognition of its relevance to the new problem at hand.

The question is how intentions and effectivities form. Intentions are dynamically constituted through one's activity; they are neither a property of the context nor a property of the individual (Barab et al., 1999; Shaw et al., 1997; Young, Depalma, & Garrett, 2002). Effectivities arise through individuals' histories of participation; what one is able to do is indeed an artifact of what one has been able to do in the past. Thus, an individual's disposition arises through moments of participation that accrue in order to build both his effectivities and intentions for acting in particular ways. Of course, these dispositions shift based on the kinds of activity in which one is participating.

An example of how dispositions play out can be seen in the following scenario. A teacher's opening of "does anyone have any questions about what David just said" might invite one student to raise his hand and voice his confusion, while another student, who is equally confused, might not choose to voice his confusion aloud. These differences in the ways the students respond to the teacher's opening are indications of different dispositions that they have developed towards engaging. In the first case, the teacher's invitation served as affordance for the student, which he was able to both recognize and act on. The second student either lacked an intention to act (he was not interested in resolving his confusion, or did not feel comfortable in making his confusion apparent), or lacked the effectivity to recognize his confusion or to ask a question that would help to resolve his confusion. In both cases, the student's ultimate actions can best be understood in light of the affordance that was presented to him.

Affording Opportunities for Engagement

Our focus on opportunities to learn changes the goals of learning theorists quite dramatically. No longer can we consider the individual learner as the sole unit of analysis, but must also include the resources of the environment in any analysis of knowing. Our work focuses specifically on the design of learning environments, and how particular designs can afford opportunities to learn that will lead to forms of engagement likely to be recognized as "intelligent." As designers, we are obligated to consider not only our goals for learning (what, at the end of an activity, we want students to know and be able to do), but also the mechanisms of learning—how we conjecture students will actually accomplish those goals. Thus, designers must simultaneously design at two levels: a macro level, with a focus on overall engagement, and a micro level, with a focus on momentary opportunities to learn. Our overall goal is to support students to develop dispositions towards *critical engagement*, that is, a way of being in the world that involves intentionally engaging situations, dilemmas, and activities by leveraging disciplinary tools in order to resolve personally meaningful problems (Barab, Gresalfi, & Arici, 2009; Gresalfi, Barab et al., 2009). The key component of critical engagement is student agency—our goal is to position students so that they are core decision-makers, considering for themselves how their selection and use of particular disciplinary tools can help them to achieve particular outcomes. Agency is important in that, without it, the task simply becomes procedural and is one of compliance and reproduction, neither of which requires being critical.

With this in mind as a macro goal, we then must consider how to organize particular opportunities to learn such that students are able to realize this goal. Engaging critically with content is a non-trivial goal and requires that students also are able to engage procedurally, conceptually, and—crucially—*consequentially* with information (Gresalfi, Barab et al., 2009; Gresalfi & Ingram-Goble, 2008). Although procedural and conceptual engagement is familiar to readers, consequential engagement is somewhat different and involves considering *how* particular disciplinary decisions impact designed contexts. Take the example of a problem in which students are asked how many busses, each of which hold eight people, they would need to reserve in order to transport 28 people. A student who is engaging conceptually might notice that they need to divide the people evenly between the busses, and that the operation of dividing 28 by eight would help them to do so (actually carrying out that procedure would involve procedural engagement). However, a student engaging consequentially would be able to determine that he actually needs four busses, rather than the numerically accurate answer of three and one-half, because you can't have half of a bus.

Our designs take these elements of engagement seriously and carefully consider both the *types* of opportunity to learn that are important to include in designs, as well as their *strength* (c.f. Gresalfi, 2009). First, it is important to carefully consider the extent to which designs legitimately position students to engage in the ways we envision. Despite the shocked response to findings that students in American schools seem often to be able to engage only procedurally, a careful look at the curriculum—and the opportunities to learn typically offered to our students—reveals that, often, students are simply taking up the opportunities that are available to them (Boaler, 1997, 2000; Henningsen & Stein, 1997). More crucially, however, we consider how those opportunities to learn are presented and offered to students, and how their presentation serves to position students relative to the subject matter and to the immersive storyline in which they are engaging.

The extent to which opportunities to learn shape students' potential for intelligent action is, in part, a matter of timescales. We typically consider intelligence to be somewhat enduring, stretching across multiple activities and settings. Of course, as previously noted, this is a simplification of intelligence, as the contexts in which one is acting shape the extent to which one can act in a way that is recognized as intelligent at any particular moment in time. Nonetheless, one momentary experience in a classroom is not, in and of itself, sufficient for shaping an individual's intelligent behavior. Instead, we propose that developing a disposition for intelligent action develops over time across multiple opportunities to learn. What those opportunities afford are significant elements of what ultimately is constructed as intelligent action. Unpacking how particular opportunities to learn afford particular forms of engagement helps to illuminate the ways that intelligent action develops and is defined. In the sections that follow, we examine two single episodes of very different classrooms in order to focus on the affordances of opportunities to learn. Our belief is that developing the potential to engage in intelligent action ultimately develops over repeated experiences like those described below.

What is significant to notice in the two examples is that what students need to do in order to look intelligent is quite different, although both contexts are designed to demonstrate understanding of coordinate systems. Beyond the different characterization of the episodes, it is also important to reflect on how each of these learning situations might give rise to very different dispositions in the long term. More specifically, we review two different lessons that cover the same content: coordinate graphing. The first example is from a traditional lesson on coordinate graphing and highlights what we mean by procedural engagement. The second example is from a unit of our own design, intended to support consequential engagement. We unpack these two examples in terms of our three ontological elements (tasks, norms, and dispositions). We then discuss the implications of these differences for the kinds of intelligent action that students are able to execute and the alignment of those actions with traditional forms of assessment and indications of intelligence.

Example 1: Traditional Teaching

The first example comes from a classroom transcript, posted at the website: www.shodor.org/interactivate/discussions/IntroductionToTheCoo/ (accessed July 25, 2011). This website offers curriculum for math and science, and is funded by the National Science Foundation. We have chosen this example because it is representative of lessons about coordinate graphing in that it presents information first as a structured lecture, then with several resources designed for students to test and refine their understanding of the ideas presented in lecture. This is a common structure for American mathematics classrooms (Stigler, Fernandez, & Yoshida, 1996; Stigler & Hiebert, 1997). In addition, the fact that the transcript is offered through the website as an example of an introduction to the material suggests that it is an ideal presentation of the material from the perspective of the designers, and therefore is an example of implementing the materials with fidelity. In the transcript below, students are presented with information about the logistics and mechanics of coordinate graphing. Students are introduced to the procedures associated with making a coordinate graph and are given clear and precise directions for graphing accurately.

In this example, the teacher gives clear instructions about how to create a coordinate graph, the vocabulary associated with the axes, and the correct procedure for plotting points. She checks with students to ensure that they understand the instructions and are responsive to questions or confusion that might arise. The entirety of the transcript is not presented below because of space constraints. Briefly, in the lesson, the teacher first presents procedures for how to create a coordinate plot and how to label points on the axes. She introduces the idea of the axes having both positive and negative sides and teaches them the vocabulary for labeling the horizontal (x) and vertical (y) axes. She then explains the conventions for describing the location of a point (the first number in a pair denotes the point's location along the x axis, the second denotes the point's location along the y axis). Finally, she introduces the idea that points are located in one of four quadrants, and labels those quadrants so that students know to what she is referring. The transcript portion that is included below includes the first two ideas in this lecture: how to create a coordinate plot, and how to place points.

In this exchange, students are presented with strong opportunities to learn how to construct a graph and how to graph accurately. These are procedural skills that are required for accurate coordinate plotting. Taking the interaction apart in terms of our ontological elements, the *task* affords procedural engagement: there is an emphasis on careful drawing, careful counting, and accurate placement of points. Students are introduced to the vocabulary of the task, terms such as *axis* and *negative* (instead of "minus"). Likewise, students are taught how to accurately plot points

Mentor: Please, draw a straight horizontal line at the center of your graphing paper. As we count: "Zero, one, two, three . . ." we put the numbers on the line, one number per line of the graph paper. When we count backwards, we distinguish the numbers that come before zero by placing a "–" sign in front of them, so it goes: "Two, one, zero . . ." Make sure that you evenly space the numbers, since the distance from 1 to 2 should be the same as the distance from 2 to 3.

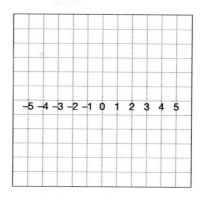

Student: Minus one, minus two, minus three . . .

Mentor: What we have now is called a "number line" or "coordinate line." It can be used to describe where a point is on the line. To give the exact "address" of a point, we just look at how far the point is from zero, using a minus symbol for numbers to the left of zero. Except we don't call it a minus sign, we refer to these numbers as "negative."

Student: So the address of this point [Student highlights 4] is 4, and the address of this point [Student highlights –5] is *negative 5*.

Mentor: Excellent. Now we want to get more freedom of movement. We will let our points be anywhere on the paper, not only on the line. To give an address for the points that are not on the number line we will need to make a vertical number line. Draw a vertical line through the zero of the horizontal number line. Now label it with positive numbers above the horizontal number line and the negative numbers below the horizontal number line. Instead of saying horizontal number line and vertical number line all the time, let's call them by their mathematical names. The horizontal number line is called the *x*-axis and the vertical number line is the *y*-axis.

Student: Well, I would go up three blocks and then right two blocks.

Mentor: Sure. How else can we get there?

Student: We can first go two blocks to the right, and then three blocks up.

Student: Or we can go one right, three up, and one more right.

Mentor: There are many ways to get from one point to another point (how many ways, by the way?). To create a standard way of referring to points, mathematicians came to an agreement that they will always name the point after one special way of walking. Starting from zero, we go all the way to the right or to the left, counting steps: one, two. Then we go up or down: one, two, three steps up. Then we write the number of steps like that: (2, 3). Again, the first number is "left–right," the second "up–down." A negative sign means either left or down. So, if our point is (–2, –3), we go two steps to the left, and then three steps down. Do you remember the names of our number lines?

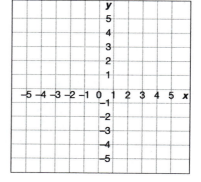

Student: Yes, the horizontal line is called the *x*-axis and the vertical line is called the *y*-axis.

FIGURE 2.1 Transcript from Classroom 1.

using the standard conventions of the discipline (plot x first, then y). The structure of this task limits other forms of engagement for students; they are asked to follow directions and to ensure that they are drawing accurately, but there is no discussion about what coordinate plotting is used for, where the conventions come from, or why it is important to have agreed-upon conventions when creating coordinate plots.

The *norms and rules* of this classroom are of course impossible to discern clearly given such a short excerpt. However, there are some indications in the interaction patterns between the teacher and the students that suggest a fairly familiar structure. Specifically, the well-documented interaction style of I–R–E (Mehan, 1979) seems to be in place: the teacher *initiates* both directions and questions, students are asked to *respond*, and the teacher *evaluates* that contribution. Students seem to feel comfortable in this classroom; they respond to questions when the teacher asks and at times volunteer information without specifically being asked to do so. Overall, the norms for valued activity, or *what it means to do math* here (Cobb, Gresalfi, & Hodge, 2009), involve following the teacher's lead, working accurately, and replicating presented information. Students need to be able to model the teacher's presentation, but there is little or no attention to other forms of engagement—conceptual, understanding how conventions shape the kinds of plots we create, or consequential, understanding how such coordinate plots might be useful.

Finally, the *dispositions* that are being fostered and rewarded in this classroom involve engaging in procedural tasks without a rationale for compliance. The affordances for engagement are very clear, and careful directions are given about coordinate graphing. The extent to which students have an intention for engaging is left solely up to the student; if they are uninterested in this content or un-interested in doing well in math, there are few extrinsic resources to persuade them. Ultimately, students' success is left to their own compliance. In terms of effectivities, the teacher is very clear and precise in her instructions, thus making it more likely that a broad range of students should be able to comply with her directions. This explicitness raises the question of the extent to which these practices foster intelligent action beyond school and testing situations in which the rules for engagement are clearly specified.

Example 2: Quest Atlantis

We now contrast this example with an excerpt from the whole-class discussion from a very different activity about coordinate graphing. Although this activity covered very similar content to the one reviewed above, the content is situated in a larger narrative that involves finding a lost archaeology professor who has been taken captive by an island because he has not respected their rules. In this unit, students learn about coordinate graphing as a tool they need to leverage in order to find the professor. Students must navigate the island in a particular way so that the island does not become further angered; thus it is imperative that students understand coordinate graphing in order to move only to parts of the island where they are allowed. In addition, students have to earn the respect of the inhabitants of the island by completing tasks that also target elements of coordinate graphing. This task is part of a larger curriculum called *Quest Atlantis* (www.questatlantis.org, accessed July 25, 2011), an immersive 3D videogame that allows students to navigate around the virtual world and speak with virtual characters in order to resolve legitimate dilemmas (Barab et al., 2009; Barab, Thomas, Dodge, Carteaux, & Tuzun, 2005; Barab et al., 2007). As with the unit discussed above, students are introduced to the mechanics of coordinate graphing, including vocabulary procedures and conventions. However, this content is situated in a larger fictional dilemma, thus positioning coordinate graphing as a tool that can be leveraged in order to solve or address larger issues.

The conversation below is a whole-class discussion that occurred in the middle of students engaging this complex dilemma. As with the example above, the teacher and students talk about conventions and vocabulary around coordinate graphing. However, unlike the example above, the talk goes beyond pure mechanics. The conversation follows students having first learned about different kinds of maps they might choose to use to be able to navigate around an island: one that is a simple map that shows landmarks without orientation, and a second that imposes the map over a grid. The students meet a wild boar who challenges the utility of using a map without a grid and begins to introduce the idea that there is more than one way to describe locations and directions—cardinal directions (N, S, E, W) and coordinate plotting (x, y). For the purposes of comparison, the excerpt from this whole-class conversation was selected to map (as closely as possible) onto the same content that was presented in the example above.

In this exchange, students are presented with strong opportunities to review the elements of a graph and how to locate points on a coordinate graph. They also have opportunities to consider the differences between the coordinate graphing system, which uses x and y coordinates, and the more familiar cartography system that locates points based on their north–south–east–west orientation.

Taking the interaction apart in terms of our ontological elements, the *task* that students are working on affords opportunities for students to engage procedurally with information, as they have to ensure that they are locating and placing points accurately on the coordinate grid. The task also creates opportunities for students to engage conceptually: students begin to think about how coordinate graphing conventions work by comparing them with conventions that they were already familiar with—those from cartography. Additionally, the task creates opportunities for students to engage consequentially with content. Student 2 revealed this consequential engagement as he began to talk about the value of having a grid over a map. Specifically, he was referring to a choice he was asked to make between different kinds of maps that students could use to help them navigate around the

T: Ivo is a wild boar, and he lives in the jungle, and he taught you some things about maps. What are some things that he taught you?

St1: Um, about the graph.

T: About the graph. This is called a graph. What else did he teach you?

St2: He taught you that Archie was completely wrong about what he did, saying that you need an actual grid to show it, and he showed you what a grid would look like on the map, and you answered questions on it. It's like . . . I had argued that it would be a lot harder to find it if I didn't have a grid.

T: OK, a grid. What does a grid look like? I know this is a graph, but what does a grid look like. Can anyone describe it for me?

St3: It would have the lines of the x- and y-axis.

T: OK, so we're saying there's a grid, there's an x- and y-axis. And what does the x- and y-axis look like, Arkham?

St3: Well, the x-axis is the one going from left to right, and the y-axis is the one going up and down.

T: Alright, go ahead. What else do you see?

St4: Um, the x-axis is the, um east and west.

T: So, like this? [Labels east and west.]

St4: Yeah, so the east and west, you know, it's the exact same thing, and the y-axis is the north and south.

T: Very good. So it really does look like a what?

St: A map

T: Excellent. What else?

St1: Usually we use the north and south first and then the east and the west, but in the graph we use first the x-axis which is west or east and then the y-axis which is north or south.

T: OK. So . . . he's saying that . . . you have a graph. On here we have north and south, and we have west and east, and if it looks like 8N 4W, they do north–south first, east–west second. Is that how we do on this? So let's say in Crypto Jungle we're at 8N 4W. What spot do you think that would be . . . in what area?

St5: That would be 4 this way . . . OK, negative four . . . around here.

T: OK, you think it would be here. [Writes (–4, 8).]

St5: Yes

T: How many people agree? [Many hands go up]

T: Do you know what we call each of these four spots? Typically we call them quadrants. This is the quadrant that Roman believes this would be in, and (–4, 8) is what we would call it on a coordinate grid.

FIGURE 2.2 Excerpt from Quest Atlantis classroom.

island. The map with the grid overlays a coordinate graph on top of the map of the island, which allow students to be more precise about the locations of various objects and characters that they need to find. The student claims having grids makes it much easier to navigate around the island. Indeed, this is one of the reasons behind the precise conventions for coordinate graphing: being able to communicate clearly to other people about the location of points. The task allows students to recognize the affordances of those conventions for realizing their own purposes and goals.

It is difficult to discern the *norms* of the classroom from a mere excerpt of conversation. However, the exchanges between the teacher and the students in this transcript have a markedly different tone from the exchanges reviewed above. It is clear that the teacher is still in charge of this conversation; she is standing at the overhead projector and is noting students' observations. However, the teacher herself provides very little information beyond repeating what students volunteer. She asks open questions and requires that students offer information, ideas, and explanations, rather than offering them herself. Thus, what it means to do math here ultimately looks quite different from the first classroom and involves connecting ideas with contexts of use; in their contributions, students offered facts and information, as in Classroom 1, but also shared opinions and meanings.

The dispositions that students are likely to develop in this classroom involve taking up opportunities, not only for procedural engagement, but also more conceptual and consequential engagement. The affordances for this engagement come in large part from the task the students are completing, but also from the way the teacher positioned the students relative to the task: she herself is more of a guide as the students review their gameplay than she is a director of the students' thinking. As a consequence, there are more diverse opportunities for students to engage content in different ways. Students' contributions range from procedural answers, much like those observed in the earlier episode, to more conceptual and consequential responses. In terms of intentionality, many students seem to recognize that their understanding of the coordinate system has implications for the consequence that they've come to care about—saving the professor.

Indeed, understanding the difference between the coordinate graphing system and the cartography system is consequential for students in order for them to engage successfully in the game. Thus, students' intention to engage is not merely about compliance and getting a good grade, but is also enhanced through their interest in and commitment to the larger narrative. This conversation impacts students' effectivities for taking up the opportunities presented in the task, in that it helps to ensure all students have access to the information that is being presented, so they can both recognize and realize its affordances. As can be seen from the tone of the conversation, much of the information the students share has been gleaned through their gameplay (specifically through conversations with Ivo the boar). However, it is possible that in their play students might have overlooked specific details or become confused about the different elements of graphing. The summarizing conversation with the teacher serves to ensure that all students have access to the underlying ideas they will need to master in order to be able to play the game successfully.

Summary

It is important to note the dual role of task design and classroom norms in affording opportunities to learn. The task itself creates a framework for engagement, by creating expectations for what content will be discussed and how it will be discussed. The task in the first classroom involved asking students to create a graph and locate particular points on that graph. In contrast, the task in the second classroom involved considering how two different systems of graphing and navigation are related. In the first example, the task positioned content as a set of facts to be learned and remembered, and positioned students as novices whose role was to acquire this information. The task in the second classroom positioned content as information to be interrogated and analyzed, and positioned students as meaning-makers. Thus, through their designs, the tasks created dramatically different opportunities to learn. However, these tasks must be further understood within the context of the norms and values of the classroom (and school context more broadly) that shaped local expectations for competent behavior.

In the first classroom, the students and the teacher seemed to share a view of mathematics engagement that involved answering questions and paying attention. The teacher did not ask students to interpret what she was saying or to interrogate it. Likewise, students did not initiate that kind of behavior themselves, suggesting that this was a typical expectation for the classroom. Classroom 2 seemed to work equally seamlessly—the teacher expected students to share what they knew and even to lead the discussion. The students appeared to be accustomed to this way of doing math, as they shared ideas and led the discussion with very little resistance. It is quite possible to imagine these tasks being conducted in classrooms that operated under very different norms, and the subsequent conversations unfolding very differently. Thus, it is only in the interaction between the tasks and the classroom norms that the opportunities to learn—and, thus, the instantiation of intelligent action—are constructed.

In examining these two lessons, which are ostensibly about the same content, we can begin to understand how intelligence is constructed through interactions and how what constitutes intelligent action is dependent on the context. What it means to be intelligent in the first classroom involves replication and accuracy. Students are recognized as intelligent if they can act within the parameters of that system. In Classroom 2, what counts as intelligent action looks quite different. Students are invited to share ideas and opinions that are not merely procedural; indeed, some of the students' utterances had very little to do with the mathematical topic under discussion. Importantly, these utterances were not considered off topic, but rather part of what it meant to do math here. These episodes are just a snapshot of one of many experiences that accrue in order to shape students' dispositions towards engaging mathematics. However, in contrasting these two cases, it is clear that the parameters of the classroom shape opportunities for students to act in particular ways and reinforce different frameworks for what intelligent behavior looks like.

Conclusions

In this chapter, we argued that intelligence, rather than being a static property of an individual, should be considered a shared accomplishment between individual and environment in the service of a particular goal. Further, in defining the ontological elements of intelligent action, we advanced a characterization that included (a) the nature of the task and how it frames activity, (b) the tools and resources that are available to support activity, (c) the norms and rules that shape how particular activities are recognized and valued, and (d) the personal histories and dispositions of the learner. More generally, if one treats intelligence as a relational act involving consequential success, then one must rethink how learning should be organized. It is clear that students have different kinds of opportunity to engage in mathematical thinking, based on the structure of the tasks and classrooms in which they are situated (Gresalfi, Martin et al., 2009). In schools, we tend to see learning as more of a compliance and acquisition process, not a participatory one that involves using disciplinary content to achieve particular outcomes. Additionally, most real-world mathematics problems do not conform themselves to the procedural structures as defined in schools; therefore, one might argue that the traditional classroom may not be effectively preparing students to act intelligently outside of schools.

The question arises about the potential link between classroom norms and broader sociopolitical structures. As previously stated, the interaction style or participation structure observed in Classroom 1 is quite common. This kind of classroom structure has evolved for a variety of reasons; it is clear that there are some particular outcomes that are well aligned with this kind of structure. Specifically, many of the tests that students are asked to take, which ultimately serve as determinants of their intelligence or at least of future opportunities, are well aligned with this kind of tightly organized procedural classroom structure. Classroom 2, on the other hand, is not as closely aligned with the kind of sequestered assessments that we typically give to students. Specifically, the teacher does not give clear directions about how graphing should be undertaken, nor is she focused on students' own creation of graphs. Instead, she focuses on students' thinking about coordinate graphing. We believe that this latter form of classroom participation is a valuable one; indeed, more valuable than one that focuses solely on procedural engagement (c.f. Barab et al., 2009; Gresalfi, Barab et al., 2009). However, it might not be the form of classroom structure that best prepares students to succeed on tests of sequestered problem solving.

If these tests of sequestered problem solving are the kinds of outcome that we care most about, then Classroom 1 truly is a better way to prepare students. We argue, however, that knowledgeable participation is about more than successful performance in standardized tests and involves being able to think about not only what to do to solve a problem, but why doing so makes sense and for what purposes it is useful. Outside of schools, most real-world mathematics problems do not usually conform themselves to the procedural structure seen in schools, particularly because problems are ill defined and do not typically specify solution methods. One might argue, therefore, that the traditional classroom may not be effectively preparing students to act intelligently outside of schools.

Importantly, the same behavior that is recognized as intelligent in Classroom 1 is less likely to be recognized as intelligent in Classroom 2, as there is a broader range of behavior that is expected and encouraged as part of what it means to be intelligent. If Classroom 2 frequently looks as it did in this excerpt, students would have opportunities to develop very different dispositions towards doing math, dispositions that involved not only procedural engagement but also conceptual and consequential engagement. Students are not simply asked to recite or apply a procedure (Whitehead, 1929), but instead are asked to engage tasks as they exist and are defined in context, with problem solvers asking themselves which procedures make sense for accomplishing what ends. This form of intelligent action is much more situated, much more dependent on available resources, and, we argue, much more relevant to the real-world context. From this perspective, it is intelligent to leverage resources and use contextual information to assess the validity of particular actions; not being able to do so should be seen as less intelligent and not more.

These contrasting cases also illuminate the complexity of our research, designed in part to examine outcome differences but also to illuminate process and mechanism with the goal of advancing theory and positively impacting how people learn. Clearly, our understanding of the extent to which curricular designs are effective depends on more than controlled comparison studies that, through their design, factor out the complexity of classroom interaction seen here. Instead, in our work we focus on the ways that elements of the classroom system shape the ways that students and teachers make meaning of the content they are working with, and therefore the ways that they together set expectations for what it means to be intelligent. Indeed, by ignoring the complexity of classroom interaction, such large-scale studies fail to help teachers and designers learn about whether and why particular designs are effective. For that reason, in our research we leverage a methodology called "design-based research."

Design-based research takes as its central goal the advancement of both theoretical and pragmatic understandings (Barab & Squire, 2004; Brown, 1992;

Cobb, Confrey, diSessa, Lehrer, & Schauble, 2003) and thus must investigate not only whether designs are effective, but also the underlying mechanisms that might account for their effectiveness. The fundamental methodology involves cycles of conjecture, design, implementation, analysis, and reflection/conjecture. In this way, designs are created based on one's initial conjectures about how people learn, and these designs are refined as the researchers gain insight into the extent to which those conjectures were sufficiently nuanced. Design-based research is an explicitly theory-building activity (Barab & Squire, 2004) and, as such, requires intentional specification of the theories that underlie both initial assumptions and interpretations of data. In particular, one's understanding or conceptualization of how people learn necessarily informs the initial designs undertaken. Thus, in the case of our understanding of intelligent action, design-based research as a methodology can help us to learn about how people come to act in ways that are recognized as more or less intelligent, depending on the tools and resources available in a particular context.

Specifically, in the case of the relational ontology specified here, design-based research as a methodology could help to frame the kinds of design that one might create in order to foster dispositions towards action that might be recognized as important in certain valued contexts. But, equally importantly, the methodology might be used to help us better understand the extent to which intelligent action is shaped through one's experiences in the world and, more precisely, how. These conjectures then become embodied in future design decisions and reexamined in new contexts and situations from which one can begin to build petite generalizations (Stake, 1995) that specify both the theory and the conditions across which it has been seen as relevant. We see such research, one that is simultaneously interventionist and naturalistic, as necessary if one is attempting to examine what it means to act intelligently.

We believe that being able to act competently in complex settings is what we should consider as intelligent, and it is this sort of disposition that is better aligned with the 21st-century competencies that will be required to be successful in our ever-changing technologically driven world. If this is the outcome that we care most about, then we need to think carefully about which classroom best prepares students to be successful in a world that recognizes intelligence in this more complex way. It is clear the ontological elements that define a particular system of activity have significant implications for the ways that intelligence can be acted out and recognized. An attempt to consider the extent to which students are intelligent without considering these kinds of opportunity is, therefore, likely to lead to an impoverished notion of the individual and an incomplete understanding of why people are able to do what they do. In contrast, when one treats intelligence as a shared accomplishment, we begin to look at a much richer ontological space for understanding why someone does or does not act intelligently. Further, such a view of intelligence is emancipatory in that it opens up the possibility that a much wider group of people can be intelligent. For this potential to be realized, we would need new classroom models that focus on positioning content in contexts of use and in supporting students in learning to leverage contextual afford-ances as part of what constitutes successful participation in schools.

References

Barab, S. A., & Plucker, J. A. (2002). Smart people or smart contexts? Cognition, ability, and talent development in an age of situated approaches to knowing and learning. *Educational Psychologist, 37*(3), 165–182.

Barab, S. A., & Squire, K. D. (2004). Design-based research: Putting a stake in the ground. *Journal of the Learning Sciences,* (13), 1–14.

Barab, S. A., Cherkes-Julkowski, M., Swenson, R., Garrett, S., Shaw, R. E., & Young, M. (1999). Principles of self-organization: learning as participation in autocatakinetic systems. *The Journal of the Learning Sciences, 8*(3 & 4), 349–390.

Barab, S. A., Gresalfi, M. S., & Arici, A. (2009). Transformational play: Why educators should care about games. *Educational Leadership, 67*(1), 76–80.

Barab, S. A., Thomas, M., Dodge, T., Carteaux, R., & Tuzun, H. (2005). Making learning fun: Quest Atlantis, a game without guns. *Educational Technology Research & Development, 53*(1), 86–107.

Barab, S. A., Zuiker, S., Warren, S., Hickey, D., Ingram-Goble, A., Kwon, E., et al. (2007). Situationally embodied curriculum: Relating formalisms and contexts. *Science Education, 91*(5), 750–782.

Boaler, J. (1997). Reclaiming school mathematics: The girls fight back. *Gender and Education, 9,* 285–305.

Boaler, J. (2000). Exploring situated insights into research and learning. *Journal for Research in Mathematics Education, 31,* 113–119.

Boaler, J., & Greeno, J. G. (2000). Identity, agency, and knowing in mathematical worlds. In J. Boaler (Ed.), *Multiple perspectives on mathematics teaching and learning* (pp. 45–82). Stamford, CT: Ablex.

Bourdieu, P. (1984). *Distinction: A social critique, of the judgement of taste.* (R. Nice, trans.). Cambridge, MA: Harvard University Press.

Brown, A. L. (1992). Design experiments: Theoretical and methodological challenges in creating complex interventions in classroom settings. *Journal of the Learning Sciences, 2,* 141–178.

Cobb, P., Confrey, J., diSessa, A. A., Lehrer, R., & Schauble, L. (2003). Design experiments in education research. *Educational Researcher, 32*(1), 9–13.

Cobb, P., Gresalfi, M. S., & Hodge, L. (2009). An interpretive scheme for analyzing the identities that students develop in mathematics classrooms. *Journal for Research in Mathematics Education, 40*(1), 40–68.

Cochran-Smith, M., & Lytle, S. L. (1999). Relationships of knowledge and practice: Teacher learning in communities. *Review of Research in Education, 24,* 249–305.

Eccles, J. S., Adler, T. F., Futterman, R., Goff, S. B., Kaczala, C. M., Meece, J. L., et al. (1983). Expectancies, values, and academic behaviors. In J. T. Spence (Ed.), *Achievement and achievement motivation* (pp. 75–146). San Francisco, CA: Freedman.

Gibson, J. J. (1979). *The ecological approach to visual perception.* Boston, MA: Houghton Mifflin.

Greeno, J. G. (1994). Gibson's affordances. *Psychological review, 101*(2), 336–342.

Greeno, J. G., & Gresalfi, M. S. (2008). Opportunities to learn in practice and identity. In P. A. Moss, D. C. Pullin, J. P. Gee, E. H. Haertel & L. J. Young (Eds.), *Assessment, equity, and opportunity to learn* (pp. 170–199). New York: Cambridge University Press.

Gresalfi, M. S. (2009). Taking up opportunities to learn: Constructing dispositions in mathematics classrooms. *Journal of the Learning Sciences, 18*, 327–369.

Gresalfi, M. S., & Ingram-Goble, A. (2008). *Designing for dispositions.* Paper presented at the International Conference of the Learning Sciences, Utrecht, the Netherlands.

Gresalfi, M. S., Barab, S. A., Siyahhan, S., & Christensen, T. (2009). Virtual worlds, conceptual understanding, and me: Designing for critical engagement. *On the Horizon (online journal), 17*(1), 21–34.

Gresalfi, M. S., Martin, T., Hand, V., & Greeno, J. G. (2009). Constructing competence: An analysis of students' participation in the activity system of mathematics classrooms. *Educational Studies in Mathematics, 70*(49–70).

Gutiérrez, R. (2004, August). *The complex nature of practice for urban (mathematics) teachers.* Paper presented at the Rockefeller Symposium on the Practice of School Improvement: Theory, Methodology, and Relevance, Bellagio, Italy.

Hand, V. (2010). The co-construction of opposition within a low-track mathematics classroom. *American Educational Research Journal, 47*, 97–132.

Henningsen, M., & Stein, M. K. (1997). Mathematical tasks and student cognition: Classroom-based factors that support and inhibit high-level mathematical thinking and reasoning. *Journal for Research in Mathematics Education, 28*(5), 524–549.

Horn, J. L., & Cattell, R. B. (1967). Age differences in fluid and crystallized intelligence. *Acta Psychologica, 26*, 1–23.

Lareau, A. (2003). *Unequal childhoods: Class, race, and family life.* Berkeley, CA: University of California Press.

McDermott, R. (1993). The acquisition of a child by a learning disability. In S. Chaiklin & J. Lave (Eds.), *Understanding practice.* Cambridge, UK: Cambridge University Press.

Mehan, H. (1979). *Learning lessons: Social organization in the classroom.* Cambridge, MA: Harvard University Press.

Perkins, D., & Ritchhart, R. (2004). When is good thinking? In D. Y. Dai, & R. J. Sternberg (Eds.), *Motivation, emotion, and cognition: Integrative perspectives on intellectual functioning and development* (pp. 351–384). Mahwah, NJ: Lawrence Erlbaum.

Perkins, D., Tishman, S., Ritchhart, R., Donis, K., & Andrade, A. (2000). Intelligence in the wild: A dispositional view of intellectual traits. *Educational Psychology Review, 12*(3), 269–293.

Schoenfeld, A. H. (1988). When good teaching leads to bad results: The disasters of "well-taught" mathematics courses. *Educational Psychologist, 23*(2), 145–166.

Shaw, R. E., Effken, J. A., Fajen, B. R., Garrett, S. R., & Morris, A. (1997). An ecological approach to the online assessment of problem-solving paths. *Instructional Science, 25*, 151–166.

Shaw, R. E., Kadar, E., Sim, M., & Repperger, D. W. (1992). The intentional spring: A strategy for modeling systems that learn to perform intentional acts. *Journal of Motor Behavior, 24*, 3–28.

Snow, R. E. (1992). Aptitude theory: Yesterday, today, and tomorrow. *Educational Psychologist, 27*, 5–32.

Squire, K. D., McKinster, J. G., Barnett, M., Leuhmann, A. L., & Barab, S. A. (2001). Designed curriculum and local culture: Acknowledging the primacy of classroom culture. *Science Education, 87*(4), 468–489.

Stake, R. E. (1995). *The art of case study research.* Thousand Oaks, CA: Sage.

Stein, M. K., Smith, M. S., Henningsen, M. A., & Silver, E. A. (2000). *Implementing standards-based mathematics instruction: A casebook for professional development.* New York: Teacher College Press.

Sternberg, R. J. (2007). Who are the bright children? The cultural context of being and acting intelligent. *Educational Researcher, 36*(3), 148–155.

Stigler, J. W., & Hiebert, J. (1997). Understanding and improving classroom mathematics instruction: An overview of the TIMSS video study. *Phi Delta Kappan, 79*(1), 14–21.

Stigler, J. W., Fernandez, C., & Yoshida, M. (1996). Traditions of school mathematics in Japanese and American elementary classrooms. In L. P. Steffe, P. Nesher, C. E. Cobb, G. A. Goldin & B. Greer (Eds.), *Theories of mathematical learning* (pp. 149–175). Mahwah, NJ: Erlbaum.

Vygotsky, L. S. (1978). *Mind and society: The development of higher psychological processes.* Cambridge, MA: Harvard University Press.

Whitehead, A. N. (1929). *The aims of education and other essays.* New York: The Free Press.

Young, M. F., Depalma, A., & Garrett, S. (2002). Situations, interaction, process and affordances: An ecological psychology perspective. *Instructional Science, 30*, 47–63.

3

THE INTERPLAY OF CREATIVE AND CRITICAL THINKING IN INSTRUCTION

Judith A. Langer

Logic takes you from A to B. Imagination takes you everywhere.
(Albert Einstein)

This chapter focuses on creative and critical thinking, their role in intellectual functioning and growth, and classroom environments that support their development and use. I begin with a discussion of what I mean by these terms and how they call for a shift in the goals and expectations of schooling, especially what gets taught and how, and then use findings from a series of design experiments to specify instructional principles that support their development.

Notions of creativity have earned a growing place in the psychology literature. However, in this chapter they are contextualized somewhat differently and therefore take on somewhat different foci. By and large, the literature tends to focus on, or make distinctions between, creativity with a "Big C" and creativity with a "small c" (Czikszentmihalyi, 1996). The Big C focus looks at creativity as an act of genius, one that is sufficiently eminent to change a field, if not the world (e.g., Koestler, 1964; Simonton, 1988; Wallace & Gruber, 1989). The small c focus, on the other hand, looks at creativity as the kind of originality that occurs, or can occur, in everyday life (e.g., Gardner, 2008; Runco, 2004; Singer, 2004). Halpern (1997) considers creativity to be defined by its outcomes, which are marked by the production of novel and appropriate responses, but not by the processes that led to those outcomes. She describes creativity as a set of processes such as ways to identify that a problem exists, developing and evaluating potential solutions, as well as judging how novel and well the problem has been solved. All three bodies of work have been important and productive, permitting greater understanding of the multiple factors and contexts that accompany original thinking.

Although, to some degree, we are all attempting to identify enabling mechanisms, I approach the issue from a somewhat different tangent, focusing less on the act of creativity than on the cognitive moves that enable the mind to seek and welcome novelties that might otherwise be excluded from consideration. These cognitive moves are brought to bear in the range of creative experiences in academic studies and life. However, they are never taught at school, rarely sanctioned and often considered the mark of a sloppy mind (Langer, 2011b). Critical thinking (e.g., Fisher & Scriven, 1997; Sternberg, 1985), on the other hand, is often presented as a set of strategic moves that apply similarly, across disciplines and goals (see Langer, 1992, 2011a, b, for discussion of these issues). At the present time, critical thinking is generally treated as the mark of good thinking, whatever the course of study or goal of the activity.

However, from my perspective, both critical and creative thinking are essential aspects of the well-developed mind (Langer, 2011a, b). Together, they offer individuals different vectors into the same issues and thus have the potential to mutually enrich understanding of material and experiences and ways in which they might be interpreted, connected to other knowledge and used in enhanced or novel ways. From this perspective, both critical and creative thinking are essential parts of the human consciousness from which humans draw when constructing meaning, but each focuses on a different approach to reasoning. Jerome Bruner (1986) contrasts them as narrative and paradigmatic thought. Suzanne Langer (1967) calls them subjective and objective reasoning. In earlier work, I made distinctions between literary and discursive orientations (Langer, 1990, 1995). Of importance in all is the identification of both creative and critical thought as necessary parts of the well-developed intellect, each different from, but as valued as, the other. Creative thought involves an open-ended stance that seeks and is responsive to the unexpected, to ambiguities or to unimagined ideas and experience, while critical thought is more focused outside the individual, on ideas, concepts, texts, images and situations as they relate to each other or to some reference point (see Langer, 2011a, b, for fuller discussions).

There is growing evidence that the processes involved in thinking creatively are also important and productive in dealing with everyday problems of life and work. For example, one study shows that computer repair people use "storytelling" to figure out how best to fix highly complex computers when their more logical analyses fail to identify the source of problems or how to fix them (Orr, 1987a, b). In such situations, computer repairers listen to each other, create scenarios and build on each others' stories until they make a breakthrough with a possible solution they can try out. They search for the unexpected. Studies of physicians, who learn throughout their professional training to rely on logical and critical reasoning, show that they try to use what they were taught when making diagnoses. However, when this method of reasoning is unproductive, studies say they engage in more open-ended "storytelling"(Elstein, Shulman & Sprafka, 1978), or they discard their more deductive approach and turn to more open-ended thinking (Groopman, 2007). In each case, use of these more open-ended meanderings led physicians to unexpected diagnoses and treatments that they had not otherwise considered. Similar studies have been done with lawyers who prepare court cases (Bruner, 2002; Putnam, 1978). Creative thinking opens new possibilities that can then be examined from a critical stance. In such situations, both critical and creative thinking are used, and both are needed. They serve different purposes that move us to orient ourselves differently to meaning.

What is Meant by Creative and Critical Thinking?

It is useful to think of critical and creative thinking as different orientations toward meaning. The question becomes, "When we are trying to make sense, what kind of meaning do we orient our minds to seek and expect?" Research (Langer, 1990, 1995, 2011a, b) suggests that there are basic differences in how we orient ourselves, in how we position ourselves to expect ideas based on our primary purpose for engaging in an activity. Two major purposes that help shape our expectations are: (1) to gain information and build concepts (for example, to learn more about economic recessions or about health-care options), or (2) to engage in a more fluid and open-ended experience where we are not sure to where it might lead (like embarking on making the unexpected diagnoses Groopman [above] describes, or curling up with a good book). The first would be motivated primarily by an information-getting, retrieval, connecting and/or applying purpose, whereas the second would be motivated primarily by a search and see purpose. Together, they are "mind in action," meaning-making moves with distinct functionality and motivation. Together, they contribute to the intellect, and it is their joint availability that permits us to engage in the kinds of flexible cognitive interplay that support intellectual functioning and intellectual growth.

Maintaining a Point of Reference

The goal of a critical orientation is to understand something more fully, to analyze, critique or refine an understanding, to apply it and to gain or share information about it. I call this orientation maintaining a point of reference. In point of reference thinking, the cognitive search is for relevant ideas that will fill out or refine understanding or reaction to a topic, concept or point. Our sense of the whole provides a steady reference point. As understandings unfold, the new information may clarify or disturb our sense of the whole, but rarely changes it. We rely on our perception of the constancy of the whole in order to monitor initial understandings (or misunderstandings) and weigh the contribution of the new information to our ideational quest.

Our goal in maintaining a point of reference is to build understandings or concepts, especially when we: (a) already have a good sense of what the topic or point of view is, but know little about it and want to access more information or related ideas; (b) already know something about the topic or point of view but wish to develop, deepen or extend our understandings; or (c) when we want to use content generatively, as a stepping stone to making new connections or creating new uses for that knowledge. I refer to this orientation as point of reference because the "point" refers to the fact that there is usually a particular kind of content we are after, and that is where we aim our thinking. The "reference" suggests that we use this point as a way to monitor what we let in or filter out; we check with or refer to it. Because, from the beginning, we have some sense of the content or concept we are after, the point of reference serves as our sense of the whole, the endpoint we are working toward. As we move along, we try to refine understandings and remove ambiguities, guided by the point of reference. Once established, our notion of that point of reference rarely changes, unless there is a substantial amount of data that leads us to rethink that initial sense of the content/endpoint we were after.

Exploring Horizons of Possibilities

In comparison, the goal of a creative orientation is to engage in an open-ended search, a sort of reconnaissance mission during which we enter spaces and experiences where ideas or concepts might come to mind that we had neither anticipated nor imagined. I refer to it as exploring horizons of possibilities because, in a creative experience, we are guided by the open-ended search for ideas. Uncertainty and ambiguity are welcomed, because the goal is to let the various experiences lead us to meaning. To do this, we not only call on what we can imagine, but also what we cannot yet imagine, in response to ideas or stimuli that we meet along the way of our search.

Our goal in exploring horizons of possibility is to create a new conceptualization, especially when: (a) we wish to think about or develop something new; (b) when there is a problem we are having difficulty solving; or (c) when we are not sure where we are headed but want to move beyond. This orientation involves us in a personal search for experiences from which ideas can emerge. In selecting the label "exploring horizons of possibilities", I chose the word horizons because, as we ponder the ideas or concepts that come to mind, we change our supposition of where our overall quest or understanding of the material might go. I use the word possibilities because creative thinking is guided by openness to new experience, welcoming of unanticipated imaginings—by the opening of possibilities. We take on new ideas and try to understand their immediate meanings for the moment, as well as look ahead for implications of their contribution to the whole. When exploring horizons of possibilities, our sense of the whole, where we are going in our quest and what it will become, changes and unfolds as our explorations unfold. The sense of the whole exists as a constantly moving horizon of possibilities. These possibilities emerge out of the growing concept or understanding itself, with all its uncertainties and ambiguities.

Thus, in creative orientations, our sense of whole, or endpoint, is always ready to shift, whereas in a critical orientation it is steady—foreseen and maintained. The envisionments or understandings that are built along the way and what they contain are developed in relation to that sense of the whole. That sense of the whole serves as a guide, keeping our inquiry within bounds that are relevant. In contrast, the creative endpoint is always in a state of change because, along the way, we are moved to explore possibilities that new experiences or ideas bring to mind.

The Case of Charles Darwin

In both point of reference and horizons of possibility orientations we ask questions, judge appropriateness, make comparisons, connections, syntheses, evaluations, etc. However, in the creative orientation we do these in a more exploratory manner, seeking possibilities along the way, with the open-ended search as a guide. Although critical thinking is also open to new interpretations and changing endpoints, these generally occur through our setting of successive points of reference, as in a sequence of scientific experiments based on serial and successively informed hypotheses. Here, however, I am positing other ways in which science as well as everyday thinking can get done. I am suggesting that, instead of seeing the two orientations as mutually exclusive, we look to ways in which they can serve complementary purposes. Let us look to the voyage of Charles Darwin as an example.

Darwin's revelations during his round-the-world voyage on the *Beagle*—how his questions began, how his thoughts developed and how he reached his findings and explained them to the society of his time—are good examples of creative and critical thinking. Throughout his voyage, Darwin kept careful notes that were eventually known as the Red and Blue Notebooks (Darwin, 2002–2009). The Red Notebook was the first and primarily contains his initial observations and speculations, with possible supporting or contradicting data considered and explored. Here we can see his early questions, his exploratory attempts at explanations and his movement toward a theory that he would later be able to explain, elaborate upon and defend. His writings give us a window into his thought processes. In an autobiography edited by his son Francis Darwin (Darwin, 1987), he says:

> From my early youth I have had the strongest desire to understand or explain whatever I observed—that is to group all facts under some general laws. These causes combined have given me the patience to reflect or ponder for any number of years over any unexplained problem. As far as I can judge, I am not apt to follow blindly the lead of other men. I have steadily endeavored to keep my own mind free so as to give up any hypotheses, however much beloved, (and I cannot resist forming one on every subject),

as soon as facts are shown to be opposite it . . . This has naturally led me to distrust deductive reasoning . . . Of these [mental qualities], the most important have been—the love of science—unbound patience in reflecting over any subject—industry in observing and collecting—and a fair share of invention as well as common sense.

As a young man on the *Beagle*, he wished to solve his problem about relationships among the discrepant forms of life he was beginning to find, but he had no idea where to turn or in what realm his solution might be found. I posit that the traits he describes in his memoirs led him primarily to explore horizons of possibility, to enter points of reference and then to explore some more. Over time, his speculations about cause began to take shape. In his autobiography (Barlow, 1958), he explains:

> During the voyage of the Beagle I had been deeply impressed by discovering in the Pompean formation great fossil animals covered with armour like that on the existing armadillos; secondly, by the manner in which closely allied animals replace one another in proceeding southwards over the Continent; and thirdly, by the South American character of most of the productions of the Galapagos archipelago . . . It was evident that such facts as these, as well as many others, could be explained on the supposition that species gradually become modified; and that subject haunted me. (pp. 118–119)

These three discoveries occurred over a long period of time, as the *Beagle* took him from one part of the world to another, bringing him into contact with yet other potentially related species. During the voyage, his openness to exploring possible relationships among the species he collected permitted a build-up of experience to lead him to "invent a theory and see how many classes of facts the theory would explain" (from a letter he wrote, cited by Koestler, 1964, p. 135). Koestler claims that Darwin plaited "disjointed threads into a braid," which became his theory of evolution of the species.

Although a creative orientation led Darwin to the theory, once it became a reference point in need of explanation and defense, a critical orientation permitted him to build upon and bolster it. However, *The Origin of the Species* was not published until 23 years after the voyage. When Darwin returned to England, he gave some of his finch specimens to John Gould, a distinguished expert, asking for his comments. Michalko (2008) states that Gould didn't quite know what to make of the samples. "He assumed that since God made one set of birds when he created the world, the specimens from different locations would be identical." From such responses Darwin "was aware of the disturbing consequences of his ideas on contemporary society—thus he carefully modified his presentation of his ideas and sought to persuade others to the scientific and philosophical soundness of his ideas" (Bowler, 1996). I would posit that during the intervening years, from developing his theory to publication of his book, Darwin's reasoning reflected both orientations, but most often point of reference, because he already knew the point he wished to make and also the nature of the opposition to it that needed a strong rebuttal. The narrow path offered by point of reference thinking would be most efficacious. However, even here, he may have engaged in more open-ended searches to find areas of explanation or rebuttal he might not otherwise have considered.

Darwin offers an example where both creative and critical thinking were needed to produce his breakthrough. His work was first an "inspired theory" of evolution that grew from Humboldt, Hilaire and Lamarck.

> To counteract "prejudice" [in the society of his day] he had to assemble and build massive pillars of fact in support of the slender bridge of his theory . . . Without those pillars, assembled with heroic patience and effort, the bridge would have collapsed in the ensuing storm. Here is one of the cases where the process of elaboration, verification, and confirmation—the long donkey-work following the brief flash of insight—is more decisive than the discovery itself. (Koestler, 1964, p. 137)

Although I consider the interplay of creative and critical thought to have been more of an ongoing interplay, with one being given a more important role than the other at different points in time, Koestler's analysis is a sound example of how the two orientations can work together fruitfully.

Pedagogical Principles to Support Creative and Critical Thinking

I have intended the preceding sections to make the case that both critical and creative thinking are important aspects of the well-functioning mind, that together they are helpful in bringing about, building upon, rounding out and moving beyond current knowledge and behaviors. They contribute to the kinds of mind called for by Gardner (2008) and Pink (2005), for example. They have also been called for by Runco (1994; Runco and Chand, 1994), whose more recent work argues that creativity involves both convergent and evaluative thinking and that evaluative thinking is necessary for creative behaviors. Yet we have evidence from national assessments (e.g., see National Assessment of Educational Progress (NAEP) assessments over time) as well as recent studies (e.g., Applebee & Langer, 2009) that only a very small percent of students across the United States have actively challenging experiences in class that ask them to engage in extended and thoughtful discussion or writing that calls upon these thinking abilities. Further, the very small percentage of students in the "proficient" categories on NAEP have remained remarkably unchanged over the 40 years of its administration. Clearly, there is an aspect of instruction in need of rethinking:

how to help students to learn to approach material with which they are more or less familiar, how to think flexibly and deeply, and how to control their own cognitive approaches to the content to hand.

To do this, I engaged in several series of design experiments, first in English language arts and English classes (grades 6–12), and later in the four core academic disciplines: social studies/history, mathematics, science and English (grades 6–12), as well as in grades K–5 and special education classes (see, especially, Langer, 1995, 2011a, b). The goal was to identify the principles of effective instruction that support critical and creative thinking, as they have been posed here.

In a series of studies at the Center for English Learning & Achievement (CELA), my colleagues and I examined the features of curriculum and instruction that are present in cognitively engaged classrooms my studies show are closely associated with the development of critical and creative thinking. (See, for example, Applebee, 1996; Applebee, Langer, Nystrand & Gamoran, 2003; Langer, 2011b, 2001; Nystrand, 1997.) This work is based on a sociocognitive view (e.g., Langer, 1985, 1987a, 1995, 2004) of learning. For schooling, this view holds that the social environment of school—what people do, why they do it, and what is valued and modeled as learning on a day-to-day basis—affects cognition. The studies led us to identify a set of principles that underlie classrooms where the sociocognitive contexts provide authentic and thoughtful discipline-appropriate experiences, where students have opportunities to engage with disciplinary content and solve disciplinary problems and are given room to make sense using both creative and critical orientations appropriate for their purposes at the time.

Principles of Effective Curriculum and Instruction

Let us look at the features of classrooms that support these kinds of thinking. As you will see, the focus is not on rote learning or recitation, but neither is it solely on critical thinking as a generic set of strategies, decontextualized from the learner's purpose, knowledge or the discipline itself. Instead, classes that have creative and critical thinking as the goal are places where teachers invite and help students to use the kinds of thinking that are most appropriate and efficacious. Students learn to engage in highly literate conversations, ones that are thoughtful and thought provoking, where the course content is learned and refined by way of exploring as well as examining the ideas. Students go beyond the information given and engage in generative thinking. They learn to be creative and critical thinkers and learners as they are also learning the content and linking it in networks with other new and existing ideas.

Our studies show that there are three critical features of curriculum and instruction that support the kind of thinking I am discussing. They are: maintaining envisionment-building classrooms; establishing curricular connections; and orchestrating substantive discussion, all in the context of demanding subject matter. I will discuss each feature, in turn.

Maintaining Envisionment-Building Classrooms

Envisionments (see Fillmore, 1981; Langer, 1987b, 1990, 1995, 2011a, b) are developing understandings. They are made up of what we do or do not understand at any point in time. They are the dynamic sets of related ideas, questions, images, hunches, anticipations, agreements, rejections, arguments and elaborations that fill our minds during the range of experiences where we gain, express and share our thoughts and understandings. They are always in a state of developing, or available to further develop. They are meanings-in-motion. In envisionment-building classrooms, students' growing understandings are at the center of class work. Their mental envisionments of the content keep developing, and their teacher, with scaffolding in the form of hints, questions, models and direct telling (based on the teacher's judgment of need), helps them do so. Classroom cultures that encourage this kind of meaning development are suffused with the following:

1. Class time is used to help students develop their understandings of the material and to generate new and related ideas. Class sessions are not used as a time for review and recitation, where the focus is on filling in the parts the students didn't "get." The point here is to provide additional experience and scaffolding, from a different angle or context, to help students approach, understand and use the material effectively. Writing, speaking, listening, and media and sign use are tools used by students as well as teachers to help the students think and manipulate the content and their thoughts about it.
2. Issues and topics are examined from a variety of perspectives, as ways to help students problematize and clarify ideas and create links. Students have opportunities to engage in debates, not only with each other, but with unseen others, and to examine distinct points of view in the field and across history and cultures.
3. Student question–asking is seen as a natural, normal and desirable aspect of learning. Students are encouraged to ask thoughtful questions that can move their understandings along. For example, they are asked to come up with good questions for the class or group to discuss.
4. Students are expected to examine and question their ideas, analyze and explain them and go beyond the given, including considering unexpected or novel outcomes.
5. Students are encouraged to provide and weigh evidence, question and evaluate its appropriateness or potential usefulness. They aim to develop airtight defenses, with examples, whatever the origin of their sources or cognitive orientation.
6. Students have opportunities to connect beyond the lesson, in conceptually generative ways that may lead to the development of new constructs, not only in applicative ways.

A range of instructional scaffolds is offered by the teacher to support envision-ment building. However, these are replaced with new ones that help students "up the ante" in what they seek, understand and communicate. The teacher's goal is to create "minds-on classes" (Langer, 2011a, b), where students are truly engaged in critical and creative meaning building.

Establishing Curricular Connections

The second instructional feature that supports critical and creative orienta-tions focuses on the opportunities students have to make curricular connections (Applebee, 1996). Following are curricular features that support this:

1. The teacher's curricular decisions are guided by the goal of creating activities that invite students to make cognitive links to new content and constructs by seeing them in the context of large and potent issues within the field of study or within the world, in ways that make the new content more cognitively connected, more memorable and more available for future use.
2. In planning and during class time, continuity and connections are given great importance. Conceptual connections are made within and across lessons, units, courses and grades—for the students, not just the teachers. Therefore, the connections are made overt, pointed out, and are discussed from the students' as well as teacher's perspectives.
3. The language arts are interrelated with the course content. Therefore, reading, writing, speaking, listening and other signs and symbols used to make sense of the content are used as tools to think, explore ideas, examine them and to learn. They are used as much to grow understandings as to receive and communicate information.
4. Skills, content and purpose are interrelated in ways that bring students into the "know" about how task and purpose shape orientations to thinking and the particular content thought about, as well as the structure of presentation, argument and word choice.

Orchestrating Substantive Discussion and Writing

The third instructional feature is the opportunity for teachers to encourage and oversee students' uses of language and sign, of speaking and writing, to engage in substantive and interactive discussions and thinking (Close, Hull, & Langer, 2005; Nystrand, 1997). Here, teachers and students ask thought-provoking questions about the content that lead to high-level discussions about the topic. These are essential interactions that extend over time, where students learn to agree, disagree, explain, elaborate, challenge ideas, offer alternatives, examine them and engage in sustained and substantive conversation that moves ideas along. Because they extend over time and invite multiple voices, envisionments have room and time to develop and be built upon.

1. Teachers plan authentic discipline-appropriate activities and ask authentic questions that require students to think about, voice, question and build ideas.
2. Teachers help students engage in uptake, connecting to one another's comments.
3. They learn to listen to, evaluate, critique, connect to and build beyond what they and others have offered.
4. Teachers guide students to engage in substantive dialogue and thought. Content is inspected, compared, analyzed, as well as seen in relation to important and discussable issues, with substantive student interaction about them.
5. When called for, teachers up the ante, posing questions or introducing new elements that move thought and discussion to a different dimension or deeper level.

When these three features of curriculum and instruction undergird the pedagogy of the classroom, students have extensive opportunities to approach the content from both critical and creative perspectives, to gain the ability to judge when and under what situations one or the other might be productive, and to gain knowledge of ways to control the language as well as understand the concepts of the various disciplines they are studying. Over time, teachers help students learn to engage the types of thinking that are most appropriate for the task, their purpose and their level of knowledge. Students, in turn, learn to engage in highly literate conversations about the content, ones that are thoughtful and thought provoking, during which the course content is learned and refined through exploring and examining ideas. Students go beyond the information given and engage in generative thinking. They learn to be creative and critical thinkers as they are learning the content.

Critical and Creative Thinking in Social Studies

But what does this look like in the classroom? Let us look at Cara Monteiro's sixth-grade class, with students from a diverse array of backgrounds, home languages, academic performance and interests. They were studying Ancient Egypt.

To begin, they saw a play about King Tut and took notes, jotting any questions or thoughts they had along the way. Then they met in groups to discuss their questions. After a time, each group was told to come up with one question that would be good for the entire class to discuss. Since the topic was quite new to them, during their group discussions and the first whole-class discussion, the students primarily explored horizons of possibility. They tried to reflect on what they had seen and to make connections to related things they may have seen or heard—as a way to gain some initial sense of Tut, his times and his reign. In response to questions they had asked, they searched the internet for information about ancient Egyptian culture and read the part of their textbook on the pharaohs. Here, as they had a point of reference they were after, critical thinking was the dominant approach to thinking. During each viewing or reading, the students did journal jots, made readers' marks to identify parts they didn't understand or questioned the connections they were making. They engaged in several classroom discussions where both kinds of thinking were evident, but point of reference thinking more so as they gathered relevant data.

Next, Monteiro asked them to fill in an "open-mind" diagram—to depict all that was in their minds, all they had learned about leadership in ancient Egypt, from their multiple sources. Discussion followed. Both critical and creative thinking were used, and these orientations varied from student to student based on prior knowledge as well as the issues that concerned them. Later, they took part in a "stand and deliver" activity, for which Monteiro gave them four examples of what King Tut might have done in a particular situation. The students chose one of the four and explored and defended that point of view with evidence, moving between both kinds of thinking to do this. Student engagement was unusually high during this activity, and students' envisionments were visibly developing.

At this point, Monteiro felt her students were on the road to deeper understanding of the problems of leadership in Tut's era, but she wanted to push their ideas further. To do this, she developed a discussion guide with open-ended questions meant to move students to and through various kinds of deeper comprehension. The questions required the students to return to their texts to ask questions and clarify things they didn't understand yet and to discuss them. They had to agree, disagree with, add to or challenge one another's views, and to explain and defend their own—with evidence. Point of reference thinking was used as students explained and defended their ideas, but sometimes they stepped back and explored new possibilities. This turned into a highly substantive discussion of whether King Tut had played a part in his own death. They discussed problems of leadership in an era of religious and political turmoil, analyzed the essence of heroism, and related these problems to other leaders they had studied.

Across this series of lessons, each of the three principles of effective curriculum and instruction discussed above were very much in operation: throughout the lessons, students' envisionments were continually building; engagement was high; and meaning-in-motion was what the students, as well as Ms. Monteiro, expected. In addition to the connections Ms. Monteiro injected into the class, the students themselves tried to make connections, both to human behavior and present-day politics. Further, the interplay of point of reference and horizons of possibility thinking contributed to the knowledge they were developing.

Critical and Creative Thinking in English

Arthea Brooks, a middle-school English teacher at Garrison School, provides another example. She wanted her students to write persuasive essays and also to understand the implications of the First Amendment for individuals' lives (a topic they were studying in social studies). This activity left a good deal of room for students to engage in both point of reference and horizons of possibility thinking. After having her students read the First Amendment, they discussed it. Using point of reference thinking, they had time to ask questions, comment on parts of it and narrow in on some initial understanding of its meaning. Then they did a "quick write" about what the First Amendment means, what it protects and what it might mean for their lives. Here, some students engaged in point of reference, others in horizons of possibility thinking and some both kinds, based on the way they interpreted the task as well as the extent of their knowledge. When they didn't get started at all, Brooks posed questions to invite them into the way of thinking she thought would be most helpful for them at that time. She asked questions such as:

- "What are some things you've heard people say (or write) that they couldn't have if they didn't have freedom of speech? Any ideas? Let's talk about it."
- "Think about what we discussed. What does freedom of speech allow people to do without fear? What kinds of things can they say?"
- "Are there any ways in which freedom of speech might affect your parents, your family, or even yourself? What might it be like if you didn't have it?"

After discussing their quick writes, they read a magazine article about the First Amendment that gave a few examples of ways in which community and individual rights had been protected under that amendment. Students then worked in groups to brainstorm other examples of First Amendment protections they had heard about, read about, or could imagine. Brooks followed this with a discussion of what it would be like without these protections, including in other countries where this might be so. The students then made a T-chart, with examples from daily life of behaviors and beliefs that exist because of the First Amendment and those that might occur without the First Amendment, primarily calling for point of reference thinking, but leaving room for horizons of possibility thinking as a way "into the topic." After discussion, they had an opportunity to plan and then give a persuasive speech (with guidance) about the benefits of First Amendment rights, from their own perspectives. This activity called primarily for point of reference thinking and, as with the other activities, offered practice in content literacy (reading, writing, discussing social studies content in discipline-appropriate ways).

But even then, Ms. Brooks wasn't finished. She brought up the subject of curfews, an issue the class had discussed in response to one of their earlier readings. She asked the students how they felt about having a 10:00 p.m. curfew in their community, and then to role-play reactions from the differing perspectives of community members: policemen, elders, parents, businesses, etc. The discussion primarily involved point of reference thinking, as the students struggled to step into the shoes of their elders. Then, she helped them prepare to write a persuasive paper by asking them to think about (1) their point of view, (2) how it could be supported under First Amendment rights, and (3) particular people in their community and what they would need to say to convince those people of their point of view. This last activity, as well as the persuasive paper, called for point of reference thinking to bolster a logically structured persuasive argument.

Overall, Ms. Brooks gave her students many opportunities to practice a range of point of reference and horizons of possibility thinking strategies as a way to come to understand particular benefits of First Amendment rights. Through the experiences, the point of reference and horizons of possibility thinking, her students engaged with and reinforced each other in extending their understandings. Beyond this, with her guidance, they also learned some cognitive moves to use in approaching the issues, deepening their understandings of them and making them their own.

Assessment

Throughout the series of design experiments, it was necessary to design assessments that would let us know if the students were "on the right track" in engaging in the flexible thinking we sought. These assessments changed over time, as our own understandings and knowledge grew. For example, early in the work, when we were developing and testing the underlying phenomena, we tape-recorded both class discussions and think-alouds (see, for example, Langer, 1990) and subjected the transcripts to various kinds of discourse analysis and coding of cognitive orientations. Later, as we developed classroom interventions, we created cognitive category checklists, with a column for inserting evidence or examples of both teacher and student behaviors. Later, the categories were refined, and classes were subjected to quarterly ratings, and sample rubrics were developed.

Constraints and Concerns in Design Research

Over time, we found that there are several practical constraints and challenges in implementing such a curriculum of thinking. First, and most important of course, is the administrator and teacher "buy-in." They need to want to do it, to believe it will help them attain a goal they considered important. This worked in our favor. As I describe in both *Envisioning Knowledge* and *Envisioning Literature,* 2nd edition, schools that engaged in our studies became aware that the students in our experimental classes thought more flexibly and deeply than did those who did not receive the treatment. Over time, teachers asked to work with us. When we worked with large numbers of a faculty in a school, administrators told us their students were doing better on the high-stakes tests, and they too wanted to work with us. Word spread. Of course, there are other constraints such as time. Often we negotiated needed time for collegial professional activity. With administrator support, what was once a problem became more easily arranged. Being aware of the constraints and working within them, while also trying to change, seems always a factor to be reckoned with.

Capacity Building

With the support of administrators and teachers, and with an open and communicative school environment where teachers and students made presentations and showed exhibitions of the work to the Board of Education and parent groups, capacity building became a given. In one instance, the Assistant Superintendent for Instruction, who believed in a "bubble-up" approach to instructional change, invited teachers in various disciplines to participate if they would like. Many did. Later, a middle-school team of teachers wished to work together (with our guidance) to develop thinking communities. Student successes that stemmed from our interventions were discussed at professional meetings and in the teachers' lounge. The social context of professionalism changed, as did the teachers' goals, approaches and activities. Over time, we learned that capacity building is possible, but takes individual nurturing—with no blueprint right for all. But community building, sharing and communicating—building on strengths while moving toward widespread change—with student and teacher gains and enthusiasm always at the forefront seem the most facilitative way to build capacity.

Research Challenges

Of course, the research challenges are great. Design experiment research is by nature messy, and will continue to be so. What we have learned over time is that setting small, clear and observable learning goals is an imperative, along with continually updated assessment instruments to track them. Further, these goals must be set for teachers as well as students, with a full teacher-learning as well as student-learning component built into the design. We try to engage teachers in the same kinds of activity-based environment we hope them to offer their students. We help them reflect on their own thinking and learning. From our perspective, teacher learning, reflection and discussion (about our pedagogy and approaches), and an interactive professional community are the primary goals. Feedback, mutual support and self-sustaining growth within a professional learning community are critical. Without teacher conceptual change, the kind of student learning we are after cannot fully develop (see Langer, 2004, 2009, for fuller discussion).

Conclusion

Educators and policymakers across the world are interested in higher-level creative and critical thinking and how it can successfully be taught. In addition to its contribution to academic success, it is of critical importance in the global workplace and is key to economic growth. At the same time, the field of education has little empirical guidance as to what these look like in the context of curriculum and instruction, or how they operate in situ. In particular, we do not have a well-developed tradition of talking about or teaching creative thinking in ways that can be used in schools, and critical thinking has often become routinized, separated from the disciplinary activities it is meant to enhance. In this chapter, I have attempted to offer a description of key elements that identify the unique features of both orientations, as well as some characteristics of curriculum and instruction that can guide their "organic" incorporation into the living classroom. Further, I have demonstrated ways in which creative and critical thinking can be experienced within the context of the classroom—both within the content of the discipline and within the context of students' ongoing attempts to make sense, raise questions, develop understandings and take their understanding of that content to a new level. In this course of events, I suggest, both creative and critical thinking play important roles; they work together to unveil a broad base of ideas, experience and knowledge from which students productively can learn to draw as they construct meaning.

My earlier studies indicated that more effective classrooms are "minds-on," cognitively engaged classrooms that involve students both in critical and creative thinking (Langer, 2004, 2011a, b). We refer to critical thinking as "point of reference" thinking. This is the type of thinking students can best engage when they know the topic or the information they are after, what the activity is about, or how to go about solving a problem, but need to gain information to understand it more fully. It offers an information-based goal to build toward. Creative thinking, on the other hand, is conceptualized as "exploring horizons of possibilities." This kind of thinking is particularly useful when students don't fully understand what the topic is, what the activity is about, how to go about solving a problem or how to go about finding a solution. In this case, they can learn to ask questions about information and ideas that are available at the moment, and also to explore possibilities about what might contribute to their understanding. In both cases, they need to ask questions and refine answers, make connections and check them out—but the ways in which they get there are different. As demonstrated in the examples above, these types of thinking don't vie with one another. Instead, they are called upon when needed, as particular content, ideas or problems are presented. The two orientations complement each other as they enrich the kinds of understandings that develop. Together, they support students' meaning making, intellectual functioning and intellectual growth.

References

Applebee, A.N. (1996). *Curriculum as conversation*. Chicago, IL: University of Chicago Press.

Applebee, A.N. & Langer, J.A. (2009). What's happening in the teaching of writing? *English Journal, 98*, 5, 18–28.

Applebee, A.N., Langer, J., Nystrand, M. & Gamoran, M. (2003). Discussion-based approaches to developing understanding: Instruction and achievement in middle and high school English, *American Educational Research Journal, 40*, 3, 685–730.

Barlow, N. (1958). *The autobiography of Charles Darwin 1809–1882*. New York: W.W. Norton.

Bowler, P.J. (1996). *Evolution: The history of an idea*. Berkeley, CA: University of California Press.

Bruner, J. (1986). *Actual minds: Possible worlds*. Cambridge, MA: Harvard University Press.

Bruner, J. (2002). *Making stories: Law, literature and life*. Cambridge, MA. Harvard University Press.

Close, E.A., Hull, M. & Langer, J.A. (2005). Writing and reading relationships in literacy learning. In Indrisano, R. & Paratore, J.R., *Learning to write/writing to learn: Theory and research in practice*. Newark, DE: International Reading Association, 176–194.

Czikszentmihalyi, M. (1996). *Creativity: Flow and the psychology of discovery and invention*. New York: HarperCollins.

Darwin, C. (2002–2009*). The complete works of Charles Darwin*. (Available online at: http://darwin-online.org.uk).

Darwin, F. (Ed.) (1987). *The autobiography of Charles Darwin* [as published in *The life and letters of Charles Darwin*]. (Available online at: www.guttenberg.org/etext).

Elstein, A., Shulman, L. & Sprafka, S. (1978). *Medical problem-solving: the analysis of clinical reasoning*. Cambridge, MA: Harvard University Press.

Fillmore, C. (1981). *Ideal and real readers*. Proceedings of the 32nd Georgetown University Round Table Conference.

Fisher, A. & Scriven, M. (1997). *Critical thinking: Its definition and assessment*. Point Reyes, CA: Edge Press; and Noriwch: Centre for Research in Critical Thinking.

Gardner, H. (2008). *5 minds for the future*. Cambridge, MA: Harvard Business School Press.

Groopman, J. (2007). *How doctors talk*. Boston, MA: Houghton Mifflin.

Halpern, D.F. (1997). *Critical thinking across the curriculum: A brief edition of thought and knowledge*. Mahwah, NJ: Lawrence Erlbaum.

Koestler, A. (1964). *The act of creation: The study of the conscious and unconscious in science and art*. New York: Dell.

Langer, J.A. (1985). A sociocognitive approach to language learning. *Research in the Teaching of English, 19*, 4.

Langer, J.A. (1987a). *Language, literacy & culture: Issues of society and schooling*. Norwood, NJ: Ablex.

Langer, J.A. (1987b). How readers construct meaning: An analysis of performance on standardized test items. In Freedle, R. (Ed.), *Cognitive and linguistic analyses of standardized test performance*. Norwood, NJ: Ablex.

Langer, J.A. (1990). The process of understanding: Reading for literary and informational purposes. *Research in the teaching of English, 24*, 3, 229–260.

Langer, J.A. (1992). Speaking of knowing: Conceptions of understanding in academic disciplines. In Herrington, A. and Moran, C. (Eds.), *Writing, teaching, and learning in the disciplines*. New York: Modern Language Association.

Langer, J.A. (1995). *Envisioning literature: Literary understanding and Literature instruction* (1st ed.). New York: Teachers College Press.

Langer, J.A. (2001). Beating the odds: Teaching middle and high school students to read and write well. *American Educational Research Journal, 38*, 4, 837–880.

Langer, J.A. (2004). *Getting to excellent: How to create better schools.* New York: Teachers College Press.

Langer, J.A. (2009). Contexts for adolescent literacy. In Christenbury, L., Bomer, R. & Smagorinsky, P. (Eds.), *Handbook of adolescent literacy research.* New York: Guilford Press, 49–64.

Langer, J.A. (2011a). *Envisioning knowledge: Building literacy in the academic disciplines.* New York: Teachers College Press.

Langer, J.A. (2011b). *Envisioning literature: Literary understanding and literature instruction* (2nd ed.). New York: Teachers College Press.

Langer, S. (1967). *Mind: An essay on human feeling.* Cambridge, MA: Harvard University Press.

Michalko, M. Available online at: www.creativity-portal.com/articles/michael-michalko-darwin (accessed May 8, 2009).

Nystrand, M. (1997). *Opening dialogue.* New York: Teachers College Press.

Orr, J. (1987a). Storytelling as cooperative diagnostic activity. *Field Service Manager: The Journal of the Association of Field Service Managers International,* June, 47–60.

Orr, J. (1987b). *Talking about machines.* Palo Alto, CA: Army Research Institute.

Pink, D. (2005). *A whole new mind.* New York: Riverhead Books.

Putnam, H. (1978). *Meaning and the moral sciences.* London: Routledge & Kegan Paul.

Runco, M.A. (1995). Idea evaluation and creativity. In Runco, M.A. (Ed.), *Critical creative processes.* Cresskill, NJ: Hampton Press, 69–94.

Runco, M.A. (2004). Everyone has creative potential. In Sternberg, R.J., Grigorenko, E.L. & Singer, J.L. (Eds.), *Creativity: From potential to realization.* Washington, DC: American Psychological Association, 21–30.

Runco, M.A. & Chand, I. (1994). Evaluative thinking and creativity. In Runco, M.A. (Ed.), *Problem finding, problem solving and creativity.* Norwood, NJ: Ablex.

Simonton, D.K. (1988). *A psychology of science: Scientific genius.* New York: Cambridge University Press.

Singer, J.L. (2004). Concluding comments: Crossover/creativity or domain specificity? In Sternberg, R.J., Grigorenko, E.L. & Singer, J.L. (Eds.), *Creativity: From potential at realization.* Washington, DC: American Psychological Association.

Sternberg, R. (1985). Teaching critical thinking, Part 1: Are we making critical mistakes? *Phi Delta Kappan, 67*, 3, 194–198.

Wallace, D.B. & Gruber, H.E. (1989). *Creative people at work: Twelve cognitive case studies.* New York: Oxford University Press.

4

DEVELOPING VALIDITY AND RELIABILITY CRITERIA FOR ASSESSMENTS IN INNOVATION AND DESIGN RESEARCH STUDIES

Anthony E. Kelly

The past 15 years have seen increasing freedom for educational researchers to develop and pursue innovative research methods. While there have been, in my opinion, some retrograde moves in the acceptance of alternative research methods (e.g., Kelly, 2008a), a welcome consensus has begun to emerge that the "paradigm wars" (Gage, 1989) between qualitative and quantitative are counterproductive. There is a growing acceptance of mixed methods, especially in complex educational settings (e.g., Johnson & Onwuegbuzie, 2004).

Moreover, in the United States, a new balance has been struck in Department of Education funding among randomized controlled trials and other research methods, especially those related to "design engineering."[1] This proposed shift shares many of the features of design research (i.e., a "Design—Educational Engineering—and Development (D–EE–D) infrastructure"; see Bryk, 2009). This change of emphasis[2] occurs in concert with historic spending in educational research and development that forms part of the American Recovery and Reinvestment Act (ARRA[3]).

For example, in 2009, the White House directed the US Department of Education to spend $650 million on an *Investment in Innovation* fund, hoping to reinvigorate the US economy through the development and testing of innovative programs (via development, validation, and scale-up grants).[4] This fund, together with the Department's *Race to the Top*[5] program, represents by far the largest investment in education reform in US history (a combined $5 billion).[6]

Similarly, industry leaders (i.e., Intel, Microsoft, Cisco), recognizing the importance of critical thinking, creativity, and other "21st century skills" are funding university-led research on how to identify, assess, and support learning tied to innovative practices and materials (www.atc21s.org/home/ and www.p21.org/, accessed December 15, 2010).

At the US National Science Foundation (NSF), funded research is expected to address National Science Board directives to pursue "potentially transformative" research. This directive applies not only to applied programs such as Discovery Research K12 (DRK12) and basic research programs such as the Research and Evaluation on Education in Science and Engineering (REESE), but similar calls are also found in larger programs such as the Mathematics and Science Partnerships (Hora et al., 2009), and in informal science education projects (e.g., http://caise. insci.org; www.informalscience.org, accessed December 15, 2010). In informal science education, the problem of conducting research on learning in open-ended exhibits and discovery experiences is an area of active exploration (Friedman, 2008; National Research Council, 2009a).

Novel research approaches and methods are seen as opening new windows on learning processes outside of laboratory settings, particularly when there is a need to teach advanced or novel subject matter within and outside of formal education (e.g., Kelly, Lesh, & Baek, 2008).

Conducting Rigorous Research in Emergent Contexts

The central challenge for researchers and evaluators is how to conduct evidence-based research in contexts and areas of application (such as the above) that are, by design, novel, unprecedented, and emergent. Too often, researchers and evaluators find themselves at a loss about how to design studies around innovations and—as important—to collect data on learning that are viewed by peer researchers as valid and reliable.

An Example of Emergent Research Designs in the MSP Program

Many projects in NSF's Mathematics and Science Partnership (MSP) portfolio attempt to address innovations in science, technology, engineering, and mathematics (STEM) learning (Hora et al., 2009). In their review of 47 projects, Hora et al. (2009) found that 80 percent of the total projects reviewed did not specify an explicit a priori research design because of their exploratory or complex nature. As a result, the role of data collection and measurement in these MSP projects was too often ad hoc. Hora et al. (2009) observed: "Indeed, in situations where *an emergent approach to project design and implementation is consistent with the discovery mission of NSF, some of these challenges may be unavoidable*" (p. 20; emphasis added).

Hora et al. (2009) summarized the problem thus:

> Many PIs may have difficulty in determining which variables to measure, how to measure them, and how to design a robust research and/or evaluation project [. . .] [and that some projects] make claims about their

success by describing their implementation efforts, rather than by presenting data that substantiate outcomes. (pp. 18, 24)

The problems facing MSP Principal Investigators (PIs) in designing and conducting credible research in innovative situations are faced equally by researchers and evaluators who choose to respond to the historic Federal and industry funding opportunities for "break-the-mold" education experiences, both formal and informal, under current ARRA funding models.

Design-Based Research

Considering the demands for studies of emergent learning environments, it would appear, on first blush, that design research methods would be ideal for engaging the many policy calls for innovative practices and subject matter in education. Design-based researchers in education (e.g., Kelly, Lesh, & Baek, 2008) recruit the creativity of students and instructors, not only in prototyping solutions, but also in enacting and implementing the innovation, and in documenting the constraints, complexities, and trade-offs that occur. A design-based team strives to conduct just-in-time theory generation and testing concerning design processes, and the learning and teaching of content (Barab & Squire, 2004).

Design research is differentiated from other research methods by its location in what Stokes (1997) called the use-inspired basic research (or Pasteur's) quadrant (see Dede, 2005a): its proponents strive to respond to theory development and testing in field settings (e.g., Confrey, 2006; Lamberg & Middleton, 2009; Plomp & Nieveen, 2008). Collins, Joseph, and Bielaczyc (2004) located the emerging methodology among other methods thus:

Ethnography provides qualitative methods for looking carefully at how a design plays out in practice, and how social and contextual variables interact with cognitive variables. Large-scale studies provide quantitative methods for evaluating the effects of independent variables on the dependent variables. Design experiments are contextualized in educational settings, but with a focus on generalizing from those settings to guide the design process. They fill a niche in the array of experimental methods that is needed to improve educational practices.

Since Brown's (1992) seminal work on design research methods in education, an impressive amount of scholarship has ensued, including this volume, special issues of journals (e.g., *Educational Researcher*, Kelly, 2003; *Educational Psychologist*, Sandoval & Bell, 2004; *Journal of the Learning Sciences*, Barab & Squire, 2004; *Educational Technology*, Dede, 2005b), and books (e.g., Kelly, Lesh, & Baek, 2008; Plomp & Nieveen, 2008; Reinking & Bradley, 2008; Van den Akker, 1999; Van den Akker, Gravemeijer, McKenney, & Nieveen, 2006). These sources, alone, account for research projects of over 30 individual researchers.

The approach of using iterative design cycles and rapid prototyping is being extended to sets of interrelated studies across programs of research (e.g., Bannan-Ritland, 2003; Clements, 2007; Middleton, Gorard, Taylor, & Bannan-Ritland, 2008; Reeves, 2006; Roschelle, Tatar, & Kaput, 2008; Schwartz, Chang, & Martin, 2008; Van den Akker et al., 2006).

Design Assessment: A Crucial Missing Piece from Design Research

However, a recent review of design research studies (Kelly, Baek, Lesh, & Bannan-Ritland, 2008) strongly encouraged greater attention to issues of measurement and assessment. Evidence from valid and reliable assessments is necessary for design researchers to decide if a proposed prototype is inadequate, if a prototype is promising and should be refined, or if a refined prototype warrants rigorous and comprehensive experimentation (see Clements, 2008; Sloane 2008b). In fact, without reliable and valid measures of student learning, the entire value of a research study is in question, even with otherwise rigorous research designs (e.g., Kelly & Yin, 2007; Sloane, 2008a; Shavelson, Phillips, Towne, & Feuer, 2003).

Thus, while the enterprise of design research continues to produce high-quality work (e.g., Lamberg & Middleton, 2009), criticism of its ad hoc data collection practices is growing. For example, Roschelle (2009), an action editor of the *Journal of the Learning Sciences*, noted that:

> A majority of submitted [design research] papers make only post hoc and ad hoc assessment arguments for the learning gains they describe; in many cases the assessments are simply adopted from existing tests—but these tests were designed for entirely different purposes, and may not even be instructionally sensitive! In other cases, the assessment process appears unplanned and unprincipled. This gravely weakens the quality of the research. Further, it weakens both what the investigators could learn from their design research and also their preparedness to take their designs to the next level of scale. *If there is one thing we could do to improve the design research funded by NSF, it would be to advance the planning, design, instrumentation, and analysis of assessment arguments.* (Emphasis in the original)

The Need for a Psychometrics of Dynamic Learning Situations

Emergent research methods studying innovations in education must directly engage questions of the validity and reliability of the evidence gathered. Without such an effort, design research methods will face growing obstacles to getting published in leading journals, program evaluation in research portfolios may be questioned, and initiatives such as the $650 million *Investment in Innovation* spending (and similar programs in industry) will risk avoiding innovation for the safer harbor of traditional approaches. Consider, for example, that the progression proposed for the $650 million *Investment in Innovation* is from development to validation to scaling studies—exactly the progression claimed for design research (e.g., Bannan-Ritland, 2003; Clements, 2008). However, without valid and reliable assessment data, on what basis will projects at one level be judged ready for the next?

If the large investment of time and money in innovation research is to be fully realized, a critical gap must be filled in test design and psychometric theory. What are needed are principles to guide rapid feedback to teachers, researchers, and subject matter experts concerning instructional targets that, themselves, may be fluid and under-theorized (e.g., Cobb & Gravemeijer, 2008).

Innovative education requires more than traditional content mastery. The learners (researcher, teacher, and student) must self-regulate and monitor their own progress toward mastery and understanding of an ill-defined concept or outcome—skills that arguably characterize higher-order thinking and reasoning (Bloom, 1976; Boekarts, 1996; Klahr, 2000). The issue of measuring higher-order thinking is central to current policy debates about how to foster creative and innovative production worldwide.[7] I show how higher-order thinking may be addressed within a design research project by using an example from engineering education, below. In short, it is important to ascertain if assessments are measuring what are called the substantive thinking skills assumed during instruction or intervention (see Nitko & Brookhart, 2006, and below).

Are Existing Standardized Tests Adequate for Measuring Design Iterations?

Traditionally, researchers and evaluators have used two main forms of assessment, summative and formative (Nitko & Brookhart, 2006). Current psychometric theories (e.g., item response theory) are largely tied to the results of the former: well-designed, standardized summative tests (e.g., Embretson & Reise, 2000).

The limitations of standardized summative assessments for classroom-level innovation were explicitly outlined by the National Research Council (2009b). Its Board on Assessment and Testing advised the US Department of Education about approaches to measuring the impact of its proposed *Race to the Top* program:

> The choice of appropriate assessments for use in instructional improvement systems is critical. Because of the extensive focus on large-scale, high-stakes, summative tests, policymakers and educators sometimes mistakenly believe that such tests are appropriate to use to provide rapid feedback to guide instruction. This is not the case.
>
> Tests that mimic the structure of large-scale, high-stakes, summative tests, which lightly sample broad domains of content taught over an extended

period of time, are unlikely to provide the kind of fine-grained, diagnostic information that teachers need to guide their day-to-day instructional decisions.

In addition, an attempt to use such tests to guide instruction encourages narrow focus on the skills used in a particular test—"teaching to the test"—that can severely restrict instruction. Some topics and types of performance are more difficult to assess with large-scale, high-stakes, summative tests, including the kind of extended reasoning and problem-solving tasks that show that a student is able to apply concepts from a domain in a meaningful way.

The use of high-stakes tests already leads to concerns about narrowing the curriculum towards the knowledge and skills that are easy to assess on such tests; it is critical that the choice of assessments for use in instructional improvement systems not reinforce the same kind of narrowing. (pp. 10–11)

Instead, the Board expressed the need for new methods of assessing learning for emerging and problem-oriented tasks, but regretted their nascent state:

Assessment of complex reasoning and problem-solving skills typically demands assessment formats that require students to generate their own extended responses rather than selecting a word or phrase from a short list of options. Automated scoring of such "constructed responses" is an active field of psychometric research: to date, however, except for automated scoring of written essays, the "state of the art" extends only to small demonstration projects not large-scale applications. (pp. 10–12)

A similar critique of standardized tests was given by Lane (2004) in her NCME Presidential address, where she called for a richer and balanced assessment portfolio for classroom research to address the limitations of standardized summative measures (see also, Bryk & Hermanson, 1993).

Are Current Formative Tests Adequate for Measuring Design Iterations?

Formative assessment has a long history in education (Black & Wiliam, 1998; Bloom, 1968; Cowie & Bell, 1999; Scriven, 1967). According to Heritage, Vendlinski, & Herman (2009, p. 24):

Formative assessment is a systematic process to continuously gather evidence and provide feedback about learning while instruction is under way. The feedback identifies the gap between a student's current level of learning and a desired learning goal (Sadler, 1989). In the process of formative assessment, teachers elicit evidence about student learning using a variety of methods and strategies—for example, observation, questioning, dialogue, demonstration, and written response . . . Other times they review evidence after a lesson or series of lessons. *In all instances, they need to infer the gap between the students' current learning and desired instructional goals,* identifying students' emerging understanding or skills so that they can build on these by modifying instruction to facilitate growth. (Emphasis added)

Heritage et al. (2009, p. 31), make the crucial point about the importance of teacher knowledge and understanding of the target construct for effective formative assessment:

We have concluded that while evidence may provide the basis for action, it cannot in and of itself "form" the action. Action is dependent on teachers' knowledge of how learning develops in the domain and on their pedagogical content knowledge . . . However, we see teacher knowledge as critical to effective formative assessment. It is particularly significant in knowing what to do with evidence. Until teachers have better conceptions of learning to work with, and deeper knowledge of how the elements of student learning are manifested, then the movement from evidence to action as a seamless process will remain a somewhat distant goal. This situation inevitably diminishes the potentially powerful impact of formative assessment on student learning.

Here we find a key challenge for design research methods. By definition, in cases of innovation, the appropriate construct that is understandable by teachers, teachable to the target population, and learnable by them with or without technology support is *itself* an open research question. For example, consider these cases in which the target for assessment (and instruction) is not yet settled: (a) teaching statistics to middle-school students (Cobb, McClain, & Gravemeijer, 2003); (b) teaching gene sequencing to high-school students (Sofer & Vershon, 2007); (c) teaching calculus to middle-school students with technology simulations, but without algebra (Roschelle et al., 2008); or (d) teaching concepts in the geosciences using the emerging cyberinfrastructure (Kelly & Bannan-Ritland, 2008). In fact, this problem would apply in most cases where detailed and validated learning progressions for content were unavailable or underdeveloped (Sarama & Clements, 2009a, b).

In the context of developing innovations in education, Hay and Kim (2006, p. 40) pointed out the limitations of current formative assessment models for design research:

Such integration does not mean the incremental improvement of the original instructional product. Rather, it means the commitment and the courage to use these insights to design future iterations that incorporate *dramatic shifts in thinking.* Such shifts in thinking are a necessary aspect of the design-based research approach, both advancing the quality of innovations and contributing to the field more generally. (Emphasis added)

Toward New Principles of Assessment Design for Innovation

Both current formative and summative assessments are characterized by their linkage to predetermined and more or less fixed instructional and learning targets (e.g., Nitko & Brookhart, 2006). These preset targets provide the basis for standard approaches to test design and validation. Drawing on Messick (1989) and Linn, Baker, and Dunbar (1991), Nitko and Brookhart (2006, pp. 46–47) identified the following criteria for establishing valid and reliable measures when the knowledge or skill targets are well defined:

(a) *Content evidence*: "The assessment procedure is viewed as a whole and judgments are made about representativeness and relevance of the entire collection of tasks."

(b) *Substantive evidence*: "Judgments are made about the assessment procedure as a whole to decide whether desirable, representative, and relevant thinking skills and processes are being assessed." Please see the example from engineering education, below.

(c) *Internal structure evidence*: [Asks] "Do all the assessment tasks 'work together' so that each task contributes positively toward assessing the quality of interest? Are the students' responses scored in a way that is consistent with the constructs and theory on which the assessment is based?"

(d) *External structure evidence*: "Studies show whether the results from this assessment converge with or diverge from results from other assessments in the way expected when the proposed interpretation of the students' performance is used (what is called *convergent and discriminant evidence*)."

(e) *Reliability evidence*: [Asks] "Will the same students obtain nearly the same results if the assessment [or an alternate form] was applied on another occasion? If different persons administered, graded or scored the assessment results, would the students' outcomes be the same?"

(f) *Generalization evidence*: [Asks] "Does the assessment procedure give significantly different results when it is used with students from different socioeconomic and ethnic backgrounds, but of the same ability? Will students' results from the assessment procedure be altered drastically if they are given special incentives or motives? Will special intervention, changes in instructions or special coaching significantly alter the results students obtain on the assessment?"

(g) *Consequential evidence*: [Asks] "What is the value of the intended and unintended consequences (negative and positive) of using the assessment?"

(h) *Practicality evidence*: [Asks] "Is the assessment easy for teachers to use? Do teachers agree that the theoretical concepts behind the assessment procedure reflect the key understandings they are teaching? Do the assessment results identify misunderstandings that need to be corrected?"

Evidence for each criterion depends on some *pre-established construct* against which progress toward realizing the construct is gauged.

The point of this analysis is not to replace existing test design principles and psychometrics across the board. Indeed, once the period of flux in the innovative process is successfully navigated, then the more standard formative and summative approaches can be adopted.

Rather, the goal is to argue the need to establish principles of assessment design to address open-ended, diffuse, fluid, and highly challenging learning contexts in which what are teachable, learnable, and measurable are themselves objects of research. Moreover, the new assessment criteria must honor all stakeholders in the research effort (e.g., researchers, evaluators, subject matter experts, teachers and other professionals, and students).

For these reasons, I believe that it is imperative to establish a psychometrics for test design and measurement for research studies in which:

- For content evidence, subject matter experts' models of their domains do not define the sine qua non of instruction or assessment. For innovative research, the targets of instruction and assessment must remain fluid for some period of time, as the instructional construct is often, itself, a variable in the study (Cobb et al., 2003; Lamberg & Middleton, 2009; Roschelle et al., 2008). This situation challenges traditional conceptions of *content evidence*, as the construct of content of assessment is open to change. For substantive evidence, the students' cognitions about the learning construct are not to be judged and ranked against some remote standard. Instead, students' cognitions give direct input to determine, dynamically, the *appropriateness* of instructional targets and learning constructs themselves, thus challenging traditional conceptions of substantive evidence.

- For both *internal* and *external structure evidence*, the expertise of teachers as advisers in the design and implementation of an innovation and the difficulties of students in learning are welcomed as significant factors in deciding not only the *how* of instruction, but also the *appropriateness* of what constructs are taught and how they are assessed. Therefore, teachers and students have a direct impact on deciding criteria for what constitutes both *internal* and *external structure evidence*, rather than their being objects of some outside expert's assessment assumptions, including their desire to nominate existing measures (both predictive and concurrent) as plausible candidates for correlations.

- For reliability evidence, design researchers use retrospective analyses of instructional interaction (with input from teachers and students), which can lead to significant changes to the goals and direction of the research, and the targets of instruction (e.g., Cobb et al., 2003; Lesh, Kelly, & Yoon, 2008). Under these circumstances, how should notions of *reliability evidence* be reconceptualized?

- For generalization evidence, by definition, design research studies are enacted to be nonrepresentative samples of normal learning situations (Fishman et al., 2004). In many cases, teams of adults work closely with students who often have rich technology resources made available to them and who learn in experimental settings, guided by domain experts. What are the implications of this nonrepresentativeness for deciding questions of *generalization evidence* for assessments? At least during the period of intensive innovative intervention, to whom and to what contexts do the findings apply?
- For consequential evidence, studies of innovations in learning situations tend to attract significant attention in schools, and may consume scarce resources that are (at least temporarily) unavailable for non-research students. As researchers make claims about how students are learning during innovative studies, what are the criteria for *consequential evidence* for their claims if their assessment principles and practices detract from normal and accepted classroom or learning processes?
- For practicality evidence, how should researchers establish criteria to determine various costs and trade-offs, when there is flux in instructional goals, and no clear lines of authority (at least in the early stages) in deciding what is assessed and in what manner?

New guidelines and blueprints for design-based assessment would help design-based researchers and others involved in innovation studies to:

(a) gather evidence that addresses reinvigorated validity and reliability criteria, thus strengthening their knowledge claims (Kelly & Yin, 2007);

(b) move from developmental to randomized controlled trials to scaled studies in a more efficient manner. For example, Kaput's early visions of "democratic access" to powerful mathematics (i.e., the mathematics of change) took most of 12 years to progress from prototypes to randomized controlled trials (Roschelle et al., 2008). The field needs to dramatically shorten this development progression if we are to have broader impact on society with innovation-based research;

(c) communicate the warrant for evidence to their graduate students, to teachers, parents, and other stakeholders who play critical roles in design research studies;

(d) become active participants in the ongoing debates about the scientific status of education research (e.g., Howe, 2009; Kelly, 2003, 2008a; Moss et al., 2009) and evaluation.[8]

Current Efforts Among Design Researchers

Those involved in design-based research are already engaging the concerns being raised here about valid and reliable evidence in a number of creative ways. As an example, one new assessment method, which grew out of mathematics education research and is now employed in engineering education, involves the use of model-eliciting activities. An example from engineering education is now given. For their use in mathematics education, see, for example, Lesh, Hoover, Hole, Kelly, & Post (2000) or Lesh & Lamon, 1992).

Model-Eliciting Activities Research

Model-eliciting activities are designed to determine the extent to which learners have mastered central constructs in a domain (e.g., Lesh et al., 2000). Model-eliciting activities have been used extensively for mathematical problem solving and reasoning in engineering (e.g., Diefes-Dux et al., 2004) to address deeper knowledge of engineering concepts (e.g., National Academy of Engineering, 2005) and reasoning across distributed technology networks (e.g., Hamilton et al., 2008).

The core idea in a model-eliciting activity is to have the expert propose problem-solving situations or contexts for the learner that require the learner to make explicit the manner in which she or he makes sense of the phenomenon. This approach is in contrast to traditional problem formats, where there is an emphasis on procedural knowledge, calculation, or choosing an option among distractors. The traditional objective formats, even some of the performance-assessment activities that use rubrics, require a priori detailed specification of the target knowledge domain (Nitko & Brookhart, 2006).

By contrast, when responding to model-eliciting activities in contexts of novelty or innovation, teachers, students, and researchers must determine if the subject matter expert's models are learnable, teachable, and assessable in the current context. For example, in her NSF CAREER grant, Bannan-Ritland had to negotiate between a domain expert in geomorphology who insisted that the key instructional idea in geosciences for fourth-graders was mastering the concept of geological time. The teachers objected to this instructional goal as it was appropriate for undergraduates, but not for their students, who were still learning the days of the week. Over time, the instructional goal (and associated assessments) was redesigned to engage students in documenting visible, tactile evidence of recent erosion in their own school playgrounds.

An Example of Model-Eliciting Activity from Engineering Education (adapted from Shuman, Besterfield-Sacre, & Clark, 2007)

A problem facing emergency planners is how to properly respond to an unexpected disaster. For that matter, locations of a major city's convention center and fire stations (which could provide first response and ambulance bases for an emergency situation that occurred at the convention center) are important. Part I of the learning task requires the student team to propose a model that could be used to determine an appropriate response to an incident at the convention center in which the number of victims was small (such as 10). Part II asks what cyber–physical systems data would be necessary to have in place in order to model a successful response to a disaster in which casualties exceeded 300 (the current limit for Pittsburgh hospitals, according to a recent analysis), when the triggering event also resulted in closing the three bridges below the convention center owing to possible hazardous contamination. Part III requires the team to draft a report to the city of Pittsburgh with recommendations as to how such eventualities might be incorporated into potential deployment of cyber–physical system data sensors and future emergency planning.

Note that, in this model–eliciting activity, the task or problem is a prompt designed to elicit the knowledge, skills, and tools the student team *assumes* will address the three–part problem. The demand on the student team is to create (and revise) a model, which may involve simulations, computational analyses, interlinked and cascading scenarios, and the specification of how this problem should be characterized and addressed. The problem statement does not "give away" a solution, but requires the team to express its understanding of the problem, which may expose the members' superficial analyses, which are then available for critique and assessment by *other student teams* and by the instructor. Over a number of instructional and assessment sessions, the combined problem–solving prowess of the teams of students and the instructor is tested, as new solutions are entertained and critiqued.

The design challenges facing engineers and planners of megacities are not simply ones of making more judicious use of available space, resources, and construction materials. Megacities create emergent problems across multidimensional factors (such as pollution, public health, transportation, and logistics, to name a few). Additionally, major cities face predictable catastrophes involving earthquakes, infectious diseases, terrorist threats, and the results of other hazards, including weather events (www.lsu.edu/highlights/052/pam.html, accessed December 15, 2010).

The challenges facing those who educate engineers in designing and managing megacities are pressing and accelerating and were explored in two recent workshops: one supported by the USC Engineering Department (www.megacities.usc.edu, accessed December 15, 2010), and one supported by the NSF (Kelly, 2008b). The participants agreed that megacities describe dynamic, complexly interacting structural, material, biological, and social phenomena, which pose challenges that are inadequately taught and assessed in regular undergraduate courses.

In terms of the above traditional criteria for judging the quality of assessments, it is clear from the above example, as the demands of the task escalate, that:

(a) the target of assessment is neither simple nor unitary, which makes decisions about content relevance challenging;

(b) the substantive skills assessed are not only manifold, but they are distributed across teams of problem solvers—in which roles (and associated thinking and technology skills) may change, over time;

(c) the "internal structure" of the assessment is not fixed, and parts of the assessment that were central in simpler solutions may prove peripheral in later ones;

(d) any "external structure" evidence that is fixed and simple may not show high correlation with the students' unfolding solutions, but this low correlation cannot be held against them or the model-eliciting assessment itself;

(e) traditional assumptions about reliability (either within a set of tasks, across time, or across raters) require rethinking;

(f) for "generalization evidence," it is difficult to describe the fixed elements of the task and the evolving expertise of the students to know, a priori, how to address ideas of generalization;

(g) for "consequential evidence," one could argue that this innovative form of assessment should have positive consequences for students' ability to deal, later, with emerging crises in complex settings (though further research would be required to substantiate this claim); and

(h) with better answers to the earlier criteria (and with a number of such innovative assessments within and across classes), it will be possible to decide on the "practicality evidence" of the endeavor.

A number of larger questions arise, which include:

1. Does the model of test validation from Messick (1989) and others, expressed in the criteria outlined by Nitko and Brookhart (2006) above, adequately account for context-based innovative research?

2. Which components of traditional assessment criteria work well for measuring innovation, and which need to be revised?

3. Do the traditional assessment criteria need to be extended by adding other components?

4. What aspects of the new assessment criteria are necessarily qualitative?

5. What tools are proving powerful in guiding and documenting analysis during retrospective cycles, and how can they be improved?

6. What psychometric formalisms can be validly applied to this design–phase assessment work? For example, is Cronbach's alpha appropriate? Are ideas from classical test theory adequate? Or item response theory? What is the role of nonparametric statistics?

7. Is adequate progress being made to communicate across design research projects in order to add to field-based insights and to inform ongoing development in design assessment activities and theorizing?

8. Are project-level activities appropriately using the empirical data that design researchers are gathering in their more constrained, design–cycle studies? In other words, how should data gathered in prototyping studies inform higher-level evaluation judgments?

On this final point, in addition to the need for modeling complex learning (in engineering, mathematics, or science), it is equally important to devise new research techniques that can integrate richer design-cycle data into larger components of a more complex evaluation or set of studies (see, for example, the many-stage model outlined by Sloane, 2008a). Sloane and colleagues (e.g., Sloane, Helding, & Kelly, 2008) have begun to reconceptualize interrupted time series as models for longitudinal research projects, and have argued for more sophisticated models of individual learning in dynamic settings (Sloane, 2008b; Sloane & Gorard, 2003; Sloane & Kelly, 2003, 2008).

Conclusion

In this chapter, I have argued that the press for innovation in education, which has grown in response to the dreadful economic conditions both in the US and around the world, requires greater attention to the development of emerging design research methods. More importantly, I argued that the development of improved design research methods must address, as a priority, the elucidation of a new set of criteria for establishing the validity and reliability of indicators of evidence that are used during design research cycles. When we embrace the fluid nature of innovation itself, we cannot rely blindly on the assessment criteria that were designed for learning targets that are more or less agreed upon and fixed. Rather, by exploring actual cases of design research in action (for example, Shuman's work with model-eliciting activities), we need to challenge design researchers and evaluation professionals to articulate and defend criteria that will establish a subfield of design assessment.

Notes

1   See www.edweek.org/login.html?source=http://www.edweek.org/ew/articles/2009/ 12/02/13ies.h29.html&destination=http://www.edweek.org/ew/articles/2009/12/02/ 13ies.h29.html&levelId=2100 (accessed December 5, 2010).
2   See also the deliberations of the American Evaluation Association, e.g., www.eval. org/aea08.omb.guidance.responseF.pdf (accessed December 5, 2010).
3   See www.ed.gov/policy/gen/leg/recovery/implementation.html (accessed December 5, 2010).
4   See www.ed.gov/legislation/FedRegister/proprule/2009–4/100909a.html (accessed December 5, 2010).
5   See www.ed.gov/legislation/FedRegister/proprule/2009–3/072909d.html (accessed December 5, 2010).
6   See www2.ed.gov/programs/racetothetop/index.html (accessed December 5, 2010).
7   See the OECD papers on innovation at www.oecd.org/pages/0,3417,en_41462537_ 41454856_1_1_1_1_1,00.html (accessed December 5, 2010).
8   See the American Evaluation Association's "Roadmap" at www.eval.org/EPTF/ aea10.roadmap.101910.pdf (accessed December 5, 2010).

References

Bannan-Ritland, B. (2003). The role of design in research: The integrative learning design framework. *Educational Researcher, 32,* 21–24.

Barab, S., & Squire, K. (2004). Design-based research: Putting a stake in the ground. *Journal of the Learning Sciences, 13*(1), 1–14.

Black, P., & Wiliam, D. (1998). Inside the black box: Raising standards through classroom assessment. *Phi Delta Kappan, 80*(2): 139–149.

Bloom, B. S. (1968). *Learning for mastery.* UCLA Evaluation Comment 1(2): 1–8.

Bloom, B. S. (1976) *Human characteristics and school learning.* New York: McGraw-Hill.

Boekarts, M. (1996). Teaching students self-regulated learning: A major success in applied research. In J. Georgas, M. Manthoulim, E. Besevegis, & A. Kokkevi (Eds.), *Contemporary psychology in Europe: Theory, research and applicaitons.* Bern: European Congress of Psychology.

Brown, A. L. (1992). Design experiments: Theoretical and methodological challenges in creating complex interventions in classroom settings. *Journal of the Learning Sciences, 2,* 141–178.

Bryk, A. (2009). Support a science of performance improvement. *Phi Delta Kappan, 90*(08) (April), 592–595.

Bryk, A. S., & Hermanson K. L. (1993). Educational indicator systems: Observations on their structure, interpretation, and use. *Review of Research in Education, 19,* 451–484.

Clements, D. H. (2007). Curriculum research: Toward a framework for "research-based curricula". *Journal for Research in Mathematics Education, 38,* 35–70.

Clements, D. H. (2008). Design experiments and curriculum research. In A. E. Kelly, R. Lesh, & J. Baek (Eds.), *Handbook of design research in education: Innovations in science, technology, mathematics and engineering.* New York: Routledge.

Cobb, P., & Gravemeijer, K. (2008). Experimenting to support and understand learning processes. In A. E. Kelly, R. Lesh, & J. Baek (Eds.), *Handbook of design research in education: Innovations in science, technology, mathematics and engineering.* New York: Routledge.

Cobb, P., Confrey, J., diSessa, A., Lehrer, R., & Schauble, L. (2003). Design experiments in educational research. *Educational Researcher, 32,* 9–13.

Collins, A., Joseph, D., & Bielaczyc, K. (2004). Design research: Theoretical and methodological issues. *Journal of the Learning Sciences, 13*(1), 15–42.

Confrey, J. (2006). The evolution of design studies as methodology. In R. K. Sawyer, (Ed.), *The Cambridge handbook of the learning sciences* (pp. 135–151). Cambridge, UK: Cambridge University Press.

Cowie, B., & Bell, B. (1999), A model of formative assessment in science education. *Assessment in Education, 6,* 101–116.

Dede, C. (2005a). Commentary: The growing utilization of design-based research. *Contemporary Issues in Technology and Teacher Education* [Online serial], *5*(3/4).

Dede, C. (2005b). Why design-based research is both important and difficult. *Educational Technology, 45*(1), 5–8.

Diefes-Dux, H. A., Moore, T., Zawojewksi, J., Imbrie, P. K., & Follman, D. (2004). *A framework for posing open-ended engineering problems: Model-eliciting activities.* Proceedings, 34th ASEE/IEEE Frontiers in Education Conference. Savannah, GA.

Embretson, S., & Reise, S. (2000). *Item response theory for psychologists.* Mahwah, NJ: Erlbaum.

Fishman, B., Marx, R. W., Blumenfeld, P., Krajcik, J., & Soloway, E. (2004). Creating a framework for research on systemic technology innovations. *Journal of the Learning Sciences, 13*(1), 43–76.

Friedman, A. (Ed.) (2008). Framework for evaluating impacts of informal science education projects. (Available online at: http://insci.org/resources/Eval_Framework.pdf).

Gage, N. (1989). The paradigm wars and their aftermath: A "historical" sketch of research on teaching since 1989. *Educational Researcher, 18*(7), 4–10.

Hamilton, E., Lesh, R., & Lester, F. (2008) Model-Eliciting Activities (MEAs) as a Bridge Between Engineering Education Research and Mathematics Education Research. *Advances in Engineering Education* (2)1, 1–25

Hay, K. E., & Kim, B. (2006). Design-based research—more than formative assessment? An account of the virtual solar system project. *Educational Technology, 45*(1), 34–41.

Heritage, M., Vendlinski, T., & Herman, J. (2009). From evidence to action: A seamless process in formative assessment? *Educational Measurement: Issues and Practice, 28*(3), 24–31.

Howe, K. (2009). Positivist dogmas, rhetoric, and the education science question. *Educational Researcher, 38*, 428–440.

Johnson, R. B., & Onwuegbuzie, A. J. (2004). Mixed methods research: A research paradigm whose time has come. *Educational Researcher, 33*(7), 14–26.

Kelly, A. E. (2003). Theme issue: The role of design in educational research [special issue], *Educational Researcher, 32*, 3–4.

Kelly, A. E. (Ed.) (2008a). Reflections on the US National Mathematics Advisory Panel Report [special issue], *Educational Researcher, 37*(9).

Kelly, A. E. (2008b). "*Distributed Learning and Collaboration (DLAC)": STEM issues bearing on sustainability and megacities.* National Science Foundation (# 0904173).

Kelly, A. E., & Bannan-Ritland, B. (2008). *Modeling cyber-enabled learning and teaching: Addressing methodological and measurement issues.* National Science Foundation (# 0816216).

Kelly, A. E., & Yin, R. (2007). Strengthening structured abstracts for educational research. *Educational Researcher, 36*(3), 133–138. Also appears in, *Selecting research methods*, edited by W. Paul Vogt (Illinois State University) (2008) as part of the SAGE *Benchmark in Social Research Methods* series.

Kelly, A. E., Lesh, R., & Baek. J. (Eds.). (2008). *Handbook of design research methods in education: Innovations in science, technology, mathematics and engineering learning and teaching.* New York: Routledge.

Kelly, A. E., Baek, J., Lesh, R., & Bannan-Ritland, B. (2008). Enabling innovations in education and systematizing their impact. In A. E. Kelly, R. Lesh, and J. Baek (Eds.), *Handbook of design research in education: Innovations in science, technology, mathematics and engineering.* New York: Routledge.

Klahr, D. (2000). *Exploring science: The cognition and development of discovery processes.* Cambridge, MA: Bradford Books.

Lamberg, T. J., & Middleton, J. A. (2009). Design research perspectives on transitioning from individual microgenetic interviews to a whole-class teaching experiment. *Educational Researcher, 38*(4), 233–245.

Lane, S. (2004). Validity of high-stakes assessment: Are students engaged in complex thinking? *Educational Measurement: Issues and Practice, 23*(3), 6–14.

Lesh, R. A., & Lamon, S. J. (1992). *Assessment of authentic performance in school mathematics.* Washington, DC: AAAS.

Lesh, R., Kelly, A. E., & Yoon, C. (2008). Multi-tier design experiments in mathematics, science and technology education. In A. E. Kelly, R. Lesh, and J. Baek (Eds.), *Handbook of design research in education: Innovations in science, technology, mathematics and engineering.* New York: Routledge.

Lesh, R. A., Hoover, M., Hole, B., Kelly, A., & Post, T. (2000). Principles for developing thought revealing activities for students and teachers. In A. E. Kelly & R. A. Lesh (Eds.), *Handbook of research design for mathematics and science education* (pp. 591–646). Mahwah, NJ: Lawrence Erlbaum Associates.

Linn, R. L., Baker E. L., & Dunbar, S. B. (1991). Complex, performance-based assessment: Expectations and validation criteria. *Educational Researcher, 20,* 15–21.

Messick, S. (1989). Validity. In R. L. Linn (Ed.), *Educational measurement* (3rd ed., pp. 13–103). New York: Macmillan.

Middleton, J. A., Gorard, S., Taylor, C., & Bannan-Ritland, B. (2008). The *"Compleat" design experiment: From soup to nuts.* In A. E. Kelly, R. A. Lesh, & J. Y. Baek (Eds.), *Handbook of design research methods in education: Innovations in science, technology, engineering, and mathematics learning and teaching* (pp. 21–46). New York: Routledge.

Moss, P. A., Phillips, D. C., Erickson, F. E., Floden, R. E., Lather, P. A., & Schneider, B. L. (2009). Learning from our differences: A dialogue across perspectives on quality in education research. *Educational Researcher, 38*(7), 501–517.

National Academy of Engineering (2005). *The engineer of 2020: Visions of engineering in the new century.* Washington, DC: National Academy of Engineering.

National Research Council (2009a). In M. Fenichel & H. A. Schweingruber (Eds.), *Surrounded by science: Learning science in informal environments.* Washington, DC: National Academy Press.

National Research Council (2009b). Letter report to the U.S. Department of Education on the Race to the Top Fund Board on Testing and Assessment. Available at: www.nap.edu/catalog/12780.html, accessed December 15, 2010.

Nitko, A. J., & Brookhart, S. M. (2006). *Educational assessment of students* (5th ed.). New York, Pearson.

Plomp, T., & Nieveen, N. (2008). *An introduction to educational design research.* Enschede, the Netherlands: SLO Netherlands Institute for Curriculum Development.

Reeves, T. (2006). Design research from a technology perspective. In J. van den Akker, K. Gravemeijer, S. McKenney, & N. Nieveen (Eds.), *Educational design research.* London: Routledge.

Reinking, D., & Bradley, B. A. (2008). *On formative and design experiments: Approaches to language and literacy research.* New York: Teachers College, Columbia University.

Roschelle, J., Tatar, D., & Kaput, J. (2008). Getting to scale with innovations that deeply restructure how students come to know mathematics. In A. E. Kelly, R. Lesh, & J. Baek (Eds.), *Handbook of design research methods in education: Innovations in science, technology, mathematics and engineering learning and teaching.* New York: Routledge.

Sadler, D. R. (1989). Formative assessment and the design of instructional systems. *Instructional Science, 18,* 119–144.

Sandoval, W. A., & Bell, P. L. (2004). Design-based research methods for studying learning in context: Introduction. *Educational Psychologist, 39*(4), 199–201.

Sarama, J., & Clements, D. H. (2009a). Teaching math in the primary grades: The learning trajectories approach. *Young Children, 64*(2), 63–65.

Sarama, J., & Clements, D. H. (2009b). *Early childhood mathematics education research:* Learning trajectories for young children. New York: Routledge.

Schwartz, D., Chang, J., & Martin, L. (2008). Instrumentation and innovation in design experiments: Taking the turn to efficiency. In A. E. Kelly, R. A. Lesh, & J. Baek (Eds.), *Handbook of design research methods in education: Innovations in science, technology, mathematics and engineering.* Mahway, NJ: Taylor & Francis.

Scriven, M. (1967) The methodology of evaluation. In R. E. Stake (Ed.), *Curriculum evaluation*. American Educational Research Association monograph series on evaluation, no. 1, Chicago: Rand McNally. Reprinted with revisions in B. R. Worthen & J. R. Sanders (Eds.) (1973), *Educational evaluation: Theory and practice*. Worthington, OH: Charles A. Jones.

Shavelson, R. J., Phillips, D. C., Towne, L., & Feuer, M. J. (2003). On the science of education design studies. *Educational Researcher, 32,* 25–28.

Shuman, L., Besterfield-Sacre, M., & Clark, R. (2007). *Collaborative research: Improving engineering students' learning strategies through models and modeling*. NSF award # 0717801.

Sloane, F. C. (2008a). Randomized trials in mathematics education: Recalibrating the proposed high watermark. *Educational Researcher, 37*(9), 624–630.

Sloane, F. C. (2008b). Multilevel models in design research: A case from mathematics education. In A. E. Kelly, R. A. Lesh, & J. Baek (Eds.), *Handbook of design research methods in education: Innovations in science, technology, mathematics and engineering*. Mahway, NJ: Taylor & Francis.

Sloane, F. C., & Gorard, S. (2003). Exploring modeling aspects of design experiments. *Educational Researcher, 32,* 29–31.

Sloane, F. C., & Kelly, A. E. (2003). Issues in high stakes testing programs. *Theory into Practice, 42*(1).

Sloane, F. C., & Kelly, A. E. (2008). Design research and the study of change: Conceptualizing individual growth in designed settings. In A. E. Kelly, R. Lesh, and J. Baek (Eds.), *Handbook of design research in education: Innovations in science, technology, mathematics and engineering*. New York: Routledge.

Sloane, F. C., Helding, B., & Kelly, A. E. (2008). Longitudinal analysis and interrupted time series designs: Opportunities for the practice of design research. In A. E. Kelly, R. A. Lesh, & J. Baek (Eds.), *Handbook of design research methods in education: Innovations in science, technology, mathematics and engineering*. Mahway, NJ: Taylor & Francis.

Sofer, W., & Vershon, A. (2007). *HiGene: A genome sequencing project for high schools*. National Science Foundation award #0737574.

Stokes, D. E. (1997). *Pasteur's Quadrant: Basic science and technological innovation*. Washington, DC: Brookings Institution Press.

van den Akker, J. (1999). Principles and methods of development research 3. In J. van den Akker et al. (Eds.), *Design approaches and tools in education and training* (pp. 1–14). Dordrecht: Kluwer Academic Publishers.

van den Akker, J., Gravemeijer, K., McKenney, S., & Nieveen, N. (Eds). (2006). *Educational design research*. London: Routledge.

5

DESIGN RESEARCH AND TWICE EXCEPTIONAL CHILDREN

Toward an Integration of Motivation, Emotion, and Cognition Factors for a Technology-based Intervention

Brenda Bannan

Design research can be considered a method for generation, dynamic progression and investigation of complex constructs in education. According to Kelly (2009), this method is best employed when little direct, usable theory exists and when pragmatic, research and theoretical perspectives can be combined to generate and test a new approach to a complex problem in education. Operationalizing and embedding theories of learning in a technology-based system or intervention allow for testing of that system to determine if any improvement in identified behavioral, learning or affective targets happens (Walker, 2006). Improvement in one outcome may facilitate improvement in another when dealing with complex educational problems.

Example of a Complex Educational Problem

Tom, a current middle-school student, has demonstrated significant problems in directed attention and focus in school and at home and demonstrates highly variable performance on learning tasks. In science and math, Tom is highly gifted and can engage in high-level complex reasoning. In other areas that he does not find as interesting, however, Tom struggles to regulate his attention and to complete routine school-based tasks. Tom fails to attend to details and directions; has difficulty focusing; does not seem to listen in class; has difficulty organizing his things and information; loses things easily; is distracted; has a tendency to misinterpret social situations; and shows emotional vulnerability. Tom's parents, his teachers and his psychologist have identified and documented his strengths and weaknesses but are in need of additional ways to support him and his learning.

The Complexity of Twice Exceptional Children and the Applicability of Design Research

Tom's case demonstrates the complex educational problem of providing appropriate interventions and support for twice exceptional children in schools. Twice exceptional children are "gifted children who have the potential to perform well beyond the norm of their peers, yet are not succeeding in school due to one or more learning disabilities" (Callard-Szulgit, 2008, p.10). These children struggle on a daily basis with organizational, social, academic and other delays that interfere with their learning and performance, particularly in school-based settings. Programs or structured supports for these students are often inappropriate or inadequate and focus only on remediation of weaknesses rather than strengths of these gifted but learning-disabled children (Baum & Olenchak, 2002).

Giftedness alone is a complex construct in research. Sternberg (as cited in Baum, 2004) states that, "giftedness involves more than just high IQ, that it has noncognitive and cognitive components, that the environment is crucial in terms of whether potentials for gifted performance will be realized and that giftedness is not a single thing" (p. xii). Further complicating the picture, twice exceptional students exemplify those who are technically gifted in some areas but are also diagnosed with Attention Deficit Hyperactivity Disorder (ADHD), or may possess other forms of giftedness and neurological deficits. Twice exceptional students are often difficult to identify, assess and support in school settings. Design research has perhaps the most potential of many research approaches or methods to attempt to discover more about these children, their experience of their learning environments and the effectiveness or ineffectiveness of potential teaching, learning and performance interventions designed for them. Teachers are also key constituents in a design research effort to determine how a particular intervention will be conceptualized, promoted and utilized in the classroom (Bannan-Ritland, 2008). The interventionist and participatory nature of design research can directly examine the individual child's and teacher's experiences in the classroom, as well as in other settings, to facilitate the generation, design or redesign of a targeted intervention that undergoes progressive improvement and testing of its effectiveness over time. These iterative cycles, informed by data-driven decision-making may provide improved and extremely valuable information on the experience of twice exceptional children and their teachers in situ. A design research effort with twice exceptional children may well exemplify and constitute the conceptualization or unit of analysis in research promoted by Dai (2004) as "person–situation as an indivisible unit of analysis" and operationalize cognition as a phenomenon that is "fundamentally situated, embodied and cannot be separated from one's goals, actions, emotions and feelings" (p. 427).

Design research can be structured to include data collection and analysis about children's and teacher's motivations, emotions and cognitions in a specific context and over time in order to: (1) analyze and learn about a particular learning profile and teaching context; (2) generate or enact an informed intervention based on that profile and setting; (3) formatively test and retest the intervention in the teaching and learning setting on a more limited basis with individuals and small groups; and, ultimately, (4) test and retest the intervention to attempt to identify significant variables in more confirmatory research cycles and broader implementation of the intervention. Design research is best used in complex learning situations where few integrated interventions exist and the situation is in need of generative, evaluative, formative and predictive design research (Suri, 2008). This might involve multi-method, multi-setting discovery- and confirmatory-based research methods under the broad umbrella of a design research approach. It is an interventionist and participatory form of research that attempts to capitalize at appropriate phases on applied as well as empirical research methods. The complexity of Tom's learning issues and what other twice exceptional children experience certainly warrants new approaches to help his teachers, parents and the professionals involved in his case best support him in school.

Design Research Targeting Interventions for Twice Exceptional Children

A specific design research case to attempt to address the design and prototyping of technology-based interventions for twice exceptional students is presented below; it conceptualizes an example of the application and sequence of applied and potential design research methods, data collection, analyses and application of these results in iterative cycles that exemplifies an approach to design research. This design research approach is a metamethodological view of design research as containing multiple cycles and phases of theory and system generation and testing called the Integrative Learning Design Framework (ILDF) (see Figure 5.1) (Bannan-Ritland, 2003). The complex educational problem of twice exceptional children and their challenges across school, home and other settings may best reveal the necessity for an integrative view of cognitive, emotional and motivational considerations for learning. This chapter is an attempt to walk through a design research case using the ILDF that attempts to address the more holistic and integrated view needed to support twice exceptional students' cognitive, emotional and motivational needs.

Design research can be used to generate, inform and revise insights about cognitive, motivational and/or emotional supports or interventions in education. My graduate students and I explored the application of design research processes toward the broad goal of supporting twice exceptional children for two 16-week semesters. We conducted multiple rounds of data collection with six twice exceptional children, their parents and several professionals/experts in this area.

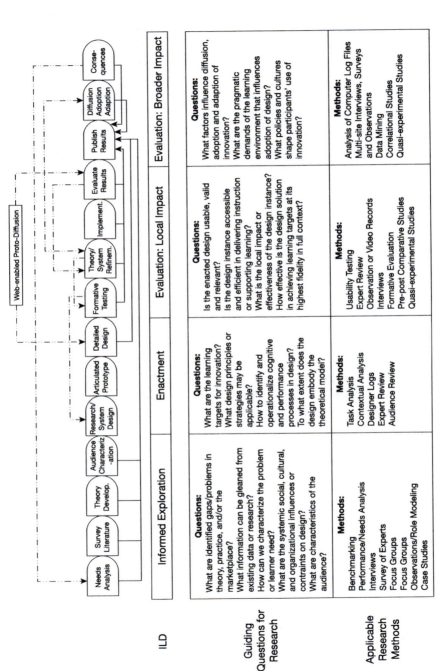

FIGURE 5.1 Questions and methods for design research by ILDF phase.

Reported here are the actual data sources collected and analyzed by ILDF phase in cycles of design research and their design outcomes. Also included in this chapter are other suggested applicable data sources, methods and analyses that might have proved useful given additional time and expertise. The additional methods/analysis techniques are conceptualized in order to attempt to push thinking forward about what other methods, both applied and basic, might be appropriate in a design research effort that attempts to integrate motivation, emotion and cognition to work toward the identification of important variables and outcomes for the improvement of educational interventions for these unique students. It is hoped that this case also exemplifies the nature of design research integrating cognition, motivation and emotion as important considerations for the advancement of teaching, learning and research.

Informed Exploration Phase

The informed exploration phase of the ILDF is to progressively and dynamically identify, describe and analyze the state of the problem or phenomenon in order to generate or advance theoretical perspectives about how people learn, progress and perform, as well as to provide insights to progress toward a targeted, designed intervention that attempts to address the problem. Most importantly, this initial phase of the ILDF is to integrate and analyze data and literature from various sources, including the applied context, as well as traditional literature and research cycles related to the broad goal. The outcomes of this phase should result in an attempt to locate the problem in context, an integration of theory, practice and research perspectives, and an improved understanding of the context, audience and problem that feeds into a defined design direction in the following enactment phase.

Needs Analysis

In this design research effort, the broad goal of attempting to support twice exceptional children and their teachers in the classroom was identified as an area in need of additional research and intervention.

To attempt to better understand the pragmatic issues as well as to frame the problem, children who were diagnosed with ADHD and identified as gifted (or twice exceptional children) and their parents were interviewed to attempt to describe the nature of their strengths and weaknesses in regard to academic settings and the specific challenges these children face. A special education teacher, a neuroscientist, a professor and director of a camp for ADHD students were later interviewed to obtain as much information as possible about these children and their experiences across the teaching/learning/home settings. In addition, the design research team supplemented their direct experience with these kids and those who support them with data collection and analysis of information from relevant online resources, organizations and conference papers (such as the proceedings from Learning & the Brain: Focused Minds, Enhancing Student Attention, Memory and Motivation Conference, 2010).

The initial needs analysis investigation or synthesis of child, parent and professional interview data and resources from the literature and applied organizations in this design research case suggested that: (1) these children are often not well understood by their parents/teachers; (2) the children demonstrate a range of organizational, behavioral and academic difficulties in school and home settings; and (3) there are limited resources for support for these children. These findings echo experts' assessment of the situation stating that the traditional school environment is often not adequately designed for twice exceptional children and "academic underachievement commonly found in these students continues to be blamed on laziness and lack of motivation; a misperception that is still too common among educators and parents" (Zeigler, 2010, p. 15). Owing to the nature of simultaneously occurring neurological strengths and weaknesses, these students often suffer in the school context because of a lack of understanding of the duality of their intellectual gifts in specific areas, such as science, math or art, and difficulties in processing and production that often negatively impact their school-based performance. Expert, parent and professional perspectives converged in our investigation to indicate that the twice exceptional are one of the least understood and least adequately served populations in schools today.

Survey of Literature

The design research team reviewed relevant research-based literature to attempt to elaborate on the findings of the needs analysis and to further expand our understanding of this unique population of students. Twice exceptional children are considered uniquely exceptional, as they typically possess high IQs, demonstrating extremes of intellectual strengths in particular areas, and yet these students also face specific challenges with attentional, organizational and executive functioning delays. Executive functioning delays are defined as "directive capacities that are responsible for a person's ability to engage in purposeful, organized, strategic, self-regulated, goal-directed processing of perceptions, emotions, thoughts and actions" (McCloskey, Perkins & Van Divner, 2009, p.15). Students themselves, as well as their teachers and parents, struggle with understanding these neurological deficits or challenges and how they manifest in school. Difficulties in identifying and addressing the needs of these children are attributed in part to the variability of their academic performance, often illustrated by an amazing level of focus at times on topics of interest, but also demonstrating a contrasting inability to deal with repetitive work at other times that requires sustained effort, step-wise problem solving, or difficulty with work that may have little intrinsic reward for them (Lovecky, 2004). These children are prone to hyper-focusing on novel areas, technologies or topics of interest, yet have significant difficulty attending to routine, non-interest tasks (e.g. such as most routine schoolwork) and also demonstrate difficulty shifting their attention to other tasks when required (Kaufmann, Kalbfleisch & Castellanos, 2000). This profile seems to be somewhat distinct from those children who are solely gifted or solely exhibit ADHD but are not gifted. For example, one study review of a group of gifted boys with ADHD reported that they demonstrated poor self-regulation, were easily frustrated, overreacted to situations, demonstrated social impulsivity and described themselves in extremes—either positively or negatively—more than boys with ADHD or gifted boys without ADHD (Moon, Zentall, Grskovic, Hall & Stormont, 2001).

In academic settings, studies have shown that gifted boys with ADHD "demonstrated underachievement, difficulties with homework and long-term projects, attending to and following directions, completing worksheets, difficulty with handwriting, and getting started with assigned reading" (Zentall, Moon, Hall & Grskovic, 2001, cited in Lovecky, 2004, p. 67). The same study indicated that many of these boys were also highly creative, preferred challenges and novelty, had special talents in science, math or social studies and demonstrated a high level of competence in spatial and mechanical skills. This population of children deserves significant study of the specific and integrated cognitive, emotional and motivational issues that illustrate how their needs, which are not currently being met in the traditional classroom, might be supported through designed and targeted technology-based interventions. This complex educational and learning problem encompassing cognitive, emotional and motivational issues is ripe for what we might learn through design research to uncover additional knowledge about these children and simultaneously attempt to design interventions to help them.

Cognitive Factors

It was important to examine what is known about the specific cognitive profile of twice exceptional children in this exploratory design research study. Gifted children with ADHD often have co-occurring learning disabilities as well. The co-occurrence between ADHD and learning disabilities (or LDs) is thought to be between 15 percent and 40 percent, with difficulties in specific cognitive functions such as inhibition of ongoing response, auditory processing, verbal working memory or response speed (Rucklidge & Tannock, 2002). Assessment of the neurological make-up of children with ADHD and their cognitive strengths and weaknesses, although typically conducted outside of schools by neuro-psychologists, is important to consider in designing and targeting educational interventions (Ek, Holmberg, DeGeer, Sword & Fernell, 2004). Neuroscientists are beginning to study executive attention that is brought to bear in school-based performance tasks requiring activation of short-term and long-term memory retrieval processes, as well as requiring significant attentional and executive control. Executive control seems to have an overarching role for regulating the allocation of cognitive, emotional and motivational effort required for learning. Executive attention is "central to the regulation of both emotion and cognitions" and is "crucial for acquiring new ideas and relating them to already learned concepts" (Posner & Rothbart, 2007, p. 81). Twice exceptional children, such as Tom, evidence difficulties in executive attention and control and, therefore, experience significant difficulty in schools.

Emotional Factors

An integrative perspective of twice exceptional students should also include a serious consideration of the emotional factors that may integrate with, or impact, cognitive goals. Immordino-Yang (2010, p. 232) advocates that thinking and emotions are interdependent and states: "brain studies reveal that thinking clearly is, in fact, an emotional process. Without emotion, people become insensitive to risk and unaware of consequences. They are less able to learn from their experiences" (p. 232).

This claim is tentatively supported by neuroscientific findings that indicate that attentional control of cognition is located in brain areas also associated with emotion (Posner & Rothbart, 2007). Immordino-Yang (2010) also points out that thinking, learning and emotion occur in social and cultural contexts tied to experience. Given this, one could postulate that the successes and failures of twice exceptional children and the associated social consequences could potentially become part of their academic knowledge and experiences, contributing negatively or positively to their self-concept as a learner. The importance of an integrated model for studying these children is highlighted when it is considered that twice exceptional children have noted difficulties with emotional self-control, tend to be more emotionally reactive and have more difficulty tolerating frustration, which may significantly impact their school experience (Lovecky, 2004). Risk factors related to depression, anxiety, bipolar and other neuro-emotional disorders can also co-occur with the ADHD diagnosis and gifted designation, increasing the possibility of neurological, academic and social problems in school. Therefore, assessment of the psychosocial and emotional functioning of twice exceptional students from multiple sources and perspectives is important to consider to attempt to plan more holistic educational interventions that may be effective (Assouline, Nicpon and Whiteman, 2010).

Motivational Factors

Twice exceptional children demonstrate many behaviors of their ADHD peers related to motivation. Recent studies of children with ADHD show that they can't generate the same degree of enthusiasm as those without ADHD for tasks they don't find intrinsically appealing. These children have trouble with tasks they find tedious, boring or uninteresting, and some experts have referred to this as "an interest deficit." This was tentatively supported in neurological research by a positron emission tomography (PET) scan study demonstrating that people with ADHD have fewer receptors and transporters in the mid brain that constitute the reward pathway or that are involved in associating stimuli with pleasurable expectations (Volkow et al., 2009). Neurological deficits in the brain's reward system may help to explain a seeming lack of motivation and attention to low-interest tasks in school for twice exceptional children. These children also seem to respond to immediate rather than delayed reward systems, as it is difficult for them to sustain attention for long-term return (Barkley, 2006).

Leveraging what we currently know about twice exceptional students and their strengths may help to support their weaknesses by focusing on their capabilities, such as associative processing (e.g. seeing new connections, noticing things no else does), generative thinking (e.g. different ways of looking at things, creative problem solving) and cultivating talent areas (e.g. visual–spatial, invention, computer programming or engineering aptitudes), rather than placing focus only on their disabilities, and as a consequence may also help to improve their motivation for learning (Lovecky, 2004). An integrative model that simultaneously considers the cognitive, emotive and motivational factors specific to this profile is central for addressing the whole child to enhance both research and educative design for these children.

Variation in Twice Exceptional Profile and Needs

However, despite some commonalities in their profiles, these children are not all alike. Diving more deeply into the literature revealed that attention and executive functioning or control vary for these individuals across domains of functioning including sensation/perception, emotion, cognition or action (McCloskey, 2010). Attempting to address individual differences in the design of educational interventions, where possible in this targeted population, is important as well. Problems with identification and fine-grain assessment of the nature and impact of these developmental and neurological delays in combination with giftedness and learning disabilities further complicate this picture. However, attempting to ground design in what we understand even about a few children possessing this unique profile may generate an improved design or intervention that can then be tested and revised with others who exhibit this profile. The next step in the design research process is to attempt to integrate what has been learned so far and then articulate initial theoretical propositions or conjectures that provide a broad target for design.

Theoretical Proposition for Designing an Intervention for Twice Exceptional Children

After expanding the team's knowledge of this profile of abilities and disabilities, the design research team interviewed special education resource teachers, a neuroscientist whose research focused on twice exceptional children and other ADHD experts, such as psychologists who interact with them. These professionals confirmed many of our findings and assumptions about these children and their needs to this point. The team attempted to integrate all the data, including the interviews with parents and professionals and interviews/observations of six twice exceptional children, with what was learned from the literature to generate an initial, broad, theoretical proposition. This proposition was then used to articulate more detailed learning targets and to further determine design features and aligned assessment methods to attempt to improve learning and performance in school settings for these students. An initial theoretical proposition was formulated that included: *to address common executive functioning delays with targeted individualized (where possible) and integrated memory, organizational and socio-emotional supports.* The type of neurological developmental delay that twice exceptional children exhibit requires an integrative view of academic, behavioral and self-regulatory interventions that could potentially be supported by technology features and functionality. This tentative proposition was also supported by a statement in the literature of specific needs surrounding twice exceptional children (Lovecky, 2004):

> Gifted children with ADHD also need a multi-pronged program that works to change the academic curriculum and to teach them specific skills in areas of deficits such as basic skills, skills related to executive functions, interpersonal skills, emotional control, etc. (p. 96)

The data sources, multiple analytic cycles and the subsequent articulated theoretical proposition conceptualized in the informed-exploration phase of the ILDF helped the team progressively frame and reframe the problem, as well as identify an important interrelationship among the multiple cognition, motivation and emotional considerations for these children. Combining our data sources and insights from direct experience with these children and their parents, as well as interviewing the professionals and teachers who work with them, further supported an integrative approach for both analysis and the technology-based intervention. Reviews of results from standardized testing, observations, self-report and parental/teacher behavioral measures in relation to an individual child were also very useful in increasing the team's understanding of some of the characteristics twice exceptional children may possess, as described in the next section.

Audience Characterization

In order to provide a focus for human–centered design processes that would further inform our theoretical propositions, we explored techniques for audience characterization found in software design. Techniques for integrating data and experience with the target audience members can be described as personas (Cooper, 2004) or role models (Constantine and Lockwood, 1999). These techniques for characterizing the audience as a point of reference for design are similar to qualitative techniques that describe an archetype or composite profile of multiple people that represent primary and secondary audiences, such as twice exceptional children and their parents or teachers. To begin to describe and characterize twice exceptional children, their parents and teachers, the design research team synthesized insights from the interview data and observation to construct three audience personas or profiles, representing a twice exceptional child, a parent and a teacher. These personas served as an important focal point to ground our design and to serve as a checkpoint for design assumptions related to our specific audiences. In addition to the direct experience with the target audience members and interview or focus group data, other forms of assessment might also be extremely valuable to elaborate on specific individual profiles and help to conceptualize specific features and functionality.

For example, a neuropsychological evaluation comprised of several assessment measures administered to an individual child from the targeted twice exceptional population can help to inform targeted intervention planning. Although representing results for an individual child, these data can provide a starting point or additional detail about these children for the purposes of design. Commonalities also exist across this profile that can be leveraged for design, such as: (1) these children typically score in the very superior or superior range of IQ testing; (2) they may also demonstrate processing deficits (e.g. such as short-term memory or processing deficits); and (3) they also can possess enhanced visuo–spatial skills that allow them to visualize, integrate and identify patterns (Lovecky, 2004). While this combination of abilities and disabilities has been demonstrated to occur more commonly in twice exceptional children, additional information about particular individuals representative of this population, such as their level of executive functioning in testing as well as realistic settings, might also be useful for design, as described below.

Dawson and Guare (2010) state that executive function deficit assessment should include several sources of information such as: (1) a detailed case history, with interview questions designed to elicit the presence or absence of executive skills in every day settings; (2) standardized behavior rating scales; (3) classroom observations; and (4) work samples (p. 14). Individual students might be assessed across all these components; however, analysis of these data can also be leveraged for generating initial features and functions of a targeted intervention at the classroom level. Knowing where and how a twice exceptional child's challenges manifest themselves in the school setting can help design researchers begin to identify theories of teaching and learning for these kids and areas for technological design and support.

Other applicable measures related to cognition, emotion and motivation of the twice exceptional might include the BASC, Conners Rating Scale, Behavior Rating Inventory of Executive Functions (BRIEF), Nagilari PASS processing approach, McCloskey Executive Function Scales, etc. (Dawson and Guare, 2010; McCloskey, 2010; Naglieri and Johnson, 2000). Any and all of these measures could provide valuable information for design research, combined with the behavioral findings or insights from relevant professionals (e.g. psychiatric, psychological, neuropsychological, school personnel observations and ratings scales), which are also potentially useful. The integration of these findings would contribute data that could possibly provide additional insight into this audience profile, but also facilitate the design of some customized features in the intervention for more individualized treatment. Twice exceptional children are often assessed through a neuropsychological evaluation that may include some or several of these measures, as well as behavioral observations in the classroom setting. For example, one child (Tom) and his parents in our target audience group offered to share his neuropsychological testing results with us and revealed the following about his profile as a fourth-grade, twice exceptional child. These data provided the team with valuable insights into this target audience to steer later design features and functionality. These results were further elaborated for the team and supported by Levin's (2002) descriptions of specific attention, memory, executive-function, language and organizational difficulties for ADHD children.

Tom's Strengths

- Auditory processing (executive function)—he can remember what he hears and repeat it.
- Receptive language—ability to listen and understand language is in very superior range (synonyms, antonyms, analogies).
- Verbal expressive—he can define words, articulate responses to questions.
- Phonological skills—analyzing, synthesizing and manipulating sound (sound blending) essential to reading are not a problem for him.
- Reading and reading comprehension ability is excellent.
- Math reasoning (word problems, graph interpretation, money and fractions, decimals, percentages) in high average range similar to children at sixth grade level.
- Verbal reasoning, expressive skills and perceptual reasoning (with weaknesses in processing speed).
- Perceptual reading, fluid reasoning, spatial processing and visual–motor integration (some variability).
- Visual spatial abstract reasoning and categorical reasoning—superior and high average ability.

Tom's Weaknesses

Attention

- Spelling and writing are deficient, spelling rules are not internalized, and delays in fine motor skills impact writing production.

- Selective or focused attention—particularly in visual matching and decision speed—demonstrated low performance, slow pace, fewer items completed than average, difficulty paying attention to one stimulus while ignoring others.

- Shifting attention—from one task to another, dependent on the degree of novelty and cognitive stimulation of task, significant trouble to attend, sequence and remember what he is doing.

- At times superficial processing and other times excessively active processing that triggers too many associations and ideas, states non-relevant ideas, loses track of flow of conversation.

- Difficulty regulating the length of his concentration—stops focusing in middle of story, explanation, etc., allocates attention to unimportant stimuli.

- Delay in planning, previewing, organizing, limited strategizing to reach a goal or complete a task.

- Difficulty self-checking or monitoring his own behavior, assessing own performance.

- Difficulty in retrieval from long-term memory (slower, but had strategy), particular trouble in naming pictures rapidly along with memory retrieval.

- Difficulty in executive function, controlling impulses, even when aware of the best course of action.

Memory

- Weakness and inconsistency in his ability to focus his attention on a particular target.

- Trouble holding a span of numbers in working memory while performing a mental operation on it, more trouble with monotonous task, math fluency.

- Trouble attending too long, non-interesting activities increase the demands to sustain his attention.

- Significant struggle to attend, sequence and remember what he is doing.

- Difficulty with divided attention to multiple stimuli or simultaneous tasks.

- Difficulty with attending to a boring task while not responding to competing stimuli.

Executive functioning

- Poor performance on making conceptual decisions and visual symbol discrimination (eighth percentile).

- Processing speed index—low average (might be impacted by attentional difficulties).

- Showed increasing difficulty in working memory tasks (saying numbers backwards, remembering series of numbers while sequencing them).
- Difficulty self-checking or monitoring his work or behavior.

Language
- Spelling in the low average range for his age and grade, with overreliance on phonetically spelling words.
- Significant difficulty constructing grammatically correct sentences.
- Problems organizing thoughts on paper, writing fluency.
- Motor memory—difficulty printing words neatly and automatically, handwriting.

Organization
- Needs cues to stay on task.
- Problems predicting and planning for daily tasks.
- Organization in preparation for, and between, classes, as well as end of day.

Motor/occupational-therapy skills
- Fine motor–visual integration was in low average and within the twenty-first percentile.
- Eye–hand coordination problems (fifth percentile).
- Visual motor speed/coordination (related to handwriting problems).

Socio-emotional
- Ratings agreed in odd behaviors, easily distracted, unable to concentrate, few skills for interacting with peers, avoiding social contact, difficulty adapting to change.
- Mother also rated difficulty in expressing feelings, communicating in ways to be understood by others.
- Teachers also rated attention problems, overly active, acts without thinking, completion of work, some rule-breaking behaviors.

It is clear that Tom's individual neuropsychological testing results represent the difficulty of addressing all of these issues in the classroom and demonstrate a complex, integrated educational challenge for design research. Reviewing these results supported the team's earlier conclusions that the profiles of these children can represent a mosaic of individual cognitive, emotional and motivational strengths and weaknesses, with some commonalities, but also differences across individuals. Despite the fact that these findings are related to a single child, the results do provide the design research team with a sensitivity to, and description of, a potential range of abilities, disabilities and behaviors that can inform the design of intervention, versus designing in a vacuum with little or no information about the unique characteristics of these children. Capitalizing on these extant data (if available) about individuals and across small groups of these students for the purposes of designing appropriate interventions could begin to facilitate a more reciprocal relationship or interplay between testing, behavioral observations and classroom outcomes. McCandliss, Kalchman and Bryant (2003) argued for a similar reciprocal relationship between brain-imaging data and specific classroom tasks. Converging all this information (e.g. cognitive, emotional, motivational, neurological, behavioral, etc.) about a single child to improve educational intervention design and research could potentially work toward assisting many children with overlapping conditions through iterative design research cycles.

Much potential also lies in the future collection, assessment and application of neurobiological and neuro-imaging data, as they provide an improved developmental picture of the interplay among cognition, emotion and motivation among these students. For example, Posner and Rothbart (2007), in simple, computerized competing responses, indicate that executive-function circuitry related to resolving conflict, for example, improves greatly between ages four and seven, with little or no improvement after age seven. Posner and Rothbart have attempted to localize attributes of executive functioning; however, recent research by Niogi et al. (in press) demonstrates that this is a distributed, decentralized processing capability. This emerging research is not directly addressed in this design research study example but holds incredible potential for the future for improving our understanding about the twice exceptional, their challenges and how to address them.

The importance of integrating various data sources and perspectives on learning in the informed exploration phase cannot be understated for this particular audience. This phase initially determined a broad problem of supporting twice exceptional children and attempted to integrate several sources and multiple cycles of reviewing existing data and collecting and analyzing data to learn more about the audience and for design (e.g. child/teacher/parent/professional interviews, focus groups, standardized testing, ratings scales, classroom observations etc.). After reviewing all of this, we refined our theoretical proposition to the following:

> Provide external, integrated support for attention, memory, organization, emotional control and overall executive functioning for twice exceptional children, as well as provide a mechanism for communication with their teachers and parents to enhance their functioning in basic skills, academic tasks and interpersonal interactions.

This phase assisted the team in defining the problem based on current literature, research and qualitative data analysis, determined what was in and out of focus for design, and presented a target learning proposition. The revision and narrowing of our theoretical proposition based on the integration of data in the exploration phase generated a design direction that constrained the problem (Rossett, 2009). The detailed audience characterization data also provided more detailed information that was employed in the next enactment phase to move toward a data-driven, rational and detailed description of the potential technology solution system.

The Enactment Phase

In the enactment phase, design researchers integrate and operationalize what is learned in the informed exploration phase into a targeted intervention or design concept. Outcomes of this phase include the integration of multiple streams of data and information, including applied experience, existing research and prior data analysis, into a conceptual design. The designed intervention articulates and embeds the emergent theoretical proposition, modeling it into a conceptual design that progressively moves from a low-fidelity prototype to a high-fidelity prototype, allowing for cycles of feedback and iterative revisions of both theory and design when put into the user's hands.

In this design research case example, we revisited our initial learning proposition to identify more specific learning targets (Nitko and Brookhart, 2007). The integration and consideration of cognitive, emotional and motivational elements for twice exceptional learners were noted in the informed enactment phase, and it therefore seemed to follow to base our learning targets on Krathwohl's affective domain. According to Krathwohl, Bloom and Masia (1964), learning is demonstrated by behaviors indicating attitudes of awareness, interest, attention, concern and responsibility, ability to listen and respond in interactions with others and ability to demonstrate those attitudinal characteristics or values that are appropriate to the situation. The team aligned the identified learning targets with the following levels of Krathwohl's affective domain (see Nitko & Brookhart, 2007).

Determine Learning Targets

Learning/Performance Proposition

Providing external support for attention, memory, organization, emotional control and executive functioning for twice exceptional children, as well as communication with their teachers and parents, may enhance their functioning in basic skills, academic tasks and interpersonal interactions.

Krathwohl Affective Domain Learning Taxonomy Level and Identified Learning Targets

Receiving

This refers to students' willingness to attend to particular phenomena of stimuli. Learning outcomes in this area range from simple awareness that a thing exists to selective attention on the part of the learner. Receiving represents the lowest level of learning outcomes in the affective domain:

- to actively listen, to differentiate among stimuli in classroom, to allocate attention, to capture information quickly, efficiently and supplement short-term memory tasks;

- to move attention from an unproductive area to a productive area; promote sequencing and organization of information.

Responding

This refers to active participation on the part of the student. At this level, he or she not only attends to a particular phenomenon but also reacts to it in some way. Learning outcomes in this area may emphasize acquiescence in responding, willingness to respond or satisfaction in responding. The higher levels of this category include those instructional objectives that are commonly classified under "interest"; that is, those that stress the seeking out and enjoyment of particular activities:

- to actively respond to cues to shift attention; to comply with cues to shift attention; to record steps in accurate sequence and call up to accomplish tasks;
- to productively sort through ideas to determine relevance to topic or task at hand; to prioritize associated information; to check with others when losing track of flow of conversation or discussion and redirect back to original focus.

Valuing

This is concerned with the worth or value a student attaches to a particular object, phenomenon or behavior. This ranges in degree from simple acceptance of a value to the more complex task of commitment. Valuing is based on the internalization of a set of specified values, but clues to these values are expressed in the student's overt behavior. Learning outcomes in this area are concerned with behavior that is consistent and stable enough to make the value clearly identifiable:

- to recognize and value on-target communication; to increase proficiency in identifying areas of high/low interest; to differentiate productive discourse from unproductive discourse in social settings; to increase awareness of over-focusing and underfocusing; to increase awareness of too many associations and ideas that promote off-track, and loss of flow of, conversation, discussion, task.

Organization

This is concerned with bringing together different values, resolving conflicts between them and beginning the building of an internally consistent value system. Thus, the emphasis is on comparing, relating and synthesizing values:

- to accept responsibility for one's own behavior; to promote forethought, systematic planning and discussion in solving social–emotional issues.

Theory/System Design and Refinement

The team analyzed current technological interventions for these children that primarily consisted of desktop, web-based information systems and determined that handheld technology was a viable option because its characteristics of mobility, communication, novelty and access were important features for this multilevel audience of twice exceptional children, teachers and parents. The team conducted a competitive analysis of other types of web-learning resource for twice exceptional children, but the learning targets seem to best align with a handheld device that could be used cross-context (e.g. home, school and professional settings, such as a counselor's or psychologist's office) and provide consistent support for the twice exceptional child.

With the learning targets aligned with Krathwohl's affective taxonomy, the team was ready to generate design ideas that often flow from, or precede, the codified learning targets. Most importantly, the learning targets needed to align with technology design features and be congruent with observations of the targeted behavior, outcome or educational outcome for assessment of improvement in learning or performance. Prior to generating a prototype, we aligned the learning difficulties that twice exceptional students face, which we discovered in our investigation in the informed exploration phase, with the appropriate learning level in Krathwohl's affective taxonomy. From there, we determined more generalized interventions that could be delivered in multiple ways (e.g. by the teacher, on paper or in a behavioral plan) and then brainstormed various handheld technology features or supports that could provide a more efficient delivery of the intent of the intervention. Many of these features demonstrated an integrative approach for cognitive, motivational and emotional factors related to twice exceptional students. We primarily targeted the affective domain in assessment, with the assumption that attempting to improve twice exceptional students' attentional, organizational and motivational goals might positively impact overall academic goals. In aligning the observation of the accomplishment of identified learning tasks, it was important to identify observable behaviors, input into the technology systems and promote overt discussions with others to provide observable evidence for reaching the targeted outcome. Table 5.1 illustrates this alignment and details each twice exceptional learning challenge, learning target, generalized intervention, aligned technology feature and observation/outcome.

With the learning targets aligned to audience needs, technology features and observational outcomes, the team began to prototype handheld device features. Initial prototypes were represented in wire frames that are low-fidelity representations of technology features and functions, in order to provide a draft of initial design ideas for input by experts and the target audience. This low-fidelity wire frame prototype is deliberately structured to be malleable in the early design conceptualization stages to allow for feedback and revisions.

Once the design features are decided upon, then the conceptualized prototype can progress toward more high-fidelity representations. The team mocked up a physical prototype that twice exceptional children could hold in their hands while providing feedback on the design and input into additional features or functions. In this manner, the targeted users interacted with the design team in a participatory design experience, with several of their ideas taking shape in the design. For example, these children have difficulty focusing and need sensory input to focus (e.g. such as walking while they are talking, fidgeting or manipulating an object such as a pencil). One of the children who provided feedback on the initial concrete prototype came up with the idea to build a special backing on the device to allow for twiddling with it, such as a finger-tracing path or koosh-ball-like backing, which was then formulated into the design. Participatory design sessions and feedback on early prototypes by the target user audience is crucial for improved, iterative design. The team was able to produce a conceptual and mock-up physical prototype for these purposes.

Evaluation: Local Impact

In two semesters and with a lack of programming or grant resources, it was difficult to progress beyond the enactment phase in the IDLF progression with this prototype. However, if the project was continued through grant support or other means, and in order to flesh out a design research example integrating cognition, emotion and motivation for learning, it behooves us to consider what might have been possible in the next phases of the design research process. With defined learning targets and outcomes, as well as a high-fidelity prototype, it would be possible to collect formative evaluation on the use of the device, with additional input/reaction from target audiences, as well as analysis of progression of improvement on the targeted behavioral outcomes.

Usability Testing

In order to be effective, the device must first be usable and should be evaluated for usability by a select group of target users. Observing the use of the device in context by several users who could provide direct feedback on the features and functionality of the device in school is warranted in this phase to determine if the design is accomplishing the intended outcomes. Teachers, parents and professionals could also provide input on the usefulness or feasibility of the technology, as well as the viability of any outcome reports for their purposes. Several rounds of usability testing and implemented iterative revisions based on the results would be ideal in progressively increasing the number of users trying out the handheld device, from several users to small-group field testing, and ultimately cross-context situations such as the feasibility of transfer of the device and use of data from school to home to professional settings.

TABLE 5.1 Alignment of twice exceptional learning challenge, learning target, generalized intervention, aligned technology feature and observation/outcome

Challenge	Target	Intervention	Technology Feature	Observations/Outcomes
Selective or focused attention—particularly, visual matching and decision speed—low performance, slow pace, fewer items completed than average, difficulty paying attention to one stimulus to accomplish task (Levin, 2002, p. 27)	*Receive:* To actively listen, to differentiate among stimuli in classroom, to allocate attention, to capture information quickly, efficiently and supplement short-term memory tasks	Promote directed attention, highlight salient information, allow for more time for completion of tasks, record attention shifts, highlight core visual information	Teacher-to-student alert system—visual, vibrational, sound cue when off-task; set interval timed cue; child rating of level of attention; timer function; highlight and capture of salient information and directions (e.g. such as assignments on board or directions)	*Observation:* Automatically record number of times flashed combined with child ratings of attention and inattention, what information child captures and records *Outcome:* Reduced number of times cueing needed, increased number of child rating positively his or her own attentional control or refocusing of attention over time *Educational outcome:* Child learns to self-monitor his own attentional control over time; quality of information capture to reduce load on short-term memory; teacher/parent becomes more aware of and sensitive to child's attentional delays and is represented graphically over time for information and motivation

Shifting attention—from one task to another, dependent on the degree of novelty and cognitive stimulation of task, significant trouble to attend, sequence and remember what child is doing (Levin, 2002, p. 90)	*Receive:* To move attention from an unproductive area to productive area, promote sequencing and organization of information *Respond:* To actively respond to cue to shift attention, to comply with cue to shift attention, to record steps in accurate sequence and call up to accomplish tasks	Promote interest and motivation through novel technology, track progress on task, consistently provide warnings and cues when off-task, to provide opportunity to record tasks, sequence tasks and store a step-wise approach to tasks for recall	Novel, handheld device, pervasive across school and home contexts; record number of times attention shifts, record number of math problems completed in 10 minutes in game-like manner, try to beat own score; attend and enter important information for task sequencing, organizing and recall, checking off what tasks are completed over time	*Observation:* Number of times attention shifts to inappropriate source recorded by teacher, parent and child; number of problems (or other academic task) completed in defined time period; step-wise problem solving with major subtasks entered by child, review by teacher/parent for capture of salient information, review sequenced of recorded tasks for quality of step-wise problem solving and later reference, recording of task breakdown and progressive accomplishment *Outcome:* Self-monitoring of attention shifts, redirection by child and teacher, use of self-motivational mechanisms such as competition and reward to keep focus on academic task; identification and breakdown of important subtasks in complex task; recording of accomplished steps and cueing what remains to be done.

TABLE 5.1 Continued

Challenge	Target	Intervention	Technology Feature	Observations/Outcomes
				Educational outcome: Child learns to attend to most important information (e.g. directions from teacher), break down tasks into subtasks and organize tasks in sequence and refer back to what is needed to accomplish next—improvement in task organization, sequencing and recorded accomplishment to begin to internalize processes
At times superficial processing and other times excessively active processing in areas of high interest that triggers too many associations and ideas, states non-relevant ideas, loses track of flow	*Respond*: To productively sort through ideas to determine relevance to topic or task at hand; to prioritize associated information; to check with others when losing track of flow of conversation or discussion and redirect back to original focus	Variable attention—self monitoring when overfocusing, overvaluing with too many ideas and underfocusing with too little information provided treated at surface level; when off-topic and when treating content too lightly To identify high interest areas that are valued and determine course of action related to them but refocus if get lost in flow—off topic	Identification of high- or low-interest task; production and recording of ideas to be sorted and establish relationships through concept mapping; self-monitoring of number of ideas and rating of relevance to topic or task; when engaged in high interest areas that are valued	*Observation*: Child able to be identify high-/low-interest areas, quickly capture thoughts through metacognitive prompts, to review for relevance to original topic *Outcome*: sort through many ideas and prioritize ideas according to task/topic at hand, self monitor or determine when lost track of flow of ideas

	Value	Strategy	System action	Outcome
	Valuing: To increase proficiency in identifying area of high/low interest; to differentiate productive discourse with unproductive discourse in social settings; to increase awareness of overfocusing and underfocusing; to increase awareness of too many associations and ideas that promote off-track and loss of flow of conversation, discussion, task		Prompts in high interest area—record ideas, with many ideas entered without connections, system prompts meta-cognitive question such as "Am I getting off topic?" Highlight prioritized ideas for follow through and what action student will take. In low interest areas (those with few ideas and no connections on concept map), system prompts, "Have I thought this through enough?"	*Educational outcome:* Child develops sensitivity to his or her overfocusing/ underfocusing wandering off task and refocusing
Difficulty self-motivating, self-checking or monitoring work or behavior	Value: To increase proficiency in completion of tasks through self-monitoring and self-motivation	Reward systems when meet expectations (commitment to complete work, values and complies with routine, completion of task, etc.) Externalizing, communication monitoring and motivational support across home and school contexts	Accumulates points to cash in for identified, valued task (e.g. computer–game time), keeps track across school, home, professional contexts, prints out reports and gives immediate feedback	*Observation:* Point values over time for level of value, commitment and completion of tasks. *Outcome:* Monitoring, checking, parent recording across contexts, tracking and completion of tasks. *Educational outcome:* Internalizing self-monitoring of valuing work commitment, relevant action and motivational rewards consistently across home and school contexts

TABLE 5.1 Continued

Challenge	Target	Intervention	Technology Feature	Observations/Outcomes
Difficulties with socio-emotional regulation, finds some social interactions confusing, does not know what to do in social settings	*Organization:* To recognize importance of social relationships; to actively pursue friendship opportunities; to accept responsibility for one's own behavior; to promote forethought, systematic planning and discussion in solving social–emotional issues	Use "what if" questions in regard to social interactions: "What if you do this in this situation, what will happen? How do you think so and so will feel if . . .?" Promote asking previewing questions such as: "What if you said this, what would the teacher/friend think? "What is the best thing to do about the situation?" "What are some other things you could consider doing/saying?"	Prompts recording of social difficulties, confusions and interactions; fill in blank prompts what if thinking to attempt to pre-think outcomes of different actions/inactions Accessible to parents, teachers, professionals such as psychologists, etc. for review and discussion with student Journal-like entry to record confusing, difficult social exchanges such as being called a name, attempting to make a friend or start a conversation	*Observation:* Recording of socio-emotional problems and generation and recording of possible solutions *Outcome:* Reflection and discussion of socio-emotional problems with peers, misunderstandings, and generation/discussion about possible courses of action with parents/teachers and professionals *Educational outcome:* Promoting overt, systematic problem solving about social and emotional concerns with others

Technology also easily affords the capture and analysis of formative data, such as student input of information of goals, tracking of step-wise problem solving or preserving counts of number of times performance targets are triggered, such as those related to attention, etc. Analyzing these data, along with other evaluative and assessment outcomes related to overall behavior and school performance, at multiple points over time could provide a rich assessment of a twice exceptional child's progress, as well as inform redesign of the intervention. Other evaluative and assessment measures leveraged in earlier phases of the ILDF might also be implemented in the evaluation phases, such as teacher/parent/professional/self-report behavioral ratings, standardized assessments related to attention and executive functioning and school-based assessment to determine if any qualitative or quantitative formative progress is demonstrated.

Applicable Experimental Research Designs

As the population of twice exceptional children is limited in any single school or context, research designs, such as those that could be applied when the sample size is one or when there is a limited number of individuals considered as one group, could be implemented in a design research effort examining cognitive, motivation and emotional outcomes. Single-subject research design or single-case experimental design studies might provide a useful analysis of executive functioning support embedded in a handheld technology device for twice exceptional children. These designs are typically implemented to examine the behavioral change an individual exhibits as a result of some treatment or intervention. In single-subject designs, each participant serves as her or his own control, similar to a time-series design. The participant is exposed to non-treatment and treatment phases, and performance is measured during each phase (Gay & Airasian, 2003, p. 383). This type of measure was used in a design research effort when examining the impact of a technology-based intervention teaching geological change to children with disabilities at the upper elementary level (Martinez, 2008).

Evaluation: Broad Impact

Data could be collected related to the implementation, use and effectiveness of handheld technology devices, promoting external processes of self-regulation related to attention, motivation and socio-emotional targeted outcomes for this population of children. Data from twice exceptional children, their parents and professionals who interact with them could be connected through an online database or content learning management system that aggregates these data, provides analysis reports and structures feedback for designers on the impact of implementation of these devices for individuals and groups of children over time and across contexts. Similar technology applications currently exist that could provide tracking of information for a distributed, national sample of twice exceptional learners and the use, effectiveness and iterative revision of the handheld technology device over time. This type of multilevel assessment of a technology intervention, where student log-file data are automatically tracked as performance assessments, has been used in science to track changes in inquiry skills over time both within and across domains (Buckley, Gobert & Horowitz, 2006). Existing learning technologies such as content management systems could be used in this manner to aggregate student input of forethought, performance and self-reflection when designed to track an individuals' progress over time, as well as provide opportunities to intersect input from parents/teachers and professionals with self-monitoring and reflection (Kitsantas & Dabbagh, 2010).

Longitudinal analysis techniques such as those used to investigate systematic change or growth over time might also be used to determine twice exceptional children's initial status and growth on targeted measures. Latent growth curve methodology could potentially be used to investigate systematic change, or growth, and interindividual variability in tracking changes in executive functioning (Duncan, Duncan, Stryker, Li & Alpert, 1999). This type of statistical technique was used to investigate resilience and changes in mental health of children of alcoholics and could potentially be used in a similar manner to investigate changes in the level of executive functioning over time for twice exceptional children (Carle, 2007). As stated by Carle (2007), this type of analysis:

> can examine: 1) whether variation in an outcome exists across time; 2) the form of this variation, e.g., linear, nonlinear, etc.; 3) whether groups vary in their averages across time, e.g., treatment vs. control; and 4) whether similarity exists in the rate of change across groups.

This information of progression or change over time of level of executive functioning exhibited with use of handheld technology intervention would be very useful in determining a developmental progression when attempting to externalize attentional control, step-wise problem solving and social-emotional decision-making for twice exceptional children.

Conclusion

This chapter has presented an overview of the progression of a design research study using a specific case example of attempting to address the intersection of cognitive, emotional and motivational abilities and disabilities of twice exceptional children. Design research, when viewed as a multi-method, metamethodological approach containing multiple research, analysis and design cycles, represents perhaps one of the best approaches to examine complex educational challenges such as those faced by twice exceptional children in the classroom. It is hoped that this chapter can begin to contribute to the dialogue of ways to improve both research and design of interventions in the classroom to directly impact children's cognitive, emotional and motivational potential.

References

Assouline, S.G., Nicpon, M.F. & Whiteman, C. (2010). Cognitive and psychosocial characteristics of gifted students with written language disabilities. *Gifted Child Quarterly, 54*(2), 102–115.

Bannan-Ritland, B. (2003). The role of design in research: The integrative learning design
framework. *Educational Researcher, 32*(1), 21–24.

Bannan-Ritland, B. (2008). Teacher design research: An emerging paradigm for teacher
professional development. In A.E. Kelly, R. Lesh and J. Baek (Eds.), *Handbook of design research
methods in education: Innovations in science, technology, engineering and mathematics learning and
teaching.* New York: Routledge.

Barkley, R.A. (2006). *Attention deficit hyperactivity disorder: A handbook for diagnosis.* New York:
The Guilford Press.

Baum, S. (2004). *Twice exceptional and special populations of gifted students.* Thousand Oaks, CA:
Corwin Press.

Baum, S. & Olenchak, F.R. (2002). The alphabet children: GT, ADHD and more.
Exceptionality, 10(2), 77–91.

Buckley, B.C., Gobert, J.D. & Horowitz, P. (2006). *Using logfiles to track students' model based
inquiry.* Proceedings of the 7th International Conference on the Learning Sciences (Eds. Barab,
S., Hay, K. and Hickey, D.), Bloomington, IN, pp. 57–63.

Callard–Szulgit, R. (2008). *Twice-exceptional kids: A guide for assisting students who are both academically
gifted and learning disabled.* Lanham, MD: Rowman & Littlefield.

Carle, A.C. (2007). *Understanding longitudinal growth modeling: An applied illustrative example
examining resilience and changes in mental health among children of alcoholics.* Proceedings of the
135th Annual Meeting and Exposition of the American Public Health Association. Accessed
at http://apha.confex.com/apha/135am/techprogram/paper_150667.htm.

Constantine, L.L. & Lockwood, A.D. (1999). *Software for use: A practical guide to the models and
methods of usage-centered design.* Upper Saddle River, NJ: Pearson Addison-Wesley.

Cooper, A. (2004). *The inmates are running the asylum: Why high tech products drive us crazy and
how to restore the sanity.* Upper Saddle River, NJ: Sams-Pearson Education.

Dai, D.Y. (2004). Epilouge: Putting it all together: Some concluding thoughts. In R.J.
Sternberg & D.Y. Dai (Eds.), *Motivation, emotion and cognition: Integrative perspectives on intellectual
functioning and development* (pp. 419–432). Mahwah, NJ: Lawrence Earlbaum Associates.

Dawson, P. & Gaure, R. (2010). *Executive skills in children and adolescents.* New York: Guilford
Press.

Duncan, T.E., Duncan, S.C., Strycker, L.A., Li, F. & Alpert, A. (1999). *An introduction
to latent variable growth curve modeling: Concepts, issues, and applications.* Mahwah, NJ: Lawrence
Erlbaum

Ek, U., Holmberg, K., de Geer, L., Sword, C. & Fernell, E. (2004). Behavioural and learning
problems in schoolchildren related to cognitive test data. *Acta Pediatr, 93*, 976–981.

Gay, L.R. & Airasian, P. (2003). *Educational research: Competencies for analysis and applications.*
Columbus, OH: Merrill Prentice Hall.

Immordino-Yang, M.H. (2010). *Emotions, social relationships, and the brain: Implications for the
classroom.* Proceedings of the 26th Conference of Learning and the Brain: Focused Minds,
Enhancing Attention, Memory and Motivation, Washington, DC, pp. 232–239.

Kaufmann, F., Kalbfleisch, M.L. & Castellanos, F.X. (2000). *Attention deficit disorders and gifted
students: What do we really know?* Monograph, University of Connecticut, Storrs, CT: National
Research Center on the Gifted and Talented.

Kelly, A.E. (2009). When is design research appropriate? In T. Plomp & N. Nieveen (Eds.),
An Introduction to educational design research (pp. 73–87). Enschede: SLO Netherland Institute
for Curriculum Development.

Kitsantas, A. & Dabbagh, N. (2010). *Learning to learn with integrative learning technologies: A practical guide for academic success.* Charlotte, NC: Information Age Publishing.

Krathwohl, D.R., Bloom, B.S. & Masia, B.B. (1964). *Taxonomy of educational objectives: Handbook II: Affective domain.* New York: David McKay Co.

Levin, M. (2002). *Educational care: A system for understanding and helping children with learning differences at home and in school.* Cambridge, MA: Educators Publishing Service.

Lovecky, D.V. (2004). *Different minds: Gifted children with AD/HD, Asperger Syndrome, and other learning deficits.* London: Jessica Kingsley Publishers.

Martinez, P. (2008). Impact of an integrated science and reading intervention (INSCIREAD) on bilingual students' misconceptions, reading comprehension and transferability of strategies. Unpublished dissertation: George Mason University.

McCandliss, B. Kalchman, W. & Bryant, P. (2003). Design experiments and laboratory approaches to learning: Steps toward collaborative exchange. *Educational Researcher, 32,* 14–16.

McCloskey, G. (2010). *Executive function and classroom learning production.* Presentation at the 26th Conference of Learning and the Brain: Focused Minds, Enhancing Attention, Memory and Motivation, Washington, DC.

McCloskey, G., Perkins, L.A. & Van Divner, B. (2009). *Assessment and intervention for executive function difficulties.* New York: Taylor & Francis.

Moon, S.M., Zentall, S.S., Grskovic, J.A., Hall, A. & Stormont, M. (2001). Emotional and social characteristics of boys with AD/HD and giftedness: A comparative case study. *Journal for the Education of the Gifted, 24,* 207–247.

Naglieri, J.A. & Johnson, D. (2000). Effectiveness of a cognitive strategy intervention to improve math calculation based on the PASS theory. *Journal of Learning Disabilities, 33,* 591–597.

Niogi, S.N., Mukherjee, P., Ghajar, J. & McCandliss, B.D. (in press). Individual differences in distinct components of attention are linked to anatomical variations in distinct white matter tracts. *Frontiers in Neuroanatomy.*

Nitko, A.J. & Brookhart, S.M. (2007). *Educational assessment of students.* Upper Saddle River, NJ: Pearson Merrill Prentice Hall.

Posner, M.I. and Rothbart, M.K. (2007). *Educating the human brain.* Washington, DC: American Psychological Association.

Rossett, A. (2009). *First things fast: A handbook for performance analysis.* San Francisco, CA: Pfeiffer.

Rucklidge, J.J. & Tannock, R. (2002). Neuropsychological profiles of adolescents with ADHD: Effects of reading difficulties and gender. *Journal of Child Psychology and Psychiatry, 43,* 988–1003.

Suri, J.F. (2008). Informing our intuition design research for radical innovation. *Totman Magazine,* 52–57.

Volkow, N.D., Wang, G., Kollins, S.H., Wigal, T.L., Newcorn, J.H., Telang, F., Fowler, J.S., Zhu, W., Logan, J., Ma, Y., Pradhan, K., Wong, C. and Swanson, J.M. (2009). Evaluating dopamine reward pathway in ADHD. *Journal of the American Medical Association, 302*(10), 1084–1091.

Walker, D. (2006). Toward productive design studies. In Van den Akker, J. Gravemiejer, K. McKenny, S. & Nieveen, N. (Eds.), *Educational design research* (pp. 8–13). New York: Taylor & Francis.

Zeigler-Dendy, C.A. (2010). *Understanding the impact of ADHD and executive function deficits on learning and behavior.* Presentation at the 26th Conference of Learning and the Brain: Focused Minds, Enhancing Attention, Memory and Motivation, Washington, DC.

Zentall, S.S., Moon, S.M., Hall, A.M. & Grskovic, J.A. (2001). Learning and motivational characteristics of boys with AD/HD and/or giftedness. *Exceptional Children, 67,* 499–519.

PART II

Models, Tools, and Pragmatics

6

DESIGNING A LEARNING ECOLOGY TO SUPPORT THE DEVELOPMENT OF RATIONAL NUMBER

Blending Motion and Unit Partitioning of Length Measures

Richard Lehrer and Erin Pfaff

Students in the first six years of schooling are routinely expected to understand mathematics that were originally developed over the course of centuries. A challenge for schooling, as well as for development, is to design classroom learning environments where this sociohistoric scale is compressed, but the intellectual accomplishments represented by these forms of mathematics are neither eradicated nor oversimplified. Design involves the intentional transformation of a setting for learning and is based upon conjectures about how the features of the designed setting will support learning and development. Our approach to design begins with envisioning how a particular set of mathematical ideas might be approached, often with an eye toward capitalizing on foundations that are not typically developed in schooling. In this chapter, we describe a hypothetical pathway for developing understanding of rational numbers by situating them as measures of length. We aim to illustrate that, although atypical, grounding rational number development in the development of spatial measure affords a fruitful alternative approach to instruction about mathematical concepts and operations that are often challenging for students to learn.

Because classroom settings are complex ecologies, successful design requires a working model of how components of the design, including tasks, inscriptions, material means, forms of argument, and the recurrent patterns of activity (activity structures) that help frame forms of student participation, are collectively constituted and orchestrated (Lehrer, 2009). We have organized this chapter to illuminate these components, beginning with a conceptual analysis of how central ideas of measure secure a foundation for rational number. After outlining how properties of rational number and operations on them are viewed from the perspective of length measure, we report the results of a four-month design study in an ethnically and intellectually diverse sixth-grade classroom located in an urban setting. Design study is a general approach to studying development and learning in which intervention and investigations are conducted as part of a coordinated enterprise (Brown, 1992). Design research presumes the need to conduct multiple iterations of the design. Lessons learned during one iteration are tested for viability in the next, so that generalization arises from replication. We are reporting the results of an initial iteration of the design, and, hence, our conclusions are tempered by anticipation of iterations to follow.

Pathways for the Development of Rational Number

In this section, we outline two alternative pathways for the development of rational number. One is the traditional emphasis on rational number as an extension of whole number. Because this is the dominant approach, we do not expand it, other than to review some of its demonstrated limitations. The second pathway begins with developing conceptions of measure and then proceeds to treat rational numbers as measured quantities.

Rational Number as an Extension of Whole Number

On the surface, rational number, an integer ratio of two whole numbers, appears a simple extension of whole number. Indeed, this is the traditional instructional approach: children are introduced to rational numbers as expansions of whole numbers. Unfortunately, when taught in this manner, children typically confuse rational with whole numbers so systematically that the resulting synthesis is termed the "whole-number bias" (Ni & Zhou, 2005), a term referring to children's tendencies to use whole-unit counting schemes when trying to interpret rational number. These tendencies surface most often as considering, for example, ¼ as larger than ⅓ because four is larger than three, adding across numerators and denominators when adding fractions, and rejecting the idea that there are numbers between 0 and 1 (Mack, 1995; Ni & Zhou, 2005). Expecting consistency with what they know about whole numbers as discrete counting units, students have difficulties understanding fractions as ratios of units or even as numbers, preferring instead to think of fractions as parts of a whole, with attendant difficulties thinking about the meaning of a rational number such as ⅔, because the number of parts exceeds the whole (Thompson & Saldanha, 2003). It is not entirely clear whether difficulties such as these should be laid entirely at the doorstep of whole numbers, but, as a practical matter, there is a high incidence of student difficulty when learning about fractions from this perspective.

Rational Measure as an Extension of Linear Measure

In this section, we propose an alternative perspective for rational number, with its origins in measuring instead of counting. Although we will describe extensions to linear measure, we situate this effort more broadly in a program of research that aims to involve students in the invention and critique of measures.

Measure

Measure is often considered as a humdrum of mere technical knowledge and mistaken as an ordinary accomplishment. Consequently, measurement often warrants no more than teaching students *how* to use an instrument, such as a ruler in early grades or perhaps a pH meter in later grades. Yet, in science, technology, engineering, and mathematics disciplines, measure and theory are interlocking, so that measurement is one of the principal ways in which knowledge is generated (Crosby, 1997; van Fraassen, 2008). Consider, for example, the history of an everyday measure, temperature, now so ordinary that the only novelty worth mentioning is when the reading exceeds or falls below some threshold. Nonetheless, the development of a measure of temperature occupied considerable material and intellectual resources. There were uncertainties about whether changes in the volumes of gases were in fact quantitatively proportional to changes in temperature, and whether a scale could be developed with a zero point, a matter not settled until there was enough confidence in the kinetic theory of gases (van Fraassen, 2008). The historical lesson is that during formation, before the relation between theory and measure has stabilized, measure is anything but ordinary. Formation of a measure calls into question assumptions about the characteristics of the system being measured, and it is often the case that understanding of these characteristics and that of their measure proceed hand in hand (Latour, 1999; van Fraassen, 2008).

Measuring space

The dialectical character of measure and theory is no less true of fundamental qualities of space, such as length, than it is of phenomena such as temperature. But, from an educational vantage, qualities of space and their measures have the added virtue of being more broadly accessible through their counterparts in everyday bodily activity. For example, in a pinch, the measure of a length can be accomplished with parts of one's body. Moreover, length need not be static, but can be experienced as motion along a path. Accordingly, we initiate children's first steps toward understanding the dialectical nature of measure by engaging them in the measure of length.

Our general approach is to rely on familiar, bodily experiences of space, such as walking from one place to another, and to engage students in inventing measures

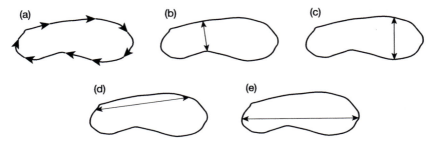

FIGURE 6.1 When a foot is used to measure a distance traveled, students often focus on different aspects of the foot, as illustrated by (a)–(e).

of the resulting path lengths (Lehrer, 2003). From these familiar situations, we position students to develop understanding of the role played by measurement units and scales by orienting instruction toward making these elements of measure visible and problematic. For example, a ready measure of the distance traveled between one point and another in a large-scale space can be obtained by iterating one's feet (Lehrer, Jacobson, Kemeny, & Strom, 1999). However, a system of measure must also explicitly address issues that the mere act of walking solves, such as the general role of the iteration of identical and rigid lengths to accumulate a measured quantity. This transition from activity to measure is not trivial, and it is what makes the activity mathematical, and not merely a stroll. For example, to foster a transition from activity to measure in a situation like this, we challenge children to create foot-strip measuring tapes that transport measure from the plane of everyday action to mathematical activity. Constructing the tape entails making decisions about which aspect of the foot should be represented on the tape (see Figure 6.1), how the beginning and end of a unit should be symbolized, and how units should be accumulated to create measures (Lehrer, Jaslow, & Curtis, 2003).

Approaching spatial measure by blending motion and unit also positions students to develop two important resources for thinking about number, as sug-gested by Lakoff and Nunez (2001). First, numbers can be viewed as metaphoric extensions of units of length measure, such as feet, so that a number corresponds to a measured length, which is most typically expressed as a ratio of a measured length to a second, unit length. (These ratios of lengths need not correspond to integers, but, in the work reported here, the ratios are all expressed by integers.) Arithmetic operations follow as the entailments of acting in the world with these measuring sticks. For example, joining segments of length along a straight line corresponds to addition. Second, by emphasizing motion and distance traveled, numbers are point-locations, with zero as the origin of measure. As we later describe more completely, we sought to capitalize on the blend of these metaphors for number, measuring sticks and motion-location, as foundations for learning about rational number as measured lengths.

In summary, involving students in the construction of unit and scale establishes lengths-as-measured-quantities, so that lengths can be compared indirectly, either additively by finding difference, or multiplicatively, by a "times as long" relation (Smith & Thompson, 2007; Thompson, 1993; Thompson & Saldanha, 2003). As we elaborate later, scales support the important conceptual work of establishing an origin of measure and specifying hierarchical relations among units of measure. The conceptual trajectory we outline in the sections that follow is rooted in forms of activity that situate the development of rational number concepts within this network of conceptions about linear measure.

Partial units

The initial step in our conjectured extension of whole-unit linear measure to rational number is to create a need for measured quantities that are not whole numbers. As students construct rulers, we arrange, or children select, objects to measure whose length is not a whole-number multiple of the unit of measure. To resolve this problem, students split—equally partition—units of length measure, which are represented by rectangular strips of paper where the length is much greater than the width, so that the paper functions to highlight the intended attribute of length while simultaneously providing a visible and manipulable tool for thought. As we shall describe more fully, partitioning has many entailments (Confrey, 1994; Confrey & Smith, 1995; Steffe, 2002, 2004). But, in this first step, the scope is narrow: Units have part-length corresponding to the magnitude of the split. We begin with two-splits, which even young children find within reach, perhaps owing to the operation of an early-developing analog system of magnitude estimation that allows kindergarten and first-grade children to predict the outcomes of halving (Barth, Baron, Spelke, & Carey, 2009). The ubiquity of bilateral symmetry likely plays a role as well.

A two-split creates two *congruent* parts. The symbolization ½ means that the original unit has been partitioned into two congruent parts and that there is one copy of this scaled unit length. The original unit is twice as long as the scaled, split unit, so that two copies or iterations of this re-scaled length are as long as the original unit length. This relation can be established by congruence of lengths: Two iterations of the split unit are congruent with the original unit. More generally, a/b is interpreted as a copies of one/b unit length, where b refers to the number of equal partitions of the original unit. Thinking of one/b is congenial to the part–whole interpretation of fractions as well: The unit has been split into two parts, and ½ means possessing one of these parts. However, the measure model provides a few additional, more useful entailments. First, measure begins at zero, so ½ u is a point between zero u and one u. That is, ½ unit is a quantity, just like any other measured quantity (taught in more traditional ways, students often deny that fractions are quantities). Second, by the embodied metaphor of motion, length measure is a distance traveled, and so iteration and distance traveled can be

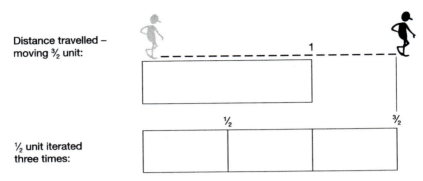

FIGURE 6.2 Coordinating distance traveled and unit iteration.

coordinated in that a/b corresponds to traveling in one/b intervals a times. The top panel of Figure 6.2 corresponds to a distance traveled of ¾ unit, while the bottom panel corresponds to three iterations of ½ unit. As we will explain more fully, students can use strips of paper that represent a unit length and then enact continuous travel, beginning at zero and then continuing to travel as they encounter each crease on the partitioned unit strip, so that, starting from zero, they travel ½ unit, ¾ unit, ⅜ unit and so on. The rational number representation thus provides waystations along the path traveled, and fractions can represent quantities greater than one. The metaphors of rigid body and motion are blended by coordinating travel and iteration: a/two represents a iterations of ½ and the distance traveled between zero and a/two (Lehrer et al., 1999, 2003). This blend of stick and motion-location also suggests that number-measures are continuous.

Composing Splits

Beginning with natural language of ½ of one unit, we next introduce students to compositions of splits, beginning with compositions of two splits. These are signaled in natural language as ½ of ½ of one unit and are composed literally and recursively with paper-strip units, in the context of the need to measure length more precisely with partial units. This recursive process is demonstrated in Figure 6.3.

Recursive folding of the unit results in new forms of a/b, initially with b as four, then as eight, 16, and so on. We encourage relational reasoning by natural language: one unit is four times as long as ¼ unit, and one unit is eight times as long as ⅛ unit. The entailment of the latter is that eight copies or iterations of ⅛ unit are the same length as one unit. We encourage teachers to physically separate the one/b unit and the unit, so that, for example, students can see that eight iterations of ⅛ unit indeed create a measure of one unit. The test of this assertion is congruency. Measured lengths are once again revisited as a iterations of one/b units and as distances traveled. This perspective makes the markings on

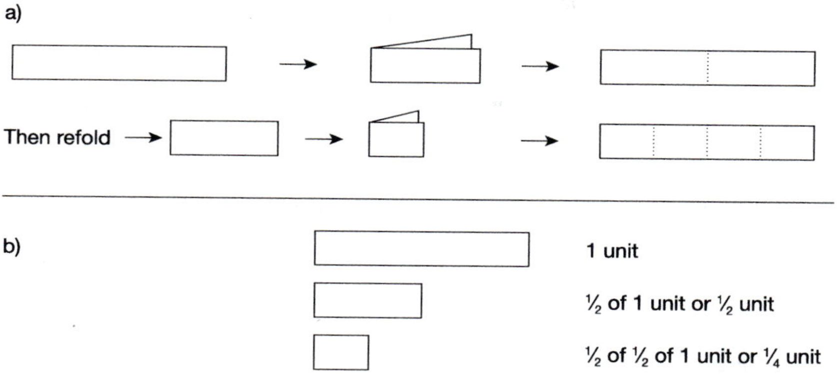
a)
Then refold
b)
1 unit
$\frac{1}{2}$ of 1 unit or $\frac{1}{2}$ unit
$\frac{1}{2}$ of $\frac{1}{2}$ of 1 unit or $\frac{1}{4}$ unit

FIGURE 6.3 Composing splits recursively.

the path traveled denser, as students learn that there are quantities, such as $\frac{3}{8}$ unit, that lie between $\frac{1}{4}$ unit and $\frac{2}{4}$ unit. And, in measurement contexts, we can put this distinction to use to obtain more precise measures.

For most students, the exponential behavior of these compositions is surprising. Many students initially believe that the result of a two-split of four will be six, not eight. By composing splits, students are positioned to view equivalence as the same distance traveled or a point on the ruler, so that, for example, $\frac{1}{2}$ unit is marked also as $\frac{2}{4}$ unit and as $\frac{4}{8}$ unit. This expands their initial sense of equivalence as the special case of one unit and $\frac{2}{2}$ unit. As we will explain more fully, students often conflate equivalence and identity, and it is disconcerting for some to find that, although traveling from zero to $\frac{1}{2}$ unit and from zero to $\frac{4}{8}$ units reaches the same destination, the means of travel are not identical, because there are different intermediate intervals along the way. The same is true of expressions of one unit as $\frac{2}{2}$ unit, $\frac{4}{4}$ unit, $\frac{16}{16}$ unit, and so on. For consistency, we introduce an interpretation of *a* units as *a*/one units, meaning, for example, that when we write six units, the interpretation is that six units is the result of six iterations of one unit, and so it can be written as 6/1. Moreover, the operation of splitting a unit can be undone and the unit restored by iteration. Given one/*b*, then *b* iterations of one/*b* restore the unit length. This assertion can also be verified via congruence of lengths.

To continue composing splits with other factors, we take a step back and involve students in constructing three-splits by folding unit strips into three congruent partitions. We have found that these are more challenging than composing two-splits, but, thereafter, students are involved in compositions involving factors with multiples of two and three. We include ways of composing twelfths, partly because doing so exercises this form of composition and partly because inches and feet are representative of this class of composition in the US. Students also conduct investigations of commutativity. For example, in what sense is the result of $\frac{1}{2}$ of $\frac{1}{3}$ of one unit the same as $\frac{1}{3}$ of $\frac{1}{2}$ of one unit?

Scaling Coordinates Multilevel Unit Relations

A ruler represents two major accomplishments that are coordinated to reduce measure to reading a value. One we have described as the development of units and their partitions, so that measure can be as precise as needed for the purposes at hand. The second is the relation of units that constitutes a scale. Scaling involves challenges about the origin of a measure—any point on the scale can stand in for zero—and, more subtly, scaling describes multilevel unit relations. The first level is that of the unit. If the measurement unit need not be partitioned, then accumulating units by single-unit iteration suffices to obtain a measure. A second level is introduced by partitioning. Now the partition must be related to the unit partitioned. Hence, partitioned units coordinate units and the partition factor (e.g., two, three), so that, for example, a/b unit is interpreted by relation to one unit. A third level occurs when partitions and units must be composed, so that they can be accumulated. A common example is the foot ruler. The foot unit is partitioned into 12, representing splitting by factors of two and three. But each of these one-twelfths is further partitioned by a composition of two-splits, often resulting in 16 further partitions. To interpret ¾₆ or 1¾₆ on such a foot-scale requires coordination across these units and splits of units, an exemplar of the general problem of coordinating multiple levels of reference when interpreting a rational number (e.g., Izsak, 2008; Izsak, Orrill, Cohen, & Brown, 2010; Steffe, 2002). Scaling is designed to facilitate this coordination. The flip side is that developing a scale poses the challenge of developing a scheme for coordinating unit, unit partitions, and compositions of units and partitions. Scale development is an important step in developing rational number knowledge, because students can partition units without necessarily developing a representation of a coordinated, unit-of-units structure (Hackenberg, 2007).

Linking Partition to Multiplication

The next step in the sequence is to link these physical operations of splitting to mathematical operations. We begin with multiplication and the linguistic hedge "of." This is an avenue toward thinking about fractions as operators and not simply as points on a line. Hence, the result of two of (times) one unit is two units, and the result of ½ of (times) one unit is ½ unit. There are two senses of multiplication at play. One is the familiar sense of multiplication as repeated addition, so that $3 \times ¾$ unit is the same as three iterations of ¾ unit, for a total of ⁹⁄₄ units traveled. The copy metaphor is one of iteration and exemplifies multiplication as repeated addition.

There are also tight connections of multiplication to similarity and scaling, and thus a different sense of multiplication. For $a/b \times e$ unit, if $a < b$, then the effect on the e unit is contraction. For example, ½ × 3 unit contracts three units by a factor of two. If $a > b$, the effect on the e unit is dilation, and if $a = b$, the effect is the identity. Although they are complementary, iteration and scaling are distinct images of multiplication. Scaling is often important in thinking about natural systems, including organismic and population growth (Lehrer & Schauble, 2006). These images of multiplication are eventually related to the standard algorithm for multiplication of fractions, so that $a/b \times c/d$ unit $= ac/bd$ unit. However, we distinguish multiplication of a unit length by a scalar from multiplication of a unit length by another unit length. That is, $\frac{1}{2} \times \frac{1}{3}$ unit contracts $\frac{1}{3}$ unit to $\frac{1}{6}$ unit, but $\frac{1}{2}$ unit $\times \frac{1}{3}$ unit results in the creation of area and a measure of $\frac{1}{6}$ unit^2.

Addition

Addition corresponds to joining or gluing lengths, so that $\frac{1}{2}$ unit $+ \frac{1}{3}$ unit, for example, is illustrated by a continuation of travel, so that, having traveled $\frac{1}{2} u$, the traveler continues motion in the same direction for another $\frac{1}{3} u$. To arrive at a single measure, the units of length must be common, and it is this need that motivates re-expression of units in equivalences. Hence, equivalence establishes commensurate measure. Because multiplication precedes addition on this pathway, we have established that multiplication by one does not change the resulting length of the unit. Hence, $c/c \times a/b$ unit, where $c > 0$, results in an equivalent measure. Subtraction follows a similar path, but the emphasis now is on the difference between two commensurate measures, so that a/b unit $- c/b$ unit $= (a - c)/b$ unit, or the distance traveled from location c/b to location a/b.

Division

We approach division as a form of rescaling to make the inverse relation between multiplication and division more transparent. Beginning with a whole number unit of measure, such as four units, we rescale by another unit (such as $\frac{1}{2}$ unit). The result (eight) is a scalar that acts on the rescaling unit to restore the original unit. In other words, eight iterations of the $\frac{1}{2}$ unit ($8 \times \frac{1}{2}$ unit) restores the original measure of four units. The magnitude of the length is unaffected, but its measure is transformed.

This metaphor of rescaling by a measure less than one times as long is then extended to related cases, such as $\frac{3}{2}$ units divided by $\frac{1}{2}$ unit results in three: Three iterations of $\frac{1}{2}$ restores the original measure of $\frac{3}{2}$ units. In contrast, when the rescaling measure is greater than one times as long as the original measure, such as three units divided by $\frac{3}{2}$, the rescaling results in a new measure less than that of the original measure, two units, and the original measure is restored by $2 \times \frac{3}{2}$ units or two iterations of the rescaling unit. A further example of rescaling factors greater than one: $\frac{1}{2}$ unit divided by two units. Here, the scaling unit is twice as long as the original unit. The result is $\frac{1}{4}$, and $\frac{1}{4}$ iteration of the two unit restores the original measure of $\frac{1}{2}$ unit. To simplify the scalar relation between original and rescaling units of measure, both can be measured in commensurate or equivalent measure, with the result expressed as their ratio. For example, 4 units/½ unit can be re-expressed as ½ unit divided by ½ unit, with the result of eight, so that eight iterations of the ½ unit restores the original measure. In all of these instances, iterations are supported by distance traveled, so that students can see that the path length is invariant, but the measure of its distance varies with the unit of rescaling. A special case is rescaling by one, which leaves the measure unchanged.

Trying Out the Conceptual Model: A Design Study

This conceptual model for extending measured quantities to rational number is based on earlier work with younger children who were participating in forms of mathematics education featuring investigation of geometry and measure (Lehrer et al., 1999, 2003). However, we were uncertain about the viability of the approach with students who had a different history of education, especially those already reasoning about fractions as extensions of whole numbers in ways characterized as the whole-number bias. Accordingly, we conducted an initial design study in a sixth-grade classroom in an urban public school located in the southeastern region of the United States. The school primarily serves underrepresented youth: The percent of children attending the school who qualify for free or reduced lunch ranges from 60 to 90 from year to year. Participants ($n = 23$, 8 male) were racially and ethnically diverse. Two students' families moved during the year, resulting in 21 students at the end of the year.

The students in this classroom appeared to have many of the conceptions about fractions associated with whole-number bias. For example, during a mathematics class we observed early in the school year, many students added fractions by rote calculation of the sums of numerators and denominators, so that the result of $\frac{3}{10} + \frac{8}{10}$ was considered $\frac{11}{20}$, or even $\frac{8}{100}$. (The latter solution reflected some students' recollections that denominators needed to be multiplied when adding.) Sense checking did not seem to inform the results of this operation, and, for most, operations on fractions were purely a matter of computation (Thompson & Thompson, 1994); they could not explain why the algorithms worked. Assessments further indicated that many students judged $\frac{5}{10}$ as a larger fraction than $\frac{3}{4}$, while others thought that fractions must always be less than one. In addition, a few students ($n = 5$ of 23) appeared to have some whole-number counting difficulties that are not typical of students of this grade and age. For example, two students could not skip count by 10 off decade (e.g., 17, 27), and relied instead on a counting-on strategy. Another dropped back to one if the counting sequence was interrupted. Hence, we concluded that the students in the classroom also represented high diversity with respect to their previous experience of mathematics.

In the design study, we intended to introduce students to linear measure and to situate rational number as measured quantities. The approach we described previously guided the development of problems and tasks to support student learning. One of the authors (RL) served as the mathematics instructor. The regular classroom teacher remained in the classroom and provided additional assistance. Lessons were videotaped, and at least one, and occasionally two, observer(s) took field notes. Field notes and lesson reflections provoked adjustment of instruction. For example, the following reflections about students' coordination of partial units during an early lesson contributed to the next lesson:

(a) For the student who labeled each ⅛ partition as "⅛," we can address this by asking two students with two different rulers (one cumulative, one not) to measure a long object using the rulers. [The reference is to partitioning without scaling, so that the ruler's scale consistently marked each partition as the unit fraction.]

(b) The students are primarily using a part–whole model for partitions and they are thinking about measures as counts. Hence, their rulers label the centers of the partitions [and not endpoints of segments] . . . They have not yet reconciled accumulation with the symbolic design of their rulers—in other words, integrating unit conceptions with scale. The distance-traveled metaphor seems especially important as a means for thinking of fractions as partitioned unit-lengths, rather than simply as parts. We need to do more of "close your eyes, start at zero, and let your fingers travel x units." I think ⅔, etc. would make sense to a majority of the children, but I need to check on this conjecture.

Reflections about cases of student behavior were supplemented by written and formative assessments that we developed as the lessons progressed. For example, to probe the effectiveness of the motion metaphor for supporting rational number, on the fourth day of instruction, we conducted a formative assessment. Students folded a paper strip unit into eighths with their eyes closed, just using touch. This allowed us to observe whether or not students understood that partitions must be congruent. Then, again with eyes closed, we asked students to travel from the beginning of the strip by moving their fingers along it over various unit–partition distances, including those that exceeded one. This allowed us to obtain evidence about how motion supported student reasoning about iteration of unit partitions. Closing eyes also introduced an element of fun and challenge to the assessment.

As the classroom teacher required students to write summaries about each lesson in a math journal, we also sampled from students' writings to inform further instruction. These sources of ongoing evidence about learning contributed to the emerging design of approximately 30 lessons.

Sources of data for analysis of learning were classroom videos, written assessments, flexible interviews, and students' mathematics journals. The flexible interviews were administered to individual students four months after the conclusion of instruction to get a sense of the longer-term intelligibility of reasoning about rational numbers as measured quantities. The interview was designed to probe how students tended to think about equivalence among units, and its implication for the density of rational numbers. The interview also probed students' understandings of measure interpretations of operations on rational measures, including addition, multiplication, and division. The questions were posed in contexts of linear and area measure, although the focus here is on linear measure. Each interview typically lasted between 45 and 60 minutes. Interviews were conducted by the authors and video-recorded for further analysis.

To condense these data, we have organized the findings to illuminate student reasoning about critical elements of the measure approach. These illuminations draw from classroom video, field notes, and student journals. For each element, such as composing splits, we illustrate the reasoning of one or more students to reflect typical forms of understanding, and take note of some of the challenges and opportunities that students and we encountered. We conclude this section with the results obtained from the flexible interviews conducted as the school year concluded. These provide a broader view of the resources that students could conceivably bring to bear as they continue learning about rational number.

Illuminations of Student Reasoning

We began instruction by posing a problem of finding the distance between two landmarks in a large-scale space, which could be determined with any tool at students' disposal, other than conventional rulers. The task was chosen for its affordances of motion—a common solution was to walk—and iteration—a common solution was to accumulate footsteps. The task also induced students to consider the nature of units. For example, students debated about what constituted a "normal step" and how these might be compared across individuals. Students assembled their normal steps as foot-strip rulers (Lehrer et al., 1999), a task that provoked further consideration of how to label units and made obvious the need for partial units to measure other objects that we provided, or that students selected. It is in this context of practical activity, the assembly of a foot-strip ruler, that we turn to the initiation of the rational-number pathway.

Partitioning, Iterating, and Scaling

The notion of "½ of" a unit was intelligible to all students. That is, all students folded a paper strip representing a unit into two congruent partitions. However, as expected, when students composed two-splits (e.g., half of half of one), they were often surprised by the results. For example, after establishing compositions of two-splits that resulted in fourths and eighths, the instructor asked students to predict the results of composing 10 two-splits of a unit. One student, Susan, initially conjectured that the resulting number of partitions would be 20, "since each time the strip is divided, it is divided by two." Although her statement about

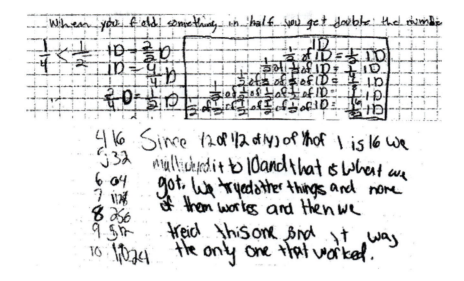

FIGURE 6.4 Susan's investigation of the results obtained by splitting a D unit.

partitioning was correct, her conclusion suggested that she was not aware of the recursive structure illuminated in Figure 6.3. After composing a few two-splits, she recognized that the number of partitions was increasing more than she expected, and, in fact, each successive composition doubled its predecessor. Her journal entry for that day is displayed in Figure 6.4, with some additional notations (e.g., ¾ u = ½ u), suggesting that Susan also considered equivalence as she explored the properties of these compositions. Note, too, that this is not yet "multiplication" as indicated by the natural language "of."

Before we introduced the travel metaphor, we noticed that many students were employing part–whole metaphors of partial units, so that iterations of partial units that exceeded the unit length were difficult to conceive. But nearly all students had little difficulty with iteration greater than one when we introduced "traveling" or "walking" by unit partitions, such as ⅝ unit and ⅞ unit. One student with a very firm conception of a fraction as part of a whole had to be literally encouraged to extend the travel beyond the unit. To do so, we aligned one of her hands with the end of the one unit and then used the other to continue to "walk" to accumulate ¹⁰⁄₈ unit. Partitioning and iterating by travel literally went hand in hand.

The symbolic expression of these relations was considerably more challenging for most students. For example, the language "one unit is eight times as long as ⅛ unit" was not initially intelligible to the majority of students, and we spent instructional time interpreting this form of expression. Symbolic description remained a consistent challenge throughout instruction, as we sought to augment practical understandings with appropriate symbolizations, including these linguistic forms of expression.

Coordinating Partitions and Units by Scaling

Following work with three-splits and their composition with two-splits, each student designed a two-unit paper tape measure. The construction materials were adding machine tape and paper strip units glued to the tape. Students exchanged tape measures and noted any difficulties they encountered when they used the tape to measure the length of different objects in the room. Figure 6.5a displays facsimiles of representative students' tape measures, which collectively indicate that many students were challenged to develop relations among units to create scales. Figure 6.5a(a) demonstrates two different partitioning schemes for the unit and two scales of measure. Figure 6.5a(b) suggests instability in the choice of one unit, as the partitions are of the two-unit structure and of the ½ unit structure, not of the unit structure. Figure 6.5a(c) illustrates partitioning of units but the absence of a scale that would allow for unit two composition and measure accumulation. The system is not notational because the same symbol marks different locations. Figure 6.5a(d) suggests the designer was reasoning about partitions as countable objects, rather than as distance traveled, because unit labels are in the center of units rather than at endpoints.

In contrast, some student solutions revealed well-developed coordination across levels of unit reference, such as those displayed in Figure 6.5b, but the diversity in students' inventions served as grist for further discussion about relations among levels of unit. For example, in the lesson immediately following, students contrasted measures of the same magnitude of length obtained with a one-unit ruler spanning the length, partitioned into eighths, with the measure obtained with a two-unit ruler spanning the length, also partitioned into eighths. During this lesson a further opportunity for splitting occurred when the unit measure fell between ⅝ unit and ⅚ unit. Proposed solutions ranged from ⅝ unit + ½ unit, ¹¹⁄₁₆ unit, and 5½ unit. Considering the distance traveled along the scale supported resolution among these choices by clarifying relations among units visually: The consequences of traveling, for example, 5½ units along the scale in

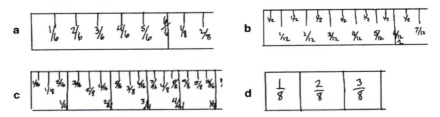

FIGURE 6.5A Invented scales of measure for two-unit rulers revealing challenges in unit coordination.

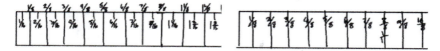

FIGURE 6.5B Invented scales that coordinate multiple levels of unit equivalence.

light of the length being measured clarified the shortcomings of this solution. Positioning students to invent scales to solve practical problems of measurement provided frequent opportunities to develop unit structures.

Equivalence

Initial discussions of equivalence centered on motion and location. Which imagined walks along the ruled length wound up in identical locations? The two–splits provided ready entrée for all students. During the eighth lesson, many students discovered that they could generate many equivalencies for any two-split. Again, we encouraged symbolization, such as $\frac{32}{64} = \frac{16}{32}$. As students observed the two–split structure of repeated doubling of the number of partitions and repeated halving of the length of each successor, the instructor asked how to go about generating any number of equivalent fractions. One student, Helen, immediately responded that the key was to multiply the original measure by $\frac{2}{4}$ or $\frac{4}{8}$ etc. The resulting measure fractions would then all be at the same place and, hence, equal. However, upon further reflection, Helen wondered how the operation could be viewed as multiplying by one. She could readily acknowledge that anything in the form of c/c was one, but she noted that, in whole–number arithmetic, multiplication by one did not change a number. She demonstrated with a few cases, such as $1 \times 10 = 10$. She went on to demonstrate that multiplying $\frac{4}{4} \times \frac{1}{16}$ unit did not result in a number literally identical to $\frac{1}{16}$, even though its location was the same! Helen's question provided an opportunity to consider equality as a relation, a problem for students in the United States, even in the realm of whole numbers. In this lesson, the instructional explanation took the form of splitting and iterating with a paper-strip model of a unit. The initial step was to four-split each one-sixth and to relate the result to the original unit as generating one-sixty-fourth. To travel the same distance from zero as $\frac{1}{16}$ unit required four iterations, thus establishing that $\frac{4}{64}$ was equivalent, but not identical, to $\frac{1}{16}$.

Helen's question spurred us to develop a written assessment that challenged students to explain how multiplication of $\frac{1}{2}$ by $\frac{1}{4}$ and $\frac{2}{2}$ could be considered as not changing a number, in light of the different results obtained by the operation. Figure 6.6 displays a student's response that shows appropriation of the instructor's explanation. However, the majority of students' responses indicated widespread confusion of identity and equality, such as, "It's not true because when you multiply by one the numbers don't split." Hence, in subsequent lessons we revisited this idea.

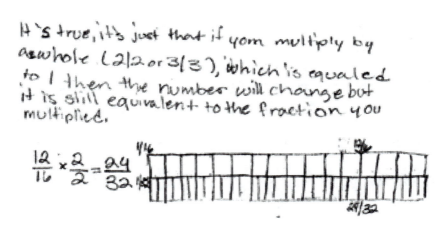

It's true, it's just that if you multiply by a whole (2|2 or 3|3), which is equaled to 1 then the number will change but it is still equivalent to the fraction you multiplied.

$$\frac{12}{16} \times \frac{2}{2} = \frac{24}{32}$$

FIGURE 6.6 A student's justification of equivalence and unit multiplication.

For example, a few lessons later, Landra explained her verification that "doing ⅔" (multiplying by one) to ¾ unit resulted in an equivalent measure, ¹⁰⁄₈ unit. She explained with the paper-strip units displayed in Figure 6.7 that first "I went all the way to ¾." The language of "I went all the way" connotes a personification of motion that made sense of improper fractions as locations. Landra continued, referring to the result of the two-split: "and when I looked at ¼ it only took to get into one," a reference clarified by the instructor as two of the ⅛ths. The teacher went on to question how the actions related to the symbolic expression, and Landra took it as self-evident with a brief gesture translating 5⅔s or 5¼s. At this point, the instructor likely should have clarified 5⅔s composite units or 10⅛s, but did not.

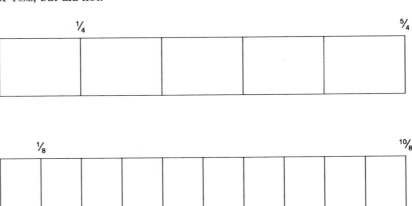

FIGURE 6.7 Coordinating partitioning and iterating with symbolization.

Kierra responded to Landra by objecting to considering $\frac{2}{2}$ as one, citing $\frac{3}{4} \times 1$ = $\frac{3}{4}$. This was reminiscent of Helen's question a few days earlier. Kierra asked: "So how'd you get $\frac{19}{8}$?" The tack taken by the instructor was to remind the students that "equal" referred to "means the same thing as," and, here, "two measured in two is the same thing as one. If I have something that is two units long, and my ruler is also two units long, and I measure it with my ruler, what will I get?" Kierra suggested one, which prompted further demonstration and comparison of two units and the two–unit ruler of identical length. The instructor formed the composite unit ruler, which relied on a unit-of-units structure, and reminded students of translation by referring to how many ruler lengths would "fit" into the two-units. After further elaboration of equal, the instructor placed strip models of $\frac{3}{4}$ unit and $\frac{19}{8}$ unit on the floor and, with Kierra, measured the same distance with fourths and eighths, noting the doubling of the number of partitions and the number of iterations required to travel the same distance in eighths compared with fourths, and then concluding that was how the expression $\frac{2}{2}$ was acting on the $\frac{3}{4}$ unit.

Putting Equivalence to Use for Developing Commensurate Measure

As we related previously, we introduced addition as an operation that joined or glued two unit lengths, or, from the perspective of motion, as an operation that continued a motion. Subtraction was introduced as a means of finding differences between unit lengths. Both of these operations gave rise to the need to find commensurate units, as in this excerpt, where students found the difference between $\frac{1}{3}$ unit and $\frac{1}{4}$ unit:

> KL: What we did was um, we folded 12 . . . and after we got the answer [folds one paper-strip unit into $\frac{1}{12} u$ and superimposes it on another unit strip folded into $\frac{1}{3} u$], we folded twelfths again and we put $\frac{1}{4}$ up against it and it was three—it was $\frac{3}{12}$. And so we marked it. Then we got the $\frac{1}{3}$ and put it up against it starting from the bottom [same origin], and we marked it. And it was only, it was only, $\frac{1}{3}$ was only $\frac{1}{12}$ longer than $\frac{1}{4}$. And I had thought the difference between uhh $\frac{1}{4}$ and $\frac{1}{3}$ would be longer than $\frac{1}{12}$.
>
> I: So it was a bit of a surprise to you?
>
> K: Yeah
>
> I: OK, so when we find differences, we call that subtraction, so [to class], they [K and partner] wrote that number sentence on the board to summarize what we just did. We found the difference between a third and a fourth (unit).

Symbolic and strip representations of units were often interwoven as students considered addition of commensurate measures. For example, when Naomi proposed with strips that 5/4 unit + 5/8 unit could be solved by finding the commensurate measure of 10/8 unit + 5/8 unit, with the result expressed as 15/8 or 1 7/8 units, Erica proposed another, symbolic solution:

> Take off the fourth (from the 5/4) for now and add it in later. And make the 5/8, 4/8 and save the eighth, and that will make it one and 1/2 (4/4 *u* + 4/8 *u*), 1/4 will make two eighths (by equivalence). Then another eighth is 3/8, and we have the 1 1/2, resulting in 1 4/8 + 3/8 = 1 7/8.

Literal reliance on splitting with strips was gradually expanded to symbolic procedures that would guarantee common measures, so that procedural and conceptual knowledge were mutually constituted, as they are in the practice of mathematics. One student invented and shared a procedure of skip counting that we collectively came to regard as finding a common multiple partitioning. The other commonly established procedure for finding commensurate partitions was multiplying factors to find common partitions. We emphasized the translation of these procedures with symbols to their counterparts with paper-strip units.

Making Sense of Multiplication

Making sense of multiplication was the most challenging but critical component of the extension of measure to rational number. Understanding multiplication required developing an operator model of rational number. Instead of points on a ruler, rational numbers acted on units, as described previously, to partition and iterate, and to stretch or shrink, with the special case of multiplication by 1, which left the length of the unit unchanged. This conceptual model was embodied by motion and partition-iteration of material, paper-strip units. It was also symbolized by a familiar notational system, $a/b \times c/d$. And, it was supported linguistically by a mathematical register of: "*x* unit is . . . times as long as *y* unit." Instruction was aimed at helping students develop each system of representation and establish coordinations among them. We illuminate some of these entailments of multiplication in the classroom.

Image of Multiplication as Stretching and Shrinking

During the ninth lesson, the instructor asked the class what happened to the length of a unit when it was multiplied by a number less than one. In rapid succession, one student said, "It splits the length," and another, "It makes it smaller." Later, another student objected that multiplication "made more." The instructor named a unit after the student who raised this objection and asked the class how to make more of this student-strip unit: "Here's one N and I want more of him." The class compared multiplying by one, which a student explained, "will stay the same length," to multiplying by two, making two copies, which stretched

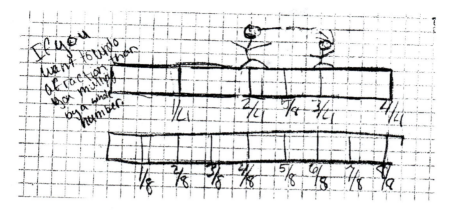

FIGURE 6.8 Student reflection about equivalence and undoing the results of partitioning.

the length. The paper-strip model verified that the new length was now twice as long as the original. The instructor then asked students to generate "something I could multiply by to shrink the N (unit)." One student proposed ½ × 1 N, and thereafter many others contributed, drawing again on two-splits, reaching a now-familiar partition of ½. The teacher noted that, symbolically, the shrinkage was ½ × 1 N. N protested to the class: "You are turning me into a shrub!" The instructor appealed to the class for a way to restore N to his original length, which occasioned a debate about the effects of 32 × ½ N vs. ³²∕₃₂ × ½ N. Undoing made an impression, as suggested by its appearance in a student journal, represented in Figure 6.8, a reflection primarily about equivalence and travel, but also including reference to the inverse. These initial steps continued to be supported throughout the sequence. For example, during a later lesson, students made "snap judgments," predicting as quickly as they could the result of a/b × c-unit, where c was any ratio of integers, for different values of a/b, as greater than, equal to, or less than the c-unit. Could a judgment be made without finding each result? If so, on what basis? In this way, we supported a general image of multiplication as scaling, comparing initial and resulting lengths of units with different scale factors.

Supporting an Image of Multiplication as Partitioning and Iterating

Iteration was treated as copying, and the unit being copied was set aside from the length being measured, because we found that, if we did not clearly distinguish these, students interpreted copying additively. For example, ¾ of one unit was interpreted by some students as a two copies of a four-split unit, because the initial fourth was already created by folding, so only two more would be required. All unit-fractions, even if unseen, were the products of multiplication. Initial steps substituted "times" for the composition of splits to create unit fractions. We referred subsequently to denominators of the scalar multiples as splitters and the numerators as copiers. Some students spontaneously related iteration to stretching and shrinking. For example, Erica suggested that, if

> you're putting a number down (putting down meant copy), so if you multiply by two, you're putting a number down two times, so if you're doing it less than one, you're not putting down a whole number, so it's kind of like it would shrink.

Erica went on to demonstrate putting down with another example: $3 \times \frac{1}{2}$ unit, showing three iterations of the $\frac{1}{2}$ unit, and compared this result with the original partitioned unit, a clear case of expansion. The class next considered the case of $1 \times \frac{1}{2}$ unit, and then the case of $\frac{1}{2} \times \frac{1}{2}$ unit:

RL: What does $\frac{1}{2} \times$ tell us to do?
S: Split it.
RL: What is the splitting number?
D: Two (Erica takes the $\frac{1}{2}$ unit and two-splits it. On the floor is the original unit, the $\frac{1}{2}$ unit, and now the $\frac{1}{4}$ unit)
RL: So what does the top number tell us to do, in Erica's terms?
S: Put it down one time. (The result is $\frac{1}{4}$ unit.)

At this point, the instructor, returning to the theme of unit multiplication, posed the question of $\frac{2}{3} \times \frac{1}{2}$ unit. Several students noted that the denominator commanded: Split it ($\frac{1}{2} u$) into two. And the numerator commanded them to put down the resulting split unit two times. The class then considered that this action resulted in the same length, but now measured as $\frac{2}{4} u$. These varied interpretations of multiplication were important for developing an operational sense of multiplication and for again revisiting the notion of equivalence as involving multiplication by one.

Developing a Language of Relation

We relied extensively on everyday meanings of "half" and "of" to initiate productive mathematical conversations, but to sustain these conversations we cultivated linguistic forms that students initially found novel. One linguistic form was "times as long," which we intended to express multiplicative relations. By partitioning and iterating unit strips, students could verify statements of relation, and we encouraged these forms of verification to establish coordination among these representational forms. For example, during the eleventh lesson, Renna claimed that two u is four times as long as $\frac{1}{2} u$. She verified this statement by demonstrating that it took four iterations of the $\frac{1}{2}$ unit to compose a two–unit length. Another student claimed that the ½ u was ¼ times as long as the two u length. Several students were not convinced. She replied: "I put together two wholes (the units) and then I looked at it as in fourths because four of these (½ u) got into two wholes." The instructor related this to travel as well: "So it takes four of these halves to travel the same distance as two u?"

Making Sense of Division

As we explained earlier, we introduced division as remeasuring or rescaling a length, grounds that had been prepared by remeasuring in the context of equivalence. The introduction revealed some of the difficulties and opportunities of this model, as suggested by the following exchange:

> RL: I'm going to put this length on the floor here and I want everyone to be able to see it. It starts here and ends there. It's just a length, I don't know what its measure is. It's just a length. Now I'm going to measure it with one of these, a J unit [named after a student].
>
> S: Three [RL iterates the J unit three times to verify].
>
> RL: Now I am going to glue two strips [J units] together and use it as my unit. If I measured this same distance . . . what's the measure going to be now?
>
> S: Two and one whole [a response suggesting difficulty maintaining unit relations].
>
> RL: I am going to ask you to look, and then you tell me what the measure is [RL iterates the composite two-unit].
>
> S: 1½.
>
> RL: Now I'm going to measure the same distance with something that is now three times as long. What is that going to be?
>
> S: One.

As we considered division as rescaling, students more readily interpreted relations where the numerator was of greater measure than the denominator, perhaps because the rescaling then could be assimilated to related ideas of "going into." Although space precludes more thorough exposition, this focus on rescaling led several students to propose an algorithm for division as a ratio of equivalent or common measures.

Epistemic Conversations

Although we have illuminated some of the ways in which the measure model was deployed to support students' modeling of rational number and operations on rational number, there were a number of side conversations that reflected a cultural clash between the instructors and the students about the nature of mathematics. To illustrate, we describe some of the conversations between instructors and this student during the course of instruction. Helen was ordinarily very articulate about her stance toward a mathematical idea and over time came to embrace a perspective on mathematics as sense making. However, in the earlier part of the year, she expressed bewilderment about our focus on something other than the results of calculations. She mentioned that "smart" people had invented mathematics, and it was the role of students to learn how to do the things they had invented. This led to a number of side conversations, such as the one that follows, which begins with the student wondering if RL hasn't noticed how much she values knowing the rules:

> S: Don't you notice how we know what—we know how to trust rules [inaudible].
>
> RL: I know, and math is about explanation as well as answers.
>
> S: Why are we? [Goes on to describe stance about smart people who tell and wonders why RL just doesn't trust them. They have our best interests in mind in the sense of responsible guardians.]
>
> RL: No, I don't trust unless I know why it works. [Invokes an imagined scene where a result is found and its trustworthiness is in doubt.]
>
> S: Well, ⅔ × ⅓, the rule's explanation is 2 × 1 / 6 × 3!
>
> RL: That's an algorithm that guarantees a result. And that's good. Now I'm just asking you to tell me, so why does that work?
>
> S: It works because that's the way the rules are.
>
> RL: Well, I agree . . . Now . . . Now I want to know—why do those rules work? Why—what are they—the people who made that rule up— What were they thinking? Math is knowing what they were thinking.

With equal parts humor and exasperation, the student suggested that she could not read minds. How was she to know what the inventors were thinking? RL replied that this was the nub of the problem. "People can't read minds, which is why you have to learn for yourself."

This conversation is emblematic of others that occurred throughout instruction. It was particularly problematic for students who had high test scores to be called to explain their mathematical thinking. They seemed to take opportunities for explanations as invitations to showcase their computational prowess, and, for one or two students, this orientation never changed. Nevertheless, over time, it appeared that the classroom culture generally became more aligned with mathematics as a sense-making enterprise. For example, a month later, the same student who had advocated mathematics as learning rules talked with the classroom teacher about her difficulties with a task involving the coordination of units of length measure to structure units of area (draw the units within a rectangle), rather than only finding the measure by the product of the lengths:

S: 'Cause I didn't know like and I never thought about this before. 'Cause I've been doing area since fourth grade but every time they just give me the number and I'll multiply. I never thought about drawing it.

T: [nodding] That's right.

H: And ever since I've been drawing it, I've been having trouble.

Flexible Interview Results

Four months after instruction, we interviewed each student ($n = 21$) to gauge how each understood elements of rational number, such as equivalence and the meaning of arithmetic operations on rational numbers. The interviews were conducted flexibly, with interviewer follow-up to determine better how students were reasoning. These follow-ups occasionally prompted shifts in reasoning. We report here our best sense of how students reasoned, given these opportunities to expand on their thinking. In the sections that follow, we summarize some of the most germane patterns of student reasoning.

Unit Sense

One of the foundations of thinking about rational numbers as measured quantities is a sense of the properties of the unit of measure. We probed this indirectly by asking students to make sense of a situation where ⅓ KM > ½ RT. Most (81 percent) suggested that the length of the KM unit must be longer than the length of the RT unit. Another suggested that KM and RT must be different units. Two students depicted lengths where ½ RT > ⅓ KM, because ½ > ⅓. The remaining student suggested a whole-number bias, reporting that 3 > 2, so that ⅓ > ½.

Equivalence and Density

The Meaning of Equivalence

Showing students a unit length, we asked how ¼ unit and ⅜ unit were alike and different. Students (95 percent) generally suggested that the expressions were alike because they were located at the same point from zero (e.g., "Both on the same box (marked distance)" and "same amount of length, eighth has more parts than the fourth," or were the same because four iterations of each would result in one unit). Many noted a relation through one: "¼ × ⅛ is ⅜, so they could be equivalent," and "Dividing ⅜ by ½ would give you ¼, so they're equivalent." An exceptional student, who also responded that 3 > 2 in the question about unit sense, suggested that ⅜ was smaller than ¼, apparently focusing on his recall of the difference between four and eight equipartitions of the same unit of length.

The Role of the Unit

To probe students' conceptions of the role of one unit in creating equivalence, students explained why $\frac{4}{4} \times \frac{2}{4}$ cm resulted in an equivalent, $\frac{8}{16}$ cm. Most (67 percent) suggested that the case was an example of a more general principle of multiplying by one and suggested other potential cases, such as $\frac{5}{5}$ and even x/x. All but one of the remaining students interpreted the question as an invitation to verify the result, suggesting, for example, that $\frac{8}{16}$ could be divided by $\frac{4}{4}$ to restore the original measure.

Density of Rational Number

We asked, "How many fractions could be between $\frac{2}{4}$ and $\frac{3}{4}$? Why do you think so?" Forty-three percent suggested that there were an infinite number, "just keep going forever," and prototypically implicated continued partitioning as the process that would result in this infinite collection. Another 43 percent suggested a finite number, generally obtained by composing two-splits or by appeal to specific cases, such as $2\frac{1}{2}/4$. Three students did not believe that there could be any fractions between $\frac{2}{4}$ and $\frac{3}{4}$. One appeared to interpret the problem as meaning that the unit of measure was a fourth, so that it made no sense to propose other fractional quantities.

Operational Sense

We posed a series of problems involving the arithmetic operations of addition, multiplication, and division. The problems were posed with unit lengths, and we asked students to demonstrate how the results they obtained would be found by transforming the unit strips.

Addition

Students solved a problem involving incommensurate measures of $\frac{1}{3}$ unit + $\frac{1}{2}$ unit. Most students (95 percent) interpreted addition as joining three-split and two-split partitioned strips, and the majority of the class (71 percent) developed a commensurate measure of $\frac{5}{6}$ unit or $\frac{10}{12}$ unit by using factors, common multiples, or literal partitions of the strips. Two students who did not develop commensurate measure estimated that the result would be "a little less than one," indicating sense making, and a third student found a common partition of sixths but did not think to generate equivalences. One student considered the problem as requiring addition across the numerators and denominators to obtain a result of $\frac{2}{5}$ and shaded in about $\frac{2}{5}$ of one unit strip.

Multiplication

Students considered three cases. The first consisted of a unit fraction scalar and a unit less than one: $\frac{1}{2} \times \frac{1}{2}$ unit. All but one student composed two two–splits of the unit length to obtain a result of $\frac{1}{4}$ unit. One student interpreted the problem as addition and generated the result of one unit. The second case involved a non–unit scalar and a unit less than one: $\frac{2}{3} \times \frac{1}{2}$ unit. Most students (86 percent) generated $\frac{2}{6}$ unit or $\frac{1}{3}$ unit, some by three–splitting the $\frac{1}{2}$ unit, some by two–splitting the $\frac{2}{3}$ unit. As they solved the problem, it was clear that some students needed the visual support of the material units to keep track of the unit relations. For example, one student initially two–split the unit, three–split the resulting $\frac{1}{2}$ unit, and then counted two of the three–splits of the $\frac{1}{2}$ unit, responding that the result was $\frac{2}{3}$, but, when asked about the original unit, he quickly said $\frac{1}{3}$ unit. The third case consisted of a scalar multiple greater than one and a unit less than one: $\frac{3}{2} \times \frac{1}{4}$ DM. Students could either use the strips provided, or, at this point, if they seemed to have a firm grounding, we proceeded algorithmically. An audiotape problem resulted in the loss of data from one student, but of the remaining 20, 75 percent obtained a result of $\frac{3}{8}$ unit, and when probed, justified, "That is 1 and $\frac{1}{2}$ of the $\frac{1}{4}$ unit." One student who did not obtain $\frac{3}{8}$ unit nevertheless suggested that the result would be about $\frac{1}{3}$ by estimating a little more than one iteration of $\frac{1}{4}$ unit.

Division

Students considered four cases. The first case consisted of a whole–unit measure divided by a partitioned unit less than one: 2 unit/$\frac{1}{2}$ unit. One student was inadvertently not asked the questions in this section of the interview. Most students (75 percent) obtained a result of four, exemplified by "4 $\frac{1}{2}$ units in two units." Of these, two students initially said that they forgot how to do division, but a prompt to consider the meaning of division or to consider it as involving remeasuring sufficed to support the result of four. The other students either confounded division with multiplication or subtraction or generated a strategy that we could not reliably classify. The second case consisted of a measure less than one divided by another unit less than one: $\frac{3}{4}$ unit/$\frac{1}{2}$ unit. Approximately 74 percent of the students generated results of $1\frac{1}{2}$. The unit relation generating this response was typified by one student as: "You have $1\frac{1}{4}$ (referring to iterating the $\frac{1}{2}$ unit as the unit of measure), but since the half is your whole, $\frac{1}{4}$ is half a half, so your answer would be one and a half." In contrast, a student who did not coordinate this unit relation said: "Here's your fourth and you're trying to find three of them, so then you're gonna remeasure in half, so it would be one half and then . . . so it would be one and a one half and a fourth." We interpret this student's last response as reverting to the original unit of measure, instead of the two–unit structure implied by $1\frac{1}{2}$. The third case consisted of a non–whole number measure greater than one divided by another unit less than one: $\frac{3}{2}$ unit/$\frac{3}{4}$ unit.

Most (82 percent) students used the strip units to arrive at a result of two via a strategy of rescaling. The last case consisted of a partitioned unit less than one divided by a whole-number unit: ½ unit/4 unit. Only 35 percent of the students were able to conceive of how the relation between the units could be employed to generate a result of ⅛. Many students found the inverse (eight), thinking about rescaling four with ½.

Reprise of Interview Results

The results of the clinical interview suggested that, months after instruction concluded, most students could use the measurement model to make sense of rational numbers. The results that appeared most robust were those about unit sense, equivalence as the same location along a numberline, relational thinking about equivalence, and understanding that the rational numberline was either finite (with some rational numbers between two landmarks) or was infinitely dense (the process of splitting implied no limit to packing rationals). A substantial majority of the class could employ the measurement model to interpret the meanings of the operations of multiplication, division, and addition. Some students who were unable to compute accurate results for these operators nonetheless used the measurement model to create reasonable estimates. Interpreting a fractional quantity divided by a whole number as shrinking the fractional quantity was challenging, perhaps because this problem was less visited during instruction as well.

Discussion

Metaphors are central to mathematics, and much of the arithmetic taught in the early years of schooling rests on what Lakoff and Nunez (2001) term the object collection metaphor. That is, numbers are regarded as representing counts of collections of things, and arithmetic operations on number are constituted in much the way that collections are constituted, such as joining two collections (addition) or separating elements of one collection from those of another (subtraction). Metaphoric projection of parts of collections results in part–whole conceptions of rational numbers, but students often confuse these rational numbers with whole numbers (Ni & Zhou, 2005).

To increase the intelligibility of rational numbers and operations on rational numbers for students, we engaged students in the development of measures of length. As we illustrated, this engagement supported two other metaphoric projections for arithmetic and rational number. The first, which Lakoff and Nunez (2001) aptly term the measuring stick metaphor, projects the experience of laying sticks or body parts, such as fingers and thumbs, end to end to measure a distance, so that every length then corresponds to a number, including rational and whole numbers (and also irrational numbers, such as the square root of two, which we do not treat here). We grounded the need for rational number in precision of measure, from which arose partitions and copy-iterations of units. These provided the means for considering measures as ratios of lengths. Unit relations were developed by coordinating partitions, units, and units-of-units as measurement scales.

The second metaphoric entailment afforded by measure was obtained by considering the lengths of the measure metaphor as potential trajectories of motion along a path. Hence, rational numbers could be considered as locations along a path of motion. And, rather than zero measure being regarded as a special case of absence of a ratio of lengths, zero was readily interpreted as the initial point of movement. By blending these metaphors, in principle, measure situated and made tractable important components of understanding of rational number, including iteration, splitting, equivalence, and unit-relations (Confrey and Smith, 1995, Steffe, 2002; Izsak, 2008).

Of course, principled rationality does not guarantee accessibility of an approach for students. However, the classroom conversations and activity during the course of this study, and the results obtained from the flexible interviews, indicated that the measure metaphor helped make rational number intelligible to students in two ways. For students who originally manifested many of the conceptions consistent with whole-number bias, the practical activity of measure provided a way to understand what had been a bewildering array of part–whole models and buggy rules for operating on fractions. Partitioning units, iterating partitioned units, and traveling partitioned-unit distances set the stage for considering relations among equivalent fractions, so that equivalence meant identical location but *not* identical measure. We emphasized the importance of motion along with the more traditional emphasis on iteration: we often noticed students finding an improper fraction such as ⅔ sensible when they viewed it as the result of a motion, indexed by an iteration, rather than as a static entity. As suggested by Lakoff and Nunez (2001), metaphoric blends are often critical for developing mathematical systems. The blend of motion and iteration appeared especially helpful for resolving apparent contradictions with previous whole-number learning, such as "multiplication makes more."

For students who were higher performing on statewide tests, the measurement model provided a way to establish a dialectic between conceptual and procedural knowledge, so that their activity became mathematical instead of only computational. As we mentioned, this re-orientation toward mathematics as meaning making represented an epistemic shift, and students appeared increasingly to enjoy the parry and thrust of argument opened by a shift toward sense making. We took this as an indicator of the development of mathematical disposition (Boaler, 2002). As suggested by Gresalfi (2009), shifts in disposition emerge when students are positioned to engage in sense-making practices, such as offering explanations and evaluating claims made by others, for prolonged periods of time. For instance, Helen's initial, exclusive focus on procedural knowledge and authority was gradually eroded by her growing awareness of the opportunities lost by exclusive reliance on sanctioned computation on the one hand (e.g., where were those units of area measure that she had learned to calculate in earlier years?) and by the opportunities generated by considering familiar results as problematic (e.g., what was the basis for claims that two fractions were equivalent?). Yet we doubt that simply relying on sense making would have been sufficient: The tasks and material embodiments of the measurement model, coupled with instruction intended to convey disciplinary values and forms of argument, co-constituted the grounds on which student activity could conceivably result in a transition in what Gee (2011) terms a "Discourse." A discourse marks a cultural accomplishment of talking and performing in a certain way. As such, student discourses were marked by hybrids of (their) historic ways of talking mathematics, oriented toward results and sanctioned rules, and an emerging alternative, oriented toward explanations and construction of relations between concepts and procedures. We supported naturalization of this alternative discourse in the classroom.

It is clear that the measurement model, while affording many opportunities for productive engagement with rational number, was not a panacea. Students often lost track of unit relations, although we supported this form of coordination by developing specialized language and measurement-scale interpretations of levels of units. The students' prior experiences with mathematical symbolization had to be recast in a new light, and putting old notational systems to new uses was often problematic, as the symbolization seemed to cue once again considering a fraction as a part of a whole. The trajectory of coordinating relations among linguistic forms, notational systems, and measurement models would likely look substantially different for students with a different prior history of education. The measurement model also has a few entailments for considering rational number that are perhaps not easily reconciled with worlds where numbers are considered as collections of objects (Lakoff & Nunez, 2001). For example, a scalar multiple of a measure distinguishes between a scalar and a quantity measured in units: 2×3 units represents a twofold dilation of a length with a measure of three units, or, alternatively, as two iterations of a length with a measure of three units. A product of two unit lengths results not in a length, but in an area. These distinctions are not important to collections, but they are critical to numbers as measured quantities.

The common standards in mathematics (www.corestandards.org, accessed August 5, 2011) specify that students become familiar with the underpinning of rational number, especially partitioning, iteration, equivalence, and location on a numberline, by the end of the elementary years of schooling. This is a laudable goal that perhaps suggests the need for alternative teaching approaches. Although future design studies are necessary to test further our conjectures about the fruitfulness of the conceptual blend of rigid stick and motion metaphors of measure as a viable pathway for developing conceptions of rational number, we are sufficiently encouraged by this first iteration to pursue further cycles of design.

References

Barth, H., Baron, A., Spelke, E., & Carey, S. (2009). Children's multiplicative transformations of discrete and continuous quantities. *Journal of Experimental Child Psychology, 103*(4), 441–454.

Boaler, J. (2002). *Experiencing school mathematics*. Mahwah, NJ: Erlbaum.

Brown, A. L. (1992). Design experiments: Theoretical and methodological challenges in creating complex interventions in classroom settings. *Journal of the Learning Sciences, 2,* 141–178.

Confrey, J. (1994). Splitting, similarity, and rate of change. In G. Harel & J. Confrey (Eds.), *The development of multiplicative reasoning in the learning of mathematics* (pp. 291–330). Albany, NY: SUNY Press.

Confrey, J., & Smith, E. (1995). Splitting, covariation and their role in the development of exponential functions. *Journal for Research in Mathematics Education, 26*(1), 66–86.

Crosby, A. W. (1997) *The measure of reality: Quantification and Western society, 1250–1600*. Cambridge, UK: Cambridge University Press.

Gee, J. P. (2011). *How to do discourse analysis. A toolkit.* New York: Routledge.

Gesalfi, M. S. (2009). Taking up opportunities to learn: Constructing dispositions in mathematics classrooms. *Journal of the Learning Sciences, 18,* 327–369.

Hackenberg, A. J. (2007). Units coordination and the construction of improper fractions: A revision of the splitting hypothesis. *Journal of Mathematical Behavior, 26,* 27–47.

Izsak, A. (2008). Mathematical knowledge for teaching fraction multiplication. *Cognition & Instruction, 26,* 95–143.

Izsak, A., Orrill, C. H., Cohen, A. S., & Brown, R. E. (2010). Measuring middle grades teachers' understanding of rational numbers with the mixture Rasch model. *Elementary School Journal, 110,* 279–300.

Lakoff, G., & Nunez, R. (2001). *Where mathematics comes from: How the embodied mind brings mathematics into being.* New York: Basic Books.

Latour, B. (1999). *Pandora's hope: Essays on the reality of science studies.* Cambridge, MA: Harvard University Press.

Lehrer, R. (2003). Developing understanding of measurement. In J. Kilpatrick, W. G. Martin, & D. E. Schifter (Eds.), *A research companion to principles and standards for school mathematics* (pp. 179–192). Reston, VA: National Council of Teachers of Mathematics.

Lehrer, R. (2009). Designing to develop disciplinary knowledge: Modeling natural systems. *American Psychologist, 64*(8), 759–771.

Lehrer, R., & Schauble, L. (2006). Cultivating model-based reasoning in science education. In R. Keith Sawyer (Ed.), *Cambridge handbook of the learning of sciences* (pp. 371–387). Cambridge University Press.

Lehrer, R., Jacobson, C., Kemeny, V., & Strom, D. (1999). Building on children's intuitions to develop mathematical understanding of space. In E. Fennema & T. A. Romberg (Eds.), *Mathematics classrooms that promote understanding* (pp. 63–87). Mahwah, NJ: Lawrence Erlbaum Associates.

Lehrer, R., Jaslow, L., & Curtis, C. (2003). Developing understanding of measurement in the elementary grades. In D. H. Clements & G. Bright (Eds.), *Learning and teaching measurement. 2003 Yearbook* (pp. 100–121). Reston, VA: National Council of Teachers of Mathematics.

Mack, N. K. (1995). Confounding whole-number and fraction concepts when building on informal knowledge. *Journal for Research in Mathematics Education, 26*(5), 422–441.

Ni, Y., & Zhou, Y. (2005). Teaching and learning fraction and rational numbers: The origins and implications of whole number bias. *Educational Psychologist, 40*(1), 27–52.

Smith, J., & Thompson, P.W. (2007). Quantitative reasoning and the development of algebraic reasoning. In J. J. Kaput, D. W. Carraher, & M. L. Blanton (Eds.), *Algebra in the early grades* (pp. 95–132). New York: Erlbaum.

Steffe, L. (2002). A new hypothesis concerning children's fractional knowledge. *Journal of Mathematical Behavior, 20,* 267–307.

Steffe, L. (2004). On the construction of learning trajectories of children: The case of commensurate fractions. *Mathematical Thinking and Learning, 6*(2), 129–162.

Thompson, P. W. (1993). Quantitative reasoning, complexity and additive structures. *Educational Studies in Mathematics, 25,* 165–208.

Thompson, P. W., & Saldanha, L. (2003). Fractions and multiplicative reasoning. In J. Kilpatrick, G. Martin, & D. Schifter (Eds.), *Research companion to the principles and standards for school mathematics.* Reston, VA: National Council of Teachers of Mathematics.

Thompson, P. W., & Thompson, A. (1994). Talking about rates conceptually, Part A: A teacher's struggle. *Journal for Research in Mathematics Education, 25*(3), 279–303.

van Fraassen, B. C. (2008). *Scientific representation.* Oxford: Oxford University Press.

7

THE PRODUCTIVE DISCIPLINARY ENGAGEMENT FRAMEWORK

Origins, Key Concepts, and Developments

Randi A. Engle

Origins

The 1990s were a time of innovation in education in the United States. New visions of teaching and learning in the disciplines were being proposed in policy documents (e.g., American Association for the Advancement of Science (AAAS), 1990; California State Department of Education, 1985; National Center for History in the Schools, 1996; National Council of Teachers of Mathematics (NCTM), 1991; National Research Council (NRC), 1996; National Science Foundation, 1997), and corresponding curricula and instructional methods were being developed in classrooms across the country. In addition, new theoretical frameworks were being actively explored to provide alternatives to the then-predominant cognitive perspective, including sociocultural perspectives (Cole, 1998; Rogoff, 1990), situative perspectives (Greeno, 1989, 1991; Lave, 1988; Lave & Wenger, 1991), distributed cognition (Hutchins, 1995), and activity theory (Engeström, 1987).

At the same time, a new way of doing educational research was emerging (Brown, 1992; Collins, 1992). Researchers, teachers, and other educational stakeholders were collaborating to iteratively design and research innovative learning environments that were providing proof that much more sophisticated forms of teaching and learning could be created than had been previously thought possible (e.g., Collins, Joseph, & Bielaczyc, 2004; D'Amico, 2006, 2010; Design-based Research Collective, 2003; diSessa & Cobb, 2004). These projects, variously called "design experiments," "design research," "problem-solving research and development," or "design–based research" (the term I will use here, see Hoadley,

2002 for justification), were developing and refining lists of "design principles" that were intended to capture the key theoretical ideas underlying these innovative learning environments while providing guidance for others to being able to recreate them elsewhere.

One key design-based research project at the forefront of this effort was the Fostering Communities of Learners (FCL) project led by Ann Brown and Joseph Campione (1990, 1994, 1996). Building on Brown's earlier successful collaboration with Annemarie Palincsar on reciprocal teaching (e.g., Brown & Palincsar, 1984) and Brown's and Campione's laboratory work on the transfer of learning (e.g., Brown, 1989; Brown, Kane, & Eccols, 1986; Campione & Brown, 1984; Campione, Brown, Ferrara, Jones, & Steinberg, 1985), Brown and Campione extended methods for supporting students' comprehension of informational texts to create a series of classroom designs that fostered students' learning about rich disciplinary content while also supporting students' discourse production and comprehension more generally. In one of a series of influential papers, Brown and Campione (1994) provided striking findings to show that elementary-school students in FCL classrooms showed improvement across the board, whether one wanted to measure basic reading comprehension, or academic discourse practices, or conceptual understanding, as compared with several different comparison classrooms. In addition, they provided an especially influential account of their design-based research methodology as "design experiments" (Brown, 1992). They also provided compelling explanations of how FCL classrooms worked, given constructivist and Vygotskian theories, research on the transfer of learning, and more (Brown & Campione, 1990; Brown et al., 1993; Brown & Campione, 1996; Brown, Metz, & Campione, 1996; Campione, Shapiro, & Brown, 1995). For example, Brown and Campione (1996) provided a compelling argument that FCL's success depended not on following a set of particular procedures, but instead on designing a system of interacting activities to realize a set of underlying "principles of learning," or what came to be called "design principles" (see Zhang, this volume, for more discussion). Soon, design-based projects around the country and the world were each specifying their own design principles.

At a conference commemorating Brown's legacy, the cognitive developmental psychologist Rochel Gelman (2001) posed a challenge to the design-based research community. She noted that the specific design principles being proposed by various projects curiously made little reference to each other, despite the fact that many investigators were in regular communication with each other. She was concerned that teachers, policymakers, research funders, and other key educational stakeholders would conclude that design-based research was diffuse and uncoordinated, and she urged the design-based research community to start coming to a consensus on at least a small set of agreed-upon principles for supporting effective learning environments.

It was in this larger context that the Productive Disciplinary Engagement (PDE) framework (Engle & Conant, 2002) was born. Faith Conant and I wrote it with an eye to providing an initial response to Gelman's challenge, by making explicit one key educational goal and a set of general core principles for achieving that goal, which we thought the design-based and mathematics and science education reform community would be likely to share. As then-emerging researchers in these fields, we had participated as legitimate peripheral participants (Lave & Wenger, 1991) in three of the key projects—FCL, Chèche Konnen (Rosebery, Warren & Conant, 1992; Conant, Rosebery, Warren, & Hudicourt-Barnes, 2001), and the Middle-school Mathematics through Applications Project (Greeno et al., 1999; Engle, 2010)—as well as in some conversations among these and other projects. Thus, we were in a particularly good position to crystallize an initial proposal of one set of general principles that would be likely to be shared among the larger community.

Our proposed principles were grounded in a detailed study of how a disciplinary discussion "took off" in two FCL classrooms (Frederick Erickson, personal communication, 1998; see Engle, Conant & Greeno, 2007). Ideas for how to conceptualize them were drawn from a wide range of existing literature from various reform-oriented teaching experiments and design-based research projects. The principles were further developed and generalized through re-analyses of additional cases of PDE from two contrasting learning environments: the Water Taste Test from the Chèche Konnen project (Rosebery, Warren, & Conant, 1992) and several investigations of the Japanese Hypothesis–Experiment–Instruction method (also known as the Itakura method after its founder; e.g., Hatano & Inagaki, 1991; Inagaki, Hatano, & Morita, 1998; Wertsch & Toma, 1995). Thus, the goal of Engle and Conant (2002) was to abstract principles that could apply across learning environments in ways that could inform both the design of a wide range of new learning environments as well as research about existing ones. Our assumption was that this would not be the last word. Our hope was to spark further discussion among the design-based research community about the principles we do and do not share.

In this chapter, I take this opportunity to further clarify the key concepts of the PDE framework, review some of the most central research that has drawn upon and developed it, and outline directions for further development of it and the larger enterprise in which it is embedded.

Key Concepts

Productive Disciplinary Engagement

To anchor the proposed principles of our framework, we focused on explaining a phenomenon characteristic of many of the newly designed learning environments: students' deep involvement in, and progress on, concepts and/or practices characteristic of the discipline they were learning about, which Conant and I dubbed PDE. The original article and research that has followed have showed that the degree and nature of PDE can be empirically investigated by separately considering evidence for: engagement; the disciplinary basis of that engagement; and the productivity of that disciplinary engagement (e.g., Duschl, Schweingruber, & Shouse, 2007, Foo & Looi, 2008; Hodge, Visnovska, Zhao, & Cobb, 2007; Mortimer & Oliveira, 2009; Venturini & Amade-Escot, 2009).

In the PDE framework, each of these three constructs is defined flexibly in order to aid in its application to a wide range of potential learning environments (Foo & Looi, 2008). At the same time, it is important in any given research investigation or educational design effort that these purposely skeletal definitions be fleshed out in ways that are explicitly responsive to one's goals and values, as well as the particular learners one is working with. In the subsections below I will provide both the skeletal definition for each construct that comprises PDE and examples of ways they have been fleshed out in research.

Engagement

We defined engagement in terms of aspects of learners' participation that can be directly accessed by researchers and practitioners. Specifically, a group of learners is more engaged to the extent that more of them are participating in an interaction, that participation has greater intensity, and each learner's participation is responsive to that of others. However, in the original paper, we cautioned that the specific measures of engagement used when fleshing out this definition need to appreciate the fact that "expressions of engagement are both culturally relative and subject to interpretation" (p. 402). Thus, what counts as "more intense" engagement or as "responsiveness" may vary depending on the cultural and other communities a student is a member of, and one should not assume that silence necessarily indicates lack of participation. Depending on one's goals and the unit of analysis, one may wish to have a single set of measures of engagement for everyone, or customize them for students from different backgrounds.

Conant and I needed to flesh out this definition to capture the degree of collective engagement of a heterogeneous group of students. Because there are no universally agreed-upon standards for what counts as "high" versus "low" engagement, to support our claim that these students were highly engaged in one particular topic, we compared the degree of the students' engagement in that topic as compared with other topics during comparable segments of interaction. We then decided to triangulate the following six different operational measures of engagement, each of which we expected would be most relevant to different subsets of the students:

(a) More students in the group sought to make, and made, substantive contributions to the topic under discussion.

(b) Students' contributions were more often made in coordination with each other, rather than independently of each other (Barron, 2000; Chi, Siler, Jeong, Yamauchi, & Hausmann, 2001).

(c) Few students were involved in unrelated 'off-task' activities.

(d) Students were attending to each other as assessed by alignment of eye gaze and body positioning (McDermott, Gospodinoff, & Aron, 1978; Schultz, Florio, & Erickson, 1982).

(e) Students often expressed passionate involvement by making emotional displays (Tannen, 1989).

(f) Students spontaneously got reengaged in the topic and continued being engaged in it over a long period of time. (Engle & Conant, 2002, p. 402)

For example, we fleshed out measure (b) about coordination by examining the degree to which students overlapped each other's speech while collaboratively completing each other's ideas. Several subsequent investigations have used all or part of these operational definitions (e.g., Engle & Faux, 2006; Foo & Looi, 2008; Hodge et al., 2007; Scott, Mortimer, & Aguiar, 2006; Venturini & Amade-Escot, 2009).

Other investigators have provided useful adaptations and extensions of our definition of student engagement to fit other types of learning environment or learner. For example, Zhang, Scardamalia, Reeve, and Messina (2009) used techniques from Social Network Analysis (Wasserman & Faust, 1994) to precisely measure collective engagement in online discussions within Knowledge Forum (Scardamalia & Bereiter, 2006). Specifically, they operationalized the idea that there is greater engagement to the extent that learners are responsive to others (what they called the degree of "complementary contributions") by measuring: "the percentage of [online] notes linked by building on, rising above, or referencing other authors; the density of the online network in terms of who linked to whose notes; [and the number of] cliques are reflected in note linking" (p. 21). To make sense of the results, they also used a comparative approach, comparing these measures across several different years of implementation of Knowledge Forum (see Zhang, this volume).

With respect to measuring the engagement of learners from diverse communities, important work has been done by members of the Chèche Konnen project (Ballenger, 1997; Hudicourt-Barnes, 2003; Warren, Ballenger, Ogonowski, Rosebery, & Hudicourt-Barnes, 2001). In collaboration with teachers, these researchers specifically consider students' cultural backgrounds when constructing methods for measuring whether and how they were engaged. They work with teachers to help construct social contexts in which students' culturally normal ways of participating in discussions are allowed, which then provide opportunities for students to engage in science in ways that are consonant with their cultural practices. For example, one pair of teachers created the participation structure of "science circle" that provided a space for their Haitian Creole students to share observations and argue about claims in ways similar to the forms of argumentative discussion common in Haitian communities (Hudicourt-Barnes, 2003; Warren et al., 2001). In so doing, they avoid formal questioning methods that discourage these and many other students from participating, which leads to under-measuring student engagement.

Disciplinary Engagement

However, just because students are genuinely engaged in some task or activity does not mean that they are engaged with the disciplinary issues, if any, that can be potentially drawn out of it (e.g., Blumenfeld, Megendoller, & Puro, 1992; Lamon et al., 1996; Pugh, Linnenbrink-Garcia, Koskey, Stewart, & Manzey, 2010). As we defined it, for engagement to be "disciplinary," there must be "some contact between what students are doing and the issues and practices of a discipline's discourse" (Engle & Conant, 2002, p. 402). We purposely kept the definition open as we were and are well aware of deep controversies about what does and does not count as "authentic" work in various disciplines (e.g., Chinn & Malhotra, 2002; Collins, Brown, & Newman, 1989; Ford & Forman, 2006; Lampert, 1992), as well as the degree to which it makes sense to embody disciplinary practices into school-based instruction, given differences in institutional positioning, societal purposes, desired outcomes, temporal horizons, prior experiences, and other constraints (e.g., Ball, 1993; Palincsar, 1989; Wineberg, 1989). To take a general principled position on those two interconnected, ongoing debates would be counterproductive. Instead, our wish is that researchers, teachers, and designers ask themselves what (if anything) is "disciplinary" about students' engagement within the learning environments they are analyzing or creating.

In our analyses of the FCL case, Conant and I argued repeatedly about the degree to which the students' engagement did and did not legitimately embody disciplinary characteristics, and if so what those might be. This resulted in a mixed evaluation in which we stated that our case was not meant to be a "model" (Engle & Conant, 2002, p. 422) of disciplinary engagement, but that the students,

> made contact with disciplinary issues and practices . . . [by being] attuned to an important value in scientific and scholarly work [that] claims need to be supported by evidence . . . [and by having] the content of the debate focused on issues and used types of evidence recognizably related to bio-logical discourse about classification. (p. 420)

This was by no means everything most educators would like students to learn about science, let alone biology, but it was also not completely disconnected from disciplinary practices either. Several other authors have followed suit, clearly specifying which aspects of a given discipline particular cases of engagement made contact with (e.g., Cornelius & Herrenkohl, 2004; Foo & Looi, 2008; Leinhardt & Steele, 2005; Scott et al., 2006; Venturini & Amade-Escot, 2009).

In general, then, our hope was that the framework would spark further discussion of what counts as "disciplinary" in particular cases and perhaps, eventually, in general. Given that, we appreciate Ford and Forman's (2006) work to use the Science Studies literature to facilitate such disciplinary analyses for engagement in science more generally. In particular, their characterization of disciplinary practice in science as including social, material, and rhetorical practices is both grounded in prior work and eminently useful in particular cases. Still, we expect that such analyses will always need to be customized, given the particular topics and subdisciplines involved in a given case of disciplinary engagement.

Productive Disciplinary Engagement

There is a similar commitment to keeping legitimately debatable issues open for debate in how to define whether a case of disciplinary engagement is "productive." My current definition is that there is productivity if one can discern "significant disciplinary progress from [the] beginning to end" of students' engagement with a particular issue (Engle, 2007a, p. 215). "What constitutes productivity depends on the discipline, the specific task and topic, and where students are when they begin addressing a problem" (Engle & Conant, 2002, p. 403).

In the FCL case, Conant and I found that, although the students did not reach a resolution consistent with current disciplinary thinking, students raised new disciplinary questions and made their arguments more sophisticated. In the Chèche Konnen case, Rosebery, Warren, and Conant (1992) showed that students were productive in that their scientific investigations led to them rejecting some of their original assumptions while also producing new knowledge. In the hypothesis–experiment–instruction method, in contrast, disciplinary progress was represented by students both becoming aware of the disciplinarily correct answer and having well-developed reasons for accepting it. "In other situations, such productivity might involve things like recognizing a confusion, making a new connection among ideas, or designing something to satisfy a goal" (Engle & Conant, 2002, p. 403). Foo and Looi (2008) documented a case of what could be considered productivity in disciplinary practices as students shifted, over time, from simply sharing individual ideas with each other to comparing, challenging, and eventually synthesizing them. Thus, it is up to particular analysts to characterize and argue for what types of disciplinary progress, if any, are characteristic of the cases they are analyzing.

Thus, it is in grappling with, and arguing about, what counts as "engagement," as "disciplinary," and as "progress" in particular cases that the notion of PDE has its power. To try to fully define these constructs ahead of time would be a futile exercise that would limit the usefulness of the framework and short-circuit the discussions we, as a field and as a society, need to keep having about what kinds of engagement count, which particular aspects of disciplines should be incorporated into learning environments, and what kinds of progress we are hoping learners will make with their engagement with academic disciplines. Still, dividing the notion of PDE into its constituent parts provides a helpful framework for structuring such critically important discussions.

Four Principles for Fostering Productive Disciplinary Engagement

Having identified the phenomenon of PDE as one that many of the newer learning environments were working to foster, Conant and I turned to what I consider to be our major contribution, which was synthesizing a set of four general principles for supporting it. For purposes of doing research, these principles collectively function as four sets of explanatory factors that need to be specified to construct an explanation for a given case of PDE or lack thereof (Duschl, 2006). By themselves, principles at this level of generality cannot capture everything that is important or unique about a particular learning environment (Scardamalia & Bereiter, 2007), but they do provide a helpful structure for constructing explanations about how PDE is supported in it. For purposes of guiding educational design efforts, these principles function in Windschitl and Thompson's (2006, p. 826) terms as "a 'top-level' organizer for thinking about instruction" that then crucially needs to be fleshed out into traditional design principles for a particular type of learning environment, and then further specified into specific curriculum materials and instructional practices (Ametller, Leach, & Scott, 2007; Tzou, 2006).

Whether designing a new learning environment or analyzing an existing case, the empirical prediction is that all four of these principles need to be embodied to some extent in a learning environment if some form of PDE is to occur. Moreover, the particular nature of the PDE that occurs will be crucially affected by exactly how the principles are embodied.

Problematizing

The first principle for fostering PDE recognizes that there must be something connected to the discipline for learners to become engaged in. It draws on Hiebert et al.'s (1996) notion of "problematizing," which itself drew on Dewey's (1910, 1929) notions of how to support reflective inquiry through engendering "perplexity, confusion, or doubt" (Dewey, 1910, p. 12). In our current use (Engle & Adiredja, 2008, in preparation), problematizing is any individual or collective action that encourages disciplinary uncertainties (Zaslavsky, 2005) to be taken up by students (see Figure 7.1). A learning environment embodies the principle of problematizing to the extent that learners are encouraged to address problems (broadly construed) that simultaneously:

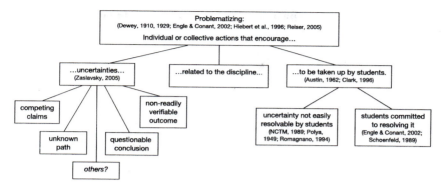

FIGURE 7.1 Process definition of problematizing (generalized from Engle & Adiredja, in preparation).

(a) engender genuine uncertainty in those particular learners, making the problems genuinely problematic to and not easily resolvable by them (e.g., Dewey, 1910, 1929; Leinhardt & Steele, 2005; Polya, 1949/1980; Romagnano, 1994; Zaslavsky, 2005);

(b) are in some way responsive to the learners' own commitments, whether based on interest, extrinsic motivations, or other reasons for learners to care to address the problems (e.g., Hiebert et al., 1996, 1997; Kuhn & Reiser, 2006; Reiser, 2004; Renninger, 2007, 2009; Schoenfeld, 1989); and

(c) in some way embody "big ideas" or other central aspects of the discipline in question, which does not necessarily need to be apparent to the learners themselves when prompted to become engaged in them (e.g., AAAS, 1990; Leinhardt & Steele, 2005; NCTM, 1991; NRC, 1996).

In particular—and here I am adapting a set of very helpful distinctions made by Zaslavsky (2005)—there are at least four kinds of uncertainty that can be aroused by successful problematizing: uncertainty about what to do, uncertainty about what to conclude, uncertainty about how to justify what one is doing or concluding, and uncertainty caused by competing alternatives about any of the three prior issues (Engle & Adiredja, 2008, in preparation). This means, therefore, that prompting an argument is not the only way to problematize the content. For example, problematizing can also be achieved by asking learners to design something new (Barron et al., 1998; Engle, 2006, 2008; Hall & Stevens, 1995). This is true, as in such cases it is often unclear exactly what the final design should look like or how to go about creating or justifying it.

In all cases, problematizing is viewed as a necessary (but not sufficient) principle that would be need to embodied in some way in a learning environment if PDE is to occur. Having some disciplinary content problematized is necessary for students to have something disciplinary that they choose to become engaged in and for which there is sufficient space for them to make substantive progress. This definition and discussion of problematizing is consistent with what Conant and I originally intended, but was not laid out nearly so clearly as we do here.

Authority

However, if students are to become truly engaged in such problems, rather than simply going through the motions of acting as if they are engaged, then it is also necessary that students have at least some degree of intellectual authority. They need to be allowed and encouraged to intellectually engage with, and be responsible for, the problems as themselves.

We claim that there are at least four kinds of intellectual authority that build upon each other: intellectual agency, authorship, contributorship, and, finally, being positioned as a local authority (see Figure 7.2). The first crucial, but most minimal, level of authority is having *intellectual agency* (Cobb, Gravemeijer, Yackel, McClain, & Whitenack, 1997; Lampert, 1990a, 1990b; Stipek et al., 1998). Learners have intellectual agency when they are "authorized" to share what they actually think about the problem in focus, rather than feeling the need to come up with a response that they may or may not believe in, but that matches what some other authority, such as a teacher or textbook, would say is correct (e.g., Hutchison & Hammer, 2010; Lamon et al., 1996; Lehrer, Carpenter, Schauble, & Putz, 2000; Magnusson & Palincsar, 1995; Scardamalia, Bereiter, & Lamon, 1994). Learners' authority is then strengthened if they become publicly recognized as authors of their own ideas, what I now refer to as *authorship* (Lampert, 1990a, 1990b; O'Connor & Michaels, 1996; Toma, 1991; Wertsch & Toma, 1995).[1] The next form of strengthening is *contributorship*, or when a learner's authoring influences the ideas of others in his or her learning environment and beyond (Schwartz, 1999; cf. Engle, Langer-Osuna, & McKinney de Royston, 2011). Finally, the strongest level of authority that a learner can have is to become socially recognized as an *authority* about some topic(s), which occurs gradually as his or her ideas become increasingly influential with others (Brown et al., 1993; Engle, Langer-Osuna, et al., 2010; Gresalfi, Martin, Hand, & Greeno, 2009).[2] Positioning as an authority can gradually expand to encompass new topics and communities who recognize a given learner's authority over them. Thus, each form of authority crucially depends on the preceding ones.

I predict that the depth and extent of a learner's engagement in a given disciplinary issue will correlate with how far up this scale of authority a given learner or learning environment has traveled. That is, we will observe the most engagement if learners become positioned as authorities over relevant topics; the next most if they have opportunities to contribute to the ideas of others; somewhat less if they are only positioned as authors; and even less if they are merely given intellectual agency. The intuition here is that, as learners are positioned with

learners "authorized" to share what they *really* think

to become recognized as "authors" of those ideas

to become "contributors" to the ideas of others

to gradually develop into local "authorities" about something

FIGURE 7.2 Hypothesized process through which learner authority can be developed (adapted from Engle, 2007b).

increasing authority over a particular topic, they are increasingly expected, by themselves and others, to be able to engage knowledgably with it (Engle, 2006).

This authority can also expand so learners do not just have authority to resolve disciplinary issues brought to them by others, but also authority over problematizing disciplinary content in the first place (Greeno, in press). I would predict this would intensify learners' engagement even more, both because of their commitment to the issues as their own problems, but also because disciplinary content would be problematized more often if learners were also involved in initiating the process. Still, even in cases in which only intellectual agency is supported, one should see learners being engaged as themselves rather than simply acting the part. In contrast, in situations in which learners are simply talked about as if they were authors, contributors, and/or authorities, but they are actually expected to serve merely as enthusiastic spokespersons for others' ideas, we would expect to see evidence of mock engagement, an elaborate performance designed to satisfy others and external constraints, but that would not necessarily involve learners developing their own ideas.

Accountability

Although designing a learning environment in which disciplinarily connected issues are problematized and making sure that students have at least a modicum of true authority may be necessary to foster authentic engagement that is at least somewhat disciplinary, it is not sufficient if learners' engagement is going to be as disciplinarily grounded and productive as it could be. With untrammeled authority, there is a very real danger that some learners will act as authorities unto themselves, developing all kinds of unsubstantiated ideas and inappropriately dominating conversations (e.g., Brown et al., 1993; Engle, Langer-Osuna, et al., 2011; Esmonde & Langer-Osuna, in press).

To address these dangers, learners' authority needs to be balanced by a particular type of accountability (Cobb et al., 1997; Engle & Conant, 2002; Ford, 2008; Lerner & Tetlock, 1999; Michaels, O'Connor, & Resnick, 2007; Warren & Rosebery, 1996; Scott et al., 2006). By accountability, we are taking the root of the word seriously and referring to a norm developed within a learning environment that learners are responsible for regularly "accounting" for how their ideas make sense, given the relevant work of others. "Others" is defined broadly to include one's peers, oneself at other times (cf. Mead, 1913), local and outside disciplinary authorities, and the discipline itself.

Our hypothesis was that being expected to explain why one's ideas make sense, given the relevant ideas of others, will provide the social conditions that will prompt learners to revise their ideas for the better. Being held accountable to oneself provides a push for greater internal intellectual coherence that can, by itself, lead to progress in a learner's substantive engagement, making it more productive. Being held accountable for explaining how one's own ideas make sense in the light of other people's ideas treats those ideas as substantive resources for revising, refining, and/or better defending one's own. Finally, being held accountable to the discipline fosters further disciplinary engagement by encouraging learners to regularly consider how their ideas and disciplinary ideas do and do not make sense in light of each other.

However, as Conant and I emphasized, if PDE is to be fostered, accountability needs to be kept in balance with authority. With learners who are not used to having true intellectual authority, initial efforts to hold them accountable to the discipline can often be misinterpreted as a message that their nascent authority is not valued and can lead to them revert to the common, school-based game of guessing what it is that the teacher or some other expert (such as a peer who everyone thinks is smart) would like them to say (e.g., Engle & Faux, 2006; Esmonde, 2009; Hamm & Perry, 2002). In this common situation, it is important to firmly establish students' intellectual agency before making major efforts to foster accountability. Practical ways of doing so include providing initial assignments in which students are graded for the degree to which they elaborate and explain their starting ideas, rather than the degree to which those ideas are already canonically correct, and responding with respectful, substantive interest whenever students appear to be genuinely sharing what they really think about a topic, especially when this involves going beyond or even challenging what teacher or text has provided.

In addition, in such situations, I believe it is wise to gradually establish accountability from the inside out (see Figure 7.3), in ways very similar to Lampert's (1992, p. 299) "continuum of justification" from more "private" to more "public" arenas. First, ask such learners to explain how their ideas make sense to themselves, then to safe peers who they do not feel intellectually intimidated by, then to more challenging peers, and finally to recognized authorities in the local learning environment and beyond (Engle, 2004; Engle & Faux, 2006). At each step

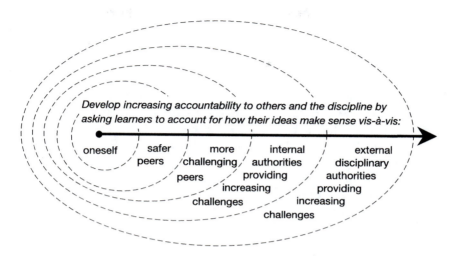

FIGURE 7.3 The inside–out accountability development hypothesis for learners not accustomed to having intellectual authority.

in being held accountable, learners improve their ideas so they are ready to be challenged more thoroughly at the next step, but without giving up on their own ideas to simply mimic those of already existing authorities. If timed well, learners will be in a position to evaluate their own (now much more well-developed) ideas and those of authorities in light of each other, revising them accordingly (Engle, 2004).

Two design-based research projects provide initial empirical evidence for the merits of this trajectory for developing learners' accountability without jeopardizing their intellectual authority. In one, an instructor of educational psychology, who in one course iteration squelched students' authority and genuine engagement in disciplinary issues by asking for accountability to the best ideas in the discipline right away, was able to fix the problem by following the inside–out trajectory, so that students gradually were held more accountable to the discipline over time, once their intellectual authority had been established (Engle & Faux, 2006). In the other, an instructor followed the inside–out trajectory of gradually holding students more and more disciplinarily accountable to their own developing definition of what a *mathematical function* is, such that, when they were presented with three textbook definitions of the concept, they correctly judged which ones were more or less mathematically sophisticated and even suggested ways each one could be improved (Engle, 2004). In addition, fostering accountability from the inside out is embedded within the commonly recommended participation structure of "think–pair–share," in which students first think about an open-ended task by themselves, then work on it with a seatmate, and finally discuss their ideas with the teacher and rest of the class.

Resources

Finally, if PDE is going to be possible, a learning environment must provide learners with access to the necessary resources for that work. As was mentioned in Engle and Conant (2002), some resources—such as sufficient time and locations in which to work, along with having access to the technological tools, artifacts, practices, or other materials for doing particular kinds of disciplinary work—directly support students' PDE. Subsequent investigators have furthered broadened the notion of resources to consider other temporal grain sizes and institutional locations. Venturini and Amade-Escot (2009) have shown that the resources affecting PDE can be as situated and momentary as when a teacher introduces a particular idea into discussion while discouraging others, while Mortimer and Oliveira (2009) have shown how the institutional constraints of particular schools can constrain available resources for supporting PDE.

Other resources support PDE crucially but indirectly by supporting the embodiment of the other principles. For example, several investigators have shown how written, computational, and other artifacts can be used to crystallize ideas in ways that can serve to help problematize issues and prompt further PDE (Engle, 2004; Furberg & Arnseth, 2009, Radinsky, 2008). Complementing this, Brian Reiser (2004) has investigated the kinds of scaffolding that serve to problematize activity and open up new opportunities for learning, versus the more classical kinds of scaffolding that serve to structure activity and guide learners to normatively valued answers or other products. Finally, in a series of careful studies, Leema Kuhn Berland and Reiser have analyzed and addressed the challenges of regularly supporting productive engagement in scientific argumentation by devising clever participation structures that serve as resources for supporting students' authority and accountability in ways that make evidence-based persuasion not just possible, but necessary, for students (Berland & Reiser, 2009, 2011; Kuhn & Reiser, 2006).

Exactly which resources are relevant for supporting PDE or the three principles in a particular situation is likely to vary dramatically depending on the topic, one's goals, and the background of the learners one is working with, among many other factors. Thus, this is a key part of the "devil in the details" that one needs to get right in particular cases when one is designing a particular learning environment. As with authority and accountability, resources need to be kept in balance with problematizing (Venturini & Amade-Escot, 2009). If insufficient resources are provided, then problematizing could be so strong that learners are unable or unwilling to act, overwhelmed with the challenge. In contrast, if too many resources are provided, then the problematic nature of the task could be reduced so much that the potential for disciplinary engagement to be productive has been squandered. This is much like Vygotsky's notion of the zone of proximal development, specifying what needs to be kept in balance for learners to stay within that zone.

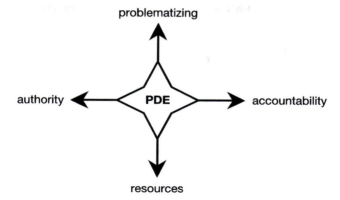

FIGURE 7.4 Fostering PDE by balancing problematizing with resources, and authority with accountability. I thank Patrice Venturini for suggesting this diagram.

Overall, then, my view is that fostering PDE involves establishing and maintaining a dynamic balance over time (see Figure 7.4). If PDE is to occur, resources need to be kept in balance with problematizing, and accountability with authority. And the stronger that all four principles are embodied together, the stronger the PDE. On the other hand, if either resources become too strong compared with problematizing, or accountability becomes too strong compared with authority, then there's a real danger of reverting to the more familiar patterns of going through the motions of completing a straightforward, school-like exercise, or simply guessing what response the teacher wants. If either happens, it may be difficult to re-establish PDE, as each is a very powerful and well-learned cultural practice (at least in US schools). So, if one needs to err, it is often best to err on the side of better supporting problematizing and authority, responding to learners' frustrations at not being able to adequately address a challenging task with some resources, and to learners' lack of awareness at how confused their initial ideas are with increased opportunities for them to account for how their ideas do and do not make sense.

In the next section, I address additional research that has drawn on, and contributed to, the PDE framework, beyond developing particular principles or further defining what PDE is or could be.

Research Drawing on the PDE Framework

I begin with claims that the PDE principles are relevant to existing programs, and then move to research that has empirically investigated cases using the principles or further developed the principles by coordinating them with other theoretical frameworks.

Claims that the PDE Principles Apply to a Range of Programs

One key goal of Engle and Conant (2002) was to make explicit a set of general principles for fostering PDE that the design-based and reform-oriented research community would be likely to share. Our first indication that this may be the case is in the number and range of times other researchers have stated that the Engle and Conant (2002) principles are characteristic of innovative learning environments with which they are familiar (though not necessarily ones they have designed). Table 7.1 compiles these claims, which mostly come from literature reviews and theoretical discussions.

As shown in the table, 14 different design-based research projects and cases of reform-oriented instruction in science and mathematics have been cited as being consistent with the PDE framework, with two additional published cases of difficulties in achieving PDE being cited by one author as being understandable in light of the principles. The first three—Lampert's "Teaching with Problems" method of reform-oriented mathematics instruction (Lampert, 1990a; 1990b; 2001), problem-based learning (or PBL; Barrows, 2000), and earlier versions of Knowledge Forum (e.g., Bereiter, 2002; Scardamalia, 2002; Scardamalia et al., 1994)—were cited as being consistent with the PDE framework by multiple authors. It is also notable that there is wide variation in the grain size and nature of the cases considered consistent with the principles, which range from particular forms of discourse all the way to complete elementary-school curricula and general approaches to instruction.

Finally, many additional pieces refer to the framework as providing a set of findings, goals, and/or methods that are important to research in the learning sciences, and/or science and mathematics education more generally (e.g., Barron & Darling-Hammond, 2008; Duschl, 2006; Gresalfi, Hand, & Hodge, 2006; Hodge, 2008; McNeill & Kuhn, 2006; National Research Council, 2008; Renninger, 2007). Thus, the PDE framework seems to capture some consensus ideas that are shared by members of our research community and are embodied in a wide variety of respected educational innovations developed during the past two decades.

Analyses that Use the Principles for Fostering PDE to Explain Cases of PDE

In addition to understanding existing programs, several empirical studies have been conducted in which the PDE principles have played a central analytical role. These analyses have explicitly used the four principles to explain why PDE was or was not observed. To give you a flavor for this work, I will briefly illustrate these kinds of analysis using three cases of PDE that have not been comprehensively analyzed using the framework before: five practices for facilitating discussions

TABLE 7.1 Claims of relevance of the PDE framework to other design-based research projects and/or reform-oriented instructional approaches

Example said to be explainable by PDE principles	Paper(s) making claim
1. Lampert's (1990a, 1990b, 2001) "Teaching with Problems" form of reform-oriented mathematics instruction	Leinhardt & Steele (2005); Nasir, Hand, & Taylor (2008); Schoenfeld (2007b)
2. Knowledge Forum to support scientific inquiry (e.g., Bereiter, 2002; Scardamalia, 2002)	Hmelo-Silver & Barrows (2008); Schoenfeld (2007a)
3. Problem Based Learning, first used in medicine	Hmelo-Silver & Barrows (2008); Hun, Tan & Koh (2006)
4. Cobb group's design-based research (DBR) in math (Cobb, Gresalfi, & Hodge, 2009; Yackel & Cobb, 1996)	Nasir et al., (2008)
5. Guided Inquiry Supporting Multiple Literacies (GISML) DBR project (Herrenkohl, Palincsar, Dewater, & Kawasaki, 1999; Palincsar, Magnusson, Marano, Ford, & Brown, 2001)	National Research Council (2008)
6. Constructing Data, Modeling Worlds DBR project (Lehrer, Schauble, Strom & Pligge, 2001)	National Research Council (2008)
7. Schoenfeld's (1985) mathematical problem-solving course (Arcavi, Kessel, Meira, & Smith, 1998) and DBR on it	Schoenfeld (2007a)
8. Hiebert et al.'s (1997) model for reform-oriented mathematics instruction	Nasir et al., (2008)
9. The reform-oriented elementary mathematics curriculum "TERC Investigations"	Stein & Kaufmann (2010)
10. The reform-oriented elementary mathematics curriculum "Everyday Mathematics"	Stein & Kaufmann (2010)
11. "Railside High School" and other similar discussion-based mathematics teaching (Boaler, 2002; Boaler & Greeno, 2000; Boaler & Staples, 2008)	Schoenfeld (2006)
12. Inquiry science classrooms studied by Hogan, Nastasi, & Pressley (2000)	Hmelo-Silver & Barrows (2008)
13. Reflective discourse in science (van Zee & Minstrell, 1997)	Scott et al., (2006)
14. Underlying strategies for "inducing comprehension activity" posited by Hatano & Inagaki (2003)	Greeno & Saxe (2007)
15. Lack of PDE found by Bianchini (1997)	Cornelius & Herrenkohl (2004)
16. Lack of PDE found by Shepardson (1996)	Cornelius & Herrenkohl (2004)

around cognitively demanding mathematical tasks, the constructive-controversy method of cooperative learning, and Bransford and Schwartz's idea of a time for telling. Then I will evaluate the basic predictions of the framework that PDE tends to occur when the PDE principles are embodied and vice versa, by summarizing the key findings from these cases and 20 others in the literature.

Five Practices for Facilitating Discussions

This model for facilitating a whole-class discussion around students' ideas (Smith, Hughes, Engle & Stein, 2009; Stein, Engle, Smith & Hughes, 2008) involves having students first work individually and then in small groups on a cognitively demanding open-ended task that will result in multiple, contrasting student responses that embed important disciplinary ideas and practices. Facilitating an effective discussion that makes disciplinary progress using students' diverse responses to such a task involves:

(a) *anticipating* as many student responses as possible and considering how each could advance one's disciplinary learning goals; (b) *monitoring* which responses students actually come up with on their own; (c) *selecting* which student and other responses for students or the teacher to present to the class; (d) *sequencing* the responses to be presented in a particular order that allows one to (e) ask pre-planned questions that will encourage students to *connect* the responses to each other by having students compare and contrast the responses with each other in order to surface important disciplinary ideas and practices. This method supports strong disciplinary connections and at least a moderate amount of support for engagement and productivity.

This method embodies the first of the four principles for fostering PDE, problematizing, by choosing and successfully implementing a mathematical task with high cognitive demand (Henningsen & Stein, 1997; Stein, Grover, & Henningsen, 1996; Stein, Smith, Henningsen, & Silver, 2000). Such tasks engender uncertainty by being ambiguous and allowing multiple possible responses; they make contact with the discipline by having students develop and justify mathematical ideas or explain connections between mathematical concepts and procedures; and they engender students' commitment to addressing them through a set of teaching strategies for helping students take up the tasks at the same level of cognitive demand that they are presented (Stein et al., 2000). Authority, in the sense of intellectual agency and authorship, is supported by having students present their responses to each other and to the class as a whole. With respect to accountability, through the practice of connecting, students are asked to account for how their responses relate to others in ways that can bring out key disciplinary ideas. In addition, selecting can be done to make sure that students are exposed to canonical or particularly innovative approaches in the discipline. Resources that support such discussions include an opaque projector or transparencies, so students can easily share and compare their written work with each other, and monitoring sheets that teachers can use to list likely students' responses, with space to note who ends up authoring them and the specific way in which they did that. Thus, students' PDE in these discussions is supported by at least moderate degrees of support for problematizing and student authority, as well as strong degrees of support for accountability and resources. Although the original research focused on discussions around mathematical tasks, I believe that these ideas can be adapted to support learners' productive engagement in discussions around similarly structured tasks in other fields as well.

Constructive Controversy

The constructive-controversy model of cooperative learning has been shown to prompt students to engage in discussions around controversial issues in more informed and nuanced ways, leading to more effective solutions and understandings of the underlying issues (Johnson & Johnson, 1995; Johnson, Johnson, & Smith, 1997, 2000). In this model, a learning group of four students is divided into pairs, each of which is responsible for preparing as convincing a case as they can for one side of a controversial pro/con issue, using prepared learning materials relevant to their side of the issue. Each pair then presents their side, defending it from rebuttals from the other side. Next—and this is crucial—the pairs switch side and present arguments for the other side, until those who originally represented that side are satisfied that they captured the essential ideas. Finally, the group as a whole designs a consensus response that takes into account the strongest arguments for each side. Thus, overall, both disciplinarity and productivity are strong in such discussions, with at least moderate levels of engagement observed.

This PDE is supported by strong embodiments of the problematizing, accountability, and resources principles and a mixed embodiment of the authority principle, which shifts over time. First, problematizing is supported both by the selection of a difficult-to-resolve controversial issue and by the challenge of designing a consensus position. Accountability is supported by the fact that students are required to account for how others' positions could make sense by having to provide arguments for each extreme position. Interestingly, in this case, the usual choice between having students' intellectual agency be fostered or having them simply try to guess the correct answer is made irrelevant, as students are instead asked to take the perspective of other people involved in the controversy. However, student authority is supported when it becomes time to create a consensus position, where students author their own resolutions for the controversy based on a deep understanding of each side. Thus, this case may represent an interesting example of an additional way, besides the inside-out accountability process, to get students who are not used to having authority to grow into this role.[3] Finally, in the most effective implementations of this approach, productive engagement is supported by careful choice of initial core articles arguing for each side, access to research resources for making those arguments more sophisticated, and sufficient time for students to carefully digest the articles and prepare their arguments.

A Time for Telling

Schwartz and colleagues have found that students get much more lasting and useful knowledge out of a lecture if it is preceded by an activity in which they actively try to grapple with the key issues that will be addressed in that lecture (Martin, Rivale, & Diller, 2007; Schwartz & Bransford, 1998; Schwartz & Martin, 2004). For example, they might be asked to try to solve the kinds of tough disciplinary problem whose solutions will be presented during the lecture. Although students usually do not produce expert-level solutions, this kind of activity better prepares them to engage with, and learn from, the lecture by helping them become aware of key issues and distinctions in such a way that they more fully appreciate the significance of the more sophisticated approaches that are shared in the lecture. These researchers found that this method of doing open-ended problem solving followed by a lecture was more productive by comparing it with three other conditions: lecture then open-ended problem solving; two sessions of lecture; and two sessions of open-ended problem solving.

Problematizing is supported in that the problem in question is an important disciplinary problem that students have difficulty solving, and their obvious difficulties in solving it lead to greater curiosity about how to solve it and appreciation for the solution once presented to them. With respect to authority, students are initially put into the position of addressing a historically important disciplinary problem for themselves, which they ideally could share with others beforehand. With respect to accountability, students learn what the disciplinarily accepted solution is and can compare it with their own solutions, which (if one follows the inside-out accountability process) ideally occurs after students have compared their solutions with each other. Finally, resources include a problem description that captures the core dilemmas or design issues to address; supportive materials or technological tools to speed up less relevant detailed work; and time for students to share and compare their own solutions prior to the lecture and to discuss their responses and understanding of the expert solution after the lecture.

Cross-Case Analysis

Showing how the four principles can be used to understand how learners' PDE is supported in otherwise dramatically different cases, analyses like these have served to demonstrate the fruitfulness of the framework. Together, such analyses can be used to begin to evaluate the overall predictions of the PDE framework.

Its most basic prediction is that, if all four principles are embodied in a learning environment, then one should expect to see some form of PDE by learners in it. The more strongly they are embodied, the stronger the PDE should be, with the specific characteristics of that engagement closely corresponding with how the principles were realized in that particular case. Conversely, if one does *not* see PDE, or only a subset of it (e.g. engagement that's not disciplinary, or disciplinary engagement that's not productive), then one or more of the principles should not be embodied in that learning environment, and there should be a connection between *how* the principles were not embodied and where PDE fell short.

In order to begin evaluating these predictions, Table 7.2 provides a synoptic overview of all known studies (plus three new analyses that will be following later in this section) that sought to explain cases, partial cases, or non-cases of PDE by using at least two of Engle and Conant's (2002) four principles. The cases are roughly ordered from top to bottom, from the strongest cases of PDE to mixed or weaker cases of PDE, followed by cases where PDE was not achieved.

In each column, I use reported findings from analyses and (when available) data from the studies as a basis for providing rough synoptic estimates of the degree to which: (a) each principle was embodied in the learning environment, and (b) each aspect of PDE was observed in it. I rated degree of embodiment as weak, moderate, strong, or mixed. Embodiment was rated as stronger to the extent that more aspects of the principle or criteria for productivity, disciplinarity, or engagement were embodied according to the authors of the study. So, for example, the authority principle was rated as being strongly embodied if students were positioned as contributors and local authorities, but only weakly if they were only given intellectual agency but were not positioned as authors, contributors, or authorities. The "mixed" designation is for complex cases where different aspects of a principle or PDE characteristic were reported to be realized to different extents (e.g., students were regularly held accountable to disciplinary norms, but hardly ever were held accountable to each others' ideas), or if the study noted significant variation over time or across learners in whether the principle or PDE characteristic was present. Obviously, this kind of coding cannot capture the nuances in each study's analyses, but it is helpful for identifying broad patterns across studies. The table specifically allows us to examine predictions about (a) whether the existence of PDE is associated with embodiment of all four principles, and (b) whether strength of embodiment is related to strength of PDE.

As shown in the table, embodiment of the PDE principles is generally associated with PDE and vice versa. The table includes 14 cases where all four principles were embodied at least moderately, as at least moderate PDE was observed, three cases where mixed embodiment of the principles co-occurred with mixed embodiments of PDE, and an additional six cases where at least one

TABLE 7.2 Evidence relevant to the validity of the PDE framework from case studies within design-based research and reform projects

	Embodiment of each principle				PDE-related outcome		
Study	Problem-atizing	Authority	Account-ability	Resources	Productivity	Disciplinarity	Engagement
Cases of PDE							
1. Engle & Conant (2002) on Chèche Konnen case	strong	strong	strong	strong	strong	strong	strong
2. Cornelius & Herrenkohl (2004)	strong	strong	strong	strong	strong	strong	strong
3. Engle & Conant (2002) on HEI	strong	moderate	moderate to strong	moderate	strong	strong	moderate
4. Leinhardt & Steele (2005) on Lampert	strong	strong	strong	strong	strong	strong	moderate
5. This chapter on "Constructive Controversy"	strong	mixed	strong	strong	strong	strong	moderate
6. This chapter on "A Time for Telling"	strong	mixed	moderate	strong	strong	strong	moderate
7. Mortimer & Oliveira (2009): lesson 1	moderate	moderate	moderate	moderate	strong	strong	moderate
8. Engle (2004) on ASTEROID courses	strong	strong	grows to strong	—	strong	strong	—
9. Scott, Mortimer & Aguiar (2006)	strong	strong	grows to strong	strong	strong	strong	strong

Study							
10. Venturini & Amade-Escot (2009)	shifting	moderate	moderate	mixed	strong	moderate	mixed
11. This chapter and Stein, et al. (2008)	moderate	moderate	strong	strong	moderate	strong	moderate
12. Imm, Stylianou & Chae (2008)	—	strong	strong	strong	—	strong	moderate
13. Engle & Faux (2006): revised class	moderate	strong	grows strong	—	—	strong	moderate
14. Engle & Conant (2002): FCL case	strong	strong	moderate	mixed	moderate	moderate	strong

Mixed cases of PDE

Study							
1. Adiredja et al. (2008)	mixed	moderate	moderate	mixed	mixed	moderate	mixed
2. Windschitl & Thompson (2006)	mixed	strong	mixed	mixed	mixed	mixed	strong
3. Greeno (in press)	mixed	mixed	mixed	strong	mixed	strong	mixed

Lack of PDE

Study							
1. Buty & Plantin (2009)	strong	mixed	weak	moderate	weak	mixed	strong
2. Mortimer & Oliveira (2009): lesson 3	—	moderate	moderate	weak	weak	moderate	weak
3. Engle & Faux (2006): Mon. class	mixed	weak	moderate	—	—	moderate	weak
4. Engle & Faux (2006): Tues. class	moderate	strong	weak	—	—	weak	moderate
5. Kuhn & Reiser (2006)	—	—	weak	weak	—	weak	—
6. Krange (2007) in Engle (2007a)	weak	weak	weak	—	weak	weak	weak

Note: "—" means the particular concept was not explicitly analyzed aspect of PDE was weak, and so were one or more of the principles. Focusing especially on the unsuccessful and mixed cases, you can see that weaker embodiment of the authority principle seems to be associated with reduced engagement. At the same time, weaker embodiment of the accountability principle seems to be associated with a reduced disciplinary grounding of that engagement, although weaker problematizing and resources may also lead to this result. Although more research would need to be done to establish a statistically reliable association between the four principles and PDE, the data are consistent with these claims. Particularly compelling to me are the existence proofs showing that, when individual principles are not embodied, then PDE is not successful in ways that make sense, given which principles were not realized and in what ways that failed to happen (e.g., Buty & Plantin, 2009; Engle & Faux, 2006; Kuhn & Reiser, 2006; Mortimer & Oliveira, 2009).

Coordinating the PDE Framework with Other Theoretical Frameworks

In recent years, investigators have expanded their analyses of particular cases of PDE to consider ways in which additional theoretical frameworks can be combined with the PDE framework in mutually enhancing ways. For example, both Scott, Mortimer, and Aguiar (2006) and Nikitina (2005) coordinated aspects of the PDE framework with key concepts from Bakhtinian theory. Below, I briefly describe two additional such efforts, highlighting how being coordinated with other theories is enriching the PDE framework. Because of space considerations, I can only provide a taste of this research; please consult the cited papers and their authors for more in-depth discussion.

Drawing on Science Studies to Develop the Notion of "Disciplinary"

One set of efforts involves drawing on various theories from Science Studies—a field in which researchers study scientists' everyday practices—to develop the key notion of "disciplinary" within the PDE framework. As noted earlier, "disciplinary" is an important element, not just for defining what counts as "productive disciplinary engagement," but also for specifying the principles of problematizing and accountability. One particularly promising set of efforts involves coordinating the PDE framework in a variety of different ways with Pickering's (1995) work on disciplinary practice (Engle, 2007a; Ford, 2008; Ford & Forman, 2006; Krange, 2007). Because Pickering's (1995) analyses spanned science, mathematics, and technology, coordinating the PDE framework with his concepts has the potential to develop the notion of what disciplinary practice is in ways that could work across disciplines.

Especially useful is a key distinction between what the learner or disciplinary researcher has independent agency for (conceptual agency) versus what he or she delegates to and holds him or herself accountable to that comes from the discipline (disciplinary agency). Pickering (1995) uses three historical cases of discovery from science, technology, and mathematics to show that agency is temporally distributed in the form of a "dance of agency" that goes back and forth between leadership by either conceptual or disciplinary agency. Krange (2007) showed how the dance of agency can unfold over time within classroom activities. This contributed to the PDE framework by beginning to provide a process-based account of how the various principles interact over time to support different kinds and levels of PDE (see Engle, 2007a). Ford (2008) coordinated Pickering's concepts with the PDE framework in additional ways. He built on a type of disciplinary agency that Pickering calls material agency to propose greater emphasis on students holding themselves and others more accountable for identifying phenomena and explaining patterns from nature. This would result in instruction that involves students in not just creating and justifying knowledge claims, but also taking on the role of critics of their own and others' ideas, in ways akin to what is prompted in academia by peer review. I look forward to further work that draws on research about actual disciplinary practices to better define what kinds of disciplinary practice we wish students to participate in, as well as how to design instruction in which they will learn to hold themselves accountable to the discipline in question.

Drawing on Socio–Historical–Cultural Theories of Mediation to Understand Resources for Problematizing

As mentioned earlier, one important kind of resource that has been noted in several investigations related to PDE or its principles is the crucial role of material artifacts, especially in supporting problematizing (Engle, 2004; Furberg & Arnseth, 2009; Radinsky, 2008). Socio-historical-cultural theories that provide more detailed accounts of how artifacts mediate human activity can be fruitfully used to help flesh out how this works. In fact, in different ways, both Cornelius and Herrenkohl (2004) and Krange (2007) have drawn on Wertsch's (1998) theory of mediation with cultural tools to enhance their understanding of cases of PDE. There is also potential in drawing on related work by Engeström (2007), who provides analyses of how artifacts can be used to surface underlying contradictions in organizations' practices that then help them create new forms of activity. This is consistent with the idea of artifacts functioning as resources for problematizing, which then leads to new forms of productive engagement. However, supporting problematizing is undoubtedly only one way that artifacts help mediate PDE (e.g., see Cole & Engeström, 2007; Lehrer & Schauble, 2007; Saxe, 2002). Thus, there is much potential for further coordinating research on PDE with the long tradition of work on mediation.

Future Directions

In this closing section, I highlight four promising research directions for additionally developing and evaluating the PDE framework in the years ahead.

More Rigorously Evaluating the Predictions of the Framework

With respect to further evaluating the predictions of the framework, this would be a particularly fruitful time to go beyond single cases in which productive engagement in a practice did or did not occur, to pursue more systematic and targeted research. Comparative case studies (Dion, 1998; Mahoney & Goertz, 1994) that only differ by whether, or how, or how extensively, one principle is embodied would provide even more compelling evidence of whether and how that principle matters for fostering productive engagement in particular practices. Design-based research studies could be created in which there is the parallel design of two or more systematically contrasting interventions to be able to support such comparative cases (Engle, Roberts, Nguyen, Yee, & the Framing Transfer Research Group, 2008). It may also be possible to pursue reasonably ecologically valid experimental work to test the principles (McCandliss, Kalchman, & Bryant, 2003) in the context of one-on-one tutoring (e.g., Cohen, Kulik, & Kulik, 1982; Graesser, Person, & Magliano, 1995). In related work (Engle et al., 2008; Engle, Nguyen, & Mendelson, 2010), we have found it possible to systematically manipulate one aspect of student authority, authorship, during a tutoring experiment. It may be possible to do so for other principles as well.

Evaluating Methods for Embodying the Principles Over Time

Most needing such testing at this point are the more specific elaborations of the principles that have been proposed by myself and others. For example, what are the pros and cons of focusing first on fostering learners' authority and then working to foster accountability from the inside out? This process for eventually developing a balance between authority and accountability contrasts markedly with standard instructional practices in some fields of endeavor, such as music and the martial arts, in which learners are first held accountable to the masters of their practice and only are allowed to have their own recognized voices once they have shown they have mastered the existing canon (Frank Lester, personal communication, March 2005; Dragan Trninic, personal communication, July 2009). And it differs from my analysis of constructive controversy, which provides yet another way accountability can be balanced. In addition, what levels of development of authority and of accountability represent a productive balance such that learners will not just be strongly engaged, but be strongly engaged in substantive matters that get somewhere?

Coordinating Individual and Collective Analyses of PDE

Finally, much work can be done to make connections between the embodiment of principles like this that are at the level of a whole classroom versus the differential opportunities to participate that are experienced by individuals (Cornelius, 2004; Esmonde, 2009; Nasir et al., 2008; Venturini & Amade-Escot, 2009). As Nasir et al., (2008, pp. 201–202) noted when discussing Engle and Conant (2002) and several other pieces like it:

> the bulk of this work considers how these features [i.e. the realized principles] support and constrain different forms of knowing and being for students in a general sense, instead of examining how they may be differentially available to particular groups of students.

This challenge is just beginning to be addressed, primarily by those who are concerned with issues of equity and who consider how classroom-level processes and outcomes relate to those that are observed in groups and individuals. Esmonde's (2009) work on how equity in opportunities to learn is affected by differences in how particular individuals are positioned vis-à-vis authority, small-group work practices, and types of activity is a fine step in this direction. In our own ongoing work, we are constructing a model about how different levels of influence in peer intellectual arguments emerge out of interactions between the degree to which students are established as authorities vis-à-vis others, their access to the resources of the conversational floor and the interactional space, and the degree to which they use those resources to make claims and present arguments for them that are accountable to existing norms for good evidence (Engle, Langer-Osuna, & McKinney de Royston, 2008, 2011).

Generalizing the Framework to Productive Engagement in Other Kinds of Enterprise

As we have applied the Engle and Conant (2002) principles, we have discovered that it is possible to generalize them so that they can explain productive engagement, not just in disciplinary practices, but in other kinds of practice and endeavor as well. Basically, wherever "disciplinary" exists in the framework—that is in "productive disciplinary engagement," within "problematizing," and as part of "accountability to the discipline," one can simply substitute characteristics of the particular enterprise in which one is hoping to promote productive engagement.

In Engle and Faux (2006), we used the principles to analyze the degree to which prospective teachers became engaged with, not just the discipline (which was educational psychology), but also with classroom experiences and practices. I then used the framework to understand how the Middle-school Mathematics through Applications Project (MMAP) successfully fostered and maintained a set of productive collaborations between researchers, teachers, and curriculum developers over more than a decade (Engle, 2006, 2008, 2010). I generalized the principles so they were consistent with both my analysis of MMAP and the literature on supporting professional learning communities (Engle, 2010). For example, the accountability principle became:

> Engendering a dynamic internal *accountability* to others and to shared norms and goals: Specifically, in the process of working together, participants are held responsible for accounting for how they are addressing both what others have done (e.g., Greeno et al., 1999; Grossman, Wineburg, & Woolworth, 2001; Lieberman & Grolnick, 1996) and agreed-upon norms and goals for the enterprise (e.g., Palincsar et al., 2001; Wood, 2007).[4] (Engle, 2010, pp. 22)

In fact, these and similar modifications for the other three principles allow the framework to be used to understand and support productive engagement in many kinds of joint enterprise, not just educational collaborations.

Conclusion

In conclusion, the framework is functioning as we had hoped, providing enough structure to guide further investigation while providing enough space for different investigators and designers to flesh it out in different ways, given their experiences, goals, and values. I now return to the hope for the future with which Conant and I ended our original paper:

> Ultimately, we hope readers will find the four principles—and the questions they raise—useful in thinking about the cases of productive disciplinary engagement with which they are already familiar, as well as those they may hope to foster in the future. (p. 40)

It is this function of the framework as a useful thinking tool, one that raises a set of interconnected questions for consideration, that I still believe will be the most important legacy of our work.

Acknowledgments

The preparation of this chapter was partially supported by a generous leave from the University of California at Berkeley. I very much appreciate the insights and contributions of my co-authors and collaborators to the ideas that I present here, among them: Jim Clark, Cynthia Coburn, Faith Conant, Frederick Erickson, Bob Faux, Lloyd Goldwasser, Jim Greeno, Elizabeth Hughes, Adam Mendelson, Xenia

Meyer, Margaret Smith, Mary Kay Stein, and Muffie Wiebe Waterman. This paper is a revision of a paper presented at EARLI 2009 and has especially benefited from the criticism and suggestions I received in discussions at that meeting from Christian Buty, Chantal Amade-Escot, Ellice Forman, Eduardo Mortimer, and Patrice Venturini. Finally, I thank David Dai, Ellice Forman, and Cindy Hmelo-Silver for their very helpful critical comments on the penultimate version of this chapter. Several weaknesses undoubtedly remain, which I hope will be addressed in subsequent work.

Notes

1   In Engle and Conant (2002), we called this same form of authority "stakeholders." The reason for making the change here is that I have found "authorship" to be more accessible to others. In addition, the root of the idea within the concept of "authority" is plainer, given the use of the same root form in both "authorship" and "authority."
2   In the ideal case, being influential with others requires the learner to have held him or herself accountable to these people and the disciplinary norms they value. This is an aspect of the principle of accountability that will be introduced next.
3   I suspect inside-out accountability to prevent students' authority from being squelched is not needed in this approach, as the controversial issue is usually a matter of social policy that most US citizens are comfortable expressing their own opinions. The challenge is having those opinions be backed up by evidence. So using structures to delay learners from expressing their own opinions until they become accountable to the evidentiary basis behind different positions makes sense.
4   Here, I am expanding Engle and Conant's (2002) original language about "disciplinary norms" to be broader, encompassing enterprises such as MMAP, in which disciplinary work is only one small part of what people are doing together. What matters is not that "disciplinary" or any other kinds of norm are being oriented to, but that participants are holding themselves accountable to those shared norms that are important for their type of enterprise.

References

Adiredja, A. P., Engle, R. A., Champney, D., Huang, A. Howison, M., Shah, N., & Ghaneian, P. (2008). Explaining student success in one PDP calculus section: A progress report. In Proceedings of the 10th Conference on Research in Undergraduate Mathematics Education. (Available online at: http://sigmaa.maa.org/rume/crume/crume2008/Proceedings/Adiredja PRE LONG.pdf)

American Association for the Advancement of Science (1990). *Science for all Americans*. New York: Oxford University Press.

Ametller, J., Leach, J., & Scott, P. (2007). Using perspectives on subject learning to inform the design of subject teaching: an example from science education. *Curriculum Journal,* 18(4), 479–492.

Arcavi, A., Kessel, C., Meira, L., & Smith, J. P. III (1998). Teaching mathematical problem solving: An analysis of an emergent classroom community. *CBMS Issues in Mathematics Education,* 7, 1–70.

Austin, J. L. (1962). *How to do things with words*. Oxford: Clarendon.

Ball, D. L. (1993). With an eye on the mathematical horizon: Dilemmas of teaching elementary-school mathematics. *Elementary School Journal, 93*(4), 373–397.

Ballenger, C. (1997). Social identities, moral narratives, scientific argumentation: Science talk in a bilingual classroom. *Language and Education, 11*(1), 1–14.

Barron, B. J. S., Schwartz, D. L., Vye, N. J., Moore, A., Petrosino, A., Zech, L., Bransford, J. D., and the Cognition and Technology Group at Vanderbilt (1998). Doing with understanding: Lessons from research on problem and project-based learning. *Journal of the Learning Sciences, 7*(3&4), 271–311.

Barron, B. (2000). Achieving coordination in collaborative problem solving groups. *Journal of the Learning Sciences, 9*, 403–436.

Barron, B. & Darling-Hammond, L. (2008). How can we teach for meaningful learning? In L. Darling-Hammond (Ed.), *Powerful learning: What we know about teaching for understanding* (pp. 11–70). New York: Jossey-Bass.

Barrows, H. S. (2000). *Problem-based learning applied to medical education.* Springfield, IL: Southern Illinois University Press.

Bereiter, C. (2002). *Education and mind in the knowledge age.* Mahwah, NJ: Erlbaum.

Berland, L. K., & Reiser, B. J. (2009). Making sense of argumentation and explanation. *Science Education, 93*(1), 26–55.

Berland, L. K., & Reiser, B. J. (2011). Classroom communities' adaptations of the practice of scientific argumentation. *Science Education, 95*(2), 191–216.

Bianchini, J. A. (1997). Where knowledge construction, equity, and context intersect: Student learning of science in small groups. *Journal of Research in Science Teaching, 34*(10), 1039–1065.

Blumenfeld, P. C., Megendoller, J. R., & Puro, P. (1992). Translating motivation into thoughtfulness. In H. H. Marshall (Ed.), *Redefining student learning: Roots of educational change* (pp. 207–239). Norwood, NJ: Ablex.

Boaler, J. (2002). *Experiencing school mathematics* (Revised and expanded edition). Mahwah, NJ: Erlbaum.

Boaler, J., & Greeno, J. (2000). Identity, agency and knowing in mathematical worlds. In J. Boaler (Ed.), *Multiple perspectives on mathematics teaching and learning* (pp. 171–200). Westport, CT: Ablex.

Boaler, J., & Staples, M. (2008). Creating mathematical futures through an equitable teaching approach: The case of Railside School. *Teachers College Record, 110*(3), 608–645.

Brown, A. L. (1989). Analogical learning and transfer: What develops? In S. Vosniadou & A. Ortony (Eds.), *Similarity and analogical reasoning* (pp. 369–412). Cambridge, UK: Cambridge University Press.

Brown, A. L. (1992). Design experiments: Theoretical and methodological challenges in creating complex interventions in classroom settings. *The Journal of Learning Sciences, 2*(2), 141–178.

Brown, A. L., Ash, D., Rutherford, M., Nakagawa, K., Gordon, A., & Campione, J. C. (1993). Distributed expertise in the classroom. In G. Salomon (Ed.), *Distributed cognitions: Psychological and educational considerations* (pp. 188–228). New York: Cambridge University Press.

Brown, A. L., & Campione, J. C. (1990). Communities of learning and thinking: Or a context by any other name. *Contributions to Human Development, 21*, 108–126.

Brown, A. L., & Campione, J. C. (1994). Guided discovery in a community of learners. In K. McGilly (Ed.), *Classroom lessons: Integrating cognitive theory and classroom practice* (pp. 229–270). Cambridge, MA: MIT Press.

Brown, A., & Campione, J. (1996). Psychological theory and the design of innovative learning environments: On procedures, principles, and systems. In L. Schauble & R. Glaser (Eds.). *Innovations in learning: New environments for education* (pp. 289–325). Mahwah, NJ: Erlbaum.

Brown, A. L., & Palincsar, A. S. (1984). Reciprocal teaching of comprehension-fostering and comprehension-monitoring activities. *Cognition and Instruciton, 1*(2), 117–175.

Brown, A.L., Kane, M. J., & Eccols, C. H. (1986). Young children's mental models determine analogical transfer across problems with a common goal structure. *Cognitive Development, 1,* 103–121.

Brown, A. L., Metz, K., & Campione, J. C. (1996). Social interaction and individual understanding in a community of learners: Influence of Piaget and Vygotsky. In A. Tryphon & J. Vonèche (Eds.), *Piaget–Vygotsky: The social genesis of thought* (pp. 146–170).

Buty, C., & Plantin, C. (2009). Argumentation and emotions in the quest for productive disciplinary engagement. In C. Buty (Chair) and R. A. Engle (organizer), *Developing and challenging the productive disciplinary engagement framework.* Symposium presented at the Conference of the European Association for Research on Learning and Instruction, Amsterdam.

California State Department of Education (1985). *Mathematics curriculum framework.* Sacramento, CA: Author.

Campione, J. C., & Brown, A. L. (1984). Learning ability and transfer propensity as sources of individual differences in intelligence. In P. H. Brooks, C. McCauley, & R. Sperber (Eds.), *Learning and cognition in the mentally retarded* (pp. 265–293). Baltimore, MD: University Park Press.

Campione, J. C., Brown, A. L., Ferrara, R. A., Jones, R. S., & Steinberg, E. (1985). Breakdowns in flexible use of information: Intelligence-related differences in transfer following equivalent learning performance. *Intelligence, 9,* 297–315.

Campione, J. C., Shapiro, A. M., & Brown, A. L. (1995). Forms of transfer in a community of learners: Flexible learning and understanding. In A. McKeough, J. Lupart, & A. Marini (Eds.), *Teaching for transfer: Fostering generalization in learning* (pp. 35–69). Mahwah, NJ: Erlbaum.

Chi, M. T. H., Siler, S. A., Jeong, H., Yamauchi, T., & Hausmann, R. G. (2001). Learning from human tutoring. *Cognitive Science, 25,* 471–533.

Chinn, C. A., & Malhotra, B. A. (2002). Epistemologically authentic inquiry in schools: A theoretical framework for evaluating inquiry tasks. *Science Education, 86,* 175—218.

Clark, H. H. (1996). *Using language.* Cambridge, UK: Cambridge University Press.

Cobb, P., Gravemeijer, K., Yackel, E., McClain, K., & Whitenack, J. (1997). Mathematizing and symbolizing: The emergence of chains of signification in one first-grade classroom. In D. Kirschner & J. A. Whitson (Eds.), *Situated cognition: Social, semiotic and psychological perspectives* (pp. 151–233). Mahwah, NJ: Lawrence Erlbaum Associates, Inc.

Cobb, P., Gresalfi, M., & Hodge, L. L. (2009). An interpretive scheme for analyzing the identities that students develop in mathematics classrooms. *Journal for Research in Mathematics Education, 40*(1), 40–68.

Cohen, P. A., Kulik, J. A., & Kulik, C. L. C. (1982). Educational outcomes of tutoring: A meta-analysis of findings. *American Educational Research Journal, 19,* 237–248.

Cole, M. (1998). *Cultural psychology: A once and future discipline.* Cambridge, MA: Harvard University Press.

Cole, M., & Engeström, Y. (2007). Cultural-historical approaches to designing for development. In J. Valsiner & A. Rosa, (Eds.), *The Cambridge handbook of sociocultural psychology* (pp. 484–507). Cambridge, UK: Cambridge University Press.

Collins, A. (1992). Toward a design science of education. In E. Scanlon & T. O'Shea (Eds.), *New directions in educational technology* (pp. 15–22). New York: Springer-Verlag.

Collins, A., Brown, J. S., & Newman, S. E. (1989). Cognitive apprenticeship: Teaching the craft of reading, writing and mathematics. In L. B. Resnick (Ed.), *Knowing, learning and instruction: Essays in honor of Robert Glaser* (pp. 453–494). Hillsdale, NJ: Erlbaum.

Collins, A., Joseph, D., & Bielaczyc, K. (2004). Design research: Theoretical and methodological issues. *The Journal of the Learning Sciences, 13*(1), 15–42.

Conant, F. R., Rosebery, A., Warren, B., & Hudicourt-Barnes, J. (2001). The sound of drums. In E. McIntyre, A. Rosebery, & N. Gonzalez (Eds.), *Classroom diversity: Connecting curriculum to students' lives* (pp. 51–61). Portsmouth, NH: Heinemann.

Cornelius, L. L. (2004). When to participate in disciplinary discourses: What happens when the conversation ends? *Proceedings of the International Society of the Learning Sciences.*

Cornelius, L. L., & Herrenkohl, L. P. (2004). Power in the classroom: How the classroom environment shapes students' relationships with each other and with concepts. *Cognition and Instruction, 22*(4), 467–498.

D'Amico, L. (2006). *The Center for Learning Technologies in Urban Schools: A case of design-based research in education.* Pittsburgh, PA: The Meta-Study, Learning Research and Development Center, University of Pittsburgh. (Available online at: www.lrdc.pitt.edu/metastudy/PDF/LeTUS_Final2006.pdf, accessed July 23, 2011).

D'Amico, L. (2010). The Center for Learning Technologies in Urban Schools: Evolving relationships in design-based research. In C. E. Coburn & M. K. Stein (Eds.), *Research and practice in education: Building alliances, bridging the divide* (pp. 37–53). Lanham, MD: Rowman & Littlefield.

Design-based Research Collective (2003). Design-based research: An emerging paradigm for educational inquiry. *Educational Researcher, 32*(1), 5–9.

Dewey, J. (1910). *How we think.* Boston, MA: Heath.

Dewey, J. (1929). *The quest for certainty.* New York: Minton, Balch & Co.

Dion, D. (1998). Evidence and inference in the comparative case study. *Comparative Politics, 30*(2), 127–145.

diSessa, A. A., & Cobb, P. (2004). Ontological innovation and the role of theory in design experiments. *Journal of the Learning Sciences, 13*(1), 77–103.

Duschl, R. A. (2006). A perspective on research in science education. In *An international conference on research and development in mathematics and science education: US panelist papers.* Washington, DC: National Science Foundation.

Duschl, R. A., Schweingruber, H. A., & Shouse, A. W. (Eds.) (2007). Participation in scientific practices and discourse. In *Taking science to school: Learning and teaching science in grades K-8* (pp. 186–210). Washington, DC: National Academies Press.

Engeström, Y. (1987). *Learning by expanding: An activity-theoretical approach to developmental research.* Helsinki, Finland: Orienta-Konsultit Oy.

Engeström, Y. (2007). Enriching the theory of expansive learning: Lessons from journeys toward coconfiguration. *Mind, Culture, and Activity, 14*(1–2), 23–29.

Engle, R. A. (2004). Revisiting previous discussions to deepen teachers' engagement with mathematics and pedagogy. In M. S. Smith (Chair), *Developing a knowledge base for teaching: Learning content and pedagogy in a course on patterns and functions.* Symposium at the annual meeting of the American Educational Research Association, San Diego, CA.

Engle, R. A. (2006). Engaging diverse stakeholders in innovative curriculum design and research: The case of the Middle-school Mathematics through Applications Project (1990–2002). Technical report for the MacArthur and Spencer Foundation Meta-study on projects that sought to reconfigure the usual relationships between research and practice. Pittsburgh, PA: Learning Research & Development Center, University of Pittsburgh. (Available online at: www.lrdc.pitt.edu/metastudy/PDF/MMAPCase 0706.pdf, accessed July 23, 2011).

Engle, R. A. (2007a). Leadership in the dance of agency during productive disciplinary engagement. *Cultural Studies in Science Education, 2,* 210–218.

Engle, R. A. (2007b, May). The power of learning communities: Lessons from research and practice. Talk presented at the *Teaching learning and technology symposium: Cultivating communities in our learning landscape*. University of California at Berkeley.

Engle, R.A. (2008). Establishing collaborations in design-based research projects: Insights from the origins of the MMAP project. In *Proceedings of the 8th International Conference of the Learning Sciences*, 216–223.

Engle, R. A. (2010). The Middle-school Mathematics through Applications Project: Supporting productive collaborations during two different phases of curriculum design. In C. E. Coburn & M. K. Stein (Eds.), *Research and practice in education: Building alliances, bridging the divide* (pp. 19–35). Lanham, MD: Rowman & Littlefield.

Engle, R. A. & Adiredja, A. A. (2008). *Increasing the cognitive demand of mathematical tasks.* Paper presented at the Research Pre-Session of the National Council of Teachers of Mathematics conference, Salt Lake City, UT.

Engle, R. A., & Adiredja, A. A. (in preparation). *Growing the cognitive demand of mathematical tasks: The role of problematizing.* Manuscript in preparation.

Engle, R. A., & Conant, F. C. (2002). Guiding principles for fostering productive disciplinary engagement: Explaining an emergent argument in a community of learners classroom. *Cognition and Instruction, 20*(4), 399–483.

Engle, R. A., & Faux, R. B. (2006). Fostering substantive engagement of beginning teachers in educational psychology: Comparing two methods of case-based instruction. *Teaching Educational Psychology, 1*(2), 3–24.

Engle, R. A., Conant, F. C., & Greeno, J. G. (2007). Progressive refinement of hypotheses in video-supported research. In R. Goldman, R. Pea, B. Barron, & S. Derry (Eds.), *Video research in the learning sciences* (pp. 239–254). Mahwah, NJ: Erlbaum.

Engle, R. A., Langer-Osuna, J., & McKinney de Royston, M. (2008). Toward a model of differential influence in discussions: Negotiating quality, authority, and access within a heated classroom argument. In B. C. Love, K. McRae, & V. M. Sloutsky (Eds.), *Proceedings of the 30th Annual Conference of the Cognitive Science Society* (2010–2015). Austin, TX: Cognitive Science Society.

Engle, R. A., Langer-Osuna, J., & McKinney de Royston, M. (2011). *Toward an interactional model of differential influence in persuasive discussions: Negotiating quality, authority, and access within student-led argument.* Manuscript under review.

Engle, R. A., Nguyen, P. D., & Mendelson, A. (2010). The influence of framing on transfer: Initial evidence from a tutoring experiment. *Instructional Science*. Published Online First and Open Access July 30, 2010. DOI: 10.1007/s11251–010–9145–2.

Engle, R. A., Roberts, S., Nguyen, P. D., Yee, P., & the Framing Transfer Research Group (2008). A design-based approach to experimental design: Investigating hypotheses about how framing influences transfer. *Proceedings of the International Conference of the Learning Sciences*. Utrecht, Netherlands.

Esmonde, I. (2009). Mathematics learning in groups: Analyzing equity in two cooperative learning structures. *Journal of the Learning Sciences, 18*(2), 247–284.

Esmonde, I. & Langer–Osuna, J. (in press). Power plays: How students in a small group negotiated mathematical discussions in hybrid spaces. *Journal for Research in Mathematics Education.*

Foo, S. Y., & Looi, C. K. (2008). Understanding elementary students' emergent dialogic argumentation in science. In *Proceedings of the International Conference of the Learning Sciences (ICLS-2008).*

Ford, M. J. (2008). Disciplinary authority and accountability in scientific practice and learning. *Science Education, 92,* 404–423.

Ford, M. J., & Forman, E. A. (2006). Redefining disciplinary learning in classroom contexts. *Review of Research in Education, 30,* 1–32.

Furberg, A., & Arnseth, H. C. (2009). The importance of socio–cultural context for understanding students' meaning making in the study of genetics. *Cultural Studies of Science Education, 4,* 211–219,

Gelman, R. (2001). [Unpublished comments]. *Conference Commemorating the Contributions of Ann Brown to Children's Learning,* Berkeley, CA.

Graesser, A. C., Person, N. K., & Magliano, J. P. (1995). Collaborative dialogue patterns in naturalistic one-to-one tutoring. *Applied Cognitive Psychology, 9*(6), 495–522.

Greeno, J. G. (1989). A perspective on thinking. *American Psychologist, 44*(2), 134–141.

Greeno, J. G. (1991). Number sense as situated knowing in a conceptual domain. *Journal for Research in Mathematics Education, 22*(3), 170–218.

Greeno, J. G. (in press). A situative perspective on cognition and learning in interaction. In T. Koschmann (Ed.), *Theories of learning and research on instructional practice.* Dordrect, NL: Springer.

Greeno, J. G. & Saxe, G. B. (2007). Conceptual growth in children and in the learning sciences: Giyoo Hatano's contributions. *Human Devleopment, 50,* 55–64.

Greeno, J. G., McDermott, R., Cole, K., Engle, R. A., Goldman, S., Knudsen, J., Lauman, B., & Linde, C. (1999). Research, reform, and aims in education: Modes of action in search of each other. In E. Lagemann & L. Shulman (Eds.), *Issues in education research: Problems and possibilities* (pp. 299–335). San Francisco, CA: Jossey-Bass.

Gresalfi, M. S., Hand, V. M., & Hodge, L. L. (2006). Creating opportunities for all: Unpacking equitable practices in mathematics classrooms. In S. Alatorre, J. L. Cortina, M. Sáiz, and A. Méndez (Eds.), *Proceedings of the 28th annual meeting of theNorth American Chapter of the International Group for the Psychology of Mathematics Education.* Mérida, México: Universidad Pedagógica Nacional.

Gresalfi, M. S., Martin, T., Hand, V., & Greeno, J. (2009). Constructing competence: An analysis of student participation in the activity systems of mathematics. *Educational Studies in Mathematics, 70*(1), 49–70.

Grossman, P., Wineburg, S., & Woolworth, S. (2001). Toward a theory of teacher community. *Teachers College Record, 103*(6), 942–1012.

Hall, R., & Stevens, R. (1995). Making space: A comparison of mathematical work in school and professional design practices. In S. L. Star (Ed.), *The cultures of computing* (pp. 118–144). Oxford: Blackwell.

Hamm, J. V., & Perry, M. (2002). Learning mathematics in first-grade classrooms: On whose authority? *Journal of Educational Psychology, 94*(1), 126–137.

Hatano, G., & Inagaki, K. (1991). Sharing cognition through collective comprehension activity. In L. B. Resnick, J. M. Levine, & S. D. Teasley (Eds.) *Perspectives on socially shared cognition* (pp. 331–348). Washington, DC: American Psychological Association.

Hatano, G., & Inagaki, K. (2003). When is conceptual change intended? A cognitive-sociocultural view. In G. M. Sinatra & P. R. Pintrich (Eds.), *Intentional conceptual change* (pp. 407–427). Mahwah, NJ: Erlbaum.

Henningsen, M., & Stein, M. K. (1997). Mathematical tasks and student cognition: Classroom-based factors that support or inhibit high-level mathematical thinking and reasoning. *Journal for Research in Mathematics Education, 28,* 524–549.

Herrenkohl, L. R., Palincsar, A. S., Dewater, L. S., & Kawasaki, K. (1999). Developing scientific communities in classrooms: A sociocognitive approach. *The Journal of the Learning Sciences, 8*(3/4), 451–493.

Hiebert, J., Carpenter, T. P., Fennema, E., Fuson, K., Human, P., Murray, H., Olivier, A., & Wearne, D. (1996). Problem solving as a basis for reform in curriculum and instruction: The case of mathematics. *Educational Researcher, 25*(4), 12–21.

Hiebert, J., Carpenter, T. P., Fennema, E., Fuson, K. C., Wearne, D., Murray, H., Olivier, A., & Human, P. (1997). *Making sense: Teaching and learning mathematics with understanding.* Portsmouth, NH: Heinemann.

Hmelo-Silver, C. E., & Barrows, H. S. (2008). Facilitating collaborative knowledge building. *Cognition and Instruction, 26,* 48–94.

Hoadley, C. (2002). Creating context: Design-based research in creating and understanding CSCL. In G. Stahl (Ed.), *Computer support for collaborative learning 2002* (pp. 453–462). Mahwah, NJ: Erlbaum.

Hodge, L. L. (2008). Student roles and mathematical competence in two contrasting elementary classes. *Mathematics Education Research Journal, 20*(1), 32–51.

Hodge, L. L., Visnovska, J., Zhao, Q., & Cobb, P. (2007). What does it mean for an instructional task to be *effective*? In J. Watson & K. Beswick (Eds.), *Mathematics: Essential research, essential practice (Proceedings of the 30th annual meeting of the Mathematics Education Research Group of Australasia),* Vol. 1, pp. 392–401). Hobart, TAS: MERGA.

Hogan, K. Nastasi, B. K., & Pressley, M. (2000). Discourse patterns and collaborative scientific reasoning in peer and teacher-guided discussions. *Cognition and Instruction, (17)*4, 379–432.

Hudicourt-Barnes, J. (2003). The use of argumentation in Haitian-Creole classrooms. *Harvard Educational Review, 73*(1), 73–93.

Hung, D., Tan, S. C. & Koh, T. S. (2006). Engaged learning: Making learning an authentic experience. In D. Hung & M. S. Khine (Eds.), *Engaged learning with emerging technologies* (pp. 29–48). Dordrecht, Netherlands: Springer.

Hutchins, E. (1995). How a cockpit remembers its speed. *Cognitive Science, 19,* 265–288.

Hutchison, P., & Hammer, D. (2010). Attending to student epistemological framing in a physics classroom. *Science Education, 94*(3), 506–524.

Imm, K. L., Stylianou, D. A., & Chae, N. (2008). Student representations at the center: Promoting classroom equity. *Mathematics Teaching in the Middle School, 13*(8), 458–463.

Inagaki, K., Hatano, G., & Morita, E. (1998). Construction of mathematical knowledge through whole-class discussion. *Learning and Instruction, 8,* 503–526.

Johnson, D. W., & Johnson, R. T. (1995). *Creative controversy: Intellectual challenge in the classroom* (3rd ed.). Edina, MN: Interaction Book Company.

Johnson, D. W., Johnson, R., & Smith, K. (1997). Academic controversy: Enriching college instruction through intellectual conflict. *ASHE-ERIC Higher Education Report, 25*(3), Washington, DC: George Washington University.

Johnson, D. W., Johnson, R. T., & Smith, K. A. (2000). Constructive controversy: The educative power of intellectual conflict. *Change, 32*(1), 28–37.

Krange, I. (2007). Students' conceptual practices in science education: Productive disciplinary interactions in a participation trajectory. *Cultural Studies of Science Education, 2,* 171–203.

Kuhn, L., & Reiser, B. (2006). *Structuring activities to foster argumentative discourse.* Paper presented at AERA, San Francisco, CA.

Lamon, M., Secules, T., Petrosino, A. J., Hackett, R., Bransford, J. D., & Goldman, S. R. (1996). Schools for thought: Overview of the project and lessons learned from one of the sites. In L. Schauble & R. Glaser (Eds.), *Innovations in learning: New environments for education* (pp. 243–288). Mahwah, NJ: Lawrence Erlbaum Associates.

Lampert, M. (1990a). Connecting inventions with conventions. In L. P. Steffe & T. Wood (Eds.), *Transforming children's mathematics education* (pp. 253–265). Hillsdale, NJ: Erlbaum.

Lampert, M. (1990b). When the problem is not the question and the solution is not the answer: Mathematical knowing and teaching. *American Educational Research Journal, 27*(1), 29–63.

Lampert, M. (1992). Practices and problems in teaching authentic mathematics. In F. K. Oser, A. Dick, & J.-L. Patry (Eds.), *Effective and responsible teaching: The new synthesis* (pp. 295–314). San Francisco, CA: Jossey-Bass.

Lampert, M. (2001). *Teaching problems and the problems of teaching.* New Haven, CT: Yale University Press.

Lave, J. (1988). *Cognition in practice: Mind, mathematics, and culture in everyday life.* Cambridge, UK: Cambridge University Press.

Lave, J., & Wenger, E. (1991). *Situated learning: Legitimate peripheral participation.* Cambridge, UK: Cambridge University Press.

Lehrer, R., & Schauble, L. (2007). A developmental approach for supporting the epistemology of modeling. *Modeling and application in mathematics education: New ICMI study series, 10*(3:3.1), 153–160.

Lehrer, R., Carpenter, S., Schauble, L., & Putz, A. (2000). Designing classrooms that support inquiry. In J. Minstrell & E. Van Zee (Eds.), *Inquiring into inquiry learning and teaching in science* (pp. 80–99). Reston, VA: American Association for the Advancement of Science.

Lehrer, R., Schauble, L., Strom, D., & Pligge, M. (2001). Similarity of form and substance: Modeling material kind. In S. M. Carver & D. Klahr (Eds.), *Cognition and instruction: Twenty-five years of progress.* Mahwah, NJ: Erlbaum.

Leinhardt, G., & Steele, M. D. (2005). Seeing the *complexity* of standing to the side: Instructional dialogues. *Cognition and Instruction, 23*(1), 87–163.

Lerner, J. S., & Tetlock, P. E. (1999). Accounting for the effects of accountability. *Psychological Bulletin, 125*(2), 255–275.

Lieberman, A., & Grolnick, M. (1996). Networks and reform in American education. *Teachers College Record, 98,* 7–45.

McCandliss, B. D., Kalchman, M., & Bryant, P. (2003). Design experiments and laboratory approaches to learning: Steps towards collaborative exchange. *Educational Researcher, 32*(1), 14–16.

McDermott, R. P., Gospodinoff, K., & Aron, J. (1978). Criteria for an ethnographically adequate description of concerted activities and their contexts. *Semiotica La Haye, (24)*3, 245–275.

McNeill, K. L., & Kuhn, L. (2006). Explanation and argumentation. In D. Fortus, et al. (organizers), *Sequencing and supporting complex scientific inquiry practices in instructional materials of middle school students.* Paper presented at NARST, San Francisco, CA.

Magnusson, S. J., & Palincsar, A. S. (1995). The learning environment as a site of science education reform. *Theory Into Practice, 34*(1), 43–50.

Mahoney, J., & Goertz, G. (1994). The possibility principle: Choosing negative cases in comparative research. *American Political Science Review, 98*(4), 653–669.

Martin, T., Rivale, S. D., & Diller, K. R. (2007). Comparison of student learning in challenge-based and traditional instruction in biomedical engineering. *Annals of Biomedical Engineering, 35*(8), 1312–1323.

Mead, G. H. (1913). The social self. *Journal of Philosophy, Psychology, and Scientific Methods, 10*, 374–380.

Michaels, S., O'Connor, C., & Resnick, L. B. (2007). Deliberative discourse idealized and realized: Accountable talk in the classroom and in civic life. *Studies in the Philosophy of Education, 27*(4), 283–297.

Mortimer, E. F., & Oliveira de Araújo, A. (2009). Productive disciplinary engagement in a Brazilian high school chemistry classroom: The lack of resources. In C. Buty (chair) and R. A. Engle (organizer), *Developing and challenging the productive disciplinary engagement framework*. Symposium presented at the conference of the European Association for Research on Learning and Instruction, Amsterdam.

Nasir, N. S. Hand, V., & Taylor, E. V. (2008). Culture and mathematics in school: Boundaries between "cultural" and "domain" knowledge in the mathematics classroom and beyond. *Review of Research in Education, 32*, 187–240.

National Center for History in the Schools (1996). *National History Standards Basic Edition.* Los Angeles, CA: Author.

National Council of Teachers of Mathematics (1989). *Curriculum and evaluation standards for school mathematics*. Reston, VA: Author.

National Council of Teachers of Mathematics (1991). *Professional standards for teaching mathematics*. Reston, VA: Author.

National Research Council (1996). *National science education standards*. Washington, DC: The National Academies Press.

National Research Council (2008). Participation in scientific practices and discourse. In R. Duschl, H. A. Schweingruber, & A. Shouse (Eds.), *Taking science to school: Learning science in grades K-8*. Washington, DC: The National Academies Press.

National Science Foundation (1997). *Foundations: The challenge and promise of K-8 science education reform* (Vol. 1, NSF 97–76). Washington, DC: Author.

Nikitina, S. (2005). Pathways of interdisciplinary cognition. *Cognition and Instruction, 23*(3), 389–425.

O'Connor, M. C., & Michaels, S. (1996). Shifting participant frameworks: Orchestrating thinking practices in group discussion. In D. Hicks (Ed.), *Discourse, learning and schooling* (pp. 63–103). New York: Cambridge University Press.

Palincsar, A. S. (1989). Less charted waters. *Educational Researcher, 18*(4), 5–7.

Palincsar, A. S., Magnussen, S. J., Marano, N., Ford, D., & Brown, N. (2001). Designing a community of practice: Principles and practices of the GIsML community. *Teaching and Teacher Education, 14*(1), 5–19.

Pickering, A. (1995). *The mangle of practice: Time, agency and science*. Chicago: University of Chicago Press.

Polya, G. (1949/1980). On solving mathematical problems in high school. In S. Krulik & R. E. Reys (Eds.), *Problem solving in school mathematics: Yearbook of the National Council of Teachers of Mathematics* (pp. 1–2). Reston, VA: NCTM. Reprinted from *California Mathematics Council Bulletin, 7*(2).

Pugh, K. J., Linnenbrink-Garcia, L., Koskey, K. L. K., Stewart, V. C., & Manzey, C. (2010). Teaching for transformative experiences and conceptual change: A case study and evaluation of a high school biology teacher's experience. *Cognition and Instruction, 28*(3), 273–316.

Radinsky, J. (2008). Students' roles in group-work with visual data: A site of science learning. *Cognition and Instruction, 26*(2), 145–194.

Reiser, B. (2004). Scaffolding complex learning: The mechanisms of structuring and problematizing student work. *The Journal of the Learning Sciences, 13*(3), 273–304.

Renninger, K. A. (2007). *Interest and motivation in informal science learning.* Commissioned report. Washington, DC: National Research Council.

Renninger, K. A. (2009). Interest and identity development in instruction: An inductive model. *Educational Psychologist, 44*(2), 105–118.

Rogoff, B. (1990). *Apprenticeship in thinking: Cognitive development in social context.* Oxford: Oxford University Press.

Romagnano, L. (1994). *Wrestling with change: The dilemmas of teaching real mathematics.* Portsmouth, NH: Heinemann.

Rosebery, A., Warren, B., & Conant, F. (1992). Appropriating scientific discourse: Findings from language minority classrooms. *The Journal of the Learning Sciences, 2*, 61–94.

Saxe, G. B. (2002). Children's developing mathematics in collective practices: A framework for analysis. *The Journal of the Learning Sciences, 11*(2&3), 275–300.

Scardamalia, M. (2002). Collective cognitive responsibility for the advancement of knowledge. In B. Smith (Ed.), *Liberal education in a knowledge society* (pp. 67–98). Chicago: Open Court.

Scardamalia, M., & Bereiter, C. (2006). Knowledge building: Theory, pedagogy, and technology. In R. K. Sawyer (Ed.), *The Cambridge handbook of the learning sciences* (pp. 97–115). New York: Cambridge University Press.

Scardamalia, M., & Bereiter, C. (2007). Fostering communities of learners and knowledge building: An interrupted dialogue. In J. C. Campione, K. E. Metz, & A. S. Palincsar (Eds.), *Children's learning in the laboratory and in the classroom: Essays in honor of Ann Brown* (pp. 197–212). Mahwah, NJ: Erlbaum.

Scardamalia, M., Bereiter, C., & Lamon, M. (1994). The CSILE project: Trying to bring the classroom into World 3. In K. McGilly (Ed.), *Classroom lessons: Integrating cognitive theory and educational practice* (pp. 201–228). Cambridge, MA: MIT Press.

Schoenfeld, A. H. (1985). *Mathematical problem solving.* New York: Academic Press.

Schoenfeld, A. H. (1989). Teaching mathematical thinking and problem solving. In L. B. Resnick & L. E. Klopfer (Eds.), *Toward the thinking curriculum: Current cognitive research* (pp. 83–103). 1989 ASCD Yearbook. Alexandria, VA: Association for Supervision and Curriculum Development.

Schoenfeld, A. H. (2006). Mathematics teaching and learning. In P. A. Alexander & P. H. Winne (Ed.), *Handbook of educational psychology* (2nd ed.). Mahwah, NJ: Erlbaum.

Schoenfeld, A. H. (2007a). Method. In F. Lester (Ed.), *Second handbook of research on mathematics teaching and learning* (pp. 69–107). New York: Macmillan.

Schoenfeld, A. H. (2007b). Problem solving in the United States, 1970–2008: Research and theory, practice and politics. *ZDM Mathematics Education, 39*, 537–551.

Schultz, J. J., Florio, S., & Erickson, F. (1982). Where's the floor? Aspects of the cultural organization of social relationships in communication at home and in school. In P. Gilmore & A. A. Glatthorn (Eds.), *Ethnography and education* (pp. 88–123). Washington, DC: Center for Applied Linguistics.

Schwartz, D. L. (1999). The productive agency that drives collaborative learning. In P. Dillenbourg (Ed.), *Collaborative learning: Cognitive and computational approaches* (pp. 197–218). Amsterdam: Pergamon.

Schwartz, D.L., & Bransford, J.D. (1998). A time for telling. *Cognition and Instruction, 16*(4), 475–522.

Schwartz, D.L., & Martin, T. (2004). Inventing to prepare for future learning: The hidden efficiency of encouraging original student production I statistics instruction, *Cognition and Instruction, 22*(2), 129–184.

Scott, P. H., Mortimer, E. F., & Aguiar, O. G. (2006). The tension between authoritative and dialogic discourse: A fundamental characteristic of meaning making interactions in high school science lessons. *Science Education, 90*(4), 605–631.

Shepardson, D. P. (1996). Social interactions and the mediation of science learning in two small groups of first-graders. *Journal of Research in Science Teaching, 33*, 159–178.

Smith, M. S., Hughes, E. K., Engle, R. A., & Stein, M. K. (2009). Orchestrating discussions of challenging tasks: Keeping your eye on the mathematics to be learned. *Mathematics Teaching in the Middle School, 14*(9), 548–556.

Stein, M. K., & Kaufman, J. H. (2010). Selecting and supporting the use of mathematics curricula at scale. *American Educational Research Journal.* Online first publication, April 19, 2010.

Stein, M. K., Engle, R. A., Smith, M. S., & Hughes, E. K. (2008). Orchestrating productive mathematical discussions: Five practices for helping teachers move beyond show and tell. *Mathematical Thinking and Learning, 10*(4), 313–340.

Stein, M. K., Grover, B. W., & Henningsen, M. (1996). Building student capacity for mathematical thinking and reasoning: An analysis of mathematical tasks used in reform classrooms. *American Educational Research Journal, 33*, 455–488.

Stein, M. K., Smith, M. S., Henningsen, M. A., & Silver, E. A. (2000). *Implementing standards-based mathematics instruction: A casebook for professional development.* New York: Teachers College Press.

Stipek, D., Salmon, J. M., Givvin, K. B., Kazemi, E., Saxe, G., & MacGyvers, V. L. (1998). The value and convergence of practices suggested by motivation research and promoted by mathematics education reformers. *Journal for Research in Mathematics Education, 29*, 465–488.

Tannen, D. (1989). *Talking voices: Repetition, dialogue, and imagery in conversational discourse.* Cambridge, UK: Cambridge University Press.

Toma, C. (1991). *Explicit use of others' voices for constructing arguments in Japanese classroom discourse: An analysis of the use of reported speech.* Paper presented at the Boston University Conference on Language Development, Boston.

Tzou, C. (2006). *Characterizing teachers' support of constructing scientific explanations from a discourse perspective.* Paper presented at the American Educational Research Association, San Francisco, CA.

Van Zee, E., & Minstrell, J. (1997). Using questioning to guide student thinking. *Journal of the Learning Sciences, 6*(2), 227–267.

Venturini, P., & Amade-Escot, C. (2009). Conditions fostering productive disciplinary engagement during a regular physics lesson in a depressed area school. In C. Buty (chair) & R. A. Engle (organizer), *Developing and challenging the productive disciplinary engagement framework.* Symposium presented at the European Association for Research on Learning and Instruction, Amsterdam.

Warren, B., & Rosebery, A. S. (1996). "This question is just too, too easy!" Students' perspectives on accountability in science. In L. Schauble & R. Glaser (Eds.), *Innovations in learning: New environments for education* (pp. 97–125). Mahwah, NJ: Erlbaum.

Warren, B., Ballenger, C., Ogonowski, M., Rosebery, A. S., & Hudicourt-Barnes, J. (2001). Rethinking diversity in learning science: The logic of everyday sense-making. *Journal of Research in Science Teaching, 38*(5), 529–552.

Wasserman, S., & Faust, K. (1994). *Social network analysis: Methods and applications.* Cambridge, UK: Cambridge University.

Wertsch, J. V. (1998). *Mind as action.* New York: Oxford University Press.

Wertsch, J. V., & Toma, C. (1995). Discourse and learning in the classroom: A sociocultural approach. In L. P. Steffe & J. Gale (Eds.), *Constructivism in education* (pp. 159–174). Hillsdale, NJ: Erlbaum.

Windschitl, M., and Thompson, J. (2006). Transcending simple forms of school science investigation: The impact of preservice instruction on teachers' understandings of model-based inquiry. *American Educational Research Journal, 43,* 783–835.

Wineberg, S. S. (1989). Remembrance of theories past. *Educational Researcher, 18*(4), 7–10.

Wood, D. (2007). Teachers' learning communities: Catalyst for change or a new infrastructure for the status quo? *Teachers College Record, 109*(3), 699–739.

Yackel, E., & Cobb, P. (1996). Sociomathematical norms, argumentation, and autonomy in mathematics. *Journal for Research in Mathematics Education, 27*(4), 458–477.

Zaslavsky, O. (2005). Seizing the opportunity to create uncertainty in learning mathematics. *Educational Studies in Mathematics, 60,* 297–321.

Zhang, J., Scardamalia, M., Reeve, R., & Messina, R. (2009). Designs for collective cognitive responsibility in knowledge building communities. *Journal of the Learning Sciences, 18*(1), 7–44.

8

DESIGNING ADAPTIVE COLLABORATION STRUCTURES FOR ADVANCING THE COMMUNITY'S KNOWLEDGE

Jianwei Zhang

Various inquiry-based collaborative learning programs have been developed to enable collaborative and productive work with knowledge among students (Barron & Darling-Hammond, 2008), often using a design-based research methodology (Collins, Joseph, & Bielaczyc, 2004). These programs suggest new learning models in line with how knowledge is processed in the real world in a knowledge-based society (Hargreaves, 1999; Paavola & Hakkarainen, 2005). Designs to scaffold inquiry and collaboration often adopt a prescriptive approach: Students work in fixed small groups to deal with assigned subtopics or tasks, following a set of procedures, steps, and scripts. Sustained, creative knowledge work needs flexible, adaptive, social structures that give participants high-level control in context (Amar, 2002; Barab et al., 1999; Chatzkel, 2003; Engeström, 2008; Sawyer, 2003; Williams & Yang, 1999). This chapter synthesizes my research to engage young students in adaptive, opportunistic collaboration for advancing knowledge as a community, suggesting a principle-based approach to classroom practice. A set of design research was conducted in elementary classrooms that implemented knowledge-building pedagogy with the support of a collaborative online environment: Knowledge Forum (Scardamalia & Bereiter, 2006).

This chapter begins with a distinction between a procedure-based and a principle-based approach to learning design, highlighting the need for principle-based, adaptive designs to cultivate creative knowledge practices. It then summarizes findings from a multi-year design research that tested three frameworks of collaboration for knowledge building. The results demonstrate the possibility and advantages of engaging young students in adaptive, opportunistic collaboration for knowledge advancement supported by a collaborative online environment. Further analyses of this design research address two additional challenges:

To identify new ways of scaffolding for opportunistic, collaborative knowledge processes; and to develop classroom strategies to represent and highlight community knowledge to the awareness of all students.

Toward Principled-Based Design for Creative Knowledge Practices

Design research aims at addressing educational problems and breaking barriers through producing and improving educational designs based on principles derived from prior research (Bereiter, 2002a; Collins et al., 2004). Thus, design research adopts a formative process that involves multiple iterations to test and refine educational designs and address emergent challenges. This process leads to not only refinement of practice but also advancement of theories and principles, contributing to sustained innovation in education (Bereiter, 2002a; Collins et al., 2004). Despite the overall emphasis on improving designs in light of principles, different learning programs approach educational designs and principles in different ways, leading to different degrees of prescription and specification (Collins, 1996; Schwartz, Lin, Brophy, & Bransford, 1999). Differences among these approaches on a procedure- to principle-based continuum have triggered ongoing debates and dialogues among researchers (Brown & Campione, 1996; Scardamalia & Bereiter, 2007) that relate to several specific areas of inquiry (see Zhang et al., 2011), including prescriptive; structured versus adaptive; open instructional design (Schwartz et al., 1999); scripted versus adaptive collaboration (Dillenbourg, 2002; Zhang, Scardamalia, Reeve, & Messina, 2009); fidelity and adaptation of curriculum implementation (Barab & Luehmann, 2003; Brown & Edelson, 2001); adoption and transformation of inquiry-based practices in international and cultural contexts (Chan, 2008; Zhang, 2010); and conceptualization and specification of learning design in design-based research (Dede, 2004).

Procedure-Based Design

Procedure-based design involves a high degree of prescription of inquiry activities in forms of project work, experiments, Webquests, and so forth. Principles of learning are not made explicit to teachers and students but inferred from procedures, which typically involve carefully sequenced activities and curriculum material coupled with pre-established prompts, scripts, and templates to keep learning progressions on course (Zhang, 2010a; Zhang, Hong, Scardamalia, Teo, & Morley, 2011). An inquiry project focuses on a pre-specified task (e.g., write a letter to the mayor about an environmental problem), with responsibilities for different components assigned to different small groups (or members of the groups), which are often fixed for the duration of an inquiry. A fixed-stage model of inquiry is adopted, with a timeline for each stage (e.g., identify questions, gather data, make presentations), making clear who will do what, in what format, and by when (Davis, 1993). Correspondingly, a theme in research on computer-supported collaborative learning (CSCL) focuses on creating collaboration scripts —a set of instructions regarding what activities should be carried out in what sequence, and how learners should interact (see Dillenbourg, 2002, for a critical review). These scripts and procedures are set up to support generative knowledge processes; however, procedure-focused implementations of learning programs often lead to over-simplified knowledge processes that limit student creative engagement (Zhang et al., 2011). The scripts and procedures lose their effectiveness because they are used too ritualistically and thus are not adapted to local contexts in reflection of the core learning principles (Brown & Campione, 1996; c.f., Rummel, Spada, & Hauser, 2009). Moreover, in setting out such plans and procedures, the designer (teacher) retains the high-level cognitive responsibility central to creative processes (see also Chinn & Malhotra, 2002) and thus exerts centralized control over classroom practices (Brown & Edelson, 2001; Tyack & Cuban, 1995), leaving them devoid of opportunities for students to take on such responsibility. Of course, reform-minded teachers need to consider day-to-day classroom procedures and routines. The argument set forth in this chapter is that a principle-based approach may help them to become generative and adaptive in designing classroom procedures in reflection of their evolving pedagogical understanding.

Principle-Based Design and Practice

Design research to generate deep and lasting innovation in education needs a principle-based approach to learning design. As Brown and Campione (1996) indicated, principles "need to be understood if the procedures are to serve their original function" (p. 322). Without adherence to the underlying principles, new learning models are reduced to surface features and "cosmetic" changes (Brown & Campione, 1996; Russell, 1998). Accordingly, a teacher may interpret a change from individual to group work as an organizational change, rather than as a need to shift to more interactive and democratic knowledge processes. Following a principle-based approach, learning principles are treated as the key element of a learning design in design research (Collins et al., 2004) and presented as explicit pedagogical design parameters, with teachers and students engaged as developers and innovators to continually invent and improve principle-based practice, aided by analysis of principles, classroom examples, and evidence of effectiveness (Zhang et al., 2011). Fidelity of classroom implementation is evaluated based on how well these principles have been enacted, instead of merely what activities have been carried out, in what sequence, and for how long.

Learning programs to cultivate creative knowledge practices particularly need a principle-based approach to classroom design and practice (Zhang, 2010a; Zhang et al., 2011). Research on knowledge creation in scientific and professional communities has revealed interactional, emergent processes underpinning sustained creative work. Members engage in emergent and opportunistic inter-actions that cannot be predicted or pre-scripted: They perform cognitive operations (e.g., induction, deduction) and share the results with peers, who then take up and use the results as the input to further reasoning. A series of incremental contributions build on one another leading to major, often unexpected advances (Dunbar, 1997). As Sawyer (2007) suggested: "the most innovative teams are those that can restructure themselves in response to unexpected shifts in the environment; they don't need a strong leader to tell them what to do" (p. 17). Correspondingly, knowledge organizations need to develop an organic, flat structure that encourages adaptability, distributed control, and emergent collabora-tion (Amar, 2002; Chatzkel, 2003; Gloor, 2006), supporting principle-based practice that is growing in many social sectors in the 21st century (Hitysse & Kennedy, 1999).

Principle-Based Design for Creative Knowledge Work in Classrooms

Educational models that engage students in authentic, creative knowledge work need to establish dynamic social systems of knowledge creation within classrooms and beyond. A principle-based approach to learning design and practice thus follows to counteract fixed routines of schooling and bring more adaptability and opportunisms to classrooms (Zhang et al., 2011; see also, Schwartz et al., 1999). Instead of pre-specifying classroom procedures for teachers and students to faithfully follow, a principle-based approach defines core values and principles to inform their understanding and decision-making, so that they can make reflec-tive interpretations, discretionary judgments, and adaptive decisions to advance their knowledge work (Zhang, 2010a). The principles are made explicit to teachers and further transparent to students through metacognitive conversations about how things should be done and what changes are needed (e.g., adaptive classroom norms); and through technological tools that convey knowledge operations, interactions, and processes. Teachers work with their students to continually invent and improve procedures derived from principles and, consequently, deepen and elaborate the principles in relation to their contexts (Zhang, 2010a; Zhang et al., 2011). Thus, design research to develop principle-based innovations requires creative engagement of teachers and their students who are willing to experiment with unproven methods and further make significant contribution to sustained educational improvement through their inventions (Bereiter, 2002a).

Can a principle-based innovation be possibly sustained and increase student productive engagement and achievement? What efforts are needed from the teachers? What conditions might be created in a school to support such efforts? To address these questions, my recent research, in collaboration with Marlene Scardamalia and colleagues (Zhang, Scardamalia, Lamon, Messina, Reeve, 2007;

Zhang et al., 2009), makes efforts to elaborate the possibility and processes of principle-based innovation for engaging students in knowledge-creation practices. A study examined the implementation of knowledge-building pedagogy and technology as a principle-based, school-wide innovation in an elementary school over a decade (Zhang et al., 2011). Knowledge building pedagogy and technology attempt to transform education in line with how knowledge is created and processed in a knowledge society (Scardamalia & Bereiter, 2006). As a principle-based innovation, knowledge building is defined by a set of principles that collectively capture dynamics of knowledge creation, such as:

- authentic problems and real ideas;
- improvable ideas;
- epistemic agency;
- knowledge-building discourse;
- idea diversity;
- collective responsibility for community knowledge;
- constructive use of authoritative sources;
- embedded and transformative assessment, and so forth (see Scardamalia, 2002, for descriptions of 12 principles).

Instead of following predefined procedures, teachers and their students develop, improve, adapt, and share classroom processes and strategies to implement the principles. Classroom procedures and structures evolve as teachers anticipate, experience, and address challenges, share classroom designs, and reflect on their progress.

Knowledge Forum—a networked, knowledge-building environment (Scardamalia & Bereiter, 2006)—conveys and supports the implementation of the principles in practice through a shared, electronic knowledge space and a set of tools to support collaborative knowledge operations (e.g. build-on, revision, synthesis). Automated tools operating in the background provide indicators of progress related to the principles (e.g., social network patterns as indicators of collective responsibility), as feedback to aid students' progress review and reflection (more details about Knowledge Forum are provided below).

In the school portrayed in the above study (Zhang et al., 2011), teachers deepen their understanding of knowledge-building principles through inventing, improving, and discussing classroom designs in accordance with the principles and reflecting on "big ideas" surrounding classroom processes, including issues related to epistemological beliefs, student development, the teacher's role, and learning progressions in specific content areas. Classroom activities and structures are improved and adapted in light of the teachers' pedagogical understanding, with students additionally engaged to make interactive input to the evolution of inquiry goals, designs, social configurations, specific activities, and evaluations. Teachers further share their designs, reflect on the principles, and identify challenging issues in weekly meetings and online journals, contributing to sustained development of knowledge-building practices across the school. As a Grade 1 teacher said: "I often will reflect on what the stumbling blocks are, talk to colleagues, reflect on their views, work again in the classroom, and then attempt to move forward with new ideas."

As a specific example, the following section synthesizes a design research conducted in a Grade 4 classroom (Zhang et al., 2009). It focused on developing sophisticated social structures to enable *collective responsibility for community knowledge*, with design efforts further made to elaborate new strategies to scaffold and represent community knowledge.

Designing Social Structures for Collective Cognitive Responsibility

Collective Cognitive Responsibility

Collective cognitive responsibility, as a knowledge-building principle, requires students to take social as well as cognitive responsibility for the state of public knowledge in their community—their community knowledge (Scardamalia, 2002). Collective cognitive responsibility characterizes authentic knowledge-creation contexts. Members in those contexts enact high-level responsibility for understanding and reviewing knowledge in the broader world; for generating and improving promising ideas (Bereiter & Scardamalia, 1993); for providing and receiving constructive criticism (Sawyer, 2007); for synthesizing multiple perspectives (Bielaczyc & Collins, 2006); for anticipating, identifying, and addressing challenges (Leonard-Barton, 1995); and for collectively defining knowledge goals as emergents of the above interactional processes (Sawyer, 2003; Valsiner & Veer, 2000). They connect their own interests and expertise with those of the community, taking responsibility for sustained advancement of collective knowledge, collaborative learning, as well as personal growth (Zhang et al., 2009).

Enabling collective cognitive responsibility among students represents a difficult design challenge, as it is averse to traditional schooling that focuses on individual achievement, with every student carrying out the same tasks following processes decided by the teacher. To take over high-level social and cognitive responsibility, students must recognize that their own ideas, like ideas in general, can be continually improved by working toward deeper ideas with greater explanatory power (Thagard, 1992). Additionally, student ideas must have an "out-in-the-world" existence (Bereiter, 2002b). They are not equivalent to personal notions or beliefs, but "community knowledge" (Scardamalia, 2002): theories, inventions, models, plans, as knowledge objects that are accessible to all. This community-knowledge space is typically absent from traditional classrooms, making it hard for students' ideas to be shared, examined, improved, and used to enable further advances. In enhanced contexts in favor of student inquiry, the current "standard best practice" engages participants in collaborative production of a finished product that integrates small-group work, with students working in fixed small-groups following predesigned scripts and procedures.

Knowledge-building pedagogy fosters students to take collective responsibility for the overall advancement of the knowledge of the community (Scardamalia, 2002), not simply the production of a finished product for a small group or sharing individual success. Knowledge Forum software conveys and supports the implementation of *collective cognitive responsibility* by providing an open, collaborative workspace, organized as *views* that hold epistemic artifacts contributed by students in forms of *notes* involving multimedia elements. Interaction tools in Knowledge Forum allow users to *build on*, make *annotations*, add *reference* links to each other's notes, and create *rise-above* notes and views to summarize, distill, advance their understanding, and create higher-order integrations of ideas (Scardamalia & Bereiter, 2006) (see a screenshot in Figure 8.1 in the following section). Collective responsibility is further enhanced through student collaborative efforts to plan and reflect on their contributions and interactions in light of specific indicators of progress, such as: developing awareness of peer contributions, as reflected through reading notes across all views (workspaces); making complementary contributions by building on and referencing peers' notes; ensuring that views are informative and helpful for the community; linking views in ways that demonstrate conceptual relationships (Scardamalia, 2002; Zhang et al., 2009).

A Design Research: Three Models Evolved over 3 Years

Can young students take on collective cognitive responsibility, and through what participatory structures? To address these questions, a recent study (Zhang et al., 2009) analyzed a three-year design research carried out by a Grade 4 teacher, who worked with three groups of students to investigate optics supported by Knowledge Forum. The knowledge-building work in each year integrated face-to-face and online processes. Students discussed diverse ideas through face-to-face discourse, conducted experiments and observations to test and advance their theories, searched libraries and the internet for reference material, and spent a great deal of time reading. They recorded and shared new ideas and resources in Knowledge Forum for sustained discourse (see Figure 8.1 for a view created in Year 3).

Through three iterations, the teacher tested increasingly sophisticated designs to implement knowledge building and engaged student input to classroom designs. With assistance from a researcher, the teacher obtained feedback data about student engagement using analytic tools underlying Knowledge Forum (e.g., note writing, reading, build-on) and reflected on his design and practice in each year in light of knowledge-building principles. He identified challenges and opportunities for improvement and refined classroom designs accordingly.

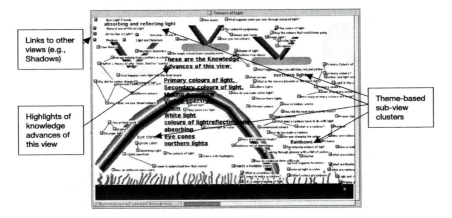

FIGURE 8.1 Discourse in the Colors of Light view.

Each small square icon in the view represents a note. A line between two notes represents a build-on connection. Using background pictures, students highlighted focal issues (absorbing and reflecting light, northern lights, eye cones, rainbows) and organized their notes accordingly. They reviewed their work and identified knowledge advances, which were highlighted using background pictures.

Year 1: Specialized Groups

In line with the current "best practice" of collaborative inquiry, the teacher adopted a specialized, fixed small-group model in the first year and used various strategies to enhance student responsibility. Students and the teacher worked together to identify areas of interest, leading to the creation of six interest-based small-groups, each working in a view in Knowledge Forum (e.g., Angles and Reflection, Colors of Light). Within these areas of specialization, students directed the inquiry processes: identifying and addressing deeper questions, locating useful materials, designing experiments, engaging in discourse in the classroom and online, and reflecting on progress. Near the end of the inquiry, each small-group synthesized the knowledge advances evident in its view, and every student wrote a portfolio note to summarize what he/she had learned. The same design was also used in the following years. The teacher tried to be an authentic member of the community, instead of the central figure. However, working with multiple fixed groups, he often faced the need to coordinate the division of labor, monitor what each group was doing, and highlight important issues and ideas emerging from one group to other groups.

To examine student collective cognitive responsibility, social network analysis (Wasserman & Faust, 1994) was applied to student online discourse data showing who had linked to (e.g. built on, rose above, referenced) whose notes, as an indicator of their collaborative efforts. The analysis revealed a teacher-mediated, small-group-based network structure in Year 1 (Figure 8. 2): Six cliques were

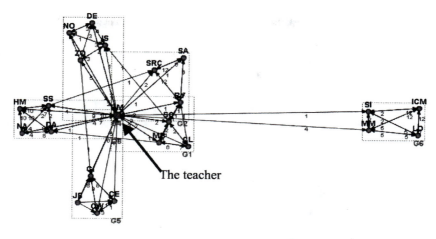

FIGURE 8.2 Social network of student online interaction in Year 1 under a
specialized-groups design.

Each member is represented as a node, and a relational tie (e.g., building on, rising
above, reference citation) between two members as a line.

identified, corresponding to the six small groups created in the classroom, with
dense ties within, and weak interactions between, the cliques. The teacher was
the single member connecting the different cliques into a whole network,
carrying much of the information flow. A network structure as such tends to
fragment the knowledge space of the community, instead of bringing diverse
intellectual input into intensive contact and coherent collaboration. As a result,
most students only reported knowledge advances related to the focus of their
own group in their portfolio notes.

Year 2: Interacting Groups

In the second year, and again based on discussion of research interests, students
were organized into six groups, each of which created a view in Knowledge Forum.
As in Year 1, each group directed their inquiry into a special area. Cross-group
interactions are encouraged, including cross-group note reading, knowledge
sharing, and, more importantly, collaboration between small groups to address
interrelated themes. Students who were working on different problems were
encouraged to design experiments to address problems that emerged at the intersection of different lines of work and construct integrative concepts. As an example,
two groups focusing on vision and lens, respectively, worked together to understand how near- and far-sightedness occur and how corrective glasses work.

Social-network analysis of student online interaction (note linking) in Year 2
revealed more sophisticated patterns of interaction (Figure 8.3), suggesting that

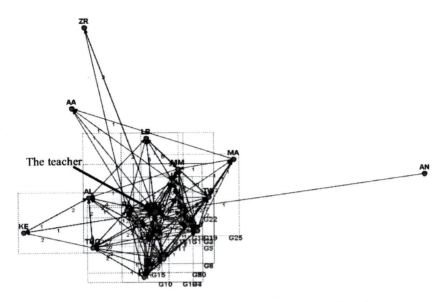

The teacher

FIGURE 8.3 Social network of student online interaction in Year 2 under an interacting-groups design.

the students had interacted with a broader network of members. The interacting-group design helped to connect the work of different groups to enable collective advancement of understanding. However, there was a clear division between central and peripheral students, and the teacher again was centrally positioned. This framework of collaboration still lacked flexibility and adaptability, and the teacher still needed to coordinate the small-groups and mediate their interactions. As he reflected: "I spend a lot of time saying what you're going to be doing, OK, go, come back, tell me what you did . . . There wasn't enough fluidity."

Year 3: Opportunistic Collaboration

In the third year, the teacher abandoned the fixed small-group structure in favor of all students starting with the same top-level goal (to understand optics). The students identified deeper issues, elaborated subgoals as their work proceeded, and created new views accordingly in Knowledge Forum. Students were responsible for the growth of knowledge in all views instead of being assigned to specific views. On a daily basis, they were free to explore problems from any view. Small-groups formed, disbanded, and regrouped, and whole-class conversations convened based on perceived needs. Students spontaneously proposed how they should proceed (e.g., "we need to conduct an experiment on . . ."), by talking to the teacher or the class, or dropping a proposal note in a pocket hung in the front of the classroom.

The teacher

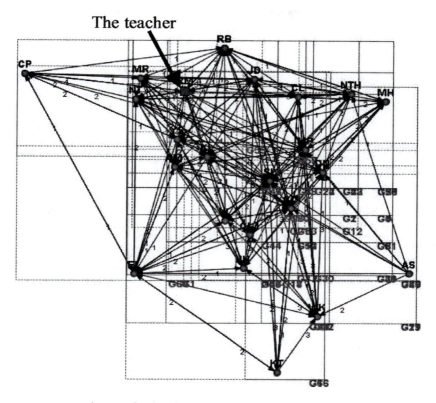

FIGURE 8.4 Social network of student online interaction in Year 3 under an opportunistic-collaboration design.

The opportunistic-collaboration design in Year 3 led to a more distributed and collectively engaged social network (Figure 8.4). The teacher was much less central in this network. Our analyses compared the three years' social networks using a number of measures (e.g., density, cohesion index, graph centralizations) supplemented with content analysis (Chi, 1997) of teacher–student exchanges. The analysis demonstrated the highest level of collective cognitive responsibilities for the third year. Content analysis was applied to student portfolio notes of each year that summarized their personal knowledge gains, indicating the advantages of opportunistic-collaboration in enabling dynamic knowledge advancement (see Zhang et al., 2009, for detailed analyses).

The design research synthesized above demonstrated new possibilities for enabling collective cognitive responsibility among young students and engaging them in dynamic, opportunistic, community-wide collaboration, in line with the view of knowledge creation as a social and emergent process (Sawyer, 2003, 2007; Valsiner & Veer, 2000). Knowledge-building principles, such as *collective responsi-*

bility for community knowledge, were treated as the key element of the learning designs in this design research. Instead of following procedures provided by the research team, the teacher invented and improved his classroom designs in each year, in light of the knowledge-building principles. He further made the principles transparent to his students through organizing metadiscourse to reflect on how things had been done and should be done, aided by Knowledge Forum and its analytic tools that provided feedback data (e.g., note reading, note linking). These strategies helped to engage his students in co-designing, improvising, and improving classroom processes to create favorable conditions for their work. The following section further elaborates how knowledge productivity is achieved and sustained through such dynamic, interactional processes.

Scaffolding for Self-Sustaining Productivity

Making emergent and opportunistic collaboration sustainable requires understanding the interactional processes and identifying scaffolding strategies adaptive to emergent processes. Scaffolding originally refers to situations in which a learner receives support from a more knowledgeable adult to perform a task that is beyond his/her independent reach (Wood, Bruner, & Ross, 1976). This concept has been recently expanded (Davis & Mayake, 2004; Pea, 2004): Scaffolding can take place face to face, as well as in computer-mediated interactions; it can be provided by multiple, distributed agents such as tutors, peers, physical artifacts, and technological tools; and the recipient can be individuals or a learning community as a whole. In procedure-based designs of inquiry, scaffolding tends to focus on structuring student learning by sequencing activities and tasks and guiding student activities through prompts, scripts, worksheets, templates, and so forth, which are provided by the teacher or technology artifacts. An unstated assumption is that the teacher (or other designer) knows the correct answer as well as the route to get there, so that he/she can play the role of a guide in the inquiry processes. Principle-based designs for dynamic, emergent knowledge processes require new and expanded ways of scaffolding. Activity sequences and scripts, when used, need to be understood by teachers and their students in light of principles and treated as adaptable and improvable (Kolodner & Gray, 2002). More importantly, scaffolding needs to take on more distributed, symmetrical, and communal forms (Davis & Mayake, 2004; Tabak, 2004) to encourage collaborative improvisation and emergence, instead of having the teacher or instructional designer chart the whole course.

To elaborate scaffolding for opportunistic, collaborative processes of knowledge building, we (Zhang & Messina, 2010) analyzed an extended iteration of the above design research: light study in Year 4. The teacher continued using the opportunistic-collaboration framework tested in Year 3, while making further efforts to foster student agency and responsibility. Content analysis (Chi, 1997) of student portfolio notes indicated productive advancement of scientific understanding. Analysis of classroom videos, online discourse, and the teacher's journal, using a grounded-theory approach (Strauss & Corbin, 1998), uncovered inter-actional processes sustaining the community's productivity and supportive roles played by the teacher. These analyses suggest *community scaffolding*: The community evolves knowledge resources, activities, and collaborative interactions over time to support its productive work (see, also, Davis & Miyake, 2004).

Idea-Accumulating Interactions

Fundamental to their collaborative productivity, students accumulate a community knowledge base—supported by Knowledge Forum—that helps to enable contin-uity across the old, current, and future work as their knowledge building proceeds. Student ideas contributed to their community space are embedded in the evolving intellectual history of the community, gaining support from the past work and further informing and enabling future idea development (Engle, 2006; Putney, Green, Dixon, Duran, & Yeager, 2000; Tabak, 2004). Specifically, community members define deeper goals for new inquiry by reviewing their previous work, identify related ideas in the community's knowledge space that can be built on, and examine their current understanding to identify promising ideas and deeper problems, which then become the focus of the next steps. Old ideas, problems, and inquiry works are circled back to the current context to inform and support the ongoing inquiry and discourse (e.g., "going back to what X said about . . ., so . . ."). Such idea connections are enhanced across a long time span through the online knowledge space. For example, the Grade 4 inquiry of light in Year 4 evolved out of the students' review of their Grade 1 work archived in Knowledge Forum, focusing on how animals adapt to their environment (including light). The old ideas and findings (e.g., white fur reflects, black fur absorbs light) became the objects of their new inquiry. Idea flow and connection penetrate boundaries between different activity contexts, leading to rich cross-referencing between classroom talks, reading, experiments, and online discussions (e.g., "Remember X's note about how light travels . . ."). This enables juxta-positioning among various inquiry activities (e.g., reading, experiments, discussions) (see also, Engle, 2006; Langer, this volume; Tabak, 2004) and between online and offline spaces.

The teacher's role in this regard focuses on facilitating historical connection of student ideas and cross-context, cross-space information flow. He models making idea connections and anchors his input (e.g., proposals of goals and actions) in student history of inquiry, such as by saying: "I'm interested in what X said earlier about . . . Then, my question is . . ." He works with students to formulate emergent and deeper inquiry themes in the contexts of student prior inquiry and helps to ground classroom conversations in relation to accumulated work and ideas.

Idea-Enriching Interactions

Students engage in knowledge-building discourse in classrooms and online, focusing on collaborative improvement of ideas beyond information sharing. In classroom-based knowledge-building conversations, students sit in a circle, with the teacher as a member of the group contributing to the conversation. Students propose problems and ideas for such conversations and build on one another's input for advancement. They collectively take charge of the flow, with the current speaker choosing the next from those who have a hand up. For example, in a whole-class knowledge-building conversation in the Year 4 inquiry of optics, students first shared their observations and ideas about how light interacts with different materials. The teacher then stepped in to highlight a student's (JL) question.

> *Teacher:* I'm interested in what JL said earlier when he was talking about opaque. He said that a mirror is opaque, because when light hits it, it can't go through. It bounces back. Then my question is: Are all opaque things reflective like mirrors? [Students answer: "No."] And if not, are there different types? . . . Like reflective and non-reflective?
>
> GM: Well, there'[re] bricks, which are still opaque. But they're not reflective. But I don't know what they are called, like that kind of opaque. JL.
>
> JL: I think all opaque materials are reflective, except not all of them reflect light back . . . OK, let's just say um like . . . a yellow carpet . . . your eyes would be able to see the yellow of it because it would only reflect yellow light. That means like that sort of like a tissue for example that would only reflect white, except the yellow carpet, since it's like green mixed with red, I believe. Then the beam of red [and green] light would touch us and your eyes would take it in as yellow.
>
> *Teacher:* So you're saying everything is reflective then. Every opaque object is reflective to some degree. Oh, I hear some people disagree. Can you pass it on? [JL: SG.]
>
> SG: What about wood? Wood isn't reflective. JL.
>
> . . .
>
> FJ: I think if wood is shiny and polished, you could see your reflection. I think it's mostly just shiny objects so it depends on what kind of wood you have, what kind of table you have, if you see your reflection. SG.
>
> SG: Like if you had a glass table.
>
> . . .
>
> DN: Um, actually all opaque objects do reflect light, because they reflect their own color. So we see them as whatever color they are.

TS: [inaudible student talking]

Teacher: Hold on, let's hear him talk.

TS: If they didn't reflect their own color, you wouldn't see a brick of red, or someone's t-shirt as purple or whatever. RP.

RP: What about black? . . . I don't think black reflects. I think that black might reflect light, but it might not. Because we had a reading today that um all the colors of the rainbow make white light and there is a note in the database about that, and everything reflects its own color. But it didn't say anything about black . . .

The students often contribute ideas using non-imperative statements (e.g., maybe . . .), open to critics and further input (Engeström, 2008). Their peers then respond to extend and elaborate these ideas; contribute supporting facts, observations, or thought experiments (e.g., let's say a yellow carpet . . .); make connections and analogies (e.g., between eye and camera); present anomalies (e.g., what about wood?) and alternative ideas; identify subordinate questions and deeper challenges (e.g. what about black?); and summarize different perspectives for deeper conceptualizations. Thus, the collaborative discourse shares characteristics of distributed and incremental idea development observed in productive research teams (Dunbar, 1997) and innovative professional communities (Engeström, 2008; Sawyer, 2007), with existing ideas and knowledge operations constantly revisited and taken up by peers to enable further advancement. The idea-enriching interactions constitute positive feedback loops fueling creative ideation—the more they know, the more they can know and generate—with existing ideas and knowledge operations becoming the input to further cognitive operations to develop new and refined ideas and identify deeper problems and challenges (Bereiter, 2002b; Engeström, 2008).

The teacher communicates his deep trust that everyone has something worth saying and can contribute to knowledge advancement. In classroom conversations, he engages in active listening; expresses interest, encouragement, and excitement (e.g., "This has been fantastic!"); asks questions on student ideas for clarification and deeper inquiry (Zhang et al., 2009); highlights interesting ideas (including misconceptions), questions (e.g., I'm interested in what X said earlier about . . .), connections, controversies, and gaps; and re-voices student ideas in relation to domain concepts to make them more explicit and precise (Hmelo-Silver & Barrows, 2008; O'Connor & Michaels, 1992).

Idea-Selecting Interactions

The positive loops fueling sustained idea generation and diversification are coupled with critical examination and selection of diverse ideas. Individual reflection functions as a bottom-level mechanism of idea examination and selection to make sure that members contribute carefully reasoned out and clearly presented ideas to address the community's goals. In their discourse entries, students identify problems to address, use scaffold labels to indicate what types of contribution they are making (e.g., "My theory," "Evidence," "I need to understand"), and elaborate both what they know and what they are not sure about. Student idea input is further examined and selected through critical dialogues among peers. Empirical evidence is collected and discussed. Competing explanations, possible anomalies, and challenging issues are raised calling for further examination of ideas. Such idea-selection interactions lead to the emergence of valid and valuable ideas from knowledge-building discourse, with misunderstandings and weak areas identified and addressed.

The teacher is cautious not to be the judge of ideas. Rather, he highlights rules of reflective contributions (e.g., contribute ideas with details) and engages students in metadiscourse to review ideas, reflect on progress, and monitor gaps, conflicts, and challenges, using identified controversies to stimulate deeper examination and analysis of ideas.

Metacognitive Interactions in Support of Distributed and Emergent Control

Community members take on collective responsibility for evolving goals and developing productive practices and structures to support their knowledge building, with the teacher and his students co-contributing to the unfolding classroom flow through an interactional process. As the teacher reflected:

> I think that one thing that has changed in me is the confidence to believe this is going to work. That I can begin without having a structure in mind, that I can really involve the children in the design of it. In fact, it is the other ways around; they involve me in their design.

A specific way to achieve distributed and emergent control is through *metadiscourse*: Reflective conversations focusing on goals, principles, rules, structures, strategies, specific plans, and progress review (see also, Scardamalia & Bereiter, 2006; van Aalst, 2009). As a part of the output of such metadiscourse, community members develop externalized support structures to increase their productivity. For example, the fourth-graders in Year 4 discussed important elements of a scientific experiment and created a list of the elements (e.g., problem, hypothesis, procedures, results) in the front page of their notebook to guide their experimental design, analysis, and reporting. They collectively monitored their participation and contributions in light of the discussed principles, plans, and support structures, requesting peer productivity, accountability, and aligned efforts.

The interactional processes summarized above elaborate how knowledge productivity emerges and is sustained in a knowledge-building community that engages opportunistic collaboration. The processes characterize various aspects of *community scaffolding* for self-sustaining productivity, with the community as the provider as well as recipient of scaffolding to evolve practices, resources, and structures for productive knowledge work. The roles of the teacher align with the interactional processes to leverage community scaffolding.

Reflective Representation of Community Knowledge

Collective cognitive responsibility requires students to understand and advance community knowledge that represents "the state of the art" understanding of their community (Bereiter, 2002b) emerged from members' interactive input. Education has been working almost exclusively with student personal and mental knowledge—concepts, understanding, and skills represented in their memory. Community knowledge represents a different realm of knowledge: External, public knowledge (e.g., theories), collectively developed and owned by a community, represented in public forms (books, journals, technical documents) (Popper, 1972; Scardamalia & Bereiter, 2006). A learning community is not only defined by collaborative processes that help individuals learn, but also by a focus on advancing collective, community knowledge (Bielaczyc & Collins, 1999; Stahl, 2006), which leverages individuals' learning of both the content and ways to make creative contributions to collective enterprise.

A design challenge thus emerges pertaining to how community knowledge can be represented so that all members—including the teacher and students —can develop a reflective awareness of its evolving status and challenges. Such reflective awareness is essential for students to take on collective responsibility: To construct a common ground for their collective work; to understand diverse ideas and horizons of possibilities (Langer, this volume); identify shared goals for deeper inquiry; position individual and collaborative efforts; identify relevant ideas to tap into, build on, and improve; and reflect on progress as they proceed (Zhang et al., 2009; see also, Hogan, Nastasi, & Pressley, 1999; Staples, 2007). Collaborative online environments support developing community knowledge in a shared online space. However, there is often a lack of effective tools to represent community knowledge emerged from distributed interactions. In online interactions that rely on a message–reply or document–comment structure, student ideas are distributed across individual messages and responses, making it difficult for participants to understand the whole picture of the extended discourse and review and synthesize group-level progress (Hewitt, 2001; Suthers, 2001; Zhang, 2009, 2010b). A parallel challenge for researchers is to develop research measures for capturing and examining progress of community knowledge in relation to individual knowledge growth (Zhang, 2004; Zhang & Chan, 2008). To address these challenges, part of our efforts in the above design research focused on identifying classroom strategies to foster reflective representation of community knowledge and developing corresponding research measures (Zhang & Sun, 2011). Several strategies are summarized below.

Metadiscourse

As noted previously, students engage in metacognitive conversations to understand what it means to work as a knowledge-building community and reflect on their work accordingly. They review progress and formulate deeper problems and goals, co-plan specific inquiries, and formulate spontaneous groups (Zhang, 2010b; Zhang et al., 2009). To aid these conversations, their Knowledge Form views and notes are sometimes projected on to a screen so they can review existing ideas and related work. The conversations address issues such as: What problems of understanding are important for our inquiry as a whole? What views (or subview areas) should be created in Knowledge Forum in line with the focal goals? What advances have we made in each area, and how can these advances be highlighted? These conversations help students to understand the landscape of their collective work, where they are individually and collectively, and how to proceed, with specific strategies identified to organize and advance their community-knowledge space.

Reflective Distilling, Sharing, and Positioning of Ideas

In their online entries, students distill and share new understanding gained from online and offline activities, often conducted by collaborative groups. Some of their notes present collective understanding, as indicated by phrases such as "*we* didn't know . . . ," "*we* learned . . . ," and "putting *our* knowledge together." Knowledge Forum adopts a visual layout of discussion webs in views (see webs of notes and build-ons in Figure 8.1). The visual layout helps students to make sense of diverse inquiry themes and their relationships and place their new contributions in the context of existing conversations (Zhang, 2010b).

Problem Highlighting and Tracing

Focal problems are highlighted using online and offline means (e.g., question list on paper) to focus the community on important goals. In their Knowledge Forum notes, students identify problems to address using note titles and problem statements or in note body (e.g. I need to understand . . .). By searching and tracing problems, students can see how their ideas have evolved in different problem spaces and identify weak areas for deeper inquiry (Zhang, 2010b; Zhang et al., 2007).

Conceptual Clustering of Online Discourse

With an increasing number of notes contributed to their views in Knowledge Forum, students engage in whole-class conversations to review the online spaces and make decisions on how the spaces should be structured, marked, and linked.

For example, the fourth-graders in the light inquiry identified important themes that emerged from their inquiry. New views were then created in line with important themes and goals, with subthemes further identified in each view (see Figure 8.1). These online structures help students to organize and highlight community knowledge and guide individual participation (e.g., note reading and writing) in addressing important goals.

Progress Documentation Using Knowledge-Building Portfolios

As students deepen their discourse, they write and update "rise-above" portfolio notes to summarize what advances have been made, through what processes, and what needs to be done to further their understanding. Doing so helps students to look backward and forward at their collective trajectory and highlight important knowledge advances for the attention of all members, enabling student-directed reflective assessment of collaborative knowledge building (van Aalst & Chan, 2007).

A set of analysis tools has been developed in our research to measure idea improvement in a community knowledge space (Zhang & Sun, 2011). For example, we analyze knowledge advances through content coding of student portfolio notes, using two four-point scales to code each idea unit: (a) epistemic complexity, from 1—unelaborated facts, 2—elaborated facts, 3—unelaborated explanations, to 4—elaborated explanations; and (b) scientific sophistication, from 1—pre-scientific, 2—hybrid, 3—basically scientific, to 4—scientific. These measures of summative artifacts are supplemented by analysis of student knowledge-building discourse, such as their growing use of domain-specific concepts and epistemic, academic words as indicators of the evolving scope and depth of the discourse (Sun, Zhang, & Scardamalia, 2010). Tracing student ideas generated in each inquiry thread—a series of discourse entries to a focal problem—and rating the scientific sophistication of each idea help to examine improvement of ideas (Zhang et al., 2007).

Concluding Remarks

This chapter highlights a distinction between procedure- and principle-based approaches to learning-environment design and elaborates on the latter through analyzing a set of design research to evolve opportunistic, collaboratively improvised classroom processes for advancing collective knowledge. Educational innovations to engage students in authentic, creative work with knowledge need a principle-based approach to evolve dynamic social systems of knowledge creation in classrooms and beyond. The design research summarized in this chapter addresses a set of challenges pertaining to enabling collective responsibility for advancing community knowledge. The results indicate that young students can take on high-level collective cognitive responsibility through adaptive, opportunistic collaboration, leading to dynamic knowledge advancement. The opportunistic process is sustained through "community scaffolding" leveraged by teacher support: members use their accumulated ideas to support the current work and inform deeper goals; interactive discourse among the members enables progressive chains of reasoning and idea build-on.

Creative-knowledge processes cannot be simply proceduralized and scripted by researchers and program designers and, then, handed over to teachers and students. Turning schools into knowledge-creation organizations in the 21st century requires embracing adaptive knowledge processes and participatory structures in line with dynamics of real-world knowledge creation, with teachers and students both making creative input to the unfolding process. In such dynamic contexts, tasks, procedures, deadlines, and division of labor will of course still exist; but these specific conditions need to be co-constructed through an interactional process in the service of student epistemic needs. Principle-based design, aligned with design research, provides a model for researchers to work closely with teachers and students to advance pedagogical theory, practice, and technology to foster collaborative and creative work with knowledge.

Acknowledgments

The body of work summarized here has been presented in several journals (e.g., *Journal of the Learning Sciences*) and conference papers (e.g., AERA, 2010; International Conference of the Learning Sciences, 2010). I want to thank my co-authors and collaborators involved in the reported work for their insights and inspiration: Carol Chan, Huang-Yao Hong, Mary Lamon, Richard Messina, Elizabeth Morley, Richard Reeve, Marlene Scardamalia, Yanqing Sun, and Chew Lee Teo. I would also like to extend my thanks to David Yun Dai, the editor of this volume, for his encouragement, suggestions, and editorial work.

References

Amar, A. D. (2002). *Managing knowledge workers: Unleashing innovation and productivity.* Westport, CT: Quorum Books.

Barab, S. A., & Luehmann, A. L. (2003). Building sustainable science curriculum: Acknowledging and accommodating local adaptation. *Science Education, 87*(4), 454–467.

Barab, S., Cherkes-Julkowski, M., Swenson, R., Garrett, S., Shaw, R. E., & Young, M. (1999). Principles of self-organization: Learning as participation in autocatakinetic systems. *Journal of the Learning Sciences, 8,* 249–390.

Barron, B., & Darling-Hammond, L. (2008). How can we teach for meaningful learning? In L. Darling-Hammond, B. Barron, D. Pearson, A. H. Schoenfeld, E. Stage, et al. (Eds.), *Powerful learning* (pp. 11–70). San Francisco, CA: Jossey-Bass.

Bereiter, C. (2002a). Design research for sustained innovation. *Bulletin of the Japanese Cognitive Science Society, 9,* 321–327.

Bereiter, C. (2002b). *Education and mind in the knowledge age.* Mahwah, NJ: Erlbaum.

Bereiter, C., & Scardamalia, M. (1993). *Surpassing ourselves*. Chicago, IL: Open Court.

Bielaczyc, K., & Collins, A. (1999). Learning communities in classrooms: A reconceptualization of educational practice. In C. M. Reigeluth (Ed.), *Instructional-design theories and models: A new paradigm of instructional theory* (pp. 269–292). Mahwah NJ: Lawrence Erlbaum Associates.

Bielaczyc, K., & Collins, A. (2006). Fostering knowledge-creating communities. In A. M. O'Donnell, C. E. Hmelo-Silver, & G. Erkens (Eds.), *Collaborative learning, reasoning, and technology* (pp. 37–60). Mahwah, NJ: Lawrence Erlbaum Associates.

Brown, A. L., & Campione, J. (1996). Psychological theory and the design of innovative learning environments: On procedures, principles, and systems. In L. Schauble & R. Glaser (Eds.), *Innovations in learning: New environments for education* (pp. 289–325). Mahwah, NJ: Erlbaum.

Brown, M., & Edelson, D. C. (2001). *Teaching by design: Curriculum design as a lens on instructional practice*. Paper presented at the Annual meeting of the American Educational Research Association, Seattle, WA.

Chan, C. K. K. (2008). Pedagogical transformation and knowledge-building for the Chinese learner. *Evaluation and Research in Education, 21*, 235–251.

Chatzkel, J. L. (2003). *Knowledge capital*. New York: Oxford University Press.

Chi, M. T. H. (1997). Quantifying qualitative analysis of verbal data: A practical guide. *Journal of the Learning Sciences, 6*, 271–315.

Chinn, C., & Malhotra, B. A. (2002). Epistemologically authentic inquiry in schools: A theoretical framework for evaluating inquiry tasks. *Science Education, 86*, 175–218.

Collins, A. (1996). Design issues for learning environments. In S. Vosniadou, E. De Court, R. Glaser, & H. Mandl (Eds.), *International perspectives on the design of technology-supported learning environments* (pp. 347–361). Mahwah, NY: Erlbaum.

Collins, A., Joseph, D., & Bielaczyc, K. (2004) Design research: Theoretical and methodological issues. *Journal of the Learning Sciences, 13*(1), 15–42.

Davis, B. G. (1993). *Tools for teaching*. San Francisco, CA: Jossey-Bass Publishers.

Davis, E. A., & Miyake, N. (2004). Explorations of scaffolding in complex classroom systems. *Journal of the Learning Sciences, 13*, 265–272.

Dede, C. (2004). If design-based research is the answer, what is the question? A commentary on Collins, Joseph, and Bielaczyc; diSassa and Cobb; and Fishman, Marx, Blumenthal, Krajcik, and Soloway in the JLS special issue on design-based research. *Journal of the Learning Sciences, 13*, 105–114.

Dillenbourg, P. (2002). Over-scripting CSCL: The risks of blending collaborative learning with instructional design. In P. A. Kirschner (Eds.), *Three worlds of CSCL. Can we support CSCL* (pp. 61–91). Heerlen: Open Universiteit Nederland.

Dunbar, K. (1997). How scientists think: Online creativity and conceptual change in science. In T. B. Ward, S. M. Smith, & S. Vaid (Eds.), *Conceptual structures and processes: Emergence, discovery and change* (pp. 461–493). Washington, DC: APA Press.

Engeström, Y. (2008). *From teams to knots: Activity-theoretical studies of collaboration and learning at work*. New York: Cambridge University Press.

Engle, R. A. (2006). Framing interactions to foster generative learning: A situative explanation of transfer in a community of learners classroom. *Journal of the Learning Sciences, 15*(4), 451–498.

Gloor, P. A. (2006). *Swarm creativity: Competitive advantage through collaborative innovation networks*. Oxford, UK: Oxford University Press.

Hargreaves, D. H. (1999). The knowledge-creating school. *British Journal of Educational Studies, 47*(2), 122–144.

Hewitt, J. (2001). Beyond threaded discourse. *International Journal of Educational Telecommunications, 7*(3), 207–221.

Hitysse, G. J., & Kennedy, S. (1999). High performing organizations. In M. J. Stahl (Ed.), *Perspectives in total quality* (pp. 105–133). Malden, MA: Blackwell.

Hmelo–Silver, C. E., & Barrows, H. S. (2008). Facilitating collaborative knowledge building. *Cognition and Instruction, 26,* 48–94.

Hogan, K., Nastasi, B. K., & Pressley, M. (1999). Discourse patterns and collaborative scientific reasoning in peer and teacher–guided discussions. *Cognition and Instruction, 7,* 379–432.

Kolodner, J. L., & Gray, J. T. (2002). Understanding the affordances of ritualized activity structures for project-based classrooms. In P. Bell, R. Stevens, & T. Satwicz (Eds.), *Keeping learning complex: International Conference of the Learning Sciences (ICLS)* (pp. 221–228). Mahwah, NJ: Lawrence Erlbaum Associates.

Leonard–Barton, D. A. (1995). *Wellsprings of knowledge: Building and sustaining the sources of innovation.* Boston, MA: Harvard Business School Press.

O'Connor, M. C., & Michaels, S. (1992). Aligning academic task and participation status through revoicing: Analysis of a classroom discourse strategy. *Anthropology and Education Quarterly, 24,* 318–335.

Paavola, S., & Hakkarainen, K. (2005). The knowledge creation metaphor—An emergent epistemological approach to learning. *Science & Education, 14,* 535–557.

Pea, R. (2004). The social and technological dimensions of scaffolding and related theoretical concepts for learning, education, and human activity. *Journal of the Learning Sciences, 13,* 423–451.

Popper, K. (1972). *Objective knowledge: An evolutionary approach.* Oxford, UK: Clarendon Press.

Putney, L. G., Green, J., Dixon, C., Duran, R., & Yeager, B. (2000). Consequential progressions: Exploring collective-individual development in a bilingual classroom. In C. D. Lee & P. Smagorinsky (Eds.), *Vygotskian perspectives on literacy research: Constructing meaning through collaborative inquiry* (pp. 86–126). Cambridge, UK: Cambridge University Press.

Rummel, N., Spada, H., & Hauser, S. (2009). Learning to collaborate while being scripted or by observing a model. *International Journal of Computer-Supported Collaborative Learning, 4*(1), 69–92.

Russell, S. J. (1998). Mathematics curriculum implementation: Not a beginning, not an end. *Hands On!, 21*(1), 6–9.

Sawyer, R. K. (2003). Emergence in creativity and development. In K. Sawyer, V. John-Steiner, S. Moran, S. Sternberg, D. H. Feldman, J. Wakamura, & M. Csikszetmihalyi (Eds.), *Creativity and development* (pp. 12–60). Oxford, UK: Oxford University Press.

Sawyer, R. K. (2007). *Group genius: The creative power of collaboration.* New York: Basic Books.

Scardamalia, M. (2002). Collective cognitive responsibility for the advancement of knowledge. In B. Smith (Ed.), *Liberal education in a knowledge society* (pp. 67–98). Chicago, IL: Open Court.

Scardamalia, M., & Bereiter, C. (2006). Knowledge building: Theory, pedagogy, and technology. In K. Sawyer (Ed.), *Cambridge handbook of the learning sciences* (pp. 97–118). New York: Cambridge University Press.

Scardamalia, M., & Bereiter, C. (2007). "Fostering communities of learners" and "knowledge building": An interrupted dialogue. In J. C. Campione, K. E. Metz, & A. S. Palincsar (Eds.), *Children's learning in the laboratory and in the classroom: Essays in honor of Ann Brown* (pp. 197–212). Mahwah, NJ: Erlbaum.

Schwartz, D., Lin, X., Brophy, S., & Bransford, J. (1999). Torward the development of flexibly adaptive instructional designs. In C. Reigeluth (Ed.), *Instructional design theories and models* (Vol. II, pp. 183–213). Mahwah, NJ: Lawrence Erlbaum Associates.

Stahl, G. (2006). Group cognition: Computer support for building collaborative knowledge. Cambridge, MA: MIT Press.

Staples, M. (2007). Supporting whole-class collaborative inquiry in a secondary mathematics classroom. *Cognition and Instruction, 25*, 161–217.

Strauss, A., & Corbin, J. (1998). *Basics of qualitative research: Techniques and procedures for developing grounded theory* (2nd ed). Newbury Park, CA: Sage.

Suthers, D. D. (2001). Collaborative representations: Supporting face to face and online knowledge-building discourse. In *Proceedings of the 34th Hawaii International Conference on the System Sciences (HICSS-34)*, January 3–6, 2001, Maui, Hawaii (CD-ROM): Institute of Electrical and Electronics Engineers (IEEE).

Sun, Y., Zhang, J., & Scardamalia, M. (2010). Knowledge building and vocabulary growth over two years, Grades 3 and 4. *Instructional Science, 38*(2), 247–271.

Tabak, I. (2004). Synergy: A complement to emerging patterns of distributed scaffolding. *Journal of the Learning Sciences, 13*, 305–336.

Thagard, P. (1992). *Conceptual revolutions.* Princeton, NJ: Princeton University Press.

Tyack, D., & Cuban, L. (1995). *Tinkering toward utopia.* Cambridge, MA: Harvard University Press.

Valsiner, J., & Veer, R. V. D. (2000). *The social mind.* Cambridge, UK: Cambridge University Press.

van Aalst, J. (2009). Distinguishing knowledge sharing, knowledge construction, and knowledge creation discourses. *International Journal of Computer-Supported Collaborative Learning, 4*, 259–287.

van Aalst, J., & Chan, C. K. K. (2007). Student-directed assessment of knowledge building using electronic portfolios in Knowledge Forum. *Journal of the Learning Sciences, 16*, 175–220.

Wasserman, S., & Faust, K. (1994). *Social network analysis: Methods and applications.* Cambridge: Cambridge University Press.

Williams, W. M., & Yang, L. T. (1999). Organizational creativity. In R. J. Sternberg (Eds.), *Handbook of creativity* (pp. 373–391). Cambridge, UK: Cambridge University Press.

Wood, D., Bruner, J., & Ross, G. (1976). The role of tutoring in problem solving. *Journal of Child Psychology and Psychiatry and Allied Disciplines, 17*, 89–100.

Zhang, J. (2004). *The growing networks of inquiry threads in a knowledge building environment.* Paper presented at the Knowledge Building Summer Institute. Ontario Institute for Studies in Education, University of Toronto.

Zhang, J. (2009). Toward a creative social Web for learners and teachers. *Educational Researcher, 38*, 274–279.

Zhang, J. (2010a). Technology supported learning innovation in cultural contexts. *Educational Technology Research and Development, 58*, 229–243.

Zhang, J. (2010b). *Enhancing creative knowledge work with collaborative technologies: Representing and mobilizing community knowledge.* Paper presented at the Annual Meeting of American Educational Research Association, Denver, CO.

Zhang, J., & Chan, C. K. K. (2008). *Examining the growth of community knowledge in an online space*. Paper presented at the Knowledge Building Workshop at the International Conference on Computers in Education (ICCE), Taipei, Taiwan.

Zhang, J., Hong, H.-Y., Scardamalia, M., Teo, C., & Morley, E. (2011). Sustaining knowledge building as a principle-based innovation at an elementary school. *Journal of the Learning Sciences, 20* (2), 262–307.

Zhang, J., & Messina, R. (2010). Collaborative productivity as self-sustaining processes in a Grade 4 knowledge building community. *Proceeding of the 9th International Conference of the Learning Sciences (ICLS 2010)*. Chicago, IL: International Society of the Learning Sciences.

Zhang, J., & Sun, Y. (2011). *Quantified measures of online discourse as knowledge building indicators*. Paper presented at the International Conference on Computer Supported Collaborative Learning (CSCL 2011). Hong Kong.

Zhang, J., Scardamalia, M., Lamon, M., Messina, R., & Reeve, R. (2007). Socio-cognitive dynamics of knowledge building in 9- and 10-year-olds. *Educational Technology Research and Development, 55*, 117–145.

Zhang, J., Scardamalia, M., Reeve, R., & Messina, R. (2009). Designs for collective cognitive responsibility in knowledge building communities. *Journal of the Learning Sciences, 18*, 7–44.

9

TRAJECTORIES OF PARTICIPATION AND IDENTIFICATION IN LEARNING COMMUNITIES INVOLVING DISCIPLINARY PRACTICES

Joseph L. Polman

Educational researchers have become increasingly interested in the role identity plays in education, and specifically in how identity and learning are linked and interrelated (e.g., Gee, 2000; Nasir & Hand, 2008; Rahm, 2007; Wortham, 2006), and as accounting for intellectual development. In my own work, I have described how school identities and affiliation group identities such as "gamers" and hip hop music fans intersected and sometimes conflicted for participants in after-school history clubs I had organized (Polman, 2006). More recently, study of an out-of-school learning environment focused on science and engineering practices and outreach work (e.g., Polman & Miller, 2008, 2010) has extended and deepened my interest. In this chapter, design-based research in these two out-of-school learning environments informs an analysis of opportunities for intellectual develop-ment relating to the disciplines of history, science, and engineering. The ways that the learning environments relate to outside communities of practice and identity groups impact both the discourse and action within the environment, and the possibilities for participants to understand and appropriate disciplinary tools for their future endeavors. Identity development, involving acts of self-positioning by individuals themselves and positioning by others over time, results in recognizable trajectories and relates to both broad sociohistorical and local models. The mastery of a discipline's "cultural tools" and practices is related to both cognitive challenges and the motivational and emotional aspects of identity positionings. In this chapter, I will examine the impacts of a history learning environment designed to foster the historical inquiry practices of interpreting events within their historical context and using primary sources; a science learning environment designed to foster the scientific inquiry practices of supporting claims with evidence and fitting within an explanatory conceptual or theoretical framework; and an engineering learning environment designed to foster the engineering practice of "design–build–test" cycles with team presentations. After presenting an analysis of cases, I will discuss implications of these findings for educators wishing to design learning environments that are "hybrids" in the sense that they incorporate powerful disciplinary thinking tools, while genuinely engaging learner interests and agency.

Theoretical Basis for Instructional Models

The overall theoretical basis for my work is a sociocultural framework for understanding human action, learning, and development (Cole, 1996; Vygotsky, 1978; Wertsch, 1991, 1998) incorporating elements of practice theory (Lave & Wenger, 1991; Wenger, 1998). The sociocultural approach allows me to track participation and identification in socially organized activity and clarify how cognition, motivation, and emotion intertwine in the course of engagement with history, science, and engineering over time. The sociocultural approach is based on the premise that individual psychological functioning (i.e., learning and development) is a product of social interaction and action embedded in contexts involving "cultural tools." These tools—including words and ideas—also have a cultural history, in the various ways that they have been used by others over time in communities of practice. In this view, intellectual development involves individuals gaining greater facility at participating in communities of practice utilizing the cultural tools of broader disciplines, while simultaneously developing identifications with those communities and their tools that support their continued use across contexts and settings.

My work in out-of-school environments for history, science, and engineering learning drew upon the broad theoretical orientation described above. In the spirit of design-based research (Design-Based Research Collective, 2003), a theoretical framework to adequately describe the empirical action in these settings has been honed over time, so that my research to date has informed a common framework for the design of learning communities involving disciplinary practices. The first element of the framework is planning for *trajectories over time*, connecting participants' pasts, present, and possible futures into recognizable pathways and storylines. The next three elements of the framework for optimizing and making sense of learning environment design are three senses of authenticity: (a) *externally authentic cultural tools*, or designing for epistemic fidelity to the cultural tools, practices, and values of intact disciplinary communities that are brokered or reified in activity (Wenger, 1998); (b) *authentic community connections* from the learning community to its wider community (Shaffer & Resnick, 1999); and (c) *authentic personal agency*, or designing for participants to have opportunities to make personal emergent meaning of the activities, related to their sense of self and agency (Rahm, Miller, Hartley, and Moore, 2003; Shaffer & Resnick, 1999). These elements are made real through acts of *positioning* and *framing* that are negotiated and taken up by the facilitators and the learners within these learning environments.

I conceptualize *trajectories over time* through the paired notions of "trajectories of participation" (Polman and Miller, 2008) and "trajectories of identification" (Dreier, 2000; Polman and Miller, 2010; Wortham, 2006). I explicate these notions in turn below.

"Trajectories of participation" refers to what commonly happens in apprenticeships (e.g., Lave and Wenger, 1991) and other communities of practice (Wenger, 1998) organized for increasingly sophisticated participation in the practices important to functioning within a given community. In the effective apprenticeships studied by Lave and Wenger, a master and sometimes a young master supervised the work of newcomers and oldtimers with varying degrees of expertise (1991, pp. 56–57). A common sequence of learning activity in these apprenticeships was newcomers acting as "legitimate peripheral participants" by seeing an overview of a process, then working on parts, starting with the finishing stages, and then moving to earlier stages. Through "partial participation in segments of work that increase in complexity and scope" (1991, p. 80), newcomers would advance their learning. Stages in this overall sequence were subdivided into a "way in" (modeling with observation) and "practice" (coaching, scaffolding, and fading) of knowledgeable skills or cultural practices. Authentic outcomes in the form of products were valued economically by the workplace and personally by the apprentices.

Participation in the practices of a community is inevitably an "identity project" as well, and involves "trajectories of identification" (Dreier, 2000; Polman and Miller, 2010; Wortham, 2006). Identity is dynamic and enacted in mediated action (Penuel & Wertsch, 1995). Other work (Polman and Miller, 2010) includes a fuller explication of my notion of trajectories of identification, but I briefly review the concept here. In their actions, community members enact connections between past, present, and future through prolepsis (Cole, 1996), and by dialogically negotiating and creating meaning and identity (Bakhtin, 1981). In the process, participants have a stance toward the tools they use (Polman, 2006; Wertsch, 1998) and pursue intentional goals that give meaning to their roles and agency, in "scenes" or interpreted contexts that welcome particular kinds of people and practices and do not invite others in (Wertsch, 1998).

My research follows other research on apprenticeship learning (Lave & Wenger, 1991; O'Connor, 2003; Wenger, 1998), cognitive apprenticeship, and "communities of learners" (Rogoff, 1994) in examining trajectories of participation and identification through the actions and development of individuals and groups utilizing valued cultural tools in communities organized for learning. In traditional apprenticeships such as that of tailors, the *authentic cultural tools* of the profession are directly embedded in a set of seamless *authentic community connections* of the apprenticeship workplace designed to produce products. In "benign" apprenticeships, *all* apprentices are expected to succeed, and their "professional development" is an investment in employees that would be a loss if employees were not successful. For this reason, apprentices in such apprenticeships commonly take on identities as "legitimate peripheral participants," and others in the workplace reinforce the expectation that all apprentices will move toward some form of full participation (i.e., the knowledgeable skills needed are all learnable). In other words, apprentices position themselves as future experts, and are positioned by others in the apprenticeship as moving toward mastery. The work of apprentices is framed as contributing to the financial well-being of the workplace and connecting to the broader society through existing webs of relationships and commerce.

Building on such studies of apprenticeships outside of school, subsequent researchers developed the "cognitive apprenticeship" model (e.g., Brown, Collins & Duguid, 1989; Collins, Brown, & Newman, 1989; Collins, Hawkins, & Carver, 1991) and the notion of communities of learners in schools (e.g., Rogoff, 1994). The cognitive apprenticeship model borrowed the instructional activities of modeling, coaching, scaffolding, and fading from traditional apprenticeships, but looked to facilitate expertise in the practices of academic disciplines, rather than workplace practices. Thus, cognitive apprenticeships implemented in schools make disciplinary practices the *externally authentic cultural tools* informing the design of instruction. Not only is the inspiration for the tools external to the school; the focus on practices within academic disciplines makes cognitive apprenticeships necessarily more abstract than practical workplace skills. Cognitive apprenticeships emphasize individuals taking up the habits of thought and belief valued in the academic community. The standard by which progress is made in such an apprenticeship is whether the learner values and can carry out practices that, for instance, a mathematician, scientist, or skilled reader could, even though the learners are *removed from the authentic community connections* of the professional workplaces in which the tools were developed.

For a number of reasons, it is not surprising that, when these notions of cognitive apprenticeship and communities of learners have been applied to schools, a number of tensions have arisen. For one thing, schools are not necessarily benign communities of practice for many of the students in them; on the contrary, students in the role of cognitive apprentices may often have tensions with other students, and power grabs may take place through negative positionings of others and positive positionings of oneself (O'Connor, 2003). In addition, owing to age grading, the expertise levels in school classes are usually "flattened" compared with traditional apprenticeships with varying degrees of oldtimers, because, in a class, the students are all mostly newcomers at approximately the same level (Polman, 2000). Finally, teachers in the "master" role in cognitive apprenticeships often do not frame their assessment of their student apprentices' work as intending to guide the students in successful performance, but rather to assign grades judging and sorting the quality of the work; this differs greatly from apprenticeships, where it is assumed all can and will succeed (Dow, 1991; Polman, 2000).

Some applications of the notion of "communities of learners" in schools, such as the whole-school reform documented by Rogoff (1994), have more successfully created opportunities for "transformation of participation" by students over time through their active involvement in meaningful endeavors with adults within school. This is often achieved through *authentic community connections* and *authentic personal agency*. For instance, project-based learning in schools and after-school programs often involves young people in creating artifacts valued by members of their community, with community members sometimes directly involved, either as facilitators or as interested audience (Bransford, Brown, & Cocking, 2000). An example is the "mutual benefit partnership" for urban environmental science work at an elementary school in Chicago, described by Bouillon & Gomez (2001). In such an activity, framing young people's work around real problems in their extended community provides "contextual scaffolds" for the learners' participation in science practices. In Wenger's (1998) terms, connections across communities of practice are provided either by *boundary objects* that move from one community to another, or by individuals *brokering* practices from one community to another. Boundary objects reify knowledge of one community in a form that can be "imported" into another community, such as a way of organizing and representing data from the science research community that is taken up by a teacher and students in a school. Brokers are people with expertise and direct experience in one community of practice, who move into another community and coach participants in the use of tools imported from the other realm, such as an experienced historian who facilitates the historical inquiry of schoolchildren. The *agency* of the young people is maintained and strengthened when their contributions are valued, not just by school teachers, but by recognition outside the school for meaningful work, in ways that facilitators seek to link to their durable sense of self (e.g., Calabrese Barton, Tan, and Rivet, 2008). An example would be an engineering design and construction project that will be used by some external group for a valued, ongoing purpose (as will be described below).

In the initiatives described below, my colleagues and I sought to involve youth participants in practices that allowed them to connect their present actions with their past experiences and possible futures. We did so by designing activities valued by disciplinary communities as well as their local community, and attempting to allow for "emergent" authenticity in terms of the participants' own agency, meanings, perspectives, and unique contributions. We hoped that this general strategy would provide a means by which trajectories of identification and participation mutually reinforce one another. In the next sections, I examine and compare these learning environments in terms of the four elements and two acts, in order to glean insights for learning environment design.

"HistoryWeb"—Historical Contextualization and Interpretation

Elsewhere (Polman, 2006), I have detailed the relationship between mastery (or increasingly sophisticated participation in a practice) and appropriation (which relates to identification) in the "HistoryWeb" learning environment. Fourth-through eighth-grade youth (aged 10–14) at two schools were recruited for this optional after-school activity through flyers and presentations offering the opportunity to use technology to make a "multimedia online history museum exhibit" about abolitionism. Thus, we were seeking to build an environment where young people could connect their past *trajectories* as computerphiles with activities during the course of the club, using computers as tools for historical inquiry and artifact creation, in hopes that they would be inspired to use both computer tools and historical thinking tools in the future. In addition, we also connected our own and the youth participants' heritage as Americans with diverse racial and ethnic backgrounds (primarily African-American and European-American) and a need to live in a diverse US society together in the future.

Most of the participants were attracted to the clubs by the lure of computer technology, but we also specifically targeted the *externally authentic cultural tools* of two historical inquiry practices: "contextualizing" events in their historical context rather than assuming the past was the same as the present, and utilizing primary-source documents. This was done in the context of researching historical struggles for freedom, specifically abolitionism and the "Underground Railroad." During the course of the club, the youth created web pages about that history and about themselves with the guidance of adults.

We maintained *authentic community connections* by arranging for the public display of the youth-created web pages at a local history museum. The museum display, created with attractive technology tools, along with the recognition from school personnel and families that contributing to it would provide, was intended to provide opportunities for participating youth to develop *authentic personal agency*. Undergraduate mentors taking an education class I taught at a nearby private university were expected to *position* the youth participants as competent and facilitate their engagement with cultural tools and practices of historical inquiry through *framing* and guiding their work in positive directions, as coaches would.

Next, I summarize the cases of two African-American students, fourth-grader "Bobby" and eighth-grader "Richard." I will describe how their experiences relate to the design of their respective learning environments with respect to the four elements of the framework and two acts described earlier.

As part of the after-school HistoryWeb club activities at his urban public elementary school, 10-year-old Bobby and between five and eight of his fourth- and fifth-grade peers designed a historically accurate, web-based simulation "game" about escaping slavery along the Underground Railroad. As mentioned earlier, this website was later exhibited to the public at a local history museum.

The activity structure was such that each child and undergraduate facilitator chose from a set of topics related to the Underground Railroad, each of which had an associated folder with print background material I had gathered from the library, including historic primary sources. The topics included choosing when and how to leave, crossing rivers, finding food, coping with bounty hunters, using disguises, following the North Star, looking for safe houses, and so on. Their folders also included large index cards on which they could storyboard each screen that would become part of their section of the game, before building it on the computer. My experience with website design and specifically storyboarding allowed me to broker a form of this additional, externally authentic cultural tool to the task and mix it with the history tools. The students' experience with the computer game Oregon Trail®, which they enjoyed playing on the school's computers during free time at the beginning and end of the after-school club, helped them understand how a web-based simulation game would lead from one choice to the next, and so on in a branching fashion. I told the students that, after all the screens were created, I would stitch them all together into a traversable whole, based on their specifications of the implications choices would have.

In the first game-creation session, Bobby chose the topic of "river crossing" and began by reading through some of the contents of the folder of materials provided to him related to the topic. In the folder were some first-person accounts of former slaves and abolitionists helping escapees across rivers to the North, and an excerpt from Harriett Beecher Stowe's (1985) *Uncle Tom's Cabin*, based on an oral history account of a slave crossing the Ohio River in winter by jumping from ice floe to ice floe. The undergraduate facilitator helped Bobby see how he could separate his ideas on the index cards that would become web pages and then connect them in what would later become links between web pages in the simulation of travel along the Underground Railroad. Bobby culled ideas from the sources and basically created a set of branching choices for crossing rivers in different seasons, utilizing ice floes or boats or swimming, and describing some of the dangers of each. Bobby came into this situation with a trajectory as a computer gamer and appropriated the externally authentic cultural tools of historical contextualization within a particular time and place (e.g., Wineburg, 2001), utilizing primary sources, as relevant to his agency in carrying out the goal of contributing to the creation of an engaging computer-simulation game himself. Thus, his identification with, and agency as, a gamer interested in becoming a game designer in the future contributed to his participation in game-design thinking that aligned with participation in historical inquiry. He positioned himself as a gamer, and he was positioned by the facilitators as a gamer; his successful participation later led to his positioning himself and his being positioned by others as a more competent history student.

Fourteen-year-old Richard's participation in his urban public middle school's after-school HistoryWeb club across one semester also showed some of the benefits of identification and participation in historical inquiry, but this was tempered with some pitfalls. During one semester, the seventh- and eighth-grade youth and undergraduate mentors at Richard's middle-school site created personal web pages and web pages on topics and in forms of their choice related to struggles against abolitionism. This was a more open-ended activity structure than that followed by Bobby: the content of their web pages was open to any form of textual and pictorial historical analysis. During the first of seven after-school sessions in the semester, Richard decided to focus on "freedom," with no further specification. In the second week, his undergraduate facilitator Sarah, who was interested in becoming an elementary-school teacher, suggested he think about tying his past and ongoing personal interest in rap music to the topic of freedom, thus trying to build on Richard's trajectories over time. During the following week, Richard and Sarah selected a song about the Underground Railroad from among a collection I had assembled for club use. Their plan included analyzing the lyrics to the song. Following this analysis, Richard would locate a present-day song that dealt with the issues of freedom and slavery, which they expected to be easy as he was very familiar with music that touched on these themes. He would analyze and describe the lyrics about the present day in parallel fashion to the old song, and also compare and contrast them.

After doing an initial analysis of a historical song I had provided the group, Richard's positioning of himself along the trajectory of a "good student" and his identification as a rap-music fan came into conflict. His facilitator Sarah was disturbed by the violence of some of the rap music he enjoyed that related to the themes of freedom and oppression. She also did not want him to use "inappropriate" lyrics, and he himself did not want to use anything with "too much cussin'." This led them both to reject the prospect of analyzing the song "Only God Can Judge Me," by Tupac Shakur (1996) because of words such as "muthafuckas" and reference to "weed." Richard chose to prioritize his positioning as a good student in a caring, collaborative relationship with an adult facilitator who did not approve of such language, especially in a context related to school (the after-school club met in the school library) and intended for adult public audiences. Thus, the authentic community connections of the public display at a nearby museum and youth work with undergraduates from the nearby university both contributed to Richard prioritizing his personal agency as a cooperative student.

As described in more detail elsewhere (Polman, 2006), the Shakur song would have provided a wonderful opportunity for Richard to use the externally authentic, historical inquiry tool of analyzing "constancy and change"; specifically, how African-Americans' struggles for freedom in the 1800s in the US had some similarities and some very important contextual differences from African-Americans' struggles for freedom in the beginning of the 21st century. Shakur's song alludes to lack of economic opportunity as "trapping" him, and blacks rather than whites threatening him with physical violence. But, since I as facilitator did not become aware of this incident until later, Richard and Sarah passed up this opportunity. The outcome might have been different, if I had brokered the historical and social-science practice of eliding selected words from quotations and discussed with Sarah the notion of encouraging an analysis of constancy and change, rather than her own preference of Richard describing a positive progression of increasing freedoms for African-Americans over time. As it turned out, Richard did participate in some historical practices of interpreting sources in the course of his web-page creation, but his identification as a rap-music fan and as a good student limited his potentially deeper involvement with historical-inquiry practices.

The contrast between Bobby's and Richard's experiences provides some lessons for how to design learning environments. It is a truism that all human beings have multiple identifications with diverse communities of affiliation and practice. Although the notion of connecting with young people's past trajectories of identification has promise, not all identifications—such as rap-music fan, computer gamer, and history student—can be made to align and mutually reinforce one another within a learning environment. In addition, there may be a lack of fit between certain combinations of trajectories over time, externally authentic cultural tools, authentic community connections, and personal agency. The affordances of one resource may become a constraint when seen in light of the other. In addition, it is notable that, in Bobby's case, the reification of historical tools was more supported through a constrained activity structure, and my brokering of game-design storyboarding tools was more successful in part owing to strong past experience with computer-software design. Richard's task was more open-ended and thus less effectively structured to constrain for historical inquiry tool use, and his undergraduate facilitator (a first-year college student) was less well prepared to act as a broker.

"ScienceTeam"—Science Demonstrations and Labs

In 2006, I began research in the "YouthScience" program, which is run by a large community-based organization in a Midwestern United States city with a mission to "stimulate interest in and understanding of science and technology throughout the community." The program works with "underserved" teenagers throughout the course of their high-school careers, providing them with a work-based, inquiry learning environment that focuses on STEM—science, technology, engineering, and mathematics (Polman & Miller, 2008, 2010). At the time of the study, the program was based in a rehabbed warehouse building, with modern meeting rooms of various sizes, ample equipment including desktop and laptop computers, informal science supplies, and a wet lab fully equipped for chemistry. The program attempted to foster participant *trajectories over time* by recruiting "teens" (as they are referred to in the program) from partner community-based programs and through strong ties to the African-American community and participants' families. The work experiences of teens in the program were directed toward a variety of community science projects, supervised by the adult staff. The job also included a large amount of what the staff termed "professional development" related to workplace skills, such as communication. The workplace skills were based on the recommendations of the Secretary's Commission on Achieving Necessary Skills (SCANS, 1991) and were explicitly intended to connect to possible future work in any professional field, with specific emphasis on STEM career possibilities.

In this chapter, I focus on two specific groups from the summer 2006 program. Across both the "ScienceTeam" discussed in this section and the "TechTeam" discussed in the next, slightly less than one-quarter of the youth would be entering ninth grade (15–16 years old), and joining the program for the first time. The remaining youth were in their second–fourth years in the program and would be entering tenth–twelfth grade. ScienceTeam was aimed primarily at teaching community groups through the *externally authentic cultural tools* of hands-on informal science activities (such as those seen commonly in museums involving household chemistry and everyday physics); in addition, they used authentic chemistry lab work along the way. ScienceTeam included 40 African-American youth and one Albanian-American youth and was divided into four groups, led by a team of individuals in their twenties, including an Asian-American woman with a biology degree, two African-American men and one African-American woman attending college, and two European-American women with college degrees and backgrounds in education. Three of them had several years' experience supervising in YouthScience, whereas the other three supervisors were either new or had only supervised for one previous period. ScienceTeam maintained *authentic community connections* by targeting the informal science activities at the same community-based organizations from which youth were recruited. The young people who participated in the program were *positioned* as valued employees of the informal science organization, and the fact that their mission was framed as an extension of the organization was meant to contribute to their sense of *authentic personal agency*.

The informal science activities the teens learned from the staff and led were like those conducted by community science programs and interactive science museums around the United States: they included interesting and engaging phenomena involving primarily chemistry and physics utilizing common household chemicals from the kitchen (e.g., baking soda) and affordable household items (e.g., balloons and straws). One example a teen group facilitated several times throughout the summer was "Gas in a Bag." It involved placing baking soda and vinegar into a plastic Ziploc bag and closing the seal quickly. The bag quickly swelled up with gas (carbon dioxide, formed through the reaction of calcium bicarbonate with vinegar) and in some cases harmlessly—but dramatically—popped open.

When leading such activities, the ScienceTeam staff taught the teens to follow a basic activity structure of:

1. introducing themselves and having the community group introduce themselves;
2. doing an "icebreaker" activity from among the large staple they'd learned in the program;
3. doing the science activity;
4. summarizing the science behind the activity; and
5. closing the session (or going onto another).

This activity structure was designed so the young people had a pattern to follow that they could lean on, even though many started out as shy public speakers, and that included reminders of, and practice at, social transitions (Steps 1 and 5); a social comfort-building activity that would help both guests and teen facilitators in the "icebreaker" (Step 2); the main science activity, with its hands-on aspects that teens had practiced ahead of time (Step 3); and a reminder to the teens to stress the science explanations for the hands-on work (Step 4). The teens worked diligently at their communication skills when interacting with community groups, but their attention to Step 4, the science behind the activities, was diminished by the teens prioritizing visitors "having fun," which all mentioned as most important to them in interviews. As the activity structure was designed to not only guide work in the sessions, but also assure that the practice and the sessions reinforced the communication skills as well as the science understanding of the teen facilitators, neglecting Step 4 had negative consequences. Evidence of this is seen in a description of the "Gas in a Bag" activity prepared by teens at the end of the summer in a poster for an open house they held for parents and partners. The poster text was as follows:

Procedure
1. Gather all your materials.
2. Then put the spoon full of baking soda in your plastic bag.
3. Slowly pour your cup full of vinegar in the bag and close it quickly.
4. Then observe the chemical change.

Materials
*   Vinegar
*   Baking Soda
*   Spoon
*   Cups
*   Plastic Bag.

Background Info

- Vinegar contains a lot of acetic acid; baking soda is sodium bicarbonate.
- When sodium bicarbonate dissolves into the vinegar it reacts with water and forms OH^- which reacts with the acetic acid (OH^- is base) to form water.

Short answer: It's an acid-base reaction.

The background information listed at the end relates to the science, but it reveals some important issues. It was quoted directly from an "Ask A Scientist" website (Argonne National Laboratory, n.d.), and it is unclear how well the teens understood what they wrote. In addition, it did not address the most striking event in the experiment: that a large amount of gas forms. This fact was addressed on the same website, but the teens did not quote that portion. Based on my observations in the course of these activities, the teens showed strong evidence of becoming more practically familiar with the phenomenon in the course of the activities and adept at communicating with visitors about how to accomplish these tasks, but they did not talk much about, or show much evidence that they understood, *why* the gas formed in the bag. The teens readily identified as science outreach workers in their interactions with the public, made possible through authentic community connections. But, although their authentic personal agency was tied closely to the externally authentic cultural tools relating to general communication, because those tools allowed them to engage their audience in the hands-on activity, their agency was *not* tied to the use of deeper scientific explanation, which would have required more understanding of the science. Neither their audience, nor their adult supervisors pushed them hard on this aspect of scientific practice, as evidenced by my observations.

A second aspect of ScienceTeam during summer 2006, which contrasts with the above example, was lab work. An example of lab work, which was carried out several times during the summer under the direction of a staff member with a science degree and experience in university-based laboratory practices, was the making of pH indicator. Unlike some chemistry labs carried out in the program, and many labs carried out in schools, this lab resulted in a product that was needed and used. The pH indicator was used in some other labs and it was also used in one of the informal science activities for other community groups led by the YouthScience teams, and it thus tied to authentic community connections. As detailed by three teens in their poster for the open house at the end of the summer, the indicator solution was created by the following procedure:

1. Cut very small pieces of red cabbage.
2. Blend red cabbage and water in a blender.
3. Strain the pulp leaving only the juice behind; the juice serves as the indicator for this activity.

The teens had a pH scale to match colors the indicator would become when it reacted with solutions at various pH levels, such as Lysol, soda, and baking soda mixed with water. As with the baking soda and vinegar, it is not clear that the teens deeply learned much conceptual knowledge of pH, because their identification as lab workers that they took up did not require participation in deeper conceptual analysis. Their lab activities did, however, familiarize them with some concepts such as pH and state change in matter, and provided them with practical experience in laboratory skills, including following procedures, precise measurement, observation, data collection and analysis, and handling and use of equipment such as test tubes, beakers, pipettes, and graduated cylinders. Thus, the pH labs related to externally authentic cultural tools directly connected to science inquiry skills valued in academic science and brokered by a lab leader with external credentials. The YouthScience program probably had better lab facilities and equipment than some of the teens' under-funded schools, or they may have been more willing to use them. As one student put it: "in physical science [at school], we didn't get to do anything with the materials and chemicals," but he preferred the hands-on experimentation they did in YouthScience, where he gave evidence that he felt some sense of agency owing to the privilege of working with expensive materials in a well-outfitted facility. For all the teens, the skills gained in ScienceTeam labs likely prepared them for some school science activities, or reinforced their experiences in school science.

"TechTeam"—Designing, Building, and Testing Greenhouse Structures

The TechTeam program at YouthScience was aimed primarily at designing and building structures while utilizing computer technology. In this case, the group had an *authentic community connection* with two community organizations that were interested in providing lower-cost and healthier food to their clients by growing edible plants (e.g., tomatoes, cabbage, herbs). In order to provide an extended growing season for edible plants, the TechTeam supervisors decided to undertake designing and building greenhouses. For this reason, most of TechTeam's time during the summer of 2006 was spent on the *externally authentic cultural tools* of designing, building, testing, and sharing practices as used by teams of engineers, followed by some construction practices, all aimed at creating affordable greenhouse structures for the partner organizations. TechTeam included 17 African-American youth and was co-led by a European-American male in his twenties with a bachelor's degree in physics, who had been supervising in the program for several years, and a supervisor new to the program who was a European-American female in her twenties with a degree in engineering and a background in international environmental education. The engineering activities were intended to connect with participants' prior trajectories as computerphiles (all the participants in this module had an ongoing interest in tech tools) and with potential futures as engineers or other professionals. As with the HistoryWeb clubs, it was hoped that participating youth in TechTeam would develop *authentic personal agency* through meaningful work on this project and through meaningful use of the computer tools for the design, building, testing, and presenting tasks.

As part of this greenhouse initiative, the TechTeam teens participated in two rounds of systematic "design–build–test," followed by meetings where teams would report on their designs and tests. Such design–build–test cycles are authentic practices used by professional engineers (Bucciarelli, 1994; Svarovsky & Shaffer, 2006) that include critical thinking combining concepts and values.

During the summer, the teens created and tested structure prototypes using PVC, wood, and metal to decide on the optimal shape for a greenhouse and then the optimal "skin" to cover the greenhouse frame. In the process followed by the TechTeam teens, they worked in collaborative teams of three or four and chose the shape they'd design and build. After they chose shapes, which included a geodesic dome, house, cube, hemisphere, half cylinder, and pyramid, they planned a design for how they'd construct it, in some cases with the aid of internet research. The teams had to work with real-world constraints of a limited set of materials (PVC, wood dowels, wire, screws, bolts, metal connectors). Each team was responsible for building one prototype, and some teams had to overcome difficulties in making their model work (e.g., strains of bending materials, using math to figure out how to make shapes work). After the models of each shape were built and preliminary models presented, the whole group came to consensus on elements that would make a structure design good for a greenhouse. These included cost, area, volume, holding weight, withstanding "pushes" from the side, cost per area, and cost per volume. Then "fair tests" for how those elements in proposed designs could be tested were needed.

Each team of three or four teens was responsible for solving the problem of how to make a "fair test" that was numeric and measurable for all the prototypes and then to collect the data. In some cases, such as holding weight and withstanding push from the side, it was difficult for the teens to figure out how to isolate and measure the variable both accurately and for fair comparison across structures with different shapes. After all data were collected, the measured outcomes were then converted into ratings on a scale, and the ratings were given weights based on their importance to the overall quality of design. Finally, the composite scores of competing designs were compared using spreadsheets and graphs to pick the better design according to the agreed-upon criteria. All this was done in the context of preparing for presentations to an external panel of experts from the National Society of Black Engineers (NSBE), and for deciding which structure to use for the teens' own greenhouse design. The first design competition led to the selection of a geodesic dome as the optimal shape. In the second round, the teens focused primarily on the "test" phase and coming up with the optimal skin material to use to cover their geodesic dome. Pairs of groups came up with tests for several factors. Again, the groups were responsible for solving problems that arose in making the test data rigorous and comparable, and the tests again led to presentations to guest NSBE experts.

The final aspect of the summer greenhouse project involved the group in constructing a prefab geodesic dome on Science Corner and building a prototype of their own affordable geodesic dome that could be duplicated for other locations. Building the prefab dome involved extensive use of tools and some assembly challenges in the hot summer.

In contrast to the ScienceTeam activities, the TechTeam greenhouse design and building activity strongly aligned externally authentic cultural tools, authentic community connections, and authentic personal agency with opportunities for the teens to create trajectories of identification and participation in fundamental practices of the discipline of engineering. The teens who designed, built, and tested structures and skins for the greenhouses had to both master practical skills of tool use and engage in more extensive analysis work to succeed in, and have a chance at winning, these competitions. The fact that they identified with the role of designers serving the public, and with competitors within their own group trying to generate the "winning" designs, both contributed to their deeper participation.

Lessons Learned

In looking across these initiatives, I draw several lessons about pathways for intellectual development, the importance of participant knowledge as well as identifications, and the role of framing. I will explicate these in turn.

In any learning environment, there are "pathways" (Nasir, 2010; Polman and Miller, 2010) that the institutional or designed context provides for the participation and identification of participants. In the case of these environments meant to involve young people in disciplinary communities of practice, these pathways combine practices from the discipline with values and expectations for how one can develop from a newcomer to the situation to a more expert and full participant. The pathways were intended in all these cases to welcome youth with multiple and complex trajectories of identification and participation outside the learning environment into the community. In the HistoryWeb context, the pathway for a game player such as Bobby to become a game designer smoothly integrated with the pathway for him as a newcomer to the historical practice of contextualization, because that contextualization directly served goals that were authentic and meaningful to him as a game player and developing designer. On the other hand, the pathway for Richard to move from an interested student to a history web-page developer was less clear to him and his facilitator, and the cultural tool of contextualization was less salient and usable than basic interpretation of sources. In the ScienceTeam context, the pathways from new science outreach worker doing demonstrations and new lab techs to more expert practitioners of those activities did not demand, in personally meaningful and authentic ways, strong conceptual understandings and scientific explanations of the material in use. On the other hand, in TechTeam, the greenhouse-design task combined authenticity in terms of the engineering practices and in the sense of the authentic personal agency and meaning the participants were making of the activity.

Relatedly, the prior trajectories of participation and identification of both the youth and adult participants came into play in the course of their work in these learning environments. The missed opportunities of Richard for deeper historical inquiry and of the ScienceTeam members for deeper scientific explanation were in part the result of their adult facilitators not having high levels of expertise in these areas. As the adults lacked expertise in historical contextualization and scientific explanation, respectively, they were less able to provide relevant scaffolding. On the other hand, one of the adults in the TechTeam context brokered her own, personal experience as an engineering student to scaffold the youth carrying out engineering practices. The knowledge of how to behave in a more expert manner is not always directly brokered by individuals moving across communities of practice, however. As Wenger (1998) has noted, "boundary objects" sometimes reify the elements of a practice, and the adult who was facilitating Bobby's work on the game design utilized the set of index cards and an activity structure for laying out web-page designs provided by me (though not coincidentally: I am someone with a background in software-design practices). As stated previously, the fact that participants bring multiple identifications with communities of practice and affiliation is both a potential asset and a potential problem in learning environments. The fact that Bobby was a gamer proved to be an asset as his involvement developed, but the fact that Richard had difficulty reconciling his identifications as a rap-music fan and as a good student limited some potential opportunities for growth.

Finally, the way that situations get framed and intersubjectively negotiated affects the opportunities for growth and development of participants. The limitations in knowledge of scientific explanation and historical contextualization led, in some cases, directly to an inability to see how information and actions related to these cultural tools of the discipline could be framed within those practices. On the other hand, Bobby and his adult facilitator were able to intersubjectively align their framing of the situation and of actions taken by him in the situation along disciplinary lines, as authentic history embedded in game design; similarly, the participants in the greenhouse-design project were able to intersubjectively align their framing of the situation and of actions taken by them in the situation along disciplinary lines, as authentic engineering work.

These experiences and design-based research studies have the potential to inform more effective learning environment design in other contexts. They point to the importance of planning for the pathways and trajectories that participants can follow as they gain in expertise, considering the relevant knowledge—in the terms used above, externally authentic cultural tools—and how it can be brokered by individuals and/or reified in boundary objects. In addition, facilitators should work to interactively frame situations so that they allow learners to make use of their incoming identifications and knowledge, while seeking to address any tensions across identifications as they arise. The authentic community connections should be utilized, if at all possible, to both enhance authentic personal agency of learners and enhance the need for rigor in regards to the cultural tools targeted. In these ways, the identifications of individuals may productively align with their participation in learning activity.

References

Argonne National Laboratory (n.d.). Vinegar & baking soda II. Newton Ask a Scientist Archive. Retrieved March 8, 2007 from www.newton.dep.anl.gov/askasci/chem99/chem99116.htm (accessed March 8, 2007).

Bakhtin, M. M. (1981). Discourse in the novel (C. Emerson, & Holquist, M., Trans.). In M. Holquist (Ed.), *The dialogic imagination: Four essays by M. M. Bakhtin* (pp. 259–422). Austin, TX: University of Texas Press.

Bouillon, L. M., and Gomez, L. M. (2001). Connecting school and community with science learning: Real world problems and school-community partnerships as contextual scaffolds. *Journal of Research in Science Teaching, 38*(8), 878–898.

Bransford, J. D., Brown, A. L., & Cocking, R. R. (2000). *How people learn: Brain, mind, experience, and school.* Washington, DC: National Academies Press.

Brown, J. S., Collins, A., & Duguid, P. (1989). Situated cognition and the culture of learning. *Educational Researcher,* (January–February), 32–42.

Bucciarelli, L. L. (1994). *Designing engineers.* Cambridge, MA: MIT Press.

Calabrese Barton, A., Tan, E., & Rivet A. (2008). Creating hybrid spaces for engaging school science among urban middle school girls. *American Education Research Journal, 45,* 68–103.

Cole, M. (1996). *Cultural psychology: A once and future discipline.* Cambridge, MA: Belknap Press of Harvard University Press.

Collins, A., Brown, J. S., & Newman, S. E. (1989). Cognitive apprenticeship: Teaching the craft of reading, writing, and mathematics. In L. B. Resnick (Ed.), *Knowing, learning, and instruction: Essays in honor of Robert Glaser* (pp. 453–494). Hillsdale, NJ: Lawrence Erlbaum Associates.

Collins, A., Hawkins, J., & Carver, S. M. (1991). A cognitive apprenticeship for disadvantaged students. In B. Means, C. Chelemer, & M. S. Knapp (Eds.), *Teaching advanced skills to at-risk students: Views from research and practice* (pp. 216–243). San Francisco, CA: Jossey-Bass.

Design-Based Research Collective (2003). Design-based research: An emerging paradigm for educational inquiry. *Educational Researcher, 32*(1), 5–8.

Dow, P. (1991). *Schoolhouse politics: Lessons from the Sputnik era.* Cambridge, MA: Harvard University Press.

Dreier, O. (2000). Psychotherapy in clients' trajectories across contexts. In C. Mattingly, and L. Garro (Eds.), *Narrative and the cultural construction of illness and healing* (pp. 237–258). Berkeley: University of California Press.

Gee, J. P. (2000). Identity as an analytic lens for research in education. *Review of Research in Education, 25,* 99–125.

Lave, J., & Wenger, E. (1991). *Situated learning: Legitimate peripheral participation.* Cambridge, UK: Cambridge University Press.

Nasir, N. S. (2010). *Examining racial and cultural influence on learning and development across multiple levels of context.* Paper presented at the Annual Meeting of the American Educational Research Association, Denver, CO.

Nasir, N. S., and Hand, V. (2008). From the court to the classroom: Opportunities for engagement, learning, and identity in basketball and classroom mathematics. *The Journal of the Learning Sciences, 17*(2), 143–179.

O'Connor, K. (2003). Communicative practice, cultural production, and situated learning: Constructing and contesting identities of expertise in a heterogeneous learning context. In S. Wortham and B. Rymes (Eds.), *Linguistic anthropology of education* (pp. 61–92). Westport, CT: Praeger.

Penuel, W. R., and Wertsch, J. V. (1995). Vygotsky and identity formation: A sociocultural approach. *Educational Psychologist, 30*, 83–92.

Polman, J. L. (2000). Designing project-based science: Connecting learners through guided inquiry. New York: Teachers College Press.

Polman, J. L. (2006). Mastery and appropriation as means to understand the interplay of history learning and identity trajectories. *The Journal of the Learning Sciences, 15*(2), 221–259.

Polman, J. L. and Miller, D. (2008). *Trajectories of participation and identification in a socio-cognitive apprenticeship.* Paper presented at the Second Congress of the International Society for Cultural and Activity Research (ISCAR), San Diego, CA.

Polman, J. L., and Miller, D. (2010). Changing stories: Trajectories of identification among African American youth in a science outreach apprenticeship. *American Educational Research Journal*, doi: 10.3102/0002831210367513.

Rahm, J. (2007). Youths' and scientists' authoring of and positioning within science and scientists' work [Electronic Version]. *Cultural Studies of Science Education, 1*, 517–544. Retrieved May 18, 2007.

Rahm, J., Miller, H. C., Hartley, L., and Moore, J. C. (2003). The value of an emergent notion of authenticity: Examples from two student/teacher—scientist partnership programs. *Journal of Research in Science Teaching, 40*(8), 737–756.

Rogoff, B. (1994). Developing understanding of the idea of communities of learners. *Mind, Culture, and Activity, 1*(4), 209–229.

Secretary's Commission on Achieving Necessary Skills. (1991). *What work requires of schools: A SCANS report for America 2000.* Washington, DC: US Department of Labor.

Shaffer, D. W., and Resnick, M. (1999). "Thick" authenticity: New media and authentic learning. *Journal of Interactive Learning Research, 10*(2), 195–215.

Shakur, T. (1996). Only God can judge me. Death Row & Interscope Records.

Svarovsky, G. N., & Shaffer, D. W. (2006). Berta's tower: Developing conceptual physics understanding one exploratoid at a time. In S. A. Barab, K. E. Hay, & D. T. Hickey, *ICLS 2006: 7th International Conference of the Learning Sciences*, (pp. 751–757). Mahwah, NJ: Lawrence Erlbaum Associates.

Vygotsky, L. S. (1978). *Mind in society.* Cambridge, MA: Harvard University Press.

Wenger, E. (1998). *Communities of practice: Learning, meaning, and identity.* New York: Cambridge University Press.

Wertsch, J. V. (1991). *Voices of the mind: A sociocultural approach to mediated action.* Cambridge, MA: Harvard University Press.

Wertsch, J. V. (1998). *Mind as action.* New York: Oxford University Press.

Wineburg, S. (2001). *Historical thinking and other unnatural acts: Charting the future of teaching the past.* Philadelphia: Temple University Press.

Wortham, S. (2006). *Learning identity: The joint emergence of social identification and academic learning.* New York: Cambridge University Press.

10

DOES PLAYING *WORLD OF* *GOO* FACILITATE LEARNING?

Valerie J. Shute and Yoon Jeon Kim

> Failure is the opportunity to begin again, more intelligently.
>
> (Henry Ford)

Introduction

There has been a great deal of interest in video games and learning in recent years (e.g., Gee, 2003; Prensky, 2006; Shaffer, Squire, Halverson, & Gee, 2005; Shute, Rieber, & Van Eck, in press). A large part of this interest is motivated by frustration with the current education system and a desire for alternative ways of teaching and learning. Scholars in this games–learning arena argue that current schools in the United States do not adequately prepare kids for success in the 21st century. That is, learning in school is still heavily geared toward the acquisition of content, with instruction too often abstract and decontextualized, and thus not suitable for this age of complexity and interconnectedness (Shute, 2007).

In contrast to what children do inside of school, many of these same children spend countless hours playing fairly complex and challenging video games. In Ito and her colleague's three-year ethnographic study (2010), they report that playing video games with friends and family is a large and normal part of the daily lives of youth. They also contend that playing video games is not solely for enter-tainment purposes. In fact, many youth enthusiastically participate in online discussion forums to share their knowledge and skills about a game with other players, or seek help in relation to challenges when needed. Kids use a variety of video- and picture-editing tools to share their playing on the internet, and sometimes even learn how to modify the game (i.e., *modding*), which requires advanced computer technology skills.

The main claim of researchers in the area of games and learning is that computer (or video) games can facilitate learning, because games provide a rich, interesting context, conducive for learning to occur (e.g., Gee, 2003; Shaffer et al., 2006). In addition to establishing context, well-designed games share many of the same features as exemplary learning environments. Some of these features include interactivity, immediate and ongoing feedback, adaptive levels of challenge, and complex problems with specific goals (Gee, 2003; Shute & Torres, in press). Well-designed games thus have the potential to elicit active and critical thinking and learning skills (e.g., Gee, 2003; Shute et al., in press; Shute, Ventura, Bauer, & Zapata-Rivera, 2009).

Learning Theory

To support the claim that well-designed games are effective learning environments, we need to examine if and how people learn in those environments, and we need to be clear about what we mean by "learning." The most widely accepted learning theory for games-and-learning research is *situated cognition* (e.g., Barab et al., 2007; Gee, 2003; Lave & Wenger, 1991; Shaffer et al., 2005). Situated cognition defines human learning, thinking, and problem solving as being embodied within a context. People learn through active experiences and critical interpretation of their experiences via personal reflection and interpersonal discussion.

In addition, *people learn in action* in video games (Gee, 2008; 2010; Salen & Zimmerman, 2005). That is, people interact with all aspects of the game and take intentional actions within the game. For its part, the game continuously responds to each action, and, through this process, the player gradually creates meaning. Clearly, how people are believed to learn within video games contrasts to how people typically learn at school, which often entails memorization of decontextualized and abstract concepts and procedures (Shute et al., 2009).

Purpose and Organization of the Chapter

The main purpose of this chapter is to provide an example of an evidence-based assessment used within a commercial game to examine any learning of educationally valuable knowledge and skills that may take place during gameplay. Our beliefs motivating this research are twofold: (a) it is important to develop valid models and assessments for complex knowledge and skills that are required for success in the 21st century; and (b) assessments can be embedded within video games to support such skills that are currently not being assessed and supported. Our goal is to illustrate how people can develop educationally valuable skills (e.g., problem solving and causal reasoning) by playing a well-designed video game that is not explicitly developed for educational purposes.

The organization of this chapter is as follows. First, we briefly summarize a few examples of games and learning research to provide a feel for what's currently being done in the area. Second, we review assessment research conducted in relation to games. This is followed by an overview of a particularly effective assessment approach called evidence-centered design (ECD). The bulk of the chapter describes the game that we used to illustrate our claims—*World of Goo* (2008)—focusing our attention on how we developed and applied our ECD models to the game. We touch on our use of Bayesian networks (Pearl, 1988; Pearl & Russell, 2003) to tie the models together. And finally, we discuss findings from an exploratory assessment study, and close with implications for future research.

Background

Examples of Games and Learning

Our first example illustrates how kids learn science content and inquiry skills as situated in an online game called *Quest Atlantis: Taiga Park* (Barab et al., 2007; Shute et al., 2010). Players enter the game as an assistant to the park ranger. As such, they have to explore Taiga Park to investigate and understand why the fish are dying in the river. Players are immediately and actively engaged in various tasks, such as collecting water samples, interviewing stakeholders, creating hypotheses, and solving problems—large and small. They also travel across time via a time machine to see the consequences of their decisions and actions. From this gameplay, the players experience (via data collection and hypothesis making/revising) scientific inquiry and evolve in their understanding about how certain science concepts are related to each other (e.g., sediment in the water from the loggers' activities causes increased water temperature, which causes decreased dissolved oxygen, which causes the fish to die). Most importantly, players have many opportunities to reflect on their actions and make meaning from their experiences.

Our next example relates to research conducted by Squire (2004), who employed a popular commercial game called *Civilization* in a world-history class for high-school students. He reported that students playing the game developed deep and complex understanding and language in relation to world history.

Not only can playing video games facilitate learning of academic subjects, it also can facilitate the acquisition of complex thinking skills (e.g., problem solving and systems thinking). For instance, as Torres (2009) reported, students who played *Gamestar Mechanic* (i.e., a video game where kids play the role of game designer) developed systems thinking skills, and students playing Taiga Park similarly acquired systems thinking skills (Shute et al., 2010).

Assessment Research

Despite these preliminary, promising results, Gee (in press) and many others (e.g., Cannon-Bowers, 2006; van Eck, 2007) are quick to point out that there is still limited empirical evidence to support the range of learning-from-games claims. In an effort to begin to validate some of the claims and to provide evidence for why and how video games are good for learning, some researchers are paying greater attention to assessment (e.g., Rupp, Gushta, Mislevy, & Shaffer, 2010; Shaffer, 2006; Shute, in press).

Two examples highlight the importance of assessment research as applied to video games. First, Shute and colleagues (2009) describe *stealth assessment*—assessment that is seamlessly woven into a learning environment, such as games or simulations. They illustrate the approach within a commercial video game called *Oblivion*. Their example demonstrates how assessment can be situated within a game environment and be used to provide formative feedback and thus support learning of important competencies that are essential for success in the 21st century (e.g., creative problem solving).

Second, Shaffer and his colleagues (Shaffer et al., 2009) describe another approach to assessment in video games called *epistemic network analysis*. This is intended to be used within epistemic games such as *Urban Science* and science.net and represents another assessment approach for use in video games. Epistemic games are designed to allow players to think and act like domain-specific experts, such as urban planners and science journalists. Their example provides a way to understand players' growth in relation to the skills, knowledge, identities, and values of experts by playing epistemic games.

One common denominator underlying the two examples described above (i.e., Shute et al., 2009; Shaffer et al., 2009) is the use of an assessment design framework called ECD (Mislevy, Steinberg, & Almond, 2003).

Overview of Evidence-Centered Design

ECD is a conceptual framework that can be used to develop assessment *models*, which in turn support the design of valid assessments. The goal is to help assessment designers coherently align (a) the claims that they want to make about learners, and (b) the things that learners say or do in relation to the contexts and tasks of interest (for an overview, see Mislevy & Haertel, 2006; Mislevy et al., 2003). There are three main theoretical models in the ECD framework: competency, evidence, and task models.

The competency model consists of student-related variables (e.g., knowledge, skills, and other attributes) about which we want to make claims. For example, suppose that you wanted to make claims about a student's ability to "design excellent presentation slides" using MS PowerPoint. Your competency-model variables (or nodes) would include technical as well as visual design skills. Your evidence model would show how, and to what degree, specific observations and artifacts can be used as evidence to inform inferences about the levels or states of competency-model variables. For instance, if you observed that a learner demonstrated a high level of technical skill but a low level of visual design skill, you may estimate her overall ability to design excellent slides to be approximately "medium"—if both the technical and aesthetic skills were weighted equally. The task model in the ECD framework specifies the activities or conditions under which data are collected. In our current PowerPoint example, the task model would define the actions and products (and their associated indicators) that the student would generate, comprising evidence for the various competencies.

There are two main reasons why we believe that the ECD framework fits well with the assessment of learning in video games. First, in video games, people learn in action (Gee, 2003; Salen & Zimmerman, 2005). That is, learning involves continuous interactions between the learner and the game, so that learning is inherently situated in context. Therefore, the interpretation of knowledge and skills as the products of learning cannot be isolated from the context, and neither should assessment. The ECD framework helps us to link what we want to assess and what learners do in complex contexts. Consequently, an assessment can be clearly tied to learners' actions within video games, and can operate without interrupting what learners are doing or thinking (Shute, in press).

The second reason that ECD is believed to work well with video games is because the ECD framework is based on the assumption that assessment is, at its core, an evidentiary argument. Its strength resides in the development of performance-based assessments where what is being assessed is latent or not apparent (Rupp et al., 2010). In many cases, it is not clear what people learn in video games. However, in ECD, assessment begins by figuring out just what we want to assess (i.e., the claims we want to make about learners), clarifying the intended goals and outcomes of learning.

We will now see how this type of assessment approach can be applied within an existing game to determine what, if anything, of value is learned during gameplay.

World of Goo

World of Goo is a physics-based puzzle game where players utilize various types of "goo ball" to build different structures to reach suction pipes (Davidson, 2009). Each level consists of a different environment as well as the required number of balls to complete the level.

Depending on the nature of the environment, there are many forces working against each other, such as gravity and buoyancy. Their combination determines the stability (i.e., equilibrium) of the goo-ball structures. Thus, a player in the *World of Goo* needs to effectively solve a number of complex and novel problems.

One level of the game that we showcase in this chapter is called "Fisty's Bog" (for more on this level, see http://worldofgoo.wikia.com/wiki/Fisty's_Bog).

Similar to other levels in the game, players need to build a structure (in this case, a bridge) by connecting goo balls together and strategically affixing balloons to the structure. Fisty's Bog begins with a player figuring out what she is supposed to do to win the level. There are no explicit hints given to the player about what she is supposed to do. The only way the player can figure out the goal of the level is by engaging in exploratory behaviors, observations, reflections, and continuous hypothesis making and testing.

ECD Models Applied

Assessment in Fisty's Bog can support diagnosis of player performance and also provide the basis for formative feedback to the player—either explicitly (to the player or teacher) or upon demand. That is, specifying relevant knowledge and skills within the competency model at a sufficiently fine grain size for Fisty's Bog allows for inferential judgments to be made related to a learner's performance.

Consider a player who did not win the level on her first attempt. Maybe the player simply did not understand the goal, or perhaps she understood the goal, but experienced procedural difficulties when trying to execute a solution. That level of detail (i.e., conceptual misunderstanding vs. procedural problems) can be much more instructionally helpful than just informing her that she failed the level.

The assessment design for Fisty's Bog began with a cognitive task analysis (see Mislevy, Steinberg, Breyer, Almond, & Johnson, 1999) consisting of four parts. First, we met with a small group of *World of Goo* experts ($n = 3$) gathered to *discuss* relevant knowledge and skills needed to succeed in Fisty's Bog. Second, think-aloud protocols were collected from five individuals with varying levels of expertise in Fisty's Bog, from complete novice to expert. The main goal of this phase was to *observe* how people with different levels of expertise play Fisty's Bog. Third, the think-aloud protocols from the five players were analyzed, and we extracted features of performance that differentiated levels of proficiency. Finally, the collected information from the analysis served as the basis for coherently structuring the ECD models, described next.

The Competency Model of Fisty's Bog

Results from our cognitive task analysis yielded three main competency-model variables that are required for successful understanding and gameplay in Fisty's Bog: problem-solving skill, causal reasoning skill, and knowledge of static equilibrium. Each is described in turn.

- *Problem solving*: Problem solving consists of figuring out what the problem is, as well as the goal, and then coming up with appropriate solutions. Novice players of Fisty's Bog were not able to immediately identify what they were expected to do in Fisty's Bog. Furthermore, novice players were unable to identify all of the available resources and obstacles relating to the problem. In contrast, expert players quickly figured out the problem, identified helpful resources and obstacles to surmount, and were able to hypothesize solutions to solve the problem.

- *Causal reasoning*: From our review of the think-aloud protocols collected during the cognitive task analysis, we noticed that novice players were unable to identify all the variables that were interrelated in Fisty's Bog. Moreover, their explanations of the relationships tended to be rather simplistic and incomplete. Conversely, experts identified most of the variables that were interrelated, and their explanations for the causal relationships were fairly complex and comprehensive.

- *Knowledge of static equilibrium*: The physics principle applied in Fisty's Bog is static equilibrium. We hypothesized that a player who understood the conditions of static equilibrium would be able to readily attain balance of the bridge-like structure by manipulating the source of forces. Initially, it was not clear whether or not knowledge of static equilibrium is a critical competency in the solution of the level, to the same degree as problem solving and causal reasoning. That is, some players who had no formal knowledge of static equilibrium were still able to win the level, if they showed sufficient problem-solving and causal-reasoning skills. However, further analysis revealed that, even though the players didn't use formal physics terms, they still had a reasonable conceptual or intuitive understanding of static equilibrium that was expressed via informal language. For example, a player said, when he was asked what he was doing, "I am trying to keep it balanced . . . trying to build sort of a zigzag structure. Once it [the bridge] gets too long, it gets heavy and falls . . . need to add balloons to balance." We did, however, observe that a player who was an expert in physics more strategically distributed goo balls and balloons, compared with other players without the formal knowledge of static equilibrium.

The competency model for Fisty's Bog is shown in Figure 10.1. To win Fisty's Bog, the first thing a player needs to do is analyze the given problem. That is, a player should be able to state the mission or goal of the particular level in the game. Subsequently, a player should be able to indicate all available resources, including goo balls, balloons, the sign, and even the subtitle of the game (which, in this case was, "Not too high, not too low"). In addition, one should be able to indicate that upper and bottom spikes serve as serious obstacles as they can pop the inflated balloons (upper spikes) or kill goo balls (bottom spikes). Finally, one needs to hypothesize potential solutions. This solution-generation process is iterative, because a player needs to carefully monitor how the system reacts when the hypothesized solution is applied and make adjustments accordingly.

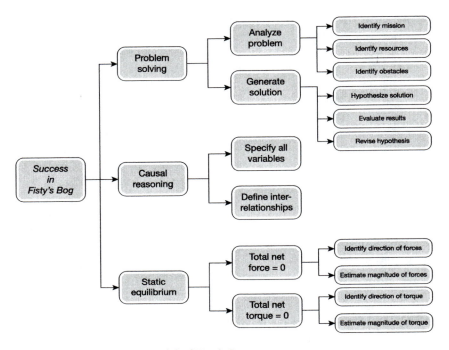

FIGURE 10.1 Competency model of Fisty's Bog.

Players should also be able to identify how the elements of the game and their interrelationships affect gameplay. For example, a player needs to understand that there are certain causal relationships among goo balls, such as sagging of the goo-ball structure, locations of balloons to counteract sagging, and the overall balance of the structure. In addition, having some informal or intuitive understanding of static equilibrium helps players to evenly distribute the weight in the structure, which helps players to build a stable structure.

The Evidence Model of Fisty's Bog

The evidence model in ECD determines how the observed actions in the game can be used as evidence to update the current states of the competency-model variables. That is, the evidence model statistically links specific observations with associated variables of the competency model, which are unobservable. The evidence model is composed of three parts: (a) *scoring rules* for indicators (i.e., how to score what a player does or says in relation to playing the game), (b) *scores* (e.g., values assigned to players' answers to questions and their causal maps), and (c) *statistical models* (e.g., probability distributions for competency-model variables for data accumulation). For example, when a player accurately identified the mission of Fisty's Bog, she would obtain a score of 1 (with a range of 0–1).

Her score is then fed back to the corresponding competency-model variable (i.e., identify the mission) using a statistical accumulation process (e.g., Bayes net).

The Action Model of Fisty's Bog

Shute et al. (2009) renamed the task model of the ECD framework to "action" model when used in games, because an action in a game is what a learner does by interacting with the environment to solve problems. The action model defines the sequence of actions that a player takes during gameplay, and each action's indicators of success (and failure). Some actions are required to be sequential to proceed within the mission, while some actions can repeatedly occur. For example, in Fisty's Bog, the first required action is to identify the goal of the current level or quest. Next, a player needs to repeatedly array goo balls and balloons to build a bridge–like structure. Table 10.1 illustrates some representative actions that a player needs to take, along with their associated indicators to succeed in Fisty's Bog.

The ECD-based models need to be tightly aligned so that they can be used for reasoning about players' proficiency in Fisty's Bog. To join all the models together, we employed a Bayesian network (or Bayes net).

TABLE 10.1 Action and indicators

Action	Indicators
Identify mission	State that the goal of this level is to reach up to the suction pipe by creating a structure that reaches to the suction pipe, and at least 6 goo balls need to be sucked into the pipe
Identify available resources	Identify the use of balloons Identify the use of goo balls to construct a bridge Identify the use of reset button (i.e., flying flies) Identify the purpose of the suction pipe Understand the meaning of the hint (not too high, not too low) Identify the use of the sign (additional hints)
Identify obstacles	Avoid upper spikes Avoid bottom spikes
Hypothesize solutions	State hypothesized solutions
Evaluate results	Analyze and articulate reasons for success Analyze and articulate reasons for failure
Revise hypothesis	Modify hypothesized solution to solve the problem in subsequent gameplay

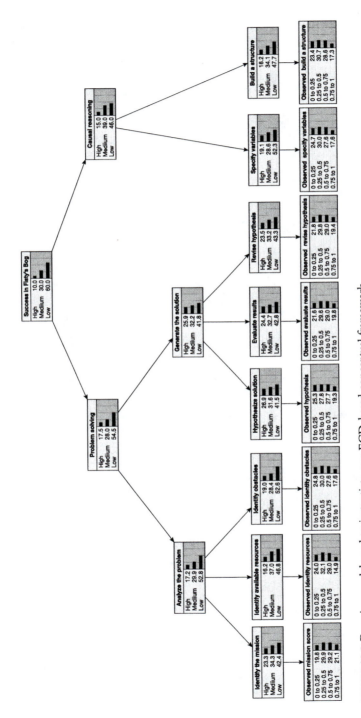

FIGURE 10.2 Bayesian model used to instantiate our ECD–based conceptual framework.

Success in Fisty's Bog

Similar to the examples described by Shute and colleagues (e.g., Shute et al., 2009, 2010), we formalized our competency and evidence models by employing a Bayes net. In this study, only two competency-model variables (e.g., problem solving and causal reasoning) were formalized and expanded. Modeling the third variable —static equilibrium—was not done because of time and computational constraints. That is, because this was an exploratory study, we first wanted to test parts of the model (problem solving and causal reasoning) that we believed exerted more influence on one's success in the game. Also, as mentioned, almost all of the individuals we observed during our cognitive task analysis phase seemed to have an intuitive understanding of static equilibrium coming into the game.

A Bayes net links together actions, evidence, and claims about competencies, which allows for probability-based reasoning of the learner's performance (Mislevy, 1994). A Bayes net can integrate evidence from a learner's performance and produce marginal probabilities for each variable of the competency model. The a priori probabilities (i.e., the priors) for the conditional probability tables of the Bayes net were obtained from the cognitive task analysis. Figure 10.2 shows our initial Bayesian model instantiating our ECD-based conceptual framework.

In the following section, we describe how our ECD-based assessment was administered and then interpret results from an exploratory study using *World of Goo*.

Exploratory Study

Method

Three undergraduate students (ages 18–22) and one graduate student (age 38) participated in this exploratory study. None had prior experience playing *World of Goo* (see Appendix A for the survey questions used to recruit participants for both the cognitive task analysis and the exploratory study). Before the participants were individually tested, we provided a warm-up exercise for the think-aloud procedure. Once each participant started playing the game, interactions with the game were automatically recorded by a screen-capturing application called Fraps (2010). This allows synchronizing of the verbal protocol with players' actions. Some structured questions were also asked while they were playing the game (Appendix B), and a behavior checklist was utilized (Appendix C) to obtain additional information regarding specific indicators.

Once each player completed or elected to quit the game, he or she was asked to draw a map explaining the causal relationships among all of the variables in the game (Appendix D). We then transcribed and analyzed the verbal protocols of the players. Table 10.2 summarizes the descriptive data of the four participants.

TABLE 10.2 Descriptive data about the participants

	S1	S2	S3	S4
Age	20	18	22	38
Gender	M	F	M	M
How often do you play video games?	Almost every day	Once a month	Never	Never
How good you are at playing games in general?	Very good	Fair	Good	Poor
Number of attempts	2	4	3	3
Completed the level	Yes	No	No	Yes

Results

To demonstrate how our ECD models were used to provide information about one's proficiency in Fisty's Bog, we compared two participants relative to their performance in the game (i.e., S3 and S4). Figures 10.3 and 10.4 indicate the overall estimated proficiency levels of S3 and S4 when the evidence is integrated into the Bayes net.

As indicated in Table 10.2, S3 didn't win the level after three attempts, while S4 won the level on his third attempt. Based solely on this information, one might conclude that S4 is a better player than S3 because he won the level, and that S4 is more likely to have higher problem–solving and causal-reasoning abilities than S3. However, when the evidence model was updated, we were able to make more valid assessments of their respective competencies, and here is why.

Problem Solving

Both S3 and S4 scored perfectly (with a value = 1.0) relative to being able to identify the mission of the game. That is, they stated that the goal of the game is to build a bridge–like structure using goo balls and pink balloons to reach the suction pipe at the other end. However, when it came to identifying resources and obstacles, S4 did not identify certain resources, such as the hint from the subtitle of the game and the utility of the reset buttons. He also didn't identify the bottom spikes as an obstacle. In contrast, S3 identified all six resources and indicated both upper and bottom spikes as obstacles. Therefore, the overall posterior probability of S3's "analyze the problem" competency was estimated as high ($p = .93$), whereas S4's posterior probability of being high in relation to that competency was less, $p = .63$.

So, both S3 and S4 played Fisty's Bog three times, and S4 won the level, whereas S3 did not. And we found that S3 identified more resources and obstacles

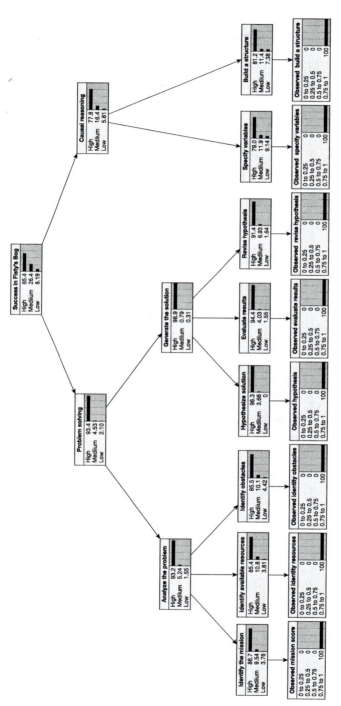

FIGURE 10.3 S3's posterior probabilities after updating the evidence model.

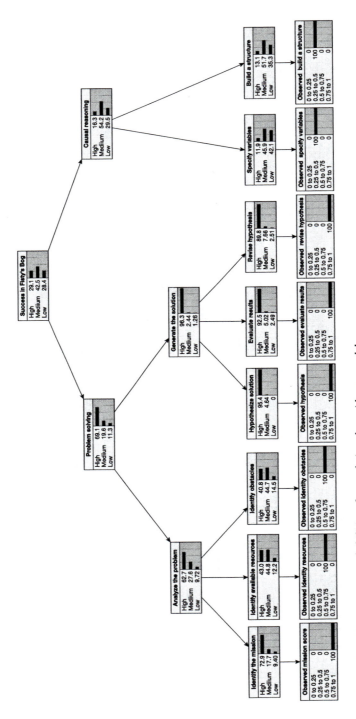

FIGURE 10.4 S4's posterior probabilities after updating the evidence model.

compared with S4. Does that finding have any bearing on learning, especially in terms of anything noteworthy? To answer this question, we further analyzed the data obtained from the captured videos, focusing on how much time each player spent in the game during their first attempt. The reason that we looked at their first-attempt data is because that is when players are more likely to be engaged in exploratory behaviors (e.g., random clicking around until something changes) compared with more purposeful actions. We found that the total amount of time S3 spent during his first attempt was 11 minutes, 51 seconds, whereas S4 spent *less than half* the time of S3, at five minutes, 38 seconds. This suggests that S3 spent more time exploring the game environment and elements compared with S4.

We further analyzed the verbal protocols of the two players during their first attempt. We wanted to see if there were any qualitative differences in terms of how they were respectively engaged. Consistent with the amount of the time they spent, S3 paid attention to every single element in the game. For example, he read and reread the hint sign three times, whereas S4 only clicked it once. S3 also tried to make sense out of the sign that was intentionally vague, whereas S4 simply said it didn't give any tips. S3 carefully evaluated each action he made, saying things such as, "I think maybe I did something right," and "Something just happened and I don't know why yet." In contrast, S4 clicked around till something accidently happened. And, instead of trying to explain why something was changed in the game, he repeated his apparently aimless clicking. Even though these differences between the two players did not predict who eventually won the level, it helped shed light on who was more actively and critically engaged during gameplay (i.e., S3).

Causal Reasoning

The causal-reasoning estimate was based on the completeness and accuracy of the causal maps that S3 and S4 produced after playing the game. Causal maps represent the players' causal knowledge about the game components. The quality of the produced causal maps is determined by the number of relevant variables included, the number of links between variables, and appropriate directions of the links (Spector, Christensen, Sioutine, & McCormack, 2001). For comparison purposes, we developed and used an *expert* (or reference) causal map that was produced from the results of the cognitive task analysis (see Figure 10.5).

When we examined the causal maps from both players relative to the expert map, we found that S3 identified 10 relevant variables that overlapped with the expert's map, whereas S4 only listed three shared variables. In addition, S3's map was more complex than S4's, as he linked all the variables with appropriate directions. Consequently, S3's diagram was seen as more complex and complete than S4's. When those data were incorporated into the Bayes net (see Figures 10.3 and 10.4), we see that, indeed, S3 has a higher estimated causal-reasoning

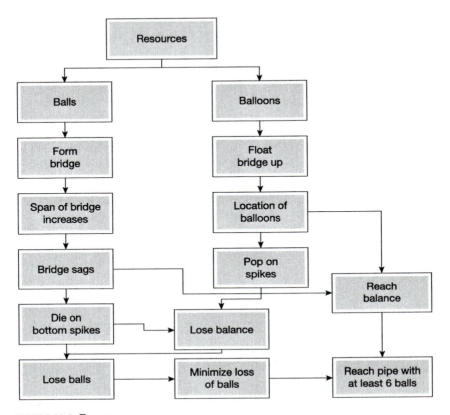

FIGURE 10.5 Expert map.

skill than S4 ($p = .78$ versus $p = .16$, respectively, in terms of the probability of being "high" on this variable).

S3's map indicates his understanding of Fisty's Bog as a system where various components of the game have causal relations. Furthermore, even though he did not explicitly use physics terms to explain these relationships, his map implies that he was able to induce the physics principle of static equilibrium (i.e., balancing two forces to make the applied net force equal to zero). On the other hand, S4's map is comparatively simplistic, suggesting that he failed to fully understand or explicate the various relations among game elements.

As illustrated by the comparisons of S3 and S4, just completing or winning Fisty's Bog does not automatically ensure the development of causal-reasoning and/or problem-solving skills. Rather, it depends on how actively and critically a learner (a) was engaged in the task (i.e., playing the game), and (b) reflected on the successes and failures during the game-play process. That is, even though S3 did not win the level, he was able to develop a higher estimated level of problem solving and causal reasoning relative to S4.

How can this result be explained? There are two important factors that affect meaningful learning in video games: reflection and failing (Gee, 2005). As Gee emphasized, the *reflection* on actions (and reactions) that take place during gameplay is crucially important for learning in video games. Furthermore, in well-designed games, *failing* is a critical part of learning. Players learn to revise their actions only as a result of failing. Therefore, "learning" in video games cannot be judged solely on the basis of whether one masters the game or wins a level. Evidently, S3 and S4 differed quite a bit in terms of their respective reflections of failure and success. This can be clearly seen in their think-aloud protocols following various attempts to win the level. When S3 failed in his first attempt, he analyzed his failure as follows:

> S3: Initially, I had no idea how to approach this game, but later I realized that you need to connect the goo balls together and use the balloons to keep the balls floated off the spikes . . . you need to make the thinnest bridge as you can across with most balloons spread out . . . so it doesn't droop. But I am out of balls now . . . I let my balloons pop and I'm kind of stuck in the middle like half-way.

On the other hand, when S4 was asked why he failed to win the level at his first attempt, he simply responded: "Because I didn't collect anything. I'm supposed to collect something."

Comparing those two responses, it seems that S3 understood the problem that he needed to solve and derived a viable solution better than S4 did after the first attempt. Moreover, S3 knew what he should do on his second attempt to win the level. Once both of them failed their second attempts, they were again asked why, to which they replied:

> S3: . . . I'm stuck because I'm out of little white flies [reset buttons] to help me get another balloon or goo balls. This time, I tried to balance out adding goo balls and balloons at the same time . . . it either rises up too fast and popped balloons, or sinks down too fast and kills goo balls . . . [I] didn't have enough balloons or goo balls to continue.

> S4: It took too long to realize the goal of the game, and my strategy wasn't good enough. If I play again, I know that I need to be careful with using the goo balls, so they don't run out.

As indicated from their answers, S3 appears to have a somewhat deeper understanding of the game than S4, and this explains why he was able to score higher than S4 in terms of problem-solving and causal-reasoning estimates, even though he didn't win the level.

Discussion

By implementing an ECD-based assessment linked to an existing causal game, we were able to examine the acquisition of certain knowledge and skills during gameplay. One interesting finding was that simply playing the game (and even winning the level) does not automatically translate into learning valuable knowledge and skills, especially to the degree, or of the kind, that can be transferred outside of the game setting. This was illustrated by the assessment results of S3 and S4. That is, even though video games have great potential as a rich context for learning, the success of learning ultimately depends on *how* one interacts with the game. Without such an understanding about the features of learners and video games, one cannot support the claim that playing video games facilitates learning.

We believe that our exploratory study has two implications to the field of video games and learning. First, employing this type of evidence-based assessment can help us to better understand the underlying learning theory in video games. That is, the present study highlights the importance of *failure* in relation to the learning processes in video games. Rather than construing it as a negative thing to be avoided (as in traditional education settings), failure should be viewed as a catalyst for reflection (e.g., *Why didn't this work, and what can I do differently next time?*). Second, ECD-based assessment can help us to make valid claims about what people do learn by playing video games, especially when the games are not explicitly educational.

We illustrated why assessment is so important in relation to video games. That is, the obtained assessment information can be used to support the development of a wide range of educationally valuable skills, including those that are not typically assessed and supported in current educational systems (e.g., causal reasoning). Because competency models are always up to date regarding a player's learning estimates, the information may ultimately be used diagnostically to direct targeted interventions or provide specific formative feedback (Shute, 2008). Moreover, information from the assessment can be used to help a player to engage in deep and critical reflection of one's actions and their consequences. However, even though reflection appears to be a key part of successful learning within video games, most game designs do not explicitly include features that facilitate reflection.

In conclusion, we described an assessment that was developed based on the ECD framework, and we illustrated how it could be used to provide the basis for valid inferences about players' learning in a particular, commercial video game. Although our preliminary results are encouraging, there is still much work to be done. More empirical studies need to be conducted to ascertain what comprises "good video games," and how they may be harnessed to facilitate people's active and critical learning and thinking (Gee, in press). We also recommend more effort by the research community to focus on identifying, modeling, and assessing what people learn. Ultimately, this can lead to a repository of valid competency models that may be reapplied in various learning environments—including other games. Finally, more examples of assessment in video games need to be tested to determine which aspects of those models are suitable, or not, for video games, or suitable for particular genres of games.

In closing, we note that the old expression, "It doesn't matter if you win or lose—it's *how* you play the game" takes on a whole new meaning relative to learning and the findings in this chapter. In particular, losing, in a curious way, may actually be a form of winning when it comes to video games and learning.

References

Barab, S. A., Zuiker, S., Warren, S., Hickey, D., Ingram-Goble, A., Kwon, E-J., Kouper, I., & Herring, S. C. (2007). Situationally embodied curriculum: Relating formalisms and contexts. *Science Education, 91*(5), 750–782.

Cannon-Bowers, J. (2006). *The state of gaming and simulation.* Paper presented at the Training 2006 Conference and Expo, Orlando, FL.

Davidson, D. (2009). From experiment gameplay to the wonderful world of goo and how physics is your friend. In D. Davidson (Ed.), *Well played 1.0: video games, values and meaning* (pp. 334–367). Pittsburgh, PA: ETS Press.

Fraps [Computer Software] (2010). (Version 3.2.2.) Beepa.

Gee, J. P. (2003). What video games have to teach us about learning and literacy? New York: Palgrave/Macmillian.

Gee, J. P. (2005). Learning by design: good video games as learning machines. *E-Learning and Digital Media, 2*(1), 5–16 Retrieved July 25, 2011 from http://dx.doi.org/10.2304/elea.2005.2.1.5.

Gee, J. P. (2008). Video games and embodiment. *Games and Culture, 3*(3–4), 253–263.

Gee, J. P. (2010). Human action and social groups as the natural home of assessment: Thoughts on 21st century learning and assessment. In V. J. Shute & B. J. Becker (Eds.), *Innovative assessment for the 21st century: Supporting educational needs.* New York: Springer-Verlag.

Gee, J. P. (in press). Reflections on empirical evidence on game and learning. To appear in S. Tobias & J. D. Fletcher (Eds.), *Computer games and instruction.* Charlotte, NC: Information Age Publishers.

Ito, M., Baumer, S., Bittanti, M., Boyd, D., Cody, R., Herr-Stephenson, B., et al. (2010). *Hanging out, messing around and geeking out: kids living and learning with new media.* The John D. and Catherine T. MacArthur Foundation Series on Digital Media and Learning. Cambridge, MA: The MIT Press.

Lave, J., & Wenger, E. (1991). *Situated learning: Legitimate peripheral participation.* Cambridge: Cambridge University Press.

Mislevy, R. J. (1994). Evidence and inference in educational assessment. *Psychometrika, 59,* 439–483.

Mislevy, R. J., & Haertel, G. D. (2006). Implications of evidence-centered design for educational testing. *Educational Measurement: Issues and Practice, 25*(4), 6–20.

Mislevy, R. J., Steinberg, L. S., & Almond, R. G. (2003). On the structure of educational assessment. *Measurement: Interdisciplinary research and perspective, 1*(1), 3–62.

Mislevy, R. J., Steinberg, L. S., Breyer, F. J., Almond, R. G., & Johnson, L. (1999). A cognitive task analysis with implications for designing simulation-based performance assessment. *Computers in Human Behavior, 15,* 335–374.

Pearl, J. (1988). *Probabilistic reasoning in intelligent systems.* San Mateo, CA: Morgan Kaufmann.

Pearl, J., & Russell, S. (2003). Bayesian networks. In M. A. Arbib (Ed.), *The handbook of brain theory and neural networks* (2nd ed., pp. 157–160). Cambridge, MA: MIT Press.

Prensky, M. (2006). *Don't bother me mom, I'm learning!: How computer and video games are preparing your kids for 21st century success and how you can help!* St. Paul, MN: Paragon House.

Rupp, A. A., Gushta, M., Mislevy, R. J., & Shaffer, D. W. (2010). Evidence-centered design of epistemic games: Measurement principles for complex learning environments. *Journal of Technology, Learning, and Assessment, 8*(4). Retrieved July 25, 2011 from http://escholarship.bc.edu/jtla/vol8/4.

Salen, K., & Zimmerman, E. (2005). Game design and meaningful play. In J. Raessens & J. Goldstein (Eds.), *Handbook of computer game studies* (pp. 59–80). Cambridge, MA: MIT Press.

Shaffer, D. W. (2006). *How computer games help children learn.* New York: Palgrave Macmillan.

Shaffer, D. W., Hatfield, D., Svarovsky, G. N., Nash, P., Nulty, A., Bagley, E., Franke, K., Rupp, A. A., & Mislevy, R. J. (2009). Epistemic Network Analysis: A prototype for 21st Century assessment of learning. *The International Journal of Learning and Media, 1*(2), 33–53.

Shaffer, D. W., Squire, K. A., Halverson, R., & Gee, J. P. (2005). Video games and the future of learning. *Phi Delta Kappan, 87*(2), 104–111.

Shute, V. J. (2007). Tensions, trends, tools, and technologies: Time for an educational sea change. In C. A. Dwyer (Ed.), *The future of assessment: shaping teaching and learning* (pp. 139–187). New York: Lawrence Erlbaum Associates, Taylor & Francis Group.

Shute, V. J. (2008). Focus on formative feedback. *Review of Educational Research, 78,* 153–189.

Shute, V. J. (in press). Stealth assessment in computer-based games to support learning. To appear in S. Tobias & J. D. Fletcher (Eds.), *Computer games and instruction.* Charlotte, NC: Information Age Publishers.

Shute, V. J. & Torres, R. (in press). Where streams converge: Using evidence-centered design to assess Quest to Learn. To appear in D. Robinson, J. Clarke-Midura, & M. Mayrath (Eds.), *Technology-based assessments for 21st century skills: Theoretical and practical implications from modern research.* New York: Springer-Verlag.

Shute, V. J., Masduki, I., & Donmez, O. (2010). Conceptual framework for modeling, assessing, and supporting competencies within game environments. *Technology, Instruction, Cognition, and Learning, 8*(2), 137–161.

Shute, V. J., Rieber, L., & Van Eck, R. (in press). Games . . . and . . . learning. To appear in R. Reiser & J. Dempsey (Eds.), *Trends and issues in instructional design and technology* (3rd ed.). Upper Saddle River, NJ: Pearson Education.

Shute, V. J., Ventura, M., Bauer, M., & Zapata-Rivera, D. (2009). Melding the power of serious games and embedded assessment to monitor and foster learning: Flow and grow. In U. Ritterfeld, M. J. Cody, & P. Vorderer (Eds.), *The social science of serious games: theories and applications* (pp. 295–321). Philadelphia, PA: Routledge/LEA.

Spector, J. M., Christensen, D. L., Sioutine, A. V., & McCormack, D. M. (2001). Models and simulations for learning in complex domains: using causal loop diagram for assessment and evaluation. *Computers in Human Behavior, 17,* 517–545.

Squire, K. (2004). *Replaying history: Learning world history through playing Civilization III.* Indiana University, IN: ProQuest Dissertations.

Torres, R. J. (2009). *Learning on a 21st century platform: Gamestar Mechanic as a means to game design and systems-thinking skills within a nodal ecology.* New York University: ProQuest Dissertations.

Van Eck, R. (2007). Six ideas in search of a discipline. In B. Shelton & D. Wiley (Eds.), *The educational design and use of computer simulation games.* Boston, MA: Sense.

World of Goo [Video Game] (2008). 2D Boy.

APPENDIX A

Your name: _____

Gender: _____

Age: _____

Highest degree earned: _____

Degree in: _____

How often do you play video games? (Please tick one option)

☐ Almost every day

☐ 3–4 times a week

☐ Once a week

☐ Once a month

☐ Never

If you regularly play video games, what kinds of video games do you play? (Please tick ALL that apply)

☐ Action (e.g., Street Fighter)

☐ Platform (e.g., Super Mario Bros)

☐ Role-playing (e.g., Dungeons & Dragons)

☐ Shooter (e.g., Halo)

☐ Simulation (e.g., The Sims)

☐ Strategy (e.g., Civilization)

☐ Others

Can you name some of the games that you played in the past?

_____

_____

_____

_____

How good you think you are at playing video (computer) games in general?

☐ Very good

☐ Good

☐ Fair

☐ Poor

☐ Very poor

APPENDIX B

Protocol Analysis prompts

In this experiment I am interested in what you say to yourself as you play the game that I will give to you. In order to do this I will ask you to THINK ALOUD as you play the game. What I mean by think aloud is that I want you to say out loud everything that you say to yourself silently. Just act as if you are alone in this room speaking to yourself. If you are silent for any length of time I will remind you to keep talking. You are also not allowed to ask me questions while you are playing the game. Do you understand what I want you to do?

Before we turn to the real experiment, I will give you a practice problem. I want you to talk while you do this problem. First I will ask you to multiply two numbers in your head.

So "think aloud" while you multiply 24 times 34.

Good! I think you are ready now. Let's go ahead and start.

Reminder: Keep talking

1   What is the goal of this level? (Identify mission)

2   How you think you can win this level? (Hypothesize solutions)

3   (Once they succeed or fail) Can you explain why you could/could not win this level?

4   (Once they succeed or fail) If you were given another chance, how would you play this time?

5   (At the end) Would you like to try again?

APPENDIX C

Behavioral Checklist

Participant's name: _____

Total # of attempts: _____

Complete the level:

☐ Yes

☐ No

Variables	Indicators	1st		2nd		3rd		4th		5th	
		Y	N	Y	N	Y	N	Y	N	Y	N
Resources	Identify the use of balloons										
	Identify the use of goo balls to construct a structure										
	Identify the use of reset button (i.e., flying flies)										
	Identify the use of the suction pipe										
	Utilized the meaning of the title as a hint (not too high, not too low)										
	Identify the use of the sign										
Obstacles	Indicate upper spikes as an obstacle										
	Indicate bottom spikes as an obstacle										

APPENDIX D

Your name: _____

List all the variables (elements) that you identified to win Fisty's Bog

_____

_____

_____

_____

_____

_____

_____

_____

_____

_____

Draw a diagram indicating causal relationships among the specified variables. (Feel free to use the back page if needed). For example:

| Hurricane Katrina | → | Loss of houses | → | Many people moved to Houston |

EPILOGUE

Where Are We, and Where Are We Going?

David Yun Dai, Jianwei Zhang, and Zheng Yan

The design research presented in this volume provides a glimpse, admittedly partial, of how the field has advanced over the past two decades or so in identifying and creating optimal conditions for promoting high-end learning and intellectual growth. The goal of this epilogue is to synthesize advances and identify challenges in design research particularly aimed at enhancing deep understanding, authentic problem solving, and critical and creative thinking. Design research as a whole goes through iterative cycles of designing, enacting, testing, and optimizing that intertwine with one another to enable sustained innovation and improvement of both educational theory and practice (Bereiter, 2002; Collins, Joseph, & Bielaczyc, 2004; Dai, this volume). Accordingly, this epilogue revisits and discusses four issues based on the work presented in the different chapters: (a) how a design is conceptualized; (b) how it is enacted to produce real advances; (c) how it is tested to demonstrate its efficacy as well as reveal its constraints and challenges; and (d) how it is formatively improved based on data collected and may be further optimized for better results.

Envisioning and Designing: Theory-Informed Innovations to Address Significant Needs

Taking a design science perspective on education research (Collins, 1992; Simon, 1969), design research focuses on identifying challenges, envisioning new possibilities, and testing new and improved designs (e.g., learning environments and interventions), with formative research findings fed back into further cycles of innovative design (Bereiter, 2002; Collins, 1992). Theory penetrates each of the above processes, informing analysis of challenges and elaboration of goals, guiding creation and improvement of designs, and justifying measures of success.

In light of their theoretical perspectives of learning and development, design researchers begin their research by defining needs of designs to address new, significant, educational goals or better solutions to existing problems. The research work represented in this volume tackles a wide range of challenges to address new and expanded educational goals: deep and transferable disciplinary understanding (e.g. Engle, this volume; Lehrer & Pfaff, this volume); sound reasoning and problem solving (Shute & Kim, this volume); critical thinking and creativity (Langer, this volume; Zhang, this volume); collaboration (Zhang, this volume); and agency and identity as lifelong learners and innovators (Engle, this volume; Polman, this volume). These competencies are highly demanded in 21st-century workplaces (Partnership for 21st Century Skills, 2008) and underlined by the latest research on learning and development (Bransford, Brown, & Cocking, 2000). The first four chapters (Dai, Gresalfi et al., Langer, and Kelly, this volume) discuss foundation issues regarding the nature and development of intelligence and intelligent actions, and how design research contributes to innovations in educational practice. Other chapters also draw on rich theoretical and research traditions and resources. Productive disciplinary engagement (Engle, this volume) builds on the Fostering Community of Learners model (FCL; Brown, 1997). Adaptive collaboration for collective knowledge advancement (Zhang, this volume) extends from knowledge building and intentional learning (Scardamalia & Bereiter, 2006).

How we conceptualize intelligence, learning, and intellectual development holds important heuristic value and has practical consequences on how we design learning environments to enhance intellectual potential and growth. For example, specifying affordances of a situation, perceiving and acting upon these affordances, and the effectivities of realizing particular affordances (Gresalfi et al., this volume) provide a framework for analyzing complex interactions between persons involved and content presented or encountered in a particular context (the nature of a task at hand, purposes of an activity organized around it, tools and resources available, norms and expectations reinforced, and positional identities or dispositions of participants to act upon the situation in an intelligent way).

As an alternative to this theory-driven approach, we can also build up design work by drawing inspirations from observations of "natural designs" and develop and design learning environments that emulate and refine "natural ways of learning" (Schank & Cleary, 1995), such as the examples of how chess players enhance their chance to win a tournament (Dai, this volume); how Darwin developed an epoch-making theory (Langer, this volume); how a human ecology rich in resources supports interest development and self-sustained learning (Barron, 2006); or how football players engage in self-evaluation and reflection after a game to increase their knowledge, enhance their skills, and nurture desired dispositions in a game situation (Derry & Lesgold, 1996).

The point of entry for design work reflects the focus of a design and understandings of a particular learning situation or problem, often achieved through collaboration with researchers from multiple disciplines (Bannan, this volume), classroom teachers (Langer, Lehrer & Pfaff, and Zhang, this volume), or other professionals (Polman, this volume). Bannan (this volume) focuses on learner-related constraints as well as potentials. Lehrer and Pfaff (this volume) examine an innovative way of representing mathematical concepts to elementary-school students. Polman (this volume) focuses on participation in learning and identity development in an informal learning setting: after-school programs. Design research can be diverse in settings, learners, and foci, but the common thread is the evolving understanding of how particular design elements work in concert to engage thought and action of desired quality and address learner-related or content-related constraints. Design elements developed and tested through a design research constitute a complex, dynamic system that plays out targeted functions and leads to deep change (Zhang, 2010). Such a system is defined, not only by activity procedures and tools, but also by a set of first principles, such as those highlighted by Engle (this volume) and Zhang (this volume). Principles underlying an innovation inform ways of viewing knowledge, learning, and teaching that imply specific approaches to learning practice and related social and technological configurations (Bielaczyc, 2006). Principles "need to be understood if the procedures are to serve their original function" (Brown & Campione, 1996, p. 322), with reflection on enactment and development of procedures further leading to deepened understanding of the principles and their consequences. The evolving understanding of principles and practices will eventually be crystallized to become what diSessa and Cobb (2004) called "ontological innovation." For example, Lehrer and Pfaff's (this volume) work represents such ontological innovation: their use of measurement as a metaphor in teaching rational numbers is not merely adding a pedagogical "trick" to the repertoire of mathematics teaching, but also reflects deep insights into how children's mathematical thinking can be facilitated by a representational medium. By the same token, the relational ontology proposed by Gresalfi et al. (this volume) repositions the locus of intelligence as situated and distributed, thus opening the door for interventions to enhance intellectual potential and growth. Maintaining a point of reference while exploring horizons of possibilities (Langer, this volume) is not merely theoretical abstraction but can be modeled as "meanings–in–motion." Moreover, assessment can no longer be just "sequestered" paper-and-pencil work that bears little resemblance to performance in real-life situations; it has to be able to document and measure real-time changes in thought and action in a situation (Gresalfi et al., this volume; Zhang, this volume). Not only so, it has to be capable of generating new insights into the affordances and constraints of a learning situation and informing ways to improve it (Kelly, this volume). Together, they call for a new epistemological grounding of knowledge claims about learning and intellectual gains, a new language for reliability and validity, which itself is no small feat as innovation.

Enacting: Implementing and Advancing Design in Practice

As a professional endeavor, design work in teaching and learning is only meaningful when it takes a pedagogical turn in putting a working hypothesis to work in authentic settings; that is, when we start to translate the conceptual into the practical. The enactment process often requires collaborative and creative efforts of teachers and researchers to elaborate, adapt, and fine-tune specific learning processes integrating various activities, material, social configurations, tools, and assessment. They implement the processes through day-to-day interactions and monitor the implementation based on data collected, in light of their target goals and principles. A perusal of the chapters in this volume indicates that advances have been made on three fronts: pedagogical devices to enhance student learning, reasoning, and problem solving; social organization of learning to reinforce particular knowledge processes, norms, commitments, and identities; and assessment to monitor progress and address emergent possibilities and constraints.

Pedagogical Innovations

Pedagogical innovations involve instructional devices and strategies that mediate learning by providing affordances for actions conducive to desired learning and thinking while addressing goal-related constraints (learner-related or otherwise). Bannan (this volume), for example, designed interventions to address learner-related constraints for twice exceptional students. Lehrer and Pfaff (this volume) developed domain-specific pedagogy (or pedagogical content knowledge) in teaching rational numbers and helping students make mathematical sense of numbers. Langer (this volume) implemented her idea of teaching for critical and creative thinking in language arts and social studies. These innovations do not merely make theory work in practical settings, but build new understandings in situ. A general theme is how to engage students in a process of inquiry that affords perspectival, instrumental, and reflective learning. Gresalfi and colleagues (this volume) discuss learning graphing in the context of mapping and finding a professor. Instead of merely learning procedures of graphing for its own sake, the consequential engagement they promote enhances instrumental learning. One may also argue that it will additionally produce reflective and perspectival gains—that is, an appreciation of what graphing techniques enable one to do in the real world.

Innovations in Social Organization of Learning

Broadly defined, social organization involves any social arrangement that defines the roles of participants and norms for an activity in a distinct manner. It is evident that, in the graphing task described above, "the way the teacher positions the students relative to the task" (Gresalfi et al., this volume) redefines the role of the teacher as well as that of the students (see also Barab, Gresalfi, & Ingram-

Goble, 2010). Building a culture of learning and thinking with committed learners has been a major impetus of research since Brown (1994) proposed her model of FCL (initially labeled "the Community of Learners," COL; Brown, 1994, p. 6). Engle (this volume) and her colleagues developed a model of productive disciplinary engagement, which is one of many follow-up endeavors in the wake of FCL to build more refined models with more clearly defined norms for learning and roles for learners. Not only do authority and accountability highlight student ownership and responsibility: problematization is another principle that predisposes students to take a critical stance on issues at hand, even issues that might appear simple and obvious. What it really does is to engage problem finding and critical thinking through questioning, argumentation, and dynamic exchanges of ideas and perspectives (see also Engle & Conant, 2002). Zhang's (this volume) lineage is also tractable. He explores adaptive collaboration for creative knowledge work on the basis of the knowledge-building pedagogy (Scardamalia & Bereiter, 2006), but with new inspiration from the research on collaborative creativity (e.g., Sawyer, 2007). The principles he lays out, such as collective cognitive responsibility, democratizing knowledge, and reflective representation of community knowledge, like maintaining a point of reference (Langer, this volume), are norms created to maintain the quality of learning and thinking at the highest level possible. Engle and Zhang reveal their common emphasis on social organization of learning (norms, roles, identities, and interactivity), and how it engages and sustains the kinds of thinking process and disposition deemed important for intellectual gains. In the same vein, Polman (this volume) tracked the parallel processes of participation and identity development that have a distinct social component.

Innovations in Technological Support

Technology includes any media, tools, and supporting systems that can be used to support particular pedagogical functions. Design researchers draw upon affordances of technology to develop innovative learning models, with research-informed learning tools created and tested as important output of their work. Lehrer and Pfaff (this volume) invented spatial measures as a medium for mathematical representations and reasoning. Other researchers developed computer-supported tools and platforms. For example, computer games afford opportunities to work and learn in a virtual environment and vastly expand the capacity to offer a variety of authentic experiences not possible without the technology (Barab et al., 2010). To a large extent, innovations in pedagogy in mediating and organizing learning are enabled by new forms of technological support. In Bannan's (this volume) case, it is a device that clients can use to enhance their cognitive functions. For Zhang (this volume), it is the online platform that provides a communal knowledge space and tools to support social interactivity, along with analytic tools to trace student activities and progress in knowledge building.

For Shute and Kim (this volume), it is the online assessment of whether all components are present and working in concert to achieve the goal of problem solving. Theoretically, technological advances enable design researchers to fine-tune particular components to the level of specificity at which engineering researchers fine-tune their system functioning. For example, a computer game may be designed to engage particular motivational processes and mechanisms at a particular point in gameplay; an assessment system can spot a particular weakness while a student is problem solving and "activate" metacognitive control for the student and suggest corrective strategies accordingly.

Assessing and Evaluating: Challenges of Design Work in Situ

Innovations in Assessment

Assessment in the context of design research means several things: assessing the overall efficacy of a design or model, as well as how specific components function; or integrating data about social and cognitive processes (e.g., engagement, collaboration, student control), individual and collective outcome (e.g., knowledge, skills, dispositions, metacognitive strategies, resources), and contextual/systematic measures (e.g., ease of adoption, sustainability, scalability, and costs) (Collins et al., 2004). Ultimately, assessment is about how well the design is doing its job at the level of individual participants: psychological, behavioral, and epistemic changes need to be documented and assessed to show how the design plays out and might be further improved. Kelly (this volume) calls on design researchers to confront this issue head-on. Shute and Kim (this volume) focus on how assessment of problem solving and causal reasoning can be done in situ (in a gameplay situation) through the use of technology. Gresalfi et al. (this volume), Zhang (this volume), and Lehrer and Pfaff (this volume) tackle assessment issues in the context of their design work. Their efforts show that it is possible to observe and assess ongoing processes to capture what has been gained and what has been changed, based on integration of multiple analyses.

Challenges in Assessment

Assessment in design research is much more than assessing "student outcomes." As a design experiment unfolds in real education settings, it is inevitable that new challenges and problems will emerge that call for modification of the initial idea, even "dramatic shifts in thinking" (Hay & Kim, 2006, quoted in Kelly, this volume). The chapters in this volume show that, indeed, it is one of the most challenging aspects of design research, particularly when it is aimed at high-end learning and higher-order thinking (deep understanding, problem solving, reasoning, critical thinking, expertise, etc.; Kelly, this volume) in socially and physically distributed learning contexts.

A starting place for testing a learning design is to ask, reflectively, some key questions: What are the purposes of a particular line of design inquiry, through what kind of design and enacting processes, with what levels of success and why (and how is it assessed)? The chapters in this volume address these questions with differential success. For the question of what levels of success a design work achieved and why, the answers are at least equivocal. In a sense, design research is still at "demo" stage, in that a typical presentation would show how a designed system works in part or as a whole. In what way the design is doing its job is often not fully elaborated. Detailed, ethnographic accounts of classroom processes, school contexts, and teacher efforts to implement and improve an innovation may provide important insights (e.g., Zhang, Hong, Scardamalia, Teo, & Morley, in press).

As design research seeks to advance principled understandings rather than merely to deliver tangible design products, it behooves design researchers to problematize their own design, very much like what we ask students to do in their inquiry (Engle, this volume). Design researchers need to be open-minded, seeking new leads and confronting disconfirming evidence. For example, during their research, Lehrer and Pfaff (this volume) found that, despite the efforts to help students make mathematic sense of quantitative relations, they still found resistance from students, and their belief that math is just computational routines and that remembering rules is more important than explaining why the rules work persisted (see also Schoenfeld, 1988). This learner-related constraint was uncovered in "epistemic conversation" with students and becomes a new leverage point to engender perspectival and reflective learning. Polman (this volume) also found that the lack of skill preparation rendered particular affordances ineffective in his after-school programs. Indeed, identifying new possibilities (feedforward) and finding new constraints (feedback) are the major mechanisms through which an initial design idea gets enriched, refined, modified, or even drastically changed in direction (see diSessa & Cobb, 2004).

To benefit the design research community, a design study needs to present a discussion of not just what the design logic is, and how design work has played out and improved over time, but how viable it is in comparison with alternatives, what evidence supports a particular approach, and what conditions are to be met for its successful adoption. This way, design studies can truly become an ongoing, evolving inquiry that seeks fundamental understanding of how the learning processes work under various conditions, rather than merely promotion of a particular model or theory. For that matter, the three criteria, effectiveness, practicality, and validity (Dai, this volume), need to be directly addressed.

Refining and Optimizing: Problems and Prospects

It is unlikely that a designed unit is completely specified in terms of content, process, and product, like a cookie-cutter solution. Conducting design research means working with an open, dynamic, evolving system of interactions, always ready to modify the way materials are presented, learning is organized, and pedagogical support deployed. A smart design is not only aimed at producing "smart" learning; it itself should be adaptive by design, responsive to changing circumstances, emergent evidence, and new opportunities. The old-fashioned technical rationality (logical positivism, canned solutions, fixed procedures) cannot solve problems in education that are by nature ill structured and not subject to simple prescription; reflective rationality is essential to ensure conceptual growth in researchers themselves (Schön, 1983). Given the uncertainties in design research, it is important to consider strategically how to experiment with, and manage, various dimensions of a design.

Authenticity

Authenticity of settings, actors, actions, and consequences (and assessment) is what distinguishes design research from traditional experimental and correlational research. It does not mean, however, only hands-on learning can be "authentic." Even second-hand, text-based learning can be made authentic by learning vicariously to think like experts (Palincsar & Magnusson, 2001). Working with ideas and producing conceptual, epistemic artifacts (e.g., theory, work plan) can be as authentic and engaging as creating material artifacts (e.g., poster, exhibition) (Scardamalia & Bereiter, 2006). Indeed, sometimes, seemingly "authentic" activities such as experiments in science classrooms can be so canned and routinized that the essence of how to investigate a particular phenomenon in a scientifically justified manner gets lost (Duschl & Duncan, 2009).

Authenticity of learning is to ensure that what students learn carries real meaning and significance for students, so as to prepare them for future learning, life-long and life-wide (Bransford and Schwartz, 1999). However, it should be pointed out that the meaning and significance can transcend everyday living and immediate experiences. In his article "After John Dewey, What?" Bruner (1979) argued that an appreciation of abstract ideas such as "commutativity" or "set theory" is an authentic experience, not because they are associated with real-life instances, but because they represent a way of thinking that is "lithe and beautiful and immensely generative" (p. 121). Authentic learning experiences not only make students more "down to earth" (making real-life connections); they should also make students fly high (envisioning new possibilities).

Authenticity of a learning environment sometimes implies cognition in the wild (Hutchins, 1995), which is not always feasible and desirable for learners. Barab and colleagues (Barab et al., 2007, 2010) delineated the quality of context for learning as a continuity from noisy to tailored. Noisy contexts are rich with contextual details, with disciplinary content embedded in real-life exploration and investigation. Tailored contexts, in contrast, feature more explicitly presented disciplinary content and can be more efficient in learning, but they lack the richness of a noisy context and can negatively affect student engagement and transfer (see also Collins, 1996). Aptitude-treatment interaction (ATI) research has long explored how student characteristics might interact with completeness of instruction (Cronbach & Snow, 1977; Snow & Lohman, 1984; see also instances of ATI in the recent research on cognitive load theory; Plass et al., 2010). If the gap-filling is indeed a hallmark of individual differences in intellectual functioning (see Dai, this volume), then design work regarding structuredness or tailoredness needs to adapt to this learner-related constraint. Incidentally, it is also worth noting that the less structured a learning environment, the more salient individual differences (Ackerman, 2003).

In the current scholarly discourse, authenticity also means organization of learning that reflects understanding of how professionals and discipline specialists think, talk, and act (Gee, 2003; Shaffer, 2004; Wineburg & Grossman, 2001). Kirschner (2009; Kirschner, Sweller, & Clark, 2006) warned about confusing pedagogy with epistemology: how disciplinarians do their research and evaluate their findings is one thing, and how to teach the disciplinary content, including the related methodology, is another. He argued that learning to think like experts is hard for children, because of knowledge deficits as well as developmental constraints. While the starting point (children's entry level) should not dictate the end state (whether they should learn to think like scientists, mathematicians, historians, etc.), pedagogy indeed should be adapted to both content-related and person-related constraints.

Complexity

If we concur that design research is dealing with a multilevel system (Dai, this volume; Fishman et al., 2004; Greeno & The Middle School Math Project Group, 1998) featuring human agency, pedagogical and social structure, and tools and resources, then how do we manage the complexities and ensuing uncertainties? For example, with authenticity, agency, and interactivity, researchers can easily lose track of how well things go, and how and when particular supporting tools and resources should be deployed. Zhang (this volume) provides some clues as to how technology might help make massively interactive systems tractable. One way to make the complexity manageable is to subject the data to multilevel analysis and then integrate relational and individual properties. Effects of interactive systems need to be accounted for at the individual level, rather than taken for granted; although the traditional reductionistic view of human functioning should be refuted, a relational ontology does not make individual accounts of intellectual processes superfluous because, without the contributions of the individual, the distributed system is devoid of its agency (see Bannan, this volume).

Emergence

Design research starts with a principle stance and some form of working hypothesis about a learning situation. How do we maintain a principle stance while being open to new possibilities, theoretically and practically? How do we balance the principled with the emergent? This is a task that fits Langer's (this volume) notion of exploring the horizons of possibilities and maintaining a point of reference. If it is indeed like building Neurath's boat in the midst of traveling in the water, then the designing process itself is a fluid conceptual development process (Carey, 1999). For example, an emergent issue from Engle's (this volume) research on teaching college educational psychology is how to manage convergence and divergence of a dynamic conservation in a way conducive to knowledge building and critical thinking, preventing premature foreclosure, while at the same time staying on course, rather than being sporadic, undisciplined, and increasingly disperse (Engle, this volume). To be true to the spirit of design research as seeking fundamental understandings of how well a particular design works and why, and how it might be improved, all basic and applied research findings in neurobiological, developmental, differential, and educational psychology should be consulted and enlisted, and all professional wisdom and insights accumulated in learning settings should be respected and honored to enrich our understanding. One thing that makes design research important is the realization that research on teaching and learning is not about discovering omnipotent universal laws and first principles, as is the case in physics, but about how to adaptively and creatively deal with emergent situations and render sustained improvement and innovation (Bereiter, 2002). In what way design research should help teachers adaptively and creatively deal with emergent situations (individual differences in prior knowledge, ability, and motivation) should also be part of its research agenda, rather than trying to find prescriptive formulas for teachers, which is unlikely to work well (Zhang, this volume). How the assessment system permits identification of progress and shortfalls in learning and thinking will become crucial if a design can indeed handle emergent issues in a timely and appropriate fashion (Kelly, this volume).

Formalism

To what extent can we achieve some form of formalism in design research? It is unlikely for design researchers to declare success if a design only states very broad principles, without some specification of processes and supporting systems to implement these principles (c.f. Bielaczyc, 2006). Indeed, a hallmark of design success is not broad abstractions, but theoretical arguments grounded in solid practices and empirical evidence that they worked. However, there seems to be a delicate balance to be maintained between structure and agency (including both teachers and learners). Whatever formalisms are stipulated, there should be a principle of agency that permits the creative implementation of a particular design. After all, designing a learning environment means designing for a particular structure of participation, a particular way of engagement and processing, a particular way of assessing to ensure progress and identification of problems. It is a form of process engineering, not that of designing a material product.

There also seems to be a trade-off between being theoretically sound and transformative and practically viable. The theoretically more stringent a model, the harder its adoption. Meanwhile, too loosely defined models tend to be ritualized and modified by educators in a way that loses their initial ethos (e.g., principles), resulting in "lethal mutation" of innovations (Brown & Campione, 1996). Educators tend to choose "domestic" models and technologies and assimilate them into existing practice without transformative change (Salomon & Almog, 1998). Kelly (this volume) discusses an instance of designing a unit on geomorphology in which a domain expert insisted on teaching fourth-graders the concept of geological time, whereas the teachers objected to this idea by arguing that children of this age are not ready for the concept. The instance reflects the classical tension Dewey (1902/1990) identified between the curriculum and the child. How to make a design theoretically refined enough for implementation with fidelity, while maintaining some level of practical flexibility so that it can be adapted to local conditions and constraints (often with fewer resources than in design research settings; see Kelly, this volume; Barab & Luehmann, 2003). The issue of formalism also brings back the issue of the extent to which we can achieve technical rationality in design research and the extent to which reflective rationality (Schön, 1983) is indispensable on the part of design researchers, as well as classroom teachers who intend to implement a particular model developed by design researchers (Brown & Edelson, 2001; Zhang et al., in press).

In concluding this commentary and reflection, we concur with Kelly (this volume) that assessment is a bottleneck for the development of design research to address critical issues in education, particularly how to develop high-level thinking skills and dispositions. To a large extent, how we assess and what we assess impact what and how students will learn. There are some advances made in assessing higher-order thinking, problem solving, and collaborative work (e.g., see Zhang, this volume; Shute & Kim, this volume). Gee and Shaffer (2010) suggest that computer games are an ideal candidate as a vehicle to assess improvements in problem solving and higher-order thinking (see also, Ketelhut, Nelson, Clarke, & Dede, 2010). Whatever approaches we might use, we should strive for technological breakthroughs in assessing action, thought, and feeling in situ, particularly documenting progress and enhanced potential and growth. Such measurements and assessment systems would accrue evidence for micro-development (Granott & Parziale, 2002) and identify transition processes in learning and development. It would be a crucial step toward an education reform aimed at high-end learning and intellectual growth.

How would this volume stand in five or 10 years? How much progress can we make by then? Perhaps only time will tell whether design research can successfully address the thorny issue of promoting high-end learning and intellectual growth, and illuminate enabling conditions and underlying processes.

The research reported in this volume gives us reason for optimism. It is our hope that this volume will be part of a continuing research-based scholarly discussion of learning in and for the 21st century for many years to come.

References

Ackerman, P. L. (2003). Aptitude complexes and trait complexes. *Educational Psychologist, 38*, 85–93.

Barab, S. A., & Luehmann, A. L. (2003). Building sustainable science curriculum: Acknowledging and accommodating local adaptation. *Science Education, 87*(4), 454–467.

Barab, S., Zuiker, S., Warren, S., Hickey, D. T., Ingram-Goble, A. A., Kwon, E. J., et al. (2007). Situationally embodied curriculum: Relating formalisms and contexts. *Science Education, 91*, 750–782.

Barab, S. A., Gresalfi, M., & Ingram-Goble, A. (2010). Transformational play: Using games to position person, content, and context. *Educational Researcher, 39*, 525–536.

Barron, B. (2006). Interest and self-sustained learning as catalysts of development: A learning ecology perspective. *Human Development, 49*, 193–224.

Bereiter, C. (2002). Design research for sustained innovation. *Bulletin of the Japanese Cognitive Science Society, 9*, 321–327.

Bielaczyc, K. (2006). Designing social infrastructure: Critical issues in creating learning environments with technology. *Journal of the Learning Sciences, 15*(3), 301–329.

Bransford, J. D., Brown, A. L., & Cocking, R. R. (2000). *How people learn: Brain, mind, experience, and school.* Washington, DC: National Academy Press.

Bransford, J. D., & Schwartz, D. L. (1999). Rethinking transfer: A simple proposal with multiple implications. In A. Iran-Nejad & P. D. Pearson (Eds.), *Review of research in education, 24* (pp. 61–101). Washington, DC: American Educational Research Association.

Brown, A. (1997). Transforming schools into communities of thinking and learning about serious matters. *American Psychologist, 52*, 399–413.

Brown, A. L. (1994). The advance of learning. *Educational Researcher, 23*, 4–12.

Brown, A. L., & Campione, J. (1996). Psychological theory and the design of innovative learning environments: On procedures, principles, and systems. In L. Schauble & R. Glaser (Eds.), *Innovations in learning: New environments for education* (pp. 289–325). Mahwah, NJ: Erlbaum.

Brown, M., & Edelson, D. C. (2001). *Teaching by design: Curriculum design as a lens on instructional practice.* Paper presented at the Annual meeting of the American Educational Research Association, Seattle, WA.

Bruner, J. (1979). *On knowing: Essays for the left hand.* Cambridge, MA: Belknap Press of Harvard University Press.

Carey, S. (1999). Sources of conceptual change. In E. K. Scholnick, K. Nelson, S. Gelman, A., & P. H. Miller (Eds.), *Conceptual development: Piaget's legacy* (pp. 293–326). Mahwah, NJ: Lawrence Erlbaum.

Collins, A. (1992) Toward a design science of education. In E. Scanlon & T. O'Shea (Eds.), *New directions in educational technology*. Berlin: Springer-Verlag.

Collins, A. (1996). Design issues for learning environments. In S. Vosniadou, E. De Court, R. Glaser, & H. Mandl (Eds.), *International perspectives on the design of technology-supported learning environments* (pp. 347–361). Mahwah, NJ: Erlbaum.

Collins, A., Joseph, D., & Bielaczyc, K. (2004) Design research: Theoretical and methodological issues. *Journal of the Learning Sciences, 13*(1), 15–42.

Cronbach, L. J., & Snow, R. E. (1977). Aptitudes and instructional methods: A handbook for research on interactions. New York: Irvington.

Derry, S., & Lesgold, A. (1996). Toward a situated social practice model for instructional design. In D. C. Berliner & R. C. Calfee (Eds.), *Handbook of educational psychology* (pp. 787–806). New York: Simon & Schuster Macmillan.

Dewey, J. (1902/1990). *The school and society, and the child and the curriculum.* Chicago: The University of Chicago Press.

diSessa, A. A., & Cobb, P. (2004). Ontological innovation and the role of theory in design experiments. *The Journal of the Learning Sciences, 13*, 77–103.

Duschl, R. A., & Duncan, R. G. (2009). Beyond the fringe: Building and evaluating scientific knowledge systems. In S. Tobias & T. M. Duffy (Eds.), *Constructivist instruction: Success or failure?* (pp. 311–332). New York: Routledge.

Engle, R. A., & Conant, F. R. (2002). Guiding principles for fostering productive disciplinary engagement: Explaining an emergent argument in a community of learners classroom. *Cognition and Instruction, 20*, 399–483.

Fishman, B., Marx, R., Blumenfeld, P., Krajcik, J. S., & Soloway, E. (2004). Creating a framework for research on systemic technology innovations. *Journal of the Learning Sciences, 13*(1), 43–76.

Gee, J. P. (2003). Opportunity to learn: A language-based perspective on assessment. *Assessment in Education, 10*, 27–46.

Gee, J. P., & Shaffer, D. W. (2010). Looking where the light is bad: Video games and the future of assessment. *Edge, 6*, 3–19.

Granott, N., & Parziale, J. (2002). Microdevelopment: A process–oriented perspective for studying development and learning. In N. Granott & J. Parziale (Eds.), *Microdevelopment: Transition processes in development and learning* (pp. 1–28). Cambridge, UK: Cambridge University Press.

Greeno, J., & the Middle School Mathematics Through Applications Project Group (1998). The situativity of knowing, learning, and research. *American Psychologist, 53*, 5–26.

Hutchins, E. (1995). *Cognition in the wild.* Cambridge, MA: The MIT Press.

Ketelhut, D. J., Nelson, B., Clarke, J., & Dede, C. (2010). A Multi-user virtual environment for building and assessing higher order inquiry skills in science. *British Journal of Educational Technology, 41*(1), 56–68.

Kirschner, P. A. (2009). Epistemology or pedagogy, that is the question. In S. Tobias & T. M. Duffy (Eds.), *Constructivist instruction: Success or failure?* (pp. 144–157). New York: Routledge.

Kirschner, P. A., Sweller, J., & Clark, R. E. (2006). Why minimal guidance during instruction does not work: An analysis of the failure of constructivist, discovery, problem-based, experiential, and inquiry-based teaching. *Educational Psychologist, 41*, 75–86.

Palincsar, A. S., & Magnusson, S. J. (2001). The interplay of first-hand and second-hand investigation to model and support the development of scientific knowledge and reasoning. In S. M. Carver & D. Klahr (Eds.), *Cognition and instruction: Twenty-five years of progress* (pp. 151–193). Mahwah, NJ: Lawrence Erlbaum.

Partnership for 21st Century Skills (2008). *21st Century Skills Education and Competitiveness Guide.* Retrieved July 25, 2011 from www.p21.org/documents/21st_ century_skills_ education_and_competitiveness_guide.pdf.

Plass, J. L., Moreno, R., & Brunken, R. (2010). *Cognitive load theory*. New York: Cambridge University Press.

Salomon, G., & Almog, T. (1998). Educational psychology and technology: A matter of reciprocal relations. *Teachers College Record, 100*(2), 222–241.

Sawyer, R. K. (2007). *Group genius: The creative power of collaboration*. New York: Basic Books.

Scardamalia, M., & Bereiter, C. (2006). Knowledge building: Theory, pedagogy, and technology. In K. Sawyer (Ed.), *Cambridge Handbook of the Learning Sciences* (pp. 97–118). New York: Cambridge University Press.

Schank, R. C., & Cleary, C. (1995). *Engines for education*. Hillsdale, NJ: Lawrence Erlbaum.

Schoenfeld, A. H. (1988). When good teaching leads to bad results: The disasters of "well-taught" mathematics courses. *Educational Psychologist, 23*, 145–166.

Schön, D. A. (1983). *Reflective practitioner*. New York: Basic Books.

Shaffer, D. W. (2004). Pedagogical praxis: The professions as models for postindustrial education. *Teachers College Record, 106*, 1401–1421.

Simon, H. A. (1969). *The sciences of the artificial*. Cambridge, MA: The MIT Press.

Snow, R. E., & Lohman, D. F. (1984). Toward a theory of cognitive aptitude for learning from instruction. *Journal of Educational Psychology, 76*, 347–376.

Wineburg, S., & Grossman, P. (2001). Affect and effect in cognitive approaches to instruction. In S. M. Carver & D. Klahr (Eds.), *Cognition and instruction: Twenty-five years of progress* (pp. 479–492). Mahwah, NJ: Lawrence Erlbaum.

Zhang, J. (2010). Technology supported learning innovation in cultural contexts. *Educational Technology Research and Development, 58*, 229–243.

Zhang, J., Hong, H.-Y., Scardamalia, M., Teo, C., & Morley, E. (in press). Sustaining knowledge building as a principle-based innovation at an elementary school. *Journal of the Learning Sciences*.

ABOUT THE CONTRIBUTORS

Brenda Bannan

Dr. Brenda Bannan is Associate Professor of Instructional Technology in the College of Education and Human Development at George Mason University in Fairfax, Virginia. Her research interests focus on the integration of design and research processes, as well as the enhanced analysis, design, and development of current technological education and training innovations. Her work in design research has been published and presented in national and international publications and conferences.

Sasha Barab

Sasha Barab is Professor in Learning Sciences and Cognitive Science at Indiana University. He holds the Barbara Jacobs Chair of Education and Technology, and is the Director of the Center for Research on Learning and Technology. His research has resulted in numerous grants, dozens of academic articles, and multiple chapters in edited books, which investigate knowing and learning in its material, social, and cultural context. The intent of this research is to develop rigorous claims about how people learn that have significant practical, pedagogical, and theoretical implications.

David Yun Dai

David Yun Dai is Associate Professor of Educational Psychology and Method-ology at University at Albany, State University of New York. His research interests include intelligence and intellectual development, gifted education and talent development. He is particularly interested in developing a functional theory of intellectual development that integrates personal (cognitive, affective, and motivational) and social–contextual factors (technical, pedagogical, and social support, mentorship, etc.).

Randi A. Engle

Randi A. Engle is an Assistant Professor and Learning Sciences Researcher at University of California at Berkeley. Her research uses tools from cognitive science and discourse analysis to understand what makes learning environments intellectually productive. She has two lines of research, one on how to foster productive engagement in the academic disciplines, and the other on the transfer of what students have learned from such engagement.

Melissa Gresalfi

Melissa Gresalfi is Assistant Professor in the Learning Sciences at Indiana University, and the Associate Director of the Center for Research on Learning and Technology. Her research considers cognition and social context by examining student learning as a function of participation in activity systems. Her current projects, funded by the National Science Foundation, the MacArthur Foundation, the Spencer Foundation, and the Department of Education, focus on investigating and designing innovative environments to support students' development of particular dispositions towards learning and engaging in mathematics, science, and beyond.

Anthony E. Kelly

Anthony E. Kelly earned his PhD at Stanford University. He served as Assistant and Associate Professor at Rutgers University, and is Professor of Educational Psychology at George Mason University. He also served as Program Officer at the US National Science Foundation in the Directorate for Education and Human Resources. He strives to foster emerging methods and domain areas in education, including research methods, cyberinfrastructure and learning, and the neural basis for learning mathematics. As a Fulbright New Century Scholar, he studied the role of the university as an innovation driver for society.

Yoon Jeon Kim

Yoon Jeon Kim is a doctoral candidate in the Instructional Systems program at Florida State University. She received her bachelor's degree in Educational Technology from the Ewha Womans University in South Korea, and currently works with her advisor, Dr. Valerie Shute, on various assessments of complex cognitive and noncognitive skills in dynamic learning environments.

Judith A. Langer

Judith A. Langer is Distinguished Professor at the University at Albany, State University of New York, where she is founder and director of the Albany Institute for Research in Education and director of the Center on English Learning and Achievement. She is an internationally known scholar in literacy education. Her research focuses on the development of the literate mind: how people become highly literate, and ways in which education can help them do so. Author of numerous research reports, articles, chapters, and monographs, she has written 11 books. She has received many awards and honors, including an Honorary Doctorate from the University of Uppsala, Sweden.

Richard Lehrer

Richard Lehrer is Frank W. Mayborn Professor of Education at Vanderbilt University's Peabody College. He has long-standing interests in the development of mathematical and scientific reasoning in environments designed to support these forms of reasoning. Current research interests include the origins and development of model-based reasoning, formative assessment of students' conceptions of statistics and chance, and the nature of mechanistic reasoning in contexts of engineering design.

Erin Pfaff

Erin Pfaff is a graduate student at Vanderbilt University. She has a BS in Mathematics and Elementary Education from Vanderbilt and spent three years teaching elementary school in Nashville, TN. Current research interests include measurement and rational-number instruction and modeling the travel of mathematical ideas in classrooms.

Joseph L. Polman

Joseph L. Polman, PhD, is Associate Professor in the Division of Teaching and Learning at the University of Missouri–St. Louis College of Education. He is interested in how people learn science, history, and other disciplinary practices through inquiry and with the support of technology, both in schools and in community-based settings. He has published a book as well as numerous research articles, chapters, and curriculum materials based on his work in these areas.

Valerie J. Shute

Valerie Shute is an Associate Professor in the Instructional Systems program at Florida State University. Her general research interests hover around the design, development, and evaluation of advanced systems to support learning. She is particularly interested in examining the effects of using well-designed games in relation to enhancing "21st century competencies."

Amanda Sommerfeld

Amanda Sommerfeld began working as a Clinical Assistant Faculty member and the Program Coordinator of the Counseling Master's program at Boston University in Fall 2009. During her doctoral studies in Counseling Psychology at the University of Wisconsin-Madison, she focused on cultural influences on child and adolescent mental health and educational advancement. Dr. Sommerfeld's current research examines the role of economic, social, and cultural capital in college access and success. She additionally conducts educational, psychological, and neuropsychological evaluations at the Child Development Network, located in Lexington, MA.

Zheng Yan

Dr. Yan is Associate Professor of Developmental Psychology at University at Albany, State University of New York. His research mainly concerns dynamic and complex relations between contemporary technologies and human development, as well as research methodology of human development. He is currently investigating children's understanding of the internet as a complex artifact and human behaviors in cyberspace as a new field of research.

Jianwei Zhang

Jianwei Zhang is currently an Associate Professor at the University at Albany. His research explores conditions and means to engage students in productive knowledge building supported by collaborative and interactive technologies, so as to inform innovative schooling in 21st-century contexts. His work has appeared in the *Journal of the Learning Sciences, Educational Technology Research and Development (ETR&D), Instructional Science*, etc., and received a number of awards, including two Outstanding Journal Articles of the Year Awards from *ETR&D*. He serves on the editorial board of the *Journal of the Learning Sciences*. More information about his work can be found at http://tccl.rit.albany.edu.

AUTHOR INDEX

SUBJECT INDEX